W9-BYS-684

Protestant Diplomacy and the Near East

Missionary Influence on American Policy, 1810–1927

◄ ►

*The publication of this book was assisted
by the Atkinson Fund*

◄ ►

Protestant Diplomacy and the Near East

Missionary Influence on American Policy, 1810-1927

Joseph L. Grabill

UNIVERSITY OF MINNESOTA PRESS • Minneapolis

© Copyright 1971 by the University of Minnesota. All rights reserved.
Printed in the United States of America at Lund Press, Minneapolis. Published in Great Britain, India, and Pakistan by the Oxford University Press,
London, Bombay, and Karachi, and in Canada by the Copp Clark Publishing Co. Limited, Toronto. *Library of Congress Catalog Card Number:
70-153504 ISBN 0-8166-0575-0*

To Clifford Lewis Grabill and Arveda Wulliman Grabill

Preface

THIS volume had casual origins. One day some years ago I sat among library stacks, letting my mind wander to the question, What has been written on the part taken by Christian missionaries in United States foreign relations? Then the Near East slipped into my thoughts. I reached without success for recollections about American missionaries in that area. Walking to the card file, I accidentally met a colleague of mine from Cyprus and quizzed him. "Yes," he said, "Protestant missionaries have been in the Near East for over a century." He recommended *The Arab Awakening* by George Antonius, in which I read that missionaries from the United States had been an impulse in the nineteenth-century literary revival among Arabs.

Later I was also reading that until the 1930s missionary and philanthropic interests were the chief American ties to the Near East. It was during the First World War and peace settlement that direct political influence by Protestants was largest. I decided to concentrate on the smaller period of time in the twentieth century without neglecting events either of the previous century or of succeeding years.

The missionaries came to intrigue me. Disturbed at times by their pretensions, I admired their verve and creativity. Despite the emotion and spirit of their lives and seasons, I sought to beware of overidentification with them. I tried while writing to be both defense attorney and prosecuting attorney of these persons, balancing their times with the 1960s, seeing people both controlled by and controlling events. Since self-awareness, let alone insight into others is incomplete, I do not know how close I have come to my goal. God alone sees things full-orbed.

An emphasis in this book is on missionaries and philanthropists as communication agents between the United States and the Near East. These people — through their evangelism, schools, relief activities, influence on public opinion, and lobbying — are seen as important American internationalists. The social contexts of the Near East, including Armenian, Arab, Nestorian, and Bulgarian nationalism, and of the United States, including American culture-religion, have important places. I have attempted a balanced treatment of emotions, ideas, leaders, institutions, and events. To interpret, particularly with an intercultural perspective, has been as weighty as to chronicle. There is content herein of potential interest to such varied observers as students of missions and Armenian Americans. This book is also one more among the many volumes dealing with the Woodrow Wilson administration.

Support has come in several forms. My parents as well as the staff of the Stark County Historical Society (Ohio) stood guard over my seclusion at various times while I wrote. Indiana University provided a grant that relieved me from financial anxiety during seven uninterrupted months. Not dodging a jeopardy of being the spouse of an historian, my wife — Doris Davis Grabill — gave many undramatic hours to typing and editing. Librarians Mary Walker and Margaret F. Ashenden, at what used to be headquarters of the American Board of Commissioners for Foreign Missions on Beacon Hill in old Boston, were solicitous. Betty Clements of the Missionary Research Library exceeded my expectations in her aid. My graduate assistant, James R. Cole, helped prepare the index.

Among persons giving counsel has been John A. DeNovo. He has made any number of penetrating comments at different stages of preparation. I have appreciated suggestions about sources from Harry N. Howard. Bayard Dodge was generous in sharing his time and knowledge. I have profited from other individuals who, like Harry Howard and Bayard Dodge, have lived in the Near East: Sydney Nettleton Fisher, Harold B. Allen, Daniel Bliss, Sarah R. Mac Neal, Luther R. Fowle, and Fred Field Goodsell. Thomas A. Bryson, Leon E. Boothe, and Kyle C. Sessions went an extra mile in their helpfulness. I feel gratitude toward Fred G. Thomas. Buffing upon my style has come from reactions to my writing by Robert H. Ferrell. My liability to him in this matter and others is large, so large that I hope he cancels part of my obligation. These as well as many unnamed people facilitated my work in ways which I hope they will recognize though they will notice, I am sure, that I have not always agreed with their counsel.

One counsellor recommended that I make explicit my use of *missionary*. I have applied this word both to individuals connected with mission boards and to educators at schools independent of mission boards (Robert College and the Syrian Protestant College — by the 1920s called the American University of Beirut). Leaders of these independent colleges for decades after their founding were clergymen, who thought of their educational functions as part of the Christian cause abroad. The president of the Syrian Protestant College in 1920 published an article, "The Modern Missionary," in which he obviously identified himself with the missionary movement. The head of Robert College in the same year described his school as a "strictly Christian missionary institution."

There are additional uses of words to be noted. I have reserved *minorities* primarily for Armenians, Arabs, and Nestorians. Some confusion exists over the roughly identical "Middle East" and "Near East." Roderic H. Davison has dealt with this problem in an article in *Foreign Affairs* of July 1960. I have stayed with the more traditional "Near East" (in this study Balkan and Caucasus areas, Persia, and the Ottoman Empire and its successor states). On proper Near East names, I have chosen indigenous usages and spellings of the 1960s except when I have felt clarity would not be enhanced.

The reader undoubtedly has a right to know about my frame of experience and reference. My childhood was spent in the home of a clergyman who resided consecutively in Ohio, California, and Indiana, and who belonged to a revivalistic group composed originally of German-speaking, rural Mennonites. This tiny group with an overseas concern had personnel in Ecuador, Jamaica, and Sierra Leone. Deputational presentations by furloughed missionaries were fascinating to me as a boy. The possibility of becoming a missionary was large during my years at a Bible college and an evangelical liberal arts school. But my Christian style has been that of an informal "minister," domestically and overseas; I have had professional roles in such organizations as a Protestant college in Ohio and as a summer mission program in the Orient and Latin America (combining evangelism and athletics). God is to me both friend and ultimate being, who is promoting integrity and maturity among people in every class and culture. Recently, as a Presbyterian "layman," I shared leadership of a church-related coffee house, which included radical youth within its clientele. My exposure to these youth has expanded the feeling that one needs mutual learning interaction with diverse individuals and groups to appropriate characteristics of integrity and maturity.

J. L. G.

Normal, Illinois
December 1969

Contents

LIST OF MAPS

LIST OF ILLUSTRATIONS BETWEEN PAGES 178 AND 179

Protestant Diplomacy and the Near East

Missionary Influence on American Policy, 1810–1927

Chapter 1

"Christianize the Nations"

AMERICAN foreign affairs and Protestant missions to the Near East began to turn a corner in the Woodrow Wilson era. Intervention in the First World War by the United States led many of its citizens to believe that their nation needed a new road away from noninvolvement in disorders of the Old World. Upstart internationalists tried to direct American diplomacy away from venerated isolationism. Of some strength in the attempted move were Presbyterian and Congregational leaders of mission churches and schools in the Ottoman Empire and Persia. Probably having more effect than public officials upon American relations with the Near East during the collapse of the Turkish Empire, these administrators, in cooperation with philanthropists, sought mandates by the United States over part or all of Turkey. They desired America thereby to facilitate autonomy or independence among subject peoples – the Armenians and the Syrian Arabs – to whom they had tethered their careers. As for the American government, it generally had abstained from the transatlantic balance of power, and the missionaries' idea that it should sponsor minorities in the Near East implied a novel course.

In the 1910s several factors helped missionaries and Americans generally to alter their opposition to a United States commitment in Turkey. An appeal to evangelize the world in one generation, proclaimed during the start of the Student Volunteer Movement in the late 1880s, had been bringing many recruits. This cry assisted Protestant Americans to take the fore in an expansion of Christianity unprecedented in modern times.[1] An international concern, of course, was inherent in the commission of Jesus to enlist disciples among every people. Publications and talks by missionaries expanded understanding in the United States of foreigners. American churches gave benevolent and technical assistance overseas, forming unconsciously an advance guard for possible direct action by Washington. Included in the missionary baggage, along with Bibles and tracts, were sewing machines and books on free government. The annexation of Hawaii in 1898 had resulted largely from the Americanization of Hawaiian society by New England missionaries; a similar process was developing in the Near East. Also, the Social Gospel was breaking down some resistance among Protestants to plans for improvement of communities and governments in foreign lands. And after the Spanish-American War, ideas of Manifest Destiny and Social Darwinism about the natural superiority of Anglo-Saxon institutions were widespread. Many missionaries to Turkey believed that the sturdy Armenians were a demonstration of struggling survival, fit for a political tie with hardy Americans.[2] When President Wilson announced self-determination of ethnic groups abroad, missionaries to Asia Minor and Syria believed they had ideal candidates upon whom America might apply Wilson's principle.

Events since 1810 had been preparing missionaries to the eastern Mediterranean as chaperons for a United States government courtship with Armenians, Arabs, and Nestorians in Turkey and Persia. It is important, therefore, to look in some detail at circumstances behind this courtship — the unfolding of Protestantism, of Ottoman-American diplomacy, and of nationalism among minorities during the nineteenth century.

ENLIGHTENMENT OF THE DEGENERATE

Missionaries had been on a frontier of United States cultural internationalism in the Turkish Empire for about a century before Wilson became President. They had first gone to proselyte Muslims and Jews and to revive Near East Christians. The first Protestants in the area had come in the sixteenth century. Permanent efforts by Protestants began when a chaplain of the British East India Company, Henry Martyn, appeared in the Near East in 1810. Martyn soon died, and Protestants in England and America made him a symbol for missionary opportunity. Members of the Church Missionary Society of the Church of England arrived in Turkey not long after Martyn's death. One decade after Martyn's appearance the initial two American missionaries, young and resourceful Levi Parsons and Pliny Fisk, landed at Smyrna (later Izmir), at which port about a dozen Yankee ships were stopping annually.

Parsons and Fisk represented the American Board of Commissioners for Foreign Missions. Students at Williams College in Massachusetts, led by angular Samuel J. Mills, had conceived the idea for the American Board while praying by a haystack near the school. Mills and some of his fellows went to Andover Theological Seminary, which orthodox Congregationalists had begun as a counter to Unitarian influence at Harvard College. These Andover seminarians in 1810 made the initial move which persuaded Congregational and Presbyterian officials to found the American Board — the first organization in the United States concerned with missions abroad. Incidentally, the seminarians established a secret missionary fraternity which by 1908 had helped recruit two hundred fifty Andover students as missionaries for the American Board.[3]

The Board arose out of various forces in New England society. The Second Great Awakening and its theology about practical Christianity (articulated by Samuel Hopkins) impelled not only foreign missions but antislavery, temperance, and peace movements. Reactions to Unitarianism helped give dynamism to traditional Calvinism. Premillennial sermons stated that preaching the Gospel to every creature was necessary before God would pitch his tent among men. A common idea was that the object of missions was moral renovation of the world — wars ceasing, every location having its school and church, every family its Bible reading and prayer. The president of Yale College, Timothy Dwight, assumed that the days of the synagogue, pagoda, mosque, and Catholic cathedral abroad were near an end. (Dwight's assumption showed that missions overseas were to be an exporting of ethnocentric, New England Protestantism.) The long history of evangelism among American Indians and frontiersmen and the example of British missions, publicized by the rise of Christian periodicals in the United States during the 1790s, spurred efforts for foreign missions. Enterprising commercial activity by merchants with Asia and Africa, backed by the Navy (as in the United States war against Tripoli), increased both international trade and communication. A final noteworthy force was the common belief that private groups, as opposed to the national government, would carry out most foreign dealings.[4]

The American Board and other Protestant organizations in the United States eventually led in completing the establishment of some form of Christianity in every region of the world. Americans were a primary force in helping Christianity become the first and only religion with a widely dispersed, intercontinental constituency. At a crest of this development in 1910 there was the World Missionary Conference in Edinburgh — an ecumenical gathering of twelve hundred Protestant missionaries from every part of the earth, presided over by the American Student Volunteer spokesman, John R. Mott. Leaders of the American Board were prominent at this conference.[5]

Thus, with comparatively cosmopolitan outlook, the American Board in the early nineteenth century was taking missions around the world. By its domestic publicity, it was also countering the provincialism of the frontiersman and his idealization of "the virgin land." [6] Appointing men and women from the Puritan heartland with purposes like the apostle Paul, the Board sent dedicated individuals to such places as Hawaii, China, and the Near East. Parsons and Fisk went to an area inhabited since the Middle Ages mainly by Muslims, but also by communities of Jews and of Armenian, Nestorian, Greek, Syrian, and other Christians.

The two missionaries, directly out of Andover Theological Seminary and soon joined by others, prepared earnestly to reach the "heathen." Parsons wrote after disembarkment at Smyrna in February 1820: "I find a great desire in my breast . . . to see a system in operation which, with the divine blessing, shall completely demolish this mighty empire of sin." He grieved for Muslims: "How many souls are shut out from the light and blessings of the gospel!" [7] The two men had received rather sophisticated instructions from the American Board to learn languages, gather information, circulate tracts and Bibles, not offend laws and customs, and instruct in private. These procedures were to be a means of evangelizing Muslims and Jews. Puritan premillennial thought believed that non-Christians in the sacred region of the Holy Land would soon bow to the Protestant revelation — a submission which would then lead to the final Kingdom of God on earth. Parsons and Fisk also were to take their message to people in traditional churches whom the Board believed to be nominal Christians.[8] After Parsons became the first American visitor to Jerusalem, the young men went to Alexandria in Egypt for reasons of health. There early in

6

1822 Parsons painfully suffered and died. An undergraduate at the Congregational school in Vermont, Middlebury College, wrote an elegy:[9]

> Thy spirit, Parsons, lur'd by seraph's song,
> Spreads its untiring wing and upward flies . . .
> Who now like him shall toil for Judah's race?
> And who like him destroy Mohammed's sway?

Fisk retreated to the headquarters of British Protestant missions at Malta, where within a year three new recruits from Andover joined him, including one with a printing press. Since Jerusalem was off limits to permanent residents and Smyrna unsafe because of the Greek war for independence, Beirut with a British consul and naval protection readily accessible became the center for the American mission. (See Map 1 on page 16.)

In Beirut and its vicinity entrenched Christian establishments resented and strongly opposed the polemical Protestants from the United States. The newcomers zealously advertised their brand of Christianity through letters and private debates; there were prohibitions against preaching in public. The missionaries had limited intercultural insight though they had more than their countrymen at home. The religious emissaries failed to understand that the individualistic, pietistic, disestablishmental, and optimistic style of the Second Great Awakening in the United States which they brought with them was a threat to the communal, liturgical, inextricably political, and status quo system of the Near East churches.[10] Christian communities in Turkey were extremely conservative. Ottoman law helped keep them so, proscribing every person's civil situation not, basically, by nearly equal standards for all free inhabitants as in the United States, but by Christian or Islamic traditions. Voluntary choice of one's religious affiliation, increasingly becoming the pattern in America, was then illegal in Turkey: for Muslims, conversion to Christianity was punishable by death. American Board missionaries interpreted this rigidity all too often in terms of the righteousness of Protestantism and the sinfulness of Ottoman life — a view which hindered realistic analysis. More important, and though they were barely aware of it, American Board personnel were a liberal force in the Ottoman domains, with as much potential for disruption as for renewal. The original wise advice from Board leaders not to offend local mores was almost impossible for the missionaries to follow. Puritanism, by its eager commitment to a city built on a hill for all to see, required conflict with competing ideas.

Progress, if any, was imperceptible during the first decade of the American mission in the Near East. A feeble start in Beirut at a school for Jewish children, with the Bible as the text, collapsed; the youngsters cut out the New Testament and sold it in the bazaar for waste paper. After highwaymen near Nazareth bludgeoned Fisk in the spring of 1825, he was not well. Colleagues applied leeches to his forehead, and a physician ordered mustard poultices for his feet, warm, wet cloths for his stomach, and regular draughts of rice water — all to no avail. Fisk died in autumn. Ecclesiastical authorities of Maronite and Greek Orthodox churches denounced the Americans and frustrated their efforts in education. Ottoman officials interdicted Bible distribution. The only "converts" were a handful of hired language teachers and translators from Armenian and Syrian Christian communities. One convert became a "martyr" after imprisonment for his change of religion and death for mysterious reasons during his incarceration. Missionaries sent young Greeks to Amherst and Yale colleges and thereby helped influence some Americans to view the Greek war for independence (successful by 1830) as a struggle between the cross and the crescent (this image was similar to pro-Armenian propaganda by missionaries later during the First World War). A large blow for missionaries came as Russo-Turkish warfare forced evacuation from Beirut to Malta, where they stayed from 1828 to 1830.

Seeing that the millennial idea about evangelizing Muslims and Jews was for the time illusory, the American Board in 1831 shifted to the spiritual enlightenment of what it called "the degenerate churches of the East." [11] In the same year it set up several stations aimed at different Christian communions: Constantinople (later Istanbul) for converting among Armenians, Smyrna and Athens among Greeks (the Board severely curtailed these Greek projects later in 1843 because of Greek Orthodox wrath), and Beirut among Syrian Arabs. Concentration for several years was on language study, Bible translation, the printing of scriptural and other religious materials (the press remained in Malta until 1834), elementary schools using the vernacular, and private evangelism. Measurable steps forward were largest among the Armenians.

At the same time that goals became oriented toward non-Muslim and non-Jewish minorities living in urban seacoast regions, missionaries turned to extending American culture to the interior. This move issued out of a courageous survey of Anatolia and Persia by Eli Smith and Harrison Gary Otis Dwight. Recently graduated from Andover and with a bride of two weeks, Dwight sailed in January 1830 from Boston. Three months later with Smith he left both Malta and his wife, Elizabeth, to make the survey. (For her the honeymoon was over. When Dwight returned in fifteen months, there was both a wife and an infant son.) Although there were no Americans and few Westerners east of Constantinople, the two pioneers felt that their responsibilities went farther from the coast than a European's hat could be seen, or a consul's arm reach. On the overland trip, the two men used one packhorse to carry supplies and camping equipment. To escape undue attention, if not trouble, they wore robes and turbans. Smith became sick with cholera several times, and twice he nearly died. Concerning one stop in a village, the travellers recorded that their room was "filled with every species of dirt, vermin, and litter . . . [and] insufferable smoke of the dried cow-dung" which was being used in the oven to bake bread. Impatient to enter their room to rest even though the baking was not finished and the smoke had not abated, they entered to find their host and others shaking their shirts in the oven "to dislodge the 'crawling creatures' that inhabited them." The creatures stuck to the sides of the bread, and, they wrote, "though we would fain have quieted our fastidiousness by imagining that they [the creatures] were purified by fire, the nature of the fuel . . . left little room upon which to found such a conception." [12] Finding Nestorian Christians in northwestern Persia, the two men enthusiastically approved Urmia (spelled *Urumia* by missionaries, later Rezaieh) as a mission site. Safely back in Constantinople in May 1831 after a journey of over two thousand miles, they prepared to publish *Researches in Armenia*, in the 1960s a neglected travel classic.[18] Their research led to a new station at Urmia, opened in 1834 by Justin Perkins; their trip led also to outposts among Armenians in eastern Asia Minor (Trabzon — then Trebizond, 1835; Erzurum, 1839). (See Map 2 on page 17.) These fresh emphases helped the Americans in 1843 to relinquish their lethargic outpost for Jews in Jerusalem to the English Church Missionary Society.

The missionaries had a dimension in their character which gave continuity to their religious duties. The first missionary to Constantinople, William Goodell, illustrated Protestant purposefulness. Born in a two-room house in Templeton, Massachusetts, Goodell remembered an experience as a boy when he undertook to mix a rum toddy for a visitor: "On tasting it I thought it too strong, and put in more water, with sugar to match. Tasting it again, I thought it was too weak and too sweet; and therefore made another change, and still another. . . . After he had gone, I thought within myself, Now, what shall we do with all this toddy; for we should be ashamed to have our parents come home and see it, and to throw any of the 'good creature' away would be quite wicked. So, taking counsel with my brothers and sisters, all but one younger than myself, we sat down, in high earnest, to see what we could do towards reducing the fearful amount. And we drank and drank till our heads turned round. . . . those were days of darkness." Goodell continued: "In those days everybody drank, old and young, rich and poor, male and female; and our whole country seemed rapidly descending on the steep and slippery side of the hill towards ruin. But New England at length arose in the greatness of her strength, and, in the firmness of her principles, signed the temperance pledge; 'and the land had rest for forty years.' " [14]

Goodell's and his missionary associates' religious purposes gave the strength to endure hardship to a larger extent than American merchants and officials. The sixty some missionaries dressed in no-nonsense black who went to Turkey before 1844 had an average of five years of advanced education, begun in such colleges as Yale, Amherst, Dartmouth, Williams, and Middlebury, in an era when only 2 per cent of the people in the United States went to college; yet they were willing to go without salaries until 1843. And they were not overcome by 30 per cent of their number's dying because of disease or misfortune.

According to observer David H. Finnie, the missionaries "on the whole . . . fared the best" among Americans in Turkey in resisting the conviction that the American touch would produce magical improvement.[15] The Protestant emissaries also did best in understanding something of the Near East mind through such means as learning the local languages.

A NEW ZION

Missionaries from the United States had a marginal chance to reform the Near East churches; they found themselves tempted to transplant a separate species of Christianity, vigorous American Protestantism, into the original Christian soil. They had started their mission with more stress on frontally criticizing rites they felt were idolatrous — an ignorant priesthood, the Virgin Mary, vestments, monasteries, a celibate clergy, and episcopal polity — than on inobtrusively complementing preexisting efforts. Their tactics did not augur well for avoiding attacks between Protestant sympathizers and leaders of the ancient Armenian and Syrian bodies. But the missionaries were prepared to accept this conflict, for in 1835 the

American Board had expressed anxiety that no Protestant sect as yet was emerging.

As the task went forward among non-Muslims, missionaries turned to a revival among Armenians. Perhaps it is well to mention that such terms as Armenian, Turkish, and Arab had shades of racial, linguistic, religious, and legal meaning. Most Armenians spoke Turkish and belonged to a religious and ethnic community called a millet, a semi-autonomous institution having civil immunities from the central government (Ottoman Greeks also had a millet). In the Armenian millet, missionaries encountered the oldest ethnic Christian organization in the world. During the first century A.D. Christianity had gotten a toehold among Armenians in the Anatolian mountains, and two centuries later, before Constantine's Edict of Toleration, the whole tribal group formally became Christian. In the early fourth century Saint Gregory the Illuminator was the chief teacher of the new faith, and from his work and name there emerged the Armenian Gregorian Church. Patriarchs devised a thirty-seven-letter alphabet, reduced the language to writing, and by 433 translated the Scriptures into Armenian. Surrounded by Islamic peoples after the ninth century, the Armenian Gregorian Church, partly for the sake of survival, retreated into a crusty ritualism. After encountering the Papacy during the Crusades, a few Armenians became Roman Catholics. Most remained in the traditional church with which they felt more identity than with the foreign Catholic movement. For weaponless Armenian Christians in Turkey, loyalty to their millet amid the subtle and occasionally direct threats of armed Muslims and of the Ottoman government provided the same emotions as nationalism and anti-Communism did after the Second World War for many Americans.

Protestants in the 1830s sought to invigorate the Gregorians. The missionaries attempted to reverse a strong, centuries-long undertow which had caused Armenians' and other Christians' slow drowning in a Muslim sea. Before the Muslim wave of the seventh century, the entire population of the Eastern Roman Empire was professedly Christian. Through conversion, and occasionally force, churches had since vanished in North Africa, and many were in hiding throughout the Ottoman Empire and Persia.[16] New England forebears of the missionaries had conquered a forest and transformed it into Puritan commonwealths; with this heritage the American religionists in Turkey were taking on with confidence their brash job of altering the Armenian way of life.

American Board missionaries hoped their idea of individual repentance and obedience to God would be more attractive than Gregorian ceremonies. Harrison Dwight and William Goodell led in translating evangelical literature and the Bible into the main language used by constituents of the old church, Armeno-Turkish (oral Turkish with an Armenian alphabet); only a tiny fraction of the Armenians could read. To deny that there was divine vibrancy in the Westerners' extemporaneous praying, discussion of Jesus as a genuine daily presence, and teaching to read the Scriptures in the contemporary idiom would be difficult. It was not long until certain businessmen, educators, and clerics showed interest in the Protestants. A young Armenian, John der Sahakian, developed a preference for personal, literate evangelicalism over communal, mystical Gregorianism. In cooperation with the missionaries, Sahakian led a small surge among Armenians, the Evangelical Union, which by 1836 included about twenty men. To missionary Goodell these "Armenian followers were signs of God's blessed Spirit" and so uplifted him that he wrote in his diary: "The good work among the Armenians . . . now seems to be carrying bishops, bankers, every thing before it. . . . We have seen nothing like this since we left America." [17]

For a while the strategy of reformulating the Armenian Gregorian Church seemed to function. Formal American Board policy begun in 1830 had been not to tear down the old churches or "build up a sect, but to make known and inculcate the great fundamental truths of the gospel." [18] A superior attitude by missionaries and establishment of a separate Evangelical Union weakened much of this stated resolve. There was also the Americans' giving of sacraments to a member of the ancient church no matter how "it may interfere with his previous ecclesiastical relations." [19] A crisis occurred when the Gregorian Patriarch, the head of the Armenian millet, viewed the Evangelical Union — backed by the American Board and British diplomacy — serious competition against the integrity of his millet. He hurled anathemas against anyone's reading Goodell's translations or dealing with the Americans. The Patriarch had Sahakian jailed. Events temporarily brought an easing of the confrontation. Egypt militarily threatened the Ottoman Empire, and the Sultan, contrary to past procedures, asked the Christian (Armenian and Greek) millets to furnish men. At a decisive battle in 1839 Egypt won. Then powers of Europe intervened to preserve the Empire. Illiberality in Turkey diminished for a time. Sahakian, freed from confinement, and the missionaries increased their distributing literature and setting up Bible study groups. The Patriarch even became a bit indulgent as the emerging Evangelical Union grew to include about one hundred people.

Willingness by both Americans and Gregorians to accommodate each other was primarily appearance, not reality. It was nearly ludicrous to expect the Protestants to labor patiently, so contrary was that to the fervid spirit which brought the New World dwellers across the Atlantic. A quiet approach was necessary for sympathy to develop. The American Board in 1843 thus modified its idea of not "tearing down" the local structures: "our object as a mission is to form *churches*, and not a *sect*. A Protestant sect may grow out of our efforts, but it is not the thing for which we labor." [20] About the same time conservatives in the Gregorian Church displayed edginess in 1844 by electing a new Patriarch, Matteos, who began to discipline pro-missionary Armenians. The climax came in 1846 when Matteos, thoroughly aroused, declared these Armenians bore the curse of God, all the saints, and himself: "whoever has a son who is such a one, or a brother, or a partner in business and gives him bread or assists him . . . let such person know that they are nourishing a venomous serpent in their houses which will one day injure them with its deadly poison and they will lose their soul. Such persons give bread to Judas," the anathema continued, "such persons are enemies of the holy faith of Christianity and destroyers of the Holy Orthodox Church of the Armenians." [21] There followed boycotts of "Protestant" Armenian shops, ostracism, torture, and imprisonment.[22]

This unfortunate denouement was caused partly by the compulsive activism of the Americans. They had to have tangible results. Home churches clamored for statistics on conversions. Concern for saving particular souls had a large place in their thinking. Instead of giving priority to one of their own best insights, that God is the primary architect of redemption in his own time, Board people gave themselves almost exclusively to their preaching rather than their servant role. Apparently, their advanced education and wealth, compared to the Armenians, made it hard for them to give themselves to the ministry of the helping hand, which was less obvious than that of the proclaiming mouth. United States missionaries abroad generally believed it more valuable to get something done than to give serious thought to theological presuppositions and implications of their actions.[23]

Possibly the aspect of the missionaries' behavior most causing divisiveness was the Protestants' messianic idea of their nation's destiny. The American Board of Commissioners for Foreign Missions in its first three decades spoke of putting an American face on ignorant, sensual, idolatrous, and selfish nations abroad, of the church in the United States stretching its arms and making "the whole world feel the strong embrace." Preoccupied with the image of "conquering" foreign territories, an annual report of the American Board quoted ex-President John Quincy Adams, who said the United States had conquered Hawaii, not with victory over military forces "but over the mind and heart by the celestial panoply of the gospel of peace and love." After a visit to the Near East in 1844, a Congregational pastor announced: "America is God's last dispensation towards the world." United States Protestants often more easily saw evils overseas than such pagan practices as slavery at home. One critic noted that the American Board was attending to the splinter in the Asian eye while neglecting the plank in the American eye.[24]

Suspicion reigning between elder and younger Christian groups in the Near East, the Protestants from the United States helped organize excommunicant Armenians. There soon were four local congregations, modeled on New England polity and doctrine, and in 1847 an Ottoman charter was granted the infant, evangelical sect of Protestant Armenians. Using British diplomacy, the new community in 1850 received millet status under Turkish law.[25] Goodell and the British ambassador to Constantinople, Stratford Canning, negotiated this political instrument. The foreign secretary of the American Board in Boston celebrated: "We owe all this, under God, to the providential fact that England had gained an empire in India and must needs preserve an unencumbered way to it." [26]

Since the Americans were to have a new Zion of their own in the Near East, embroilment in public affairs was as necessary as hydrogen to water. The missionaries did not make political maneuver a studied recourse, but they were not averse to thanking God for political help, perhaps even to making petitions for such assistance. Participation in the Ottoman millet arrangement made questions about escaping involvement irrelevant. The Puritan heritage of establishmentarianism, waning though it was, reminded the Protestants of the possible benefits of public assistance for their labors. Until 1827 Massachusetts law had charged clergymen to inspect and license schools and teachers; until 1834 it had required every citizen to support Congregational churches financially. So the American Board became enmeshed in the millet structure of the Empire, and it also became entangled with a minority which would later nourish an independence movement against the Turkish government. Further, cooperation with British diplomats and consuls, begun in the 1820s, continued — the missionaries provided a lever for British policy; Queen Victoria's officials gladly used the Americans' desire for British aid to extend imperial interests.

Evolution of the Armenian evangelical churches had a parallel among the Syrian Arabs. In 1847, under the chairmanship of Butrus al-Bustani, a group of Protestant Syrians in Beirut met and petitioned the missionaries: "We have forsaken our churches, prepared to undergo disgrace and persecution and loss, a part of which has actually fallen upon some of us. . . . If we remain in our present unorganized state, we shall be weak in ourselves and appear so to those around us. . . . Wherefore, since the formation of an evangelical church in Syria is an object which we hope to see accomplished . . . we have deemed it important that the matter should be commenced as soon as possible." [27] The first local congregation of nineteen members came into being the next year. Along with other assemblies that followed, this group became a part of the Protestant millet created in 1850.

Both the Armenian and Syrian churches and the American Board then spread. New centers opened in the Anatolian highlands among Armenians at Aintab — later Gaziantep (1848); Sivas (1851); Merzifon (then Marsovan) and Adana — later Ceyhan (1852); Diyarbakir (1853); Talas and Marash (1854); Harput (1855); and Tarsus (1859).[28] (See Maps 1 and 2 on pages 16 and 17.) By the 1860s the Americans had given enough latitude to the Armenians for the latter to begin their own congregations and start their own evangelistic societies (missionaries usually were paternal in their promotion of indigenous principles). Americans hailed the Protestant work at Aintab as a "wonder." Armenians there soon took leadership administratively and financially and developed from one congregation with eight members in 1848 to two congregations with over three hundred fifty members in 1869 (attendance at services of the two congregations in 1869 averaged nearly two thousand people).[29] In Syria progress was slower: few geographic centers beyond Beirut — Abeih (1843); Tripoli, later Tarabulus (1848); and Sidon, later Sayda (1851).

The same Yankee cultural and spiritual pride which contended with the ancient churches also irritated the local Protestants. Americans resisted Armenian music and mandated Puritan hymnals and Presbyterian psal-

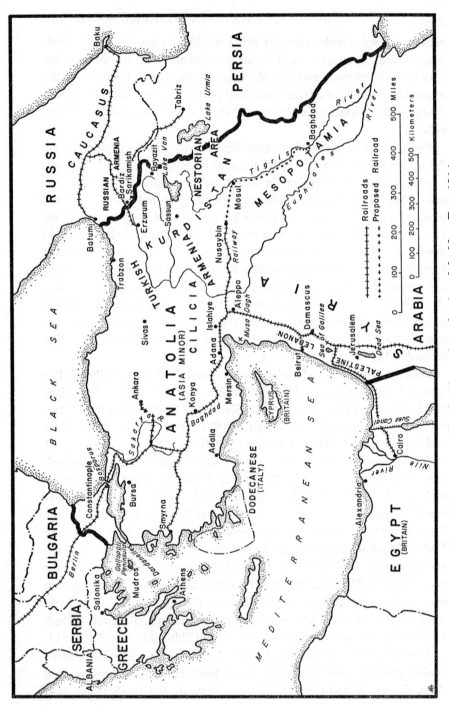

Map 1. The Ottoman Empire (heavy boundary) and the Near East, 1914

16

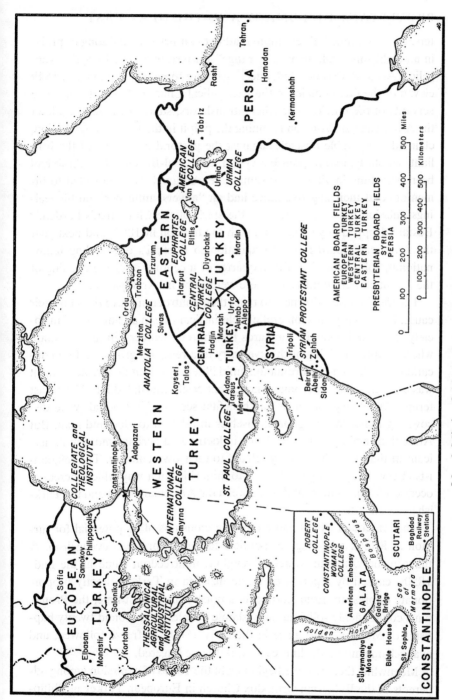

Map 2. Mission fields, stations, and colleges, 1914

17

ters, as if God tuned his ear more readily to an Isaac Watts' song of praise in an eight-tone scale than in "strange" Eastern intervals. In Syria evangelical Arabs were spoon-fed, kneeling before foreigners too long. In 1849 eleven of the fifteen males in the Evangelical Church of Beirut were paid servants of the mission — teachers, translators, stewards. Five years later the Americans, insisting on retaining the pulpit in the Beirut congregation, claimed insuperable obstacles against the pastoral candidacy of the brilliant, scholarly, and responsible Syrian, Butrus al-Bustani. This Arab had been preaching in villages for some time. Although Bustani stated to his mentors that their negative move had an "adverse influence" on his feelings, mission policy continued in the spirit of the white man's burden.[30] Bustani dropped any connection with the mission in 1857, and next year the American Board refused ordination to Bustani's outstanding fellow national, John Wortabet. For a quarter of a century after the opening of the Beirut church, until 1873, there were to be no Arab pastors.

The missionaries' slowness to relax their control ran grave risks for their cause. Inflexibility on democratic ecclesiastical rule in an authoritarian society, on New England's standards for church membership in a situation where simply surviving birth gave entry to a religious group, and on educational credentials for ordination amid illiteracy meant that Protestantism was unlikely ever to become a movement easily translated into Near East terms. Missionary standards had benefits: scores of individuals were discovering richer meaning for themselves in relation to God and man. But Armenians and Syrians were being indoctrinated perhaps more in Americanism than in a Christianity related to their own cultures. The religionists also were applying the Gospel to minorities in a way which increased occasion for misunderstanding between the Armenian millet and the Turkish government.

The American Board had a dim consciousness of its potential for turmoil as it took advantage of political factors to promote evangelism. A thaw in the Ottoman winter of religious nonfreedom came in the mid-1850s, caused by a period of Westernization in Turkey directly proportionate to pressure from European nations. For the first time, the Protestants could openly solicit among Islamic peoples, and around twenty baptisms of Muslims took place in the early 1860s. A freeze followed, and evangelism among Muslims ceased. But hope lingered.

Meanwhile there was the beginning in the 1850s of a mission among adherents of the Bulgarian Orthodox Church in European Turkey at Philippopolis (later Plovdiv). Within a little over a decade, the Protestants founded stations at Samokov and Sofia, opened schools, translated the Bible into modern Bulgarian, organized the first evangelical congregation.

Statistics on the American Board program in the Ottoman Empire for 1870 seemed of God's doing to the Presbyterians and Congregationalists from the United States, especially in contrast to the nonexistent figures for 1828 to 1830 during the exile in Malta: around twenty strong stations, mostly in Asia Minor and with two mission families on the average at each; over one hundred missionaries, including around twenty in Syria; over sixty congregations with three among the Arabs; some two thousand evangelical church members; about two hundred schools with more than five thousand students.[31]

THE GUTENBERG EPOCH

The statistics on schools showed that the missionaries were advancing education within the Ottoman Empire. As early as the 1830s the Sultan had recognized the vitality of the American Board by obtaining books and instruments from William Goodell to start two Turkish schools. The mission's own educational system evolved, and in 1850 included a few hundred students; by 1914, numbers had increased to over thirty-three thousand. Like China and Japan, the Near East was a center of aggressive United States education abroad.

The tutoring of Ottoman residents by American Protestants had begun unknowingly by Parsons, Fisk, Goodell, and others, upon their disembarkment. It astounded people within Turkey to see educated American wives without veils (presumably because of what was missing rather than what was revealed). Traditional bribery and fatalism contrasted with the honesty and optimism of the religionists from the United States. Also, American glass windows, wooden floors, wagons, clocks, sewing machines, organs, cotton gins, telegraph instruments (missionaries possibly brought the first one into the Ottoman Empire), potatoes, and tomatoes stimulated curiosity. The American Board taught Western life whether it sought to or not.

One missionary undoubtedly *sought* to teach American living standards after an overnight visit to a house with dirt floor near Kayseri (then Cesarea). The missionary's reported companions for the night included one man, two children, a dog, two birds, five donkeys, two horses, six oxen, two buffaloes, seven camels, and a legion of fleas "great in power." [32]

Mostly unaware in the early years of the disturbance they created with their alien ideas and practices, the Protestants slowly organized education for what they believed was an evangelistic reason. In the 1820s and 1830s they opened elementary schools to teach reading to Jewish, Armenian, Greek, and Arab children. Bible and psalter were the texts. It was generally not threatening, as one missionary later noted, to approach minors in the unknown society. Being teachers gave the Americans status, which they could not easily get by being preachers whom almost no one wanted to hear. Also, getting local people as paid collaborators was an entree to adults.[33] Schools met at first in missionary homes, then usually in simple structures with dirt floors, mats, and benches. The enlarging educational movement gave missionaries the opportunity to make converts among language informers and instructors. By the 1830s Armeno-Turkish and Arabic had become the main languages in teaching. As need arose to give formal training to a local staff, the first boarding institution, Bebek Seminary (a secondary school), opened in 1840 near Constantinople. Three years later a similar facility, Abeih Academy, opened in Syria. In all these situations, Near Easterners imbibed New England Christianity, which insisted on reading and practicing principles from the Bible and which differed from the unlettered Christianity they typically had known. Finally, these people also absorbed some of the American character.

Perhaps no technique helped missionary education as much as the printing press, because its efficient communication helped overcome inertia in the Near East communities. Publishing facilities, first brought to Malta in 1822, were transferred in 1834 to three locations in Turkey and Persia — Beirut, Smyrna (later moved to Constantinople), and Urmia. During the Malta period the American Board published thousands of Bibles and tracts to a total of around twenty-one million pages. Puritans from New England in 1834 could not claim the oldest printing establishment in the Ottoman Empire: an order of Roman Catholic nuns had already printed a Bible and other works in Arabic before 1825 (Arab translations of the Scriptures had existed since 750 A.D. and had been printed in Europe since the seventeenth century). But the Board took more initiative in certain areas than other publishers, improving movable type in Arabic and printing such languages as Armeno-Turkish and Bulgarian. For the first two decades after the move of publishing facilities to Beirut and Smyrna, there was concentration on materials in Armeno-Turkish and Arabic, although the Board printed works in ten languages. Almost all titles in these years were of a clearly religious nature for use by the missionaries and their assistants. The list included hymnals and Protestant moralistic tales, such as *Dairyman's Daughter* by Leigh Richmond. In midcentury elementary and secondary texts on grammar, spelling, geography, and mathematics began coming off the presses and receiving acceptance among institutions in addition to those run by the Americans. In the latter nineteenth century there was a notable series of college-level scientific and medical texts. Missionaries eventually printed an ever larger number of general works on a commercial basis, periodicals in five languages (one magazine had the largest circulation of any journal in the Ottoman Empire), dictionaries, volumes on literature and history. By 1914 missionaries had distributed an estimated eight million books, including four million Bibles.

Without creative leaders such as Elias Riggs, the Protestant presses would not have had their educational thrust. What a person was Riggs, an Amherst graduate who went to the Near East in 1830, took only one furlough (at Andover Theological Seminary) in sixty-eight years of service there, resided in Constantinople for fifty years until his death in 1901, and compiled a record of continuous, outstanding literary performance probably unmatched by any individual among nineteenth-century missionary organizations! He also was the remarkable progenitor of three children, eleven grandchildren, and two great-grandchildren who became missionaries, most of them in the Near East. Riggs had a scholar's mastery of Greek, Armeno-Turkish, Bulgarian, Arabic, Latin, Hebrew, Old Syriac, and Coptic. He wrote tracts and texts, composed or wrote over seven hundred hymns, translated folklore, assisted magazines. Monuments to his career were both a grammar and a Bible translation (started earlier by Goodell) in contemporary Armeno-Turkish. Riggs helped unify Armeno-Turkish as Martin Luther had the German tongue. Riggs also aided publication of many of the first books printed in modern Bulgarian, including the Bible.

Riggs was not the only giant among first-generation American orientalists. Eli Smith, for twenty years after arrival in Beirut in 1827 and without pills to relieve tension caused by the intricacies of thirteen conjugations and thirty-three ways of making the infinitive in Arabic, struggled with this complex language until he mastered it. During the final decade of his labors before he died in 1857, he concentrated on a fresh Arabic Bible. Other individuals, led by Cornelius Van Dyck (the author of outstanding

21

Arabic texts), completed the new translation in 1864. All this work produced a Bible adopted by diverse Arab sects and still in use in the 1960s. Among the Nestorians in northwest Persia, Justin Perkins successfully ruled over modern Syriac and brought its cadences to the Urmia press in the translation of the Bible and other works.

As Luther and his co-reformers had used movable type to help win northern Europe and eventually North America to Protestantism, so the missionaries used it to win people in Turkey. The Protestants converted Near Easterners to America's bookish culture and its individualistic and rational notion that the Bible must be widely available in the vernacular. Historian Daniel J. Boorstin has noted that America from its colonial beginning stifled anything like the Iliad or Beowulf oral cycles by publishing subliterature. The printing-press mentality of the United States thus became one of the most powerful implements the missionaries had in opening the minds of Armenians and Arabs. Within semi-tribal communities the type-set page in the privacy of the reader's home or in a school could and did expose to inquiring persons the inadequacy of many ancient authorities. Reducing cultural lag in an area which was just beginning to accept the printed word, the Protestants probably would not have been able to invade the old churches without their superior technology. The Americans' concept of God possibly made its appearance as much through Western machines and linguistically skilled missionaries as through the Spirit of the incarnate Word. One theologian in America thought that Protestants abroad acted as if lead type and paper were the light of the world. At any rate, Protestants in Turkey had an important place, along with leaders of several dozen publishing houses usually run by non-Turks, in bringing the Gutenberg epoch to the Ottoman Empire.[34] As late as the First World War, Turkey included few indigenous publishers. Many Muslims believed that since people had written the Quran by hand for centuries, Allah must dislike movable print.

With a press at one hand and equally American work tools at the other, the Protestant educational movement had such a leader as Cyrus Hamlin. Charismatic and abounding in energy, Hamlin helped start the American Board's Bebek Seminary in 1840. He soon organized an industrial annex to broaden the experience of the students. Standing at bench and anvil, Hamlin led young men in making shoes, clothes, ash pans, and sheet-iron stoves. His efforts elicited both admiration and cultural shock in nationals. Once when a person died of cholera and people would not bury the body for fear of the disease, Hamlin put a cloth saturated with vinegar over his mouth and nose and carried the corpse to a coffin. Rumors spread among Turks that he had an electrical machine which made Protestants of those whom he photographed; if the converts apostatized, he simply cut the pictures and the individuals died. Putting together a steam engine and using it to power a flour mill, he started a bakery despite the objections of his startled associates. During the Crimean War in the 1850s he and his students produced a daily peak of several thousand loaves of bread for soldiers. Profiting twenty-five thousand dollars, he turned the gains over to the mission treasury (which used the money to erect thirteen churches for Armenian Protestants). So, Hamlin was the mover in one of America's first technical assistance programs overseas, training young men in Western manufactures and finance.[35]

Soon Hamlin became interested in higher education. The American Board in 1856 temporarily decided not to finance schools but only to proclaim the Gospel. Two sons of Harrison Dwight then obtained the support of businessman Christopher Robert, who was treasurer of the American Home Mission Society, for a Christian college independent of the American Board. Robert, in turn, recruited Hamlin, who left the Board to pursue the enterprise. Opening in a Bebek Seminary building in 1863, the college was unusual: it had more faculty members (five) than students (four), it was the first American institution of higher learning anywhere abroad, and it combined technical with classical training. Hamlin and Robert sought instructors with "fervent, symmetrical piety" and "missionary spirit." Living with the students, Hamlin employed many creative methods. Once he had two quarreling young men named Silvio and Pierre sign a formal statement. "The two high contracting parties agree," the statement declared, "that in order to preserve peace . . . one shall not call the other an ass or a dog or a pig or a thief, robber, rowdy, pezevenk or other opprobrious epithet in Italian, French, Turkish, Greek, English, Bulgarian, Armenian or any other language spoken at the Tower at Babel or since that day. Silvio shall in no case strike Pierre nor Pierre Silvio." In 1868 the college moved to the site of its campus located six miles north of Constantinople; the campus overlooked the Bosporus and the Rumeli Hisar fortress built by Mehmed the Conqueror in 1453 during the final siege of Constantinople.[36] (Illustration 1 and inset, Map 2, on p. 17.)

Throughout the years Robert College patterned itself on the best New England schools. Hamlin's son-in-law, George Washburn (who went to

Constantinople in 1858 as local treasurer of the American Board), became its second president. The main sources of finance were such Protestant philanthropists in New York as John Stewart Kennedy, William E. and Cleveland H. Dodge, and, of course, Christopher Robert, whose total contributions were more than four hundred thousand dollars. The school prided itself in its athletic program; with the completion of Dodge Gymnasium in 1904, it had both the first indoor track and basketball court in the Ottoman Empire. Developing emphases of Hamlin, it established an engineering school in 1912.

Another pioneer in education was Daniel Bliss. Syrian missionaries had started preparing in 1862 for what became the Syrian Protestant College. Recognizing that the American Board had inadequate funds, they decided that a college in Syria should be legally independent of the Board. But these men contemplated that the college be "guarded by the combined wisdom and experience of the mission," and chose Bliss from their midst to head the project.[37] Spending much time in England and the United States between 1862 and 1866, Bliss raised over a hundred thousand dollars and incorporated his project in the state of New York. From the American Board's Abeih Academy, later to merge with the Syrian Protestant College, came a model. The goal was to organize a liberal arts program which would develop the physical, intellectual, and moral potential of students from any ethnic group or religion, and especially train leaders for the local Protestant community.

In December 1866 the Syrian Protestant College (later the American University of Beirut) opened triumphantly with sixteen students and four instructors. Seeking academic quality and using Arabic as the language of instruction, Bliss soon produced departments of medicine and pharmacy. After some interval there were departments of commerce (1900), nursing (1905), and dentistry (1910). The nursing program became one of the earliest opportunities for Near East women to receive a technical education. The department of dentistry was the first in the Ottoman Empire; the school's extracurricular activity was another first. For a campus, Bliss found a location next to the azure Mediterranean Sea and beneath snow-covered Mount Lebanon. At the cornerstone ceremony for the first building, he declared: "A man white, black or yellow; Christian, Jew, Mohammedan or heathen, may enter and enjoy all the advantages of this institution . . . and go out believing in one God, in many Gods, or in no God. But it will be impossible for any one to continue with us long without

24

knowing what we believe to be the truth and our reasons for the belief." [38]
The Bliss approach to discipline was more subtle than Hamlin's. As Bliss
once approached a student who was disobeying the smoking prohibition,
the student thrust his hand and burning cigarette into his pocket. The college president extended his hand, obliging the student to reciprocate.
"How is your father?" Bliss asked. "Your mother [still shaking hands]?
Your grandmother? Give them my greetings when you write." At this
point the cigarette fell through the student's smoking coat to the ground.
Bliss saluted and passed on with no further word.

Educational internationalism from America had its most revolutionary
effect within the Ottoman Empire through a third institution, Constantinople Woman's College (later Istanbul Woman's College), which began
in 1871.[39] Thus, only a decade after the start of the first feminist school of
higher learning in the United States, Vassar College, missionaries ex-
ported to a fairly closed society an idea which was quite radical at home.
The American Board, which had by then become less conservative, nurtured Constantinople Woman's College. An incident which concerned its
head, Mary Mills Patrick, illustrated the cultural tremor the new center
caused. Vastly unlike Turkish women in harems, Miss Patrick rode a bi-
cycle on the streets of Constantinople. An old-line Turk, seeing her blithe-
ly pedaling, exclaimed: "That I should ever live to see such infamy!" [40]
The earliest Turkish girls at Constantinople Woman's College, conditioned to seclusion, often refused to sit at tables served by men and
screamed when they met male attendants on the campus. Gradually, the
thought of a liberal education for women became more popular as the
school prospered. It was fitting that in 1908 the first Turkish woman to
write in the Ottoman press, the renowned Halidé Edib, who was a graduate of Constantinople Woman's College, addressed a eulogy to her alma
mater. She lauded its humane and equalitarian ideals, and concluded: "I
love, love, love everything about the college!" [41]

The Syrian Protestant College, Robert College, and Constantinople
Woman's College became prototypes within the Ottoman Empire. Although they chiefly served students from Christian minorities, a few Muslims recognized the vigor of the colleges and sent their children. French
Roman Catholic missionaries, through St. Joseph University in Beirut
(founded in 1875), established the only school of higher education to
rival those of the Americans. The example of the three United States–
based institutions at Constantinople and Beirut inspired the American

Board during the period from 1878 to 1903 to open seven colleges — usually a combination of high school and junior college: Euphrates College (including seminary) at Harput and American College at Van in eastern Anatolia; Central Turkey College (including seminary) with campuses for men and women at Aintab and Marash, respectively; St. Paul College at Tarsus in the south and Anatolia College at Merzifon in the north; and International College at Smyrna. One other college, by 1914 no longer within the Ottoman Empire, was the Collegiate and Theological Institute at Samokov in Bulgaria. The American Board also began a pioneering school — the Thessalonica Agricultural and Industrial Institute at Salonika in Greece.[42] (See Map 2 on p. 17.)

The development of Anatolia, Central Turkey, and International colleges exemplified American Board schools. Anatolia emerged out of a high school in 1886, and served primarily youth of Armenian Protestant adults in the vicinity of Merzifon. Student enrollment by 1895 had gone over one hundred fifty and by 1903 to nearly five hundred (by then there were fifteen Americans on the staff of seventy including Edward Riggs, a son of Elias Riggs and the father of six children who would become missionaries in the Near East). In 1914 there were twenty Muslims at Anatolia. Concurrently, George E. White became president of the school, having served as treasurer and dean. White's missionary career had begun at Merzifon in 1890, after graduating from both Congregational Grinnell College in Iowa and Chicago Theological Seminary and pastoring a Congregational church for three years. Central Turkey, like Anatolia, had grown out of a high school. From its college beginning in the 1880s, it had large local support from Armenians in Aintab; before its opening an Armenian board of managers had raised sixty thousand dollars among people who were poor by American standards. A Muslim Turk helped pay for college property. Its leading professor at the men's campus in Aintab for over thirty years (until he died in 1913) was Alexan Bezjian, who specialized in physics and chemistry. This Armenian had studied at Bebek Seminary under Cyrus Hamlin and abroad at Yale. John Ernest Merrill, a grandson-in-law of Elias Riggs with a doctoral degree from the University of Minnesota, became president of Central Turkey in 1898. Merrill concentrated his research interests on Christian-Muslim relations. In the course of his thirty-eight year presidency, the school moved to Syria and changed its name to Aleppo College. International College opened in Smyrna as a secondary school in 1891, and incorporated in Massachusetts as a college in 1903. Its main financial benefactors were Mr. and Mrs. John Stewart Kennedy. Serving primarily Greek students (three hundred was the total enrollment in 1911), International innovated in its sports program and agricultural department. It installed the first electric lighting plant in Turkey (1907). From the beginning its president was Alexander MacLachlan, a graduate of Union Theological Seminary in New York.[43]

An embryonic Ottoman school system for Muslims appeared in the latter half of the nineteenth century, partly in imitation of the American and other foreign facilities. As late as 1850 there were only six secondary schools. Not until 1868 did the first Western-style secondary institution, the Imperial Ottoman Lycée, open. By the 1880s a planned system of public education had emerged. The first modern center of higher learning developed in 1900 at Constantinople.[44]

Educational missions became the vogue for Protestants from across the Atlantic much as revivalism had been in the 1820s. Americans by 1914 had developed a larger network of schools in Turkey than any other nationality group, with most strength in Anatolia among Armenians and least in Syria where British, French, and Russian missions were robust. Approximate statistics tell something: in the northern Ottoman Empire there were 2,500 college students, 4,500 pupils in fifty high schools, and 20,000 in four hundred elementary schools; in Syria there were over 6,000 enrollees in both the Syrian Protestant College and one hundred secondary and elementary institutions (making a total of 33,000 students throughout Turkey). China, India, and the Near East were the three leading areas for educational internationalism from the United States.[45]

Protestant education showed both conservation and mellowing of New England ethnocentrism. The foreign secretary of the American Board, James L. Barton, wrote in 1913 that educational missions were a part of propagating the traditional Good News, although he acknowledged that founders of the Board would not have agreed.[46] Barton intimated that raising the status of women by educating them was like Jesus' concern for protecting women against cynical divorces (the Master taught that adultery, not a whim, was just cause for a husband turning out his wife). Barton suggested that promoting ecumenical understanding by giving a Western, Christian education to members of the Near East churches was like Jesus' desire that Samaritans and Syro-Phoenicians develop sympathy for the Jewish view of God. Barton rejoiced in the increasing role of indigenous teachers in the schools; in the preparation of church, business, and professional leaders; in the influence on constitutional and educational reform within Turkey. He also worried about the increasing use of English as the mode of instruction, which was Westernizing as much as Christianizing many students, and about the decline of overt Christianity.

Emphasis on the lectern more than the pulpit had potential for retrogression within the missionary program. There was the possibility that teaching Western life would lead many Armenians and Arabs to emigrate to the United States or that it would encourage rebellion of minorities against the reactionary Ottoman government. Sultan Abdul Hamid the Second warned: "Private schools constitute a grave danger to our nation. With unpardonable carelessness we have allowed representatives of all sorts of nationalities to build schools at all times and places. What a peril they are has often been shown." [47]

THROUGH A GLASS DARKLY

While educational efforts enlarged, missionaries had become somewhat introspective and frustrated about their purposes. Should priority be on individual or social salvation, education or evangelism, philanthropy or preaching, public affairs or the church, accommodation or resistance to a different culture, cooperation with secular values or defense of pietistic ones? Of course, no single one of these alternatives were unrelated to the others, so no simple answers appeared. Further, there were indications during the late nineteenth century that the traditional self-confidence of missionaries was not quite so strong as previously. The trumpet of Parsons and Fisk no longer sounded so certainly. Among many issues, the Protestants were disturbed that the "empire of Muslim sin" was not crumbling. Missionaries became aware of mixed and anxious feelings as never before.

Organizational changes between 1863 and 1870 had helped prepare for later complexity and nervousness. As noted, Robert College and the Syrian Protestant College from their formation were not part of the American Board. Another division of the mission structure, worked out by mutual consent, was the allotment in 1870 of Syria and Persia to the newly formed Presbyterian Board of Foreign Missions and the restriction of the American Board, supported primarily by Congregational churches, to Asia Minor and European Turkey.

These disruptions at first made little informal difference among the missionaries. Cooperation and personnel movement across institutional lines was regular. Whether active primarily in schools, scholarship, publishing, or churches, all Protestants from the United States called themselves missionaries and sought to apply evangelical Christianity to the Ottoman Empire. The two separate missionary schools drew almost solely on Presbyterians and Congregationalists for teachers. Intermarriage of personnel in diversified areas, functions, and boards was typical. Sons, daughters, and brothers of former or serving missionaries often joined the Protestants in the Near East. Service there became a proud family tradition as well as a Christian and professional commitment.

The leading colleges first provided opportunity for irritants to harmony of design and deed. These centers were not directly accountable to the American or Presbyterian boards or to churches. Financial sources were individuals more often than religious groups. The Syrian Protestant College in 1878 decided to move toward instruction in English since qualified teachers in Arabic were scarce. The Presbyterian mission in Syria fought to block this choice, objecting because it had anticipated when abandoning Abeih Seminary earlier that the college would supply Protestant teachers prepared in Arabic for village schools (instruction in English would make the village-school design untenable).[48] A Presbyterian Board missionary noted that the college did not teach what his organization needed and that the school's location in a city made students unfit for work among rural people. His critique and others by his colleagues were in vain. Next, the college's training of students with various religious and ethnic origins (in contrast to previous stress on Christian Arabs) and Ottoman restrictions against discrimination toward Muslims helped lead to relaxed regulations for chapel and for Bible classes. These reasons, coupled with pressures for finances and an increased staff, aided the Syrian Protestant College in 1902 to drop requirements for professors to sign statements of faith. The school also sought philanthropists for trustees, men not necessarily ardent Christians. The Presbyterian mission in Syria at the turn of the century declared that the college, while certainly an honor to the United States and a blessing to Western Asia, was not furnishing workers to the Protestant Arab community. A similar sequence was in progress at Robert College.

Even the American Board school, Constantinople Woman's College, was having comparable experiences. By 1890 it had received a charter from the state of Massachusetts. Its president, Miss Patrick, developed autonomy by such measures as a gift of $150,000 from John D. Rockefeller. In 1908 her drive for a program free from the American Board ended with victory. Then she cultivated such industrialists as a plumbing manufacturer from Chicago, Presbyterian Charles R. Crane. She recounted that when money was hard to find, Crane "was always ready to hand it out. One could tell it by a far-away, absent-minded look in his face that he was about to announce an especially large gift. As a matter of fact, I became quite familiar with that particular look." [49]

The determination of the three independent colleges to have a more flexible mission than the American and Presbyterian boards showed that many of the Protestants in the Ottoman Empire had a new Christian style. Howard Sweetser Bliss, a son of Daniel Bliss and second president of the Syrian Protestant College, explained the modern missionary. The modern missionary, Howard Bliss felt, believes in the uniqueness of Christianity, yet does not think it is the "sole channel through which divine and saving truth has been conveyed." He is not self-righteous or disparaging of other religions. He trusts in the Bible, not as errorless, but as a spiritual document with great appeal. He proclaims Christ's love and joy, obedience to God, hope amid tragedy and sin, and concern for a benign social order. He recognizes behavior change as final proof of the Message. He allows theological variety but insists on Christ's authority. "Or, in following Him, are your lips silent in your incapacity to define Him and His influence upon you? Call Him by no name, but follow Him!" The modern missionary, Bliss concluded, seeks to bring a person to Christ "with or without a resulting change in his ecclesiastical affiliation." [50]

Howard Bliss' ideas revealed growing awareness over a half century of Saint Paul's affirmation that followers of Jesus see through a glass darkly. The human environment, whether Western or Eastern, never absorbs the whole truth of God. Not until the late nineteenth century were missionaries distinguishing between Christianity and the manners and morals of New England. It began to occur to some of them that acculturation to American Protestantism by Arabs and Armenians might be undesirable. [51]

American Board Secretary James Barton had been one of the first to express new views. The missionary, Barton declared, does not go abroad to overturn society. Rather, he goes to shed Christian light as intense as a noonday sun without denigrating feeble native tapers. "All that is good in the old religion remains, all else disappears. The missionary does not forget," Barton continued, "that Jesus came not to destroy, but to fulfil." The mission executive wrote of a multipurpose Gospel: individual redemption, sharing the Good News both through example and through printed and oral words, Christian schools, and uplifting society by fighting unsanitary conditions and poverty.[52]

Barton's statements partly reflected a mood within American public opinion. An editorial in the *Nation* during the 1890s declared that the heroic age of missions was waning. Protestants overseas, the editorial stated, should stop exaggerating the sins of the "heathen" and the virtues of the United States. Since travel, commerce, and study of comparative religion were increasing among Americans, missionaries should not use hyperbole to seek retention of their monopoly of information about foreign societies.[53] Both the *Nation*'s and Barton's views, although not identical, showed concerns less culturally bound than rather simply planting New England Protestantism in Ottoman turf.

There was a dramatic reason for Barton's expressions. Introducing minorities in the Ottoman Empire to Western affluence and ideology was helping an exodus of Near Easterners to a transatlantic Promised Land. Between 1905 and the start of the First World War there were 367,000 emigrants from Turkey to the United States, nearly 75 per cent of whom were Greeks, Arabs, and Armenians.[54] As early as the 1880s and within a period of only eighteen months, the town of Zahlah in Syria lost to America 10 per cent of its population. Many of the Zahlah emigrés had been educated in Presbyterian Board schools and 5 per cent were Protestants. Throughout Syria the stampede to the United States removed local preachers and teachers from the American mission and threatened cessation of some of its activities.

In addition to emigration, the Social Gospel — an invigorated form of the Second Great Awakening's practical Christianity — was helping alter missions in Turkey. Some Protestants from the United States were sympathetic with efforts in the homeland to focus God's judgment upon the "Great Barbecue" after the Civil War; new industrialists such as Andrew Carnegie and John D. Rockefeller often were roasting the American urban workingman by their practices. Since injustices abounded also in Ottoman life, missionaries in their schools increasingly sought to deal with these inequities by teaching Western democracy, medicine, nursing, engineering, and business. They drew upon the American revivalist heritage of Christian humanitarianism and reform to put on caps of various social services. There were dispensaries and hospitals, pioneered by an early physician, Asahel Grant, who worked in the Mosul region from 1835 to 1843. By the late nineteenth century physicians had come to reside at many mission

31

stations. Among dedicated physicians and nurses was Mary Eddy, who in 1908 established the first tuberculosis sanatorium in the Ottoman Empire, and Clarence D. Ussher, who led in trying to control typhus, cholera, and smallpox epidemics. In the year 1914 there were ten missionary hospitals and a dozen or more dispensaries, performing hundreds of major surgeries and aiding thousands of patients. A sizeable number of individuals benefited were Muslims.

Cups of educational and humane water, given not only to Protestant Armenians and Arabs but to people of Gregorian, Syrian Orthodox, and Islamic conviction, both fretted and encouraged missionaries. In a report to the World Missionary Conference of 1910 in Edinburgh, a Presbyterian missionary complained that much of the new education was not Christ-oriented and would lead to skepticism and secularism. A companion urged that the Americans renew their commitment to their Lord and the spiritual transformation of Muslim Arabs. Howard Bliss in his report to the World Missionary Conference wrote that "missionary enterprise can be best advanced through the establishment of a Christian missionary system of education," although he admitted that almost no one at the Syrian Protestant College had developed a Protestant church affiliation through that means.[55]

The statement to the Missionary Conference about revived efforts among Muslims symbolized increasing uneasiness about the Protestants' failure to go forward against Islam. Only two out of some four hundred evangelical missionaries from the West to the Ottoman Empire in the early twentieth century were working solely with Muslims. An American missionary enthusiast for Muslim outreach, Henry Jessup, had announced in 1879 an imperial approach to evangelism through a speech at Saratoga, New York, a speech later published. Jessup believed that divine providence had provided Great Britain and the United States with the political, religious, and educational appliances for solving the problem of converting Muslims. He thought of a British protectorate over Turkey, consequent legality for a follower of Muhammed to change his religion, then an aggressive attack on Islam's adherents and "nominal" Christians. In 1910 a German historian and friend of Protestant missions in the Near East, Julius Richter, set forth a proposal less patronizing than Jessup's: provision of medical and educational services to Muslims.

Much of the nervousness about goals and means in relation to Muslims, ancient Christians, education, and evangelism, was latent, particularly since there was considerable pride about the Protestant edifice in the Near East. This edifice was becoming ever more imposing. By 1914 the American Board had developed in Turkey a field larger than anywhere else in the world, having divided this field into four administrative areas: European, Western, Central, and Eastern Turkey. (See Map 2 on p. 17.) These areas included over twenty stations, one hundred fifty personnel (clergymen, physicians, wives, and unmarried women), a thousand national workers, and fifteen thousand members in one hundred thirty evangelical Armenian churches. About 75 per cent of all the Western Protestant enterprises in Asia Minor and European Turkey were under American Board control. In Syria, the Presbyterian Board had in 1914 approximately four stations, fifty on the staff, two hundred national associates, three thousand church members — an organization about the same size as England's Church Missionary Society in Palestine. The three independent missionary colleges each had several hundred students (the Syrian Protestant College was the largest with nine hundred seventy) and several dozen faculty members. As mentioned, over thirty-three thousand students attended American schools throughout the Ottoman Empire. Other groups from the United States — Reformed Presbyterian (northern Syria), Dutch Reformed (Arabia), American Bible Society, Young Men's Christian Association, Christian and Missionary Alliance, Friends, and Adventist — carried out small programs.[56] The United Presbyterian work in Egypt, an area virtually independent of the Ottoman Empire, devoted itself chiefly to the Coptic minority through about fifty schools. In size of operation the American religious activity, if compared with other United States concerns, made an impression so broad that many people in Turkey believed that to be an American in the Empire was synonymous with being a missionary.[57]

At the end of nearly a century of missions in the Near East, American Protestant enterprise had become diversified. Originally, almost all missionaries had been unbending theologically, compulsive, partisan to New England Puritanism, oriented to individual salvation and church building, reticent about direct involvement in public affairs. Such views no longer dominated in 1914. By then the missionary contingent had become a blend of individuals like the first-generation people and of individuals characterized by theological openness and by reflection on goals as well as activism. Other fresh interests were ecumenicism and readiness to accept government intervention in reaching religious ends. Parsons and Fisk had said in effect: "Evangelize Muslim and 'nominal' Christian persons as a means of overthrowing Islam and reforming the old churches. Don't interfere directly with the state and public matters." Many twentieth-century missionaries were declaring, in chorus with the World Missionary Conference: "Christianize the nations through evangelism *and* service, churches *and* schools. Don't reject aid by government assistance." [58]

Appreciation of Near East values by the Protestant internationalists was still superficial in the early twentieth century. The slogan, "Christianize the nations," showed a bias rooted too easily in the assumption that the United States was a Protestant country. The belief that the founding fathers had created a Christian nation helped this assumption (many of the seventeenth-century colonial progenitors were rascals and materialists, many leaders of the American Revolution were freethinkers and Unitarians, perhaps 5 per cent of the people in the 1780s belonged to churches). Only around 40 per cent of Americans in the 1910s were church members, including Roman Catholics. In this same decade there was evidence that the milieu of the missionary's homeland included superior feelings about "Christian" America. An important movement was a nativist, Anglo-Saxon, Protestantism directed against Roman Catholic and other urban immigrants. Progressives had the hallelujah emotion that God's truth was marching on under Woodrow Wilson. Prohibitionists were invariably Protestants who sought to force everyone to accept teetotaling. Missionary behavior in Turkey was similar; the enemy was often more an ecclesiastical rival than the devil. One Presbyterian annual report stated: "Mohammedans, Muscovites [Russian Orthodox] and Monks furnish their full quota of opposition, but the Lord Christ has bidden us go onward." [59] The Kingdom of Heaven for missionaries in 1914, as with Levi Parsons and Pliny Fisk, was still primarily an unconscious mixture of Protestantism and Americanism.

Chapter 2

The Eastern Question

MISSION blending of society and religion — usually guileless, unconscious, defensive about security of persons, property, and program — helped Protestant emissaries become important in Ottoman-American relations. Missionaries disavowed union of Church and State but not of Christianity and culture. Since they dealt with the latter dichotomy so little, they were ill-prepared to cope with upheavals in the Empire which inextricably combined politics and religion. When upsets became large in the 1890s, missionaries were then the main interest of the United States government in Turkey. Other interests concerned tourists, academicians, merchants, and naturalized Americans. There were diplomatic exchanges not directly concerning the American religionists in the two decades before 1914. But nothing during that period was larger in Turkish-American affairs than the missionaries and their difficulties.

LEDGER, PEN, AND FLAG

It did not seem in 1810 that missionaries were to become ascendant, for Yankee traders then dominated relations between the Western republic and the Ottoman Empire. Earlier the English colonies in the New World made few contacts with the realms of the Sultan, for British navigation laws had sought to give the mother country a monopoly in the East. Possibly the first American vessel to dock at an Ottoman wharf was the *Grand Turk*, built in Salem, Massachusetts, in 1782. The *Grand Turk* frequently loaded gum, carpets, figs, and raisins into its hold at Smyrna in the next decade or so. In the span from 1811 to 1820 around eighty American ships stopped at Smyrna, selling cotton goods, tobacco, gunpowder, bread-stuffs, and rum (the last being the most important item). In return, American merchants picked up such Turkish exports as nuts, silver, raw wool, and hides, and participated more and more in the opium trade between the Near East and China. After 1815 the United States government sought to assist commerce through a naval squadron in the Mediterranean, based at Minorca.

During the 1820s Henry Clay of Kentucky, who favored the Greek drive for independence from the Ottoman Empire, thundered in the House of Representatives against the pro-Turkish attitude of commercial circles in the United States: "A wretched invoice of figs and opium has been spread before us to repress our sensibilities and eradicate our humanity." [1] Throughout the Greek war American opinion was divided between merchants who longed for enlarged trade with Turkey on the one hand, and agrarian and missionary interests, which saw a vindication of Christianity and of America's self-determination in the Greek rebellion on the other. President James Monroe in 1823 came close to recognition of Greek independence. But the United States government remained aloof while commerce with the Ottoman Empire expanded.[2] (Incidentally, dislocations during the Greek-Turkish conflict resulted in a private relief enterprise, the first sustained American venture in overseas philanthropy.) [3]

Much more than missionary matters, economic concerns produced official ties between Washington and Constantinople. Yankee businessmen, supported by the Navy, had been seeking treaty relations since 1800. The chief merchant at Smyrna, David Offley, after 1811 led these businessmen. Offley's Philadelphia firm controlled about 30 per cent of the goods exchanged there. The Sultan at his headquarters on the Bosporus, the Porte, could not have cared less. New England was remote and unimaginable to him — as it was to a later Shah of Persia who ordered the preparation of camels for a trip to the White House and sent a man to a London "bazaar" to discover the caravan route to the United States. Turkey in the early nineteenth century felt no need of formal communication with the United States, especially since its ships did not touch there and its Greek minority handled most of the transactions at Smyrna. The most the Porte wanted from America was naval aid. This desire arose from a United States reputation for excellence in naval architecture, a reputation which had spread since the Barbary wars. By the 1820s Offley had become a consular representative and a promoter in the John Quincy Adams administration for an agreement with the Porte. Then came a naval disaster for the Ottoman Empire in 1827 at Navarino off the southwestern Greek coast, inflicted by European powers: during the battle the Sultan and his Egyptian subjects lost sixty of seventy-five vessels. This defeat hastened an end to Turkish dallying about a pact with the United States. Negotiations in 1830 produced a treaty of commerce and amity, including a most-favored-nation clause, and assurances that American individuals would privately assist in rebuilding the Turkish fleet. Consent to the treaty by the United States Senate came a year later. Missionaries and traders alike profited from capitulatory rights — traditional exemptions for Westerners from Ottoman jurisdiction.

The 1830s and 1840s were the heyday of a United States outreach guided by people other than those of the American Board. Merchants expanded their trade. In the 1830s Henry Eckford, an American shipbuilder who had helped construct the Lake Erie squadron of the War of 1812, and his assistant Foster Rhodes sought to modernize the Turkish Navy. The 1840s saw a reform Sultan request the aid of President James K. Polk in securing the unofficial services of two horticulturists to improve cotton in the Ottoman Empire. Polk found a Southern planter, James Bolton Davis, and a civil engineer and chemist, J. Lawrence Smith, who both entered the imperial service at kingly salaries. The two men — typical American activists — instead of revitalizing Turkey's agriculture, felt so stifled by the Ottoman bureaucracy that they soon shook Near East dust off their shoes and departed. Smith afterward said a troop of "lazy, ignorant scoundrels" had followed him around.[4]

American trade and export of technical know-how declined after 1850, hurried by high tariffs passed by the United States Congress, lack of governmental interest in the Ottoman Empire (although the naval squadron remained in the Mediterranean), British competition, European imperialism, and other factors. For decades commerce was sluggish. A sign both of small investments and of ineptitude was the misguided venture in Dollar Diplomacy, a railroad and mining scheme known as the Chester Project attempted between 1908 and 1913.[5] Business concerns opened the American Chamber of Commerce for the Near East in 1911. But economic and technical commitments by the United States were almost non-existent compared with Germany's strategic Berlin-to-Baghdad railway and with British, French, Italian, and Russian investments. At the outbreak of the First World War, America sent an infinitesimal .17 per cent of its yearly exports to the Ottoman Empire. Turkish exports to the United States then — 23 per cent of the Turkish total, including tobacco, licorice, figs, and dates — were only about 1 per cent of the full volume of imports into America. Prominent United States firms operating in Turkey were the American Tobacco Company, the Standard Oil Company of New York (Socony), the Singer Sewing Machine Company (with about two hundred agencies and stores), and the Western Electric Company of Chicago.

Religious and literary internationalists, paced by missionaries and by writers, meanwhile had become more conspicuous in American relations with the Near East than merchants. This internationalism contrasted with the political isolationism of the United States government. Alongside the Protestant establishment were various Americans, all curious about the physical habitat that nurtured the Christian Scriptures and the *Arabian Nights*. In 1835, a travel writer and son of a New York merchant, John Lloyd Stephens, had gone to this land which included both shrines and dancers. From material he gathered there, Stephens produced two best sellers on the Near East. A visitor three years after Stephens, Andover Theological Seminary professor Edward Robinson, labored with Eli Smith of the American Board to make the most systematic study of Palestine since that of Eusebius and Jerome in the fourth century. Robinson's published notes won for him the first gold medal ever given a Western-Hemisphere figure by the British Royal Geographic Society. His achievement helped form the American Oriental Society at Boston in 1842, among whose sixty-eight charter members were sixteen American Board individuals. (Missionaries were the chief sources of information about the non-Western world for decades after the Society's founding.) The work both of Robinson and Smith and of the Society spurred the appearance of archaeologists, explorers, and biblical scholars in the Holy Land. By 1900 such people had founded the American School of Oriental Research at Jerusalem.

Missionaries regularly published descriptions of their lives and environs, a pattern which became a Gutenberg ritual. Biographies and memoirs were usually pietistic, exaggerating the saintly in their subjects. One of the best among cultural works was William Thomson's two-volume view of

Syria, *The Land and the Book; or Biblical Illustrations Drawn from the Manners, Customs, Scenes, and Scenery of the Holy Land* (1859). A dignified yet chatty narrative alive with warmth and humanity, Thomson's publication went through many editions totaling nearly two hundred thousand copies. It possibly sold more than any other American title of its time save *Uncle Tom's Cabin.* The cumulative effect of missionary and other writings in the United States was both an enlarged store of knowledge and a romantic perception of the Near East.

While Americans wrote, their diplomatic representatives in Turkey had little to do but seek protection of nationals. Most of these nationals were evangelists, educators, returned emigrants, and tourists. The earliest chargé d'affaires, then minister resident, was David Porter, in Constantinople from 1831 to 1843. He conducted annual Fourth of July parties at his residence for the children of missionaries. The grandeur of the legation office filled by Porter's successors was obvious: these men from 1861 to 1876 had to pay their own rent for a Turkish house on a side street reached by a filthy alley filled with barking dogs. Another indication of the value placed upon the legation office at the Porte by the American government was selection of eccentric General Lew Wallace as both Near East expert and minister on the strength of his sentimental tale, *Ben Hur* (1880). Historian John A. DeNovo has remarked that the White House's representatives were so relaxed that such missionaries as George Washburn of Robert College and Howard Bliss of the Syrian Protestant College often felt they had to become do-it-yourself diplomats. Washburn and Bliss directly dealt with British officials in Turkey as well as with local magistrates. Troubles around the turn of the century prodded Washington to give the Constantinople officer ambassadorial rank in 1906, and to organize the Division of Near Eastern Affairs within the State Department three years later.

Despite the casualness of the United States government vis-à-vis the Ottoman Empire, it had gradually become concerned about providing security for Americans there. Secretary of State Daniel Webster in the 1840s voiced sympathy for defending Protestant individuals and institutions. Americans kept pressing for new exemptions from Ottoman law, although such attempts caused resentment among Turks. Only once was there an extension of rights beyond those in the Treaty of Amity and Commerce of 1831, and the Porte revoked this concession in 1884. Another difficulty for the United States concerned how to protect several thousand returned, naturalized Americans of Ottoman origin (in 1914 there were some thirty thousand, mostly Armenian and Arab Americans).[6] The Turkish government protested that these people took unfair advantage of their adoptive citizenship. Partly to serve such people, but more because of mission pressure, United States consuls came to reside in Aleppo (Halab), Alexandretta (Iskenderun), Baghdad, Beirut, Erzurum, Harput, Jerusalem, Mersin, Sivas, Smyrna, and Trabzon. Occasionally missionaries influenced the choice of a consul or vice-consul or took the latter office themselves. Apprehension for missionary safety increased when, in 1862, brigands murdered two missionaries. In 1883 bandits attacked two American Board members at Van, and United States diplomats asked for an indemnity (a plea denied).

By the 1890s firmness had entered into the Western republic's relations with the Sultan, giving a new dimension to cultural internationalism from the United States. Up to then, the pens of writers on the Near East had been mightier than the ledger or the flag. There were hints that the time had come when the flag might exert its strength.

RATTLING THE SULTAN'S WINDOWS

In the two decades before the Great War, the United States became conscious of the Eastern Question, the query about the future place of Turkey in the European balance of power. Missionaries belatedly sensed the need for government support against Ottoman civil disorder. At no time did the Protestants from America become agents of the State Department, even though other Western missionaries in Turkey sometimes used capitulatory rights to advance their nations' imperial interests. America, delighting that European distresses indirectly had helped its successes, traditionally abstained from the Old World's high politics. The American government had concentrated on conquering its own frontier, dominating the Caribbean, and penetrating the Far East; then in the 1890s it reluctantly began to look at the Eastern Question.

Perhaps the first large trouble signs for Protestants had come in the late 1860s when the Porte tightened regulations on mission educational institutions. It regarded them as breeding marshes for nationalism and revolution among minorities. Discomfort for missionaries intensified when in the 1880s Sultan Abdul Hamid the Second harassed their schools, occasionally closing them. Often French and Russian agents encouraged measures against American learning centers, because these agents told Ottoman officials the centers had a political object. In exasperation, the American Board in 1885 asked that the President use the United States Navy to help protect missions in the Empire. The Grover Cleveland administration refused. Only joint American-British complaints prevented disruption of schools.[7]

Fearing an insurrection among Christian minorities, Ottoman leaders became neurotic about American colleges which had an Armenian clientele. In 1892 Turks set fire to a missionary's house, and Ottoman police in 1893 burned an unfinished building of the American Board school at Merzifon, Anatolia College; the police hoped to drive the foreign Protestants out of north-central Asia Minor. The student body of Anatolia College in 1893 included ninety-four Armenians, twenty-three Greeks, and three Turks. Among the teachers Turks claimed there were two members of an Armenian revolutionary organization who had posted at the school treasonable placards printed on a college duplicator. The placards asked for a British takeover of the Ottoman Empire. Missionary George White of Anatolia College denied in his memoirs that the placards came from college duplicators. White is probably right. Revolutionaries outside Anatolia apparently put the signs on college property to create an incident inviting Western intervention. Turks charged the two Anatolia teachers with treason and condemned them to death; officials also arrested and executed several Merzifon Armenians.[8]

Pardoned and exiled because of pleas by British and American diplomats, the two Anatolia College teachers symbolized the growing import of missionaries in Ottoman-American relations. The United States government asked indemnities from the Porte for mission losses by fire in 1892 and 1893. The Sultan paid $2,200 for damage at Anatolia College.

Then came terror for the Armenians. Frustrated by small revolutionary Armenian groups, Abdul Hamid promised booty to nomadic Kurds who would pillage Armenians. The Sultan in autumn 1894 also ordered Turkish soldiers to murder Armenians at Sassun west of Lake Van. These massacres at Sassun, and later ones from September 1895 through January 1896 at Constantinople, Trabzon, Erzurum, Harput, Aintab, Marash, Urfa, and other locations, probably included at least fifty thousand Armenians. About 10 per cent of the casualties were Protestants. The chaos involved hundreds of plundered villages, hundreds of Gregorian and evangelical churches. Among many American observers the Sultan's name became Abdul Hamid the Damned. Turks had used the technique of mass killings earlier with Greeks (1822), Bulgarians (1876), and Armenians (1877 and 1878).⁹ (See Illustration 6.)

The terror of 1895 and 1896 spurred thousands of Armenians to emigrate to the United States, where they later helped their new government take an active interest in the diplomacy of dismembering the Ottoman Empire. The trickle of two thousand Armenian immigrants into the United States before 1895 had become a gush of seventy thousand by 1914. The Protestant Armenian church in Harput in one year alone lost 25 per cent of its three thousand constituents as migrants to America. Feeling like modern Plymouth Pilgrims fleeing religious persecution, these Armenians from Harput and elsewhere set up New World colonies, particularly in Boston and New York City.¹⁰

The fury of the Sultan and the Turks hit not only Armenians directly, but the American Board. Beside decimating and scattering Armenian Protestants, the turmoil endangered missionary lives when in November 1895 Turks destroyed thousands of dollars worth of Board property at Harput and Marash. The Turkish government then tried to shunt the missionaries out of eastern Asia Minor by inducing sixty Armenians at Harput to sign a statement. The document claimed that the Westerners were misleading students by prejudicing them against the Ottoman Empire and requested that Americans leave at once. The United States legation investigated this document and learned that the sixty Armenians had signed under fear of death. Missionaries stayed put.

Missionaries soon helped organize relief for thousands of Armenian orphans and widows. A clergyman from a missionary family, Frederick D. Greene, became secretary of the National Armenian Relief Committee. Clara Barton of the American Red Cross cooperated closely with the National Armenian Relief Committee. Missionary son Edwin M. Bliss (also assistant editor of the *Independent*), with assistance from Cyrus Hamlin, wrote a book on the history of the Armenian question and on the killings. Bliss described the relief movement in the United States: "Armenian Sundays were observed by many churches; collections were taken in churches, Sunday-schools, colleges, societies and mass-meetings; journals opened their columns for relief subscriptions; individuals collected funds privately; Armenians throughout the country contributed from their slender resources; and the money was forwarded promptly to the field." Red Cross and American Board personnel administered aid at mission stations and colleges throughout Asia Minor, and eventually established orphanages and homes for widows which taught carpentry, tinsmithing, baking, lace-making, and silk culture.[11]

In the meantime, United States Senator Shelby M. Cullom of Illinois introduced a resolution about the Ottoman Empire in Congress. The Cullom Resolution invited the President to ask European powers to "stay the hand of fanaticism and lawless violence" against unoffending Armenians, and promised congressional support for the President "in the most vigorous action he may take for the protection and security of American citizens in Turkey, and to obtain redress for injuries committed upon the persons or property of such citizens."

Persuading the chamber to approve his measure, Cullom helped start what became overly pro-Armenian sentiment in public consideration of the Ottoman Empire. "I am astounded and appalled," he said in January 1896, "at the brief accounts which I have had of the awful carnival of havoc, destruction, and blood which has prevailed for a time in [Turkey]. . . . There has been no war, no conflict between two contending powers, but a merciless, pitiless tornado of bloody ruin. . . . Through hundreds of Eastern villages, towns blessed with schools and colleges, with churches and missionaries, the demon of damnable and fanatical hate has spread ruin, desolation, and death. . . . The heart of all Christendom is stirred to its very depths as it witnesses the piteous pleas of the suffering Armenians beseeching the Christian world to give them protection." Cullom's style indicated images of public opinion and the imaginal environment within which the government then, and in the years ahead, developed policy toward the Ottoman Empire.[12]

The ideas of Cullom were like those of the Protestant relief propagandists. One cartoon distributed by missionaries and their associates showed Kaiser Wilhelm of Germany congratulating Abdul Hamid as they both stand over an Ottoman map strewn with Armenian skulls and bones. Undisturbed by the ruin, the Kaiser is saying: "Abd-ul my beloved friend! Let us ratify a pact. Give me my railway [Berlin-to-Baghdad railway] and keep all the massacres you want. It is true there are some crackbrains who designate you 'Great Assassin!' 'Sultan Rouge' 'Abd-ul the Damned' and what not, but do not let these literary effusions disturb you, the Pen is powerless unless backed by the Might of the Sword, and — I HAVE MY ARMY." In a corner of the cartoon an angel has written: "The Might of the HAND OF GOD is mightier than the Might of the Sword of man." [13] The head of the Women's Christian Temperance Union, Frances E. Willard, wrote an introduction to Edwin Bliss' book on the massacres. Miss Willard claimed Armenians physically resembled "our Lord" more than any other race, were brave, chaste, simple in faith like New Testament Christians, earnest, unarmed, pastoral, peaceful. She castigated Turks as cruel, vindictive, insane, fanatical, wolfish, detestable, savage, torturing Armenians "as could hardly have been excelled if the bottomless pit had vomited forth its leading spirits to urge the battle on." As to the missionary force, she believed "No band of men and women more heroic have lived since the Great Light shone forth out of Jerusalem." She thought Bliss' book "should nerve the will of every Christian man and woman to defend our Mission and our Missionaries, whose work alone can disinfect the land of the scimitar from its awful taint." Bliss' choice of words showed more restraint and less passion than Miss Willard's, but presented the same stereotypes.[14]

What was the outcome of the Cullom Resolution? President Cleveland dispatched to Turkish waters the cruisers *San Francisco* and *Marblehead*. He resisted mission pleadings, as in a public letter of Cyrus Hamlin, for aggressive gunboat diplomacy. The eighty-six-year-old Hamlin, having missionary children and grandchildren in Turkey, thought a show of American force would stop both the massacres and the attempt of Abdul Hamid to expel the Protestants and to destroy their property. (In China diplomacy at the same time the Cleveland administration had been stressing, rather than a naval demonstration, an investigation and a punishment of local officials for destruction to missionary property in Szechwan.)[15] Anti-imperialist Cleveland also was unwilling to take up feelers from Britain for a joint policy in the Ottoman Empire during the Anglo-American rapprochement after the Venezuelan boundary crisis. The United States government asked the Sultan for an indemnity of around ninety thousand dollars for damage to mission property.[16]

This indemnity question met Turkish procrastination, and lingered for some time. The Sultan felt that United States schools were a factor behind Armenian disloyalty, a notion that American Minister Alexander W. Terrell allegedly reinforced when he accused the missionaries of "fomenting rebellion." The reparation issue escalated into a matter of United States national interest, meriting mention in a presidential message to Congress. It provoked the individual who replaced Terrell during the twelve months following August 1897, James B. Angell (the former president of the University of Michigan), to ask for warships "to rattle the Sultan's windows." Missionary spokesmen in the United States complemented such belligerent talk by urging President William McKinley to take "vigorous measures." [17] McKinley considered coercion when late in 1898 a Jewish New York attorney, Oscar S. Straus, began the second of his four diplomatic missions at the Porte. But dreading an incident like that of the *Maine* leading to the Spanish-American War, McKinley believed that tension in the Caribbean required the presence of the Navy in nearby waters.[18]

McKinley's concern for the indemnity developed in part because Secretary of State John Hay was a cousin of George Washburn, influential president of Robert College. A British ambassador to the Porte was known to give new members of the diplomatic corps in Constantinople a single piece of advice: "Cultivate Dr. Washburn." Urged by this missionary educator, Americans in the United States legation at the Ottoman capital persuaded the commander of the *Kentucky*, a United States vessel passing through the Mediterranean in 1900, to bring his ship to Constantinople. There a twenty-eight-year-old chargé d'affaires, Lloyd C. Griscom, used the presence of the *Kentucky* as leverage. Seeking "to make sure the battleship did not go off," Griscom obtained a promise for the indemnity from the Sultan.[19] The Empire finally paid the sum in 1901.

In addition to the Hay-Washburn relation, there was another missionary tie with an American official which after the events of the 1890s assisted missionary interests. This association had begun as a boyhood friendship between Howard Bliss of the Syrian Protestant College and Theodore Roosevelt.[20] A bombastic soul who deplored the Armenian massacres, Roosevelt declared in 1898: "Spain and Turkey are the two powers I would rather smash than any in the world." [21] As President of the United States, Roosevelt was a spirited champion of American enterprises in the Ottoman Empire. Sending vessels on more than one occasion to bolster the American minister in Constantinople, he helped keep missionary institutions open and secure rights and property. Roosevelt aided such missionaries in jeopardy as Miss Ellen Stone, whom Macedonian bandits kidnapped in 1901. A public subscription in the United States raised seventy thousand dollars in ransom money for her. At one point, he sent a squadron to Smyrna. Defending this use of the Big Stick, Roosevelt said: "The opposition in Turkey to the just protests of our missionaries and the protests of our Minister have made it imperative that some action should be taken." [22]

All the mission upsets coupled with Ottoman anxiety were not enough to pull the United States government into the vacuum of Turkey's weakening position as a great power. An aggravation to Americans was Abdul Hamid's phobia, which drove the Sultan temporarily to ban importation of telephones and typewriters (he was afraid they would become subversive tools). Fears caused him to set up customs regulations which in one year required ripping open all safes and refrigerators to make sure they did not contain contraband. After the Young Turks deposed Abdul Hamid in 1909, President William Howard Taft pursued the Dollar-Diplomacy Chester Project. This huge railroad and economic investment plan for awhile suggested United States entrance into the Eastern Question, but the plan had collapsed by 1913. During the Italo-Turkish War of 1911 and 1912 the White House toyed with an offer of mediation, partly because the American Board and several United States peace societies asked for this step. The President abstained. During the Balkan wars of 1912 and 1913, Taft rejected mediation and contented himself with encouraging relief measures and with sending two American cruisers to the Mediterranean. Irritants, business opportunities, and wars did not lead to more than one brief United States interjection (the Chester Project) into the Ottoman position in the European balance of power.

One writer has summarized relations between Washington and Constantinople: "It should not be understood that the missionaries exploited American diplomacy or that American diplomacy exploited the missionaries." [23] Nervous about criticism of regular appeals by himself and colleagues for diplomatic assistance, American Board Secretary James Barton insisted in 1906 that they had never asked for aid in the promulgation of Protestant operations.[24] Historian Kenneth Scott Latourette apparently has supported this generalization. Latourette's thesis is that in regard to all Western missions in the nineteenth century there was an increasing separation between the spread of Christianity and empire building.[25]

However, events had not been moving against a collusion between religious or economic forces and the United States government in the Near East. For the government, both customary disinterestedness and growing awareness of great power affairs were mixed in the twenty years before 1914.

"OH WEEPING ARMENIA"

Massacres of Armenians from 1894 to 1896 and despoiling of American Board compounds showed a mission relation to nationalism among minorities in the Near East. Protestant organizations were among private groups in the Ottoman Empire facilitating identity not only among Armenians but also among Arabs, Bulgarians, and Albanians. During the First World War these ties between Americans and minorities would help draw the United States into considerations of which countries would gain the lands of the Empire.

It appears that the religionists neither endorsed intrigue by Armenians, nor preached political revolt. There is "evidence that Armenian extremists held it against the missionaries that they refrained from overtly . . . supporting the movement for Armenian independence." [26]

The missionaries' contribution to violence probably was insensitivity toward the possible results of their nearly undivided attention to Armenians instead of Turks. Missionaries apparently did not expect that invigoration of the Armeno-Turkish language by a modern Bible translation and maintenance of many schools among Armenians would encourage nationalism. American Board members neglected their indirect livening of the conflict. Instead they cried out against Ottoman injustice, and gave the Turks a terrible reputation in the United States. One Ottoman ambassador to Washington, Ahmed Rustem, remonstrated against oversimplification of his nation's affairs: "Turkey has been the object of systematic attacks on the part of the press of the United States. She is represented as being a sink of iniquity." Rustem protested that America had vices, not often magnified as were those of the Turks, and that there were virtuous as well as deplorable Turks.[27] Missionaries did not understand that they were expecting the Porte to react benignly as they trained an Armenian minority in literacy and the professions — a minority which included people who spoke of independence. The American Protestants did not imagine how they might have behaved if for several decades in their homeland a foreign educational system directed by Muslims had devoted itself to, say, Afro-Americans, with the result that the black Islamic minority became more proficient than the majority of white Americans.

What happened at Anatolia and Central Turkey colleges illustrated the Americans' insensitivity. Regarding the troubles of 1894 to 1896, George White of Anatolia admitted that the missionaries at Merzifon were "intensely interested spectators and friends" of the Armenian cause. But White believed they were not at all "actors on the stage." He thought that his removal of an Armenian revolutionary who had hidden in a school closet was evidence for nonparticipation in the Armenian cause. Yet when some years later Turks arrested several Armenian students for singing patriotic

47

songs, White took them food during the year they were in prison. He apparently did not perceive how removing a single revolutionary from a closet did not appear to Turks adequate to show impartiality in Turkish-Armenian tension, especially when compared with White's general preoccupation with teaching Armenians and his regular visits to jailed Armenian students. At Central Turkey College in Aintab, the thirty faculty members had trouble in 1909 with a secret Armenian revolutionary society among the two hundred male students (almost exclusively Gregorian and Protestant Armenians). The student revolutionary society threatened a strike to advertise its cause. Upon a recommendation from the faculty, President John Merrill closed the school for six weeks and readmitted only those students who proved they had not belonged to the society. Missionaries felt Merrill's firmness was enough to reduce Turkish fears and to prove the school's integrity in relation to Armenian-Turkish conflict. Of course, Merrill's hard line allayed Turkish suspicion more than a soft line. But the missionaries inadequately saw that the existence of the society at Central Turkey, regardless of the school's disciplining it, convinced many Turks of missionary complicity in Armenian insurrection.[28]

Missionaries were only a factor in the bad feeling between Armenians and Turks. When in 1453 the Turks had taken Constantinople, they already controlled a vast territory previously part of the old Armenian kingdom (the Armenian kingdom had lost its last vestige of statehood around 1375). In time, the Ottoman Empire expanded and overran other areas. The Turks leniently treated the Armenians, who became the favorite non-Muslim minority of the Ottoman government. Then in the Russo-Turkish wars of the 1820s and 1870s (the second followed by the Treaty of Berlin of 1878), Russia obtained parts of the Sultan's domain peopled largely by Armenians. As reprisals for Russian attacks, Turks razed Armenian villages in 1877 and 1878 and killed thousands of Armenians, particularly at Bayazit (later Dogubayazit). (See Map 1 on p. 16.) The creation of a Tsarist Armenia intensified humiliation among the separated Russian and Turkish Armenians. The Treaty of Berlin made a token statement on behalf of Armenians, who incorrectly interpreted this comment as a commitment to their freedom. Russia wanted to absorb the Armenians. Britain had a limited interest in an independent Armenia, which would be both inaccessible and peripheral to the route to India. The Treaty of Berlin stimulated nationalism among Russian and Turkish Armenians without

Western guarantees of aid, and upped the jitters among Turks without controls on Ottoman hostility.

Influenced by French and Marxist socialism, Armenians (primarily Russian) sought to force a European interposition by starting revolutionary movements. The Hunchakian party appeared in 1887 (but fragmented within a decade) and the Dashnaktsuthiun (Armenian Revolutionary Federation) arose in 1890. The only important group solely Turkish Armenian, the Armenakan, began in 1885, and stressed education and self-defense rather than revolt. Located in Van, the Armenakan had little relation to the other parties.[29] Protestant, Roman Catholic, and Gregorian leaders among the Armenians did not endorse revolution and were usually apathetic about it. The Dashnaktsuthiun developed a robust program straddling the Russian-Ottoman border, with an eastern section directed from Tiflis (later Tbilisi) in Russia and a western one from Erzurum in Turkey. This movement touched nerves of national pride among large numbers of peasants. By the middle 1890s the Dashnaktsuthiun was evolving into the first powerful secular institution in Armenian history. It menaced the status of the Gregorian Church. Attempts by the western section of the Dashnaktsuthiun to stir Turkish-Armenian brothers aggravated relations with the Porte. Turkish authorities indiscriminately jailed Armenians. Abdul Hamid sought to end talk of rebellion by the massacres, started in 1894 at Sassun and continued the next two years. Armenian revolutionaries in August 1896 temporarily seized the Ottoman Bank headquarters in Constantinople, hoping to bring European intervention. The Great Powers sought to divert the Sultan from repression to reform, but this effort miscarried. The Dashnaktsuthiun did not give up; memoirs of Armenian volunteer fighter Rouben der Minasian epitomized its work. From 1903 to 1908 Minasian operated in a roving, clandestine company varying from ten to a hundred men. This band trained Armenians around Lake Van to use arms against preying Kurds, generated propaganda, assisted threatened peasants, and administered reprisals against Turks and Kurds.[30]

The Young Turk party gave promise of better days when in 1908 and 1909 it cooperated with the Dashnaktsuthiun to depose Abdul Hamid. The new Ottoman government, led by the Young Turks (officially, the Committee of Union and Progress), restored the Constitution of 1876, which gave rights to minorities. Christians and Muslims embraced each other in the streets of Constantinople. This change of affairs caused the

Dashnaktsuthiun to abandon freedom and secret activity. The new Dashnaktsuthiun planks were Armenian autonomy and election of representatives from their party to the Ottoman Parliament. The Turkish-Armenian section of the Dashnaktsuthiun remained faithful to the Committee of Union and Progress until 1912. It then became obvious that the government's Turkification drive in each vilayet (province) would not permit Armenian autonomy. Militancy and independence again became the platform of the Dashnaktsuthiun.

Meantime in 1909 a massacre of Armenians occurred in the Adana and Tarsus areas of Cilicia. Apparently the tragedy came about as part of a counterrevolutionary attempt by the deposed Sultan. In the furious episode there were over twenty thousand deaths and destruction of approximately fifty churches and schools and five thousand houses and shops. Two American missionaries and twenty evangelical Armenian pastors died. Five missionary women were fortunate to survive a week's siege at Hadjin. British and American warships helped restore order as relief activities began among thousands of refugees. Young Turk investigation brought execution of several Armenians and Turks and compensation to injured Armenians. The government also proclaimed the innocence of Armenians generally and their loyalty to the central authority.[31]

A fundamental factor producing hostility between Turks and Armenians was the millet system. Begun in the fifteenth century, the millets were a series of nonterritorial, ecclesiastical "states" within the Ottoman structure. Each millet was a religious community receiving more faithfulness from its adherents than did the central Turk administration. Millets handled marriage, divorce, inheritance, and other personal civil matters, and nourished separate languages, courts, tax collections, and cultural and educational institutions. After 1863 the Armenians even had their own legislature, which met biennially in Constantinople under the leadership of the Gregorian Patriarch. As Westernization penetrated the Ottoman Empire, chiefly through French thought, the millets became nuclei for European-style, territorial nationalism. Partly because of pressure from the great powers, there were minuscule steps toward reform within the Ottoman Empire in 1839, 1856, 1876, and 1908. Each move in the direction of Western liberalism opted in principle for uniform laws treating religious groups and individuals equally. In actuality, these efforts papered over millet nationalism and did not come anywhere near abolishing it. External and internal conflict was too great. Such Christian minorities as the Greeks and Armenians developed interdependence with Western ideas and groups which undermined the Porte's authority and helped make the reforms dead letters. As communication between millets and the outside improved, cleavage within Turkey increased. Millet attitudes advanced from autonomy to independence and the Constantinople government's from tolerance to suppression. A sign of the nearly hopeless pulling and tearing in the Ottoman fabric was the multiplication of millets: in 1831 there were only three (Greek Orthodox, Jewish, and Armenian Gregorian); in 1914 there were seventeen.[32]

Bound up with the millet dilemma was the scrambled nature of ethnic groups within the population, especially nomadic Kurds and sedentary Armenians and Turks in Asia Minor. Muslim Kurds, as a feudal understanding, traditionally had taken a part of the unarmed Armenians' crops in exchange for protection. This symbiosis worked until Turkish-Armenian confrontation became more pointed. Abdul Hamid permanently spoiled this feudal contract by starting a Cossack style, paramilitary organization among the Kurds which was given a virtually free hand against the Armenians. Dashnaktsuthiun groups armed primarily to protect Armenians against Kurdish sackings. Kurdish-Armenian dissension was a trigger for the massacres from 1894 to 1896. But it was Turkish peasants — economically inferior to and jealous of the Armenians, led by the Ottoman army and police — who did most of the killing. Approximate population figures in the year 1914 for the six vilayets of Asia Minor with the largest numbers of Armenians exemplified the tenuous minority position of each ethnic community there: 1,000,000 Armenians (about 30 per cent), 1,000,000 Turks (about 30 per cent), and 650,000 Kurds (about 20 per cent) in a total population of over 3,000,000 people (including Greek, Nestorian, Arab, and other minorities). Throughout all of the Ottoman Empire there were probably 1,800,000 to 2,000,000 Armenians.[33] (See Map 3 on p. 52.)

Armenian-Turkish confrontation related to the pace of modernization and Westernization in Turkey. The Ottoman Empire had known no Renaissance nor Reformation. No liberal upheaval like the French Revolution. No industrial spurt toward an urban society. After its first international defeat in 1699, Turkey had become more archaic while European areas had united around kings or assemblies and had developed improved technologies. The Muslim Empire lost one piece of territory after another through military setback or bureaucratic decentralization. North Africa,

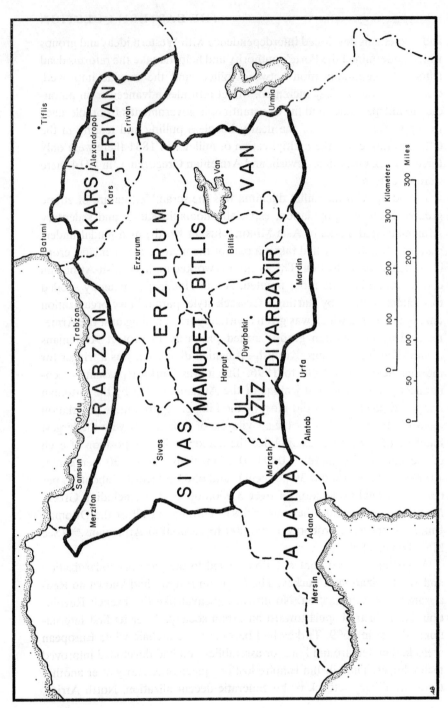

Map 3. Integral Armenia (Ottoman and Russian Armenia), 1914

most of the Balkans, and the Caucasus crumbled off in the nineteenth century. Only the balance of forces among Old World competitors for Turkey's territories and the Sultan's acceptance of some Europeanization, chiefly military and economic, prevented collapse. This selective liberalism allowed Abdul Hamid in some areas to "do what he liked — and what he liked was not liberal." [34] A growing Westernized elite in the Empire came to fruition in the Young Turks. In the impossibly brief time from 1908 to 1914, they strove to create a modern Ottoman state. But in conflicts with such enemies as Italy, Greece, and Bulgaria abroad and Armenians at home, the Committee of Union and Progress turned increasingly to assertive Turkification. A great power diplomatic intervention in 1913 and 1914 on the Armenian question failed to stop the Young Turks from attempts to modernize through stress on Turkish nationalism.

Cultural lag within the Ottoman Empire was helping make relations between Turks and Armenians a sorrowful experience, not only for them but for American missionaries. An Armenian poet has expressed for his people a mood of rumpled defensiveness, valid for any groups caught amid anxieties in Asia Minor: [35]

> Were I given a crown of rich pearls I should prize
> Far more than their beauty one tear from thy eyes,
>> Oh weeping Armenia!
> If freedom unbounded were proffered to me,
> I would choose still to share thy sublime slavery,
>> Oh my mother, Armenia!
> Were I offered proud Europe to take or refuse,
> Thee alone, with thy griefs on thy head, would I choose,
>> My country, Armenia!
> Might I choose from the world where my dwelling should be,
> I would say, still thy ruins are Eden to me,
>> My beloved Armenia!

"FREEDOM NEAR THE PYRAMIDS"

In addition to the Armenian, there were Bulgarian, Albanian, and Arab struggles for nationhood, which Protestants from the United States assisted. These bonds would affect American diplomacy at the end of the First World War.

Although Russian and other European actions were the large factors in Bulgarian independence, mission educators from the United States aided the process. As mentioned, the Protestants had begun work in Bulgaria in

1858 and eventually had opened the Collegiate and Theological Institute at Samokov. The American Board press printed approximately seventy-five of the first hundred books in modern Bulgarian, helping cultural development among the Slavic-speaking peoples of the southeast Balkans. When the Protestants dedicated an evangelical church in Sofia in 1888, Prince Ferdinand of Bulgaria attended the ceremony and donated five hundred francs to the congregation. Until 1890 Bulgarians were a majority of the graduates from Robert College; of 435 alumni between 1863 and 1903, almost half were Bulgarians. Many of these young men went into public service in their homeland, where two provinces gained autonomy within the Ottoman Empire in 1878 and full freedom thirty years later. When the Bulgarian Constituent Assembly met in 1879, former Robert College students who had knowledge of parliamentary procedure and Western government took important responsibilities. Later, many Bulgarian cabinet members, judges, diplomatic officials, and professional leaders were Robert College products.[36] George Washburn, former teacher and adviser of these alumni, became known by many as the "Father of Bulgaria." The King of Bulgaria recognized the value of Robert College to his country by decorating Washburn and the president who succeeded him, Caleb F. Gates.[37]

Albanian nationalism received support from missionaries. Protestant education started among Albanians in 1889, the same time that these people pressed for autonomy within the Ottoman Empire. Partly for political reasons, a Turkish-Albanian official visited American Board headquarters at Boston in 1899, asking for increased mission activity. In 1908 Albanians decided upon an alphabet for their language which missionaries had helped create. As Albanian independence came in 1913, Board secretary James Barton wrote that leading Albanians intended to throw off Islam for Christianity and desired the American Protestants to reorganize their institutions. One missionary during the settlement after the First World War went so far to seek protection of Albania's freedom against Italian and other threats that he became an official representative of the Albanian government to the Paris Peace Conference. (Disorders would force the closing of Board enterprise in Albania in 1922; one Protestant American family then elected to stay on independently until 1939.)[38]

Missionaries in Syria and their collaborator, Butrus al-Bustani, were a force in the Arab awakening of the nineteenth century. Bustani was the earliest Christian Arab nationalist (see pp. 15 and 18). He associated with the American Board in the 1840s and 1850s and thereafter with the Syrian Protestant College. Bustani learned Greek, Hebrew, and English from the Americans and aided them in preparing an Arabic version of the Bible. Then he began a separate career. In Beirut he edited a newspaper and three periodicals, translated many English works, wrote textbooks, helped develop a dictionary, compiled an unrivaled six-volume encyclopedia, and spurred several literary organizations. Bustani sought a non-Islamic, secular unity among all Arab-speaking people regardless of their religion. He used education in his mother tongue as his chief means and from the West selected various materials to rebuild Arab culture.[39]

An efflorescence of writing in Arabic, complementary to Bustani's flourishing, occurred during the 1870s and 1880s, partly through efforts by the Protestant schools and presses. Missionaries and Arab nationals cooperated to produce dozens of texts in anatomy, physiology, pathology, surgery, astronomy, chemistry, botany, mathematics, history, and philosophy. They also originated a medical monthly. Other works were such Bible study aids as a concordance and a dictionary. Syrians prominent in these activities were John Wortabet, Nasif al-Yaziji, and Faris Nimr; Americans included two medical missionaries on the staff at the Syrian Protestant College, George Post and Cornelius Van Dyck. In 1886 the Presbyterians in Beirut boasted that they had the largest single publishing house in the Near East. Contemporaneously, the discontinuation of Arabic as the language of instruction at the college took some of the sparkle out of the literary exuberance. But use of Arabic in the secondary and primary schools thereafter maintained some of the momentum and continued to promote Arab culture while bringing in Western influence.

Besides generating books in Arabic, the Syrian Protestant College had a part in the Arab renaissance through its graduates. Many of the alumni participated in preparing the works mentioned above and went from the college with pride in their language and customs. As of 1903, 90 per cent of the college's 576 graduates had remained in the Near East rather than leaving for a softer life abroad. These individuals founded institutions throughout the Arab world: stores, importation agencies, banks, associations, and by 1910 an alumni magazine. This alumni periodical later merged with the *Middle East Forum*, a publication of opinion and Arab nationalism.

It is hard to say how large a place the Americans had in the growing self-respect among Arabs. Throughout the nineteenth century presses at

Constantinople and Cairo had carried nearly the entire burden, as compared with the mission printers at Beirut, in a rebirth of ancient Arab literature. Such an observer as A. L. Tibawi has stated: "There is no evidence that the [Protestant] press had been an instrument in reviving a 'largely forgotten' or a 'rapidly vanishing' Arabic heritage. It was not part of its aims to revive classical Arabic literature, still less other departments of Arab culture. This is not to detract from its service, but to give it its true place in the history of American religious endeavor in Syria." [40] Writer George Antonius has evaluated the Protestants in all their efforts — including the training of Bustani and the schools — as foster parents and "pioneers; and because of that, the intellectual effervescence which marked the first stirrings of the Arab revival owes most to their labors." [41] Other data indicate that many Syrians came to view the American Revolution and the American Dream, taught by missionaries, as a model for attempts to master their destiny. The following lines, reportedly memorized by Arab secondary students and alluding to the Statue of Liberty, show this spirit: [42]

> When will you turn your face toward
>   the East, O Liberty?
> Shall the future never see a statue
>   of freedom near the Pyramids?
> Would it be possible for us to behold
>   your sister over the Mediterranean Sea?

Certain it is that after the 1880s the mission share in propelling the Arab cause forward was proportionately less. [43] Many mentors of nationalist societies and periodicals thereafter operated outside of the Ottoman-dominated homeland in the less politically smothering climate of Egypt, where the British were in charge. Winds of Arab autonomy in the Empire or of Western supervision blew strong from the expatriates in Cairo. These and other factors contributed to the report right before the First World War by the United States consul-general in Beirut that an overwhelming majority of Syrians would welcome an American or British but not a French protectorate. [44] The winsomeness of the missionaries' transatlantic country indicated that the American Protestants had aided Arab stirrings.

◄ ►

Protestant internationalism from the United States in 1914 thus was both bejeweled with evangelistic, educational, and nation-generating achievements but besmirched with political altercations. The American missionaries had moved from the rustic style of Parsons and Fisk to the elegance of the early twentieth century. By then the eastern Mediterranean had become one of the three largest centers in the world for cultural exportation from the United States. Yet the example of Yankee ingeniousness and Christian commitment was in danger, having already taken blows because of its unplanned but real embroilments in diplomacy and self-determination.

Chapter *3*

"Prelude to Point Four"

LIGHTS started going out in Europe during August 1914, dimming things for the missionaries from the United States in the Near East as well. Forces released in the Western balance of power helped begin hostilities between the Turks and the Armenians and Arabs, and also begin unprecedented trouble for the Protestants. To missionaries it was as if diabolical figures were stoking furnaces hotter than ever before. The American Protestants at first were not certain what to do.

The religionists eventually responded to the unparalleled adversity. Their trials gave opportunity to express frustrations about their purposes and methods which had been accumulating during the nineteenth century. Their reaction blended many aspects of the diversified mission behavior of 1914: evangelistic and ethnocentric zeal (as represented by the slogan "Christianize the nations"), theological flexibility, active humanitarianism, and readiness to use government aid for Protestant ends.

A FINAL SOLUTION

Commotion directly involving the emissaries from the United States arose after Turkey and its nationalities were drawn into the alignments of the First World War. When fighting in Europe started, the western section

58

of the Dashnaktsuthiun worked for Ottoman neutrality. But the Young Turks secretly chose the side of the Central Powers, by a military convention with Germany in August 1914. The Dashnaktsuthiun's western section met at Erzurum and there rejected a proposal of the Porte. The proposal stated that if Russian and Turkish Armenians would cooperate with the Committee of Union and Progress in event of an Ottoman-Russian war, the minority people would receive autonomy under the Empire for three Turkish-Armenian vilayets — Erzurum, Van, Bitlis — and for two Russian-Armenian provinces — Kars and Erivan. (See Map 3 on p. 52.) The Dashnaktsuthiun demurred, but promised to advise Ottoman Armenians to carry out their citizenship obligations. Soon after this meeting at Erzurum, the Russians appealed to the Dashnaktsuthiun-led Armenian National Council at Tiflis. The Tsar promised autonomy to six Turkish-Armenian vilayets as well as the two Russian-Armenian provinces. Earlier a Tsarist minister of foreign affairs reportedly had confided Russia's aim: "We need Armenia, but without the Armenians." Primarily because of trust in France and Great Britain as associates of Russia, the Armenian National Council accepted the Tsar's offer.

Learning of a possible conflict with Russian Armenians, the Ottoman government in September 1914 decided that aliens and Turkish Armenians would be a liability in a war against Russia. The Young Turks repudiated the hated capitulations, badges of their inferiority before Westerners. The Committee of Union and Progress began to arrest and in some cases execute Turkish Armenians. After a prodding by Germany, hostilities between the Ottoman Empire and the Allies opened early in November 1914, and the Turks called for a Holy War. Such an act by the rather irreligious Young Turks was partly cynical, to unify Arab and Turkish Muslims and to appeal to Russian Muslims. It was also an indication to Turkish Armenians that the cannon rather than the conference table might be the instrument of the Turks. The Committee of Union and Progress in December 1914 decided to attack Russian Armenia and Georgia. Led by pro-German Minister of War Enver Pasha, the Turks mobilized to capture Tiflis. Enver was a dominant leader among the Young Turks, a short, slim man with a mustache which curled upward like the Kaiser's. When Enver's forces moved across the Russian-Turkish border through the Bardiz pass, Russian-Armenian volunteers held them up at Sarikamish. (See Map 1 on p. 16.) This Armenian effort gave a Russian military unit time to group and defeat the Turks. After this failure, the Committee became

59

convinced that Turkish Armenians were traitors, that not only should the police imprison and execute them but that the Army should shoot them.[1]

American missions were not critically disturbed until Enver in April 1915 launched an assault near the city of Van against Turkish Armenians whom he considered treacherous. Van was a center of Armenianism in the Empire (60 per cent of its fifty thousand people were Armenians) and the location of both a strong evangelical organization and the Protestant school, American College. Enver's brother-in-law, Jevdet Bey, on April 16 murdered some individuals in an Armenian delegation from Van calling on him to reaffirm loyalty. Led by the Dashnaktsuthiun, about fifteen hundred Armenian men (many of whom had pledged allegiance to the Ottoman government) prepared to defend themselves and approximately thirty thousand members of their ethnic group in the walled Armenian Quarter. Within a few days an incident set off exchanges of rifle and cannon fire between Turks and Armenians. At the same time, Jevdet's troops began razing twenty nearby Armenian villages and killing many of their inhabitants. For several weeks the besieged Armenians in Van, possessing only a few hundred rifles, withstood Turkish bombardment. The eleven missionaries there, including Clarence Ussher and Ernest A. Yarrow, ministered to casualties. Ussher, the only physician in the city, worked from dawn until midnight with Armenians. Two missionary nurses served the wounded among Jevdet's soldiers at a Turkish hospital. Thousands of Armenians found refuge in the American Board compound, located next to the Armenian Quarter. Missionaries and Armenians sent messages to Russia for aid. As the Tsar's forces and Russian-Armenian volunteers neared Van the second week in May, Turkish shells fell into mission premises almost incessantly for one day, turning many buildings into rubble. The Turks fled. Next, Armenians "burned and murdered: the spirit of loot took possession of them." [2] Soon Turkish civilians found shelter and medical treatment in the American Board compound. By August 1915 the Russians had retreated toward Tiflis, with Americans and Armenians joining the exodus. Amid epidemics in this awful withdrawal, Mrs. Ussher and another missionary wife died. Ussher himself barely survived successive cases of typhus, pneumonia, and dysentery; Yarrow nearly succumbed also.

Enraged by the Van defeat, the Young Turks saw every Turkish Armenian as a foe. They completed a plan they had already conceived after the winter undoing at Sarikamish — a scheme which was to them a final solution to the Armenian matter. In May 1915 they issued a general order to kill or deport to the southern lowlands and to the Caucasus the entire Armenian population of Asia Minor, nearly all of whom were innocent of treason. Soldiers were to carry out the mission. Instructions required Turkish officials to confine their consciences or lose their jobs. Apparently two officials resigned; some of the rest refused to carry out their instructions. Yet the overall administration of the Young Turk general order was analogous to the Nazi action against Jews a generation later. The basic Turkish method in 1915 was to require Armenians with arms in a particular area to surrender them at police headquarters. There was then an attempt to murder the able-bodied and professional men by asking them to serve on road gangs, marching them out of cities, and having soldiers and nomads fall on them. Police and soldiers imprisoned and tormented recalcitrants. Usually on short notice, Turks herded together the remaining men, women, and children and sent these creatures, dispossessed of property and without adequate provisions, across Anatolian mountains and plains. Along the refugee routes local men often seized passing girls for wives. Kurds and Turks robbed, tortured, abused women. At Trabzon the executioners used another method; they transported about ten thousand Armenians on ships out into the Black Sea and forced them overboard to drown.[3]

There were several overlapping stages and areas of massacre and deportation. The Turks first began in Cilicia, where Armenians were more enterprising and less numerous than elsewhere. Minority people there who avoided the net fled to Syria or overseas to Egypt. Turning to vilayets in southeastern Anatolia like Van and Bitlis, where the density of Armenians was highest and the minority formed a troublesome zone between Russian and Turkish combatants, the Young Turks concentrated on annihilation. Ottoman scavengers operated over the summer in east-central vilayets (Erzurum, Harput, Sivas, and Trabzon) and during the autumn in western Anatolian areas, which contained small numbers of Armenians.[4]

Like the Van inhabitants, certain Armenian communities and individuals resisted or evaded deathtraps (with occasional help from humane Turks) and got through to safety. A dramatic affair concerned a mountain stronghold west of Aleppo, Musa Dagh, where eight hundred armed Armenians held off fifteen thousand Turkish regulars for over a month. The Musa Dagh defenders protected about five thousand of their people who eventually made it to the Mediterranean coast from which the French took

61

them to Egypt. German writer Franz Werfel gave a lasting splendor to these Armenians in his novel, *The Forty Days of Musa Dagh.*[5]

A sign of the agony throughout Anatolia was the story of an Armenian who reported that one night in the summer of 1915 he was in a prison at Diyarbakir, surrounded by over a thousand Armenian bodies. He watched that night as soldiers mutilated, drenched with alcohol, and set afire a compatriot. Fleeing with thousands of Armenians to the south, he saw incidents as terrible as the orgy in Diyarbakir. This escapee ended an account of his horrors with the cry: "The whole of Armenia is being cleared out. I sign this letter with my blood." [6]

Protestants from America had nightmarish experiences such as those at Bitlis. During May and June of 1915 about twelve thousand Armenian villagers from around Lake Van came into Bitlis, many with injuries (seven hundred or so stayed in the American section). The missionaries attempted to feed about eight thousand of the villagers in the hospital; they treated both Armenians and Turks as a typhus epidemic got out of control. At the end of June, soldiers came to the mission compound and arrested the Armenian men. Mission leaders thought the Turks were going to interrogate and then release their prisoners. None of the men returned, including physicians, attorneys, and clergymen. On the day Turks returned to American houses for the Armenian women, a shot barked. A young man disguised as a girl had concealed a weapon from the missionaries, who previously had made a policy of disarming all of the minority people staying in the American buildings. The young man tried to kill at least one Turk before his death; he then committed suicide. Using this incident to charge the foreigners from the United States of Armenianism, the Turks drove out the Western religionists as well as the bereaved women. This expulsion marked the end of American internationalism among Armenians in Bitlis.[7]

Merzifon differed little from Bitlis. Seven Armenian teachers of Anatolia College died. By September 1915 Turks had killed or deported the Armenian staff and students. Only fifty of over nine hundred people in the local Protestant church survived. Within a few months all but one or two missionaries had left.[8]

Why such a Turkish retribution? Large causes had to do with the millet system, scrambled ethnic groups, cultural lag, and Western interference. Specifically, Young Turk apologists have insisted that the slaughter resulted from the interplay of conspiracy among Turkish Armenians, of military opposition by Russian Armenians, and of revolt in Van. There are problems with this apology. The Dashnaktsuthiun in Turkey had eschewed revolution up until the years just before the World War when the Committee of Union and Progress decided to downgrade cooperation with minorities and to promote Social Darwinist and imperial notions then much in vogue in Germany and the West. The Young Turks pushed both Turkification to unite its polyglot country and imperial expansion to embrace Turkish-speaking groups in the Caucasus and Central Asia. A source of Turkish nationalism, which spurred the later Kemalist movement, was the writing of Turkish sociologist Ziya Gökalp. After sporadic killings of Armenians had begun late in 1914, Dashnaktsuthiun leaders tried appeasement rather than pushing independence. There is evidence that some Turkish Armenians became Allied agents. But Van Armenians were not guilty of plotting an uprising against the government.

Western nations did not interfere with the Turkish government's anti-Armenian scheme. The German government neither promoted nor welcomed the massacres; Berlin protested to Constantinople, yet refrained from determined opposition to the Ottoman killings. Extermination possibly would not have reached the proportions it did if the Allied campaign in Gallipoli had not slumped early in 1915, rendering Allied armies bound up in the Dardanelles unable to intervene.[9]

United States missionaries and diplomats at Constantinople spoke out. Turkish Minister of Interior Talaat Bey — broad-shouldered, outspoken—blandly explained to the American ambassador that the Turks were dealing with the Armenians as the United States had the Indians.[10]

By early 1916 enormous casualties had been counted among the Armenians, including the missionary constituency, the Evangelical Armenian Church. Reports have estimated that violence and starvation ended the lives of from 600,000 to 1,000,000 out of the 1,800,000 to 2,000,000 Turkish Armenians.[11] About 500,000 survivors limped out of Anatolia into beleaguered cities of the Caucasus, Syria, Mesopotamia, and Persia or else emigrated. (Approximately 300,000 went into the Caucasus and 150,000 into Syria.) In despair about 500,000 remained in Anatolia. The ruin included the death or deportation of about 80 per cent of the Protestant clergy and their assistants. A showpiece of American Board achievement was in a shambles. Mission executives in the United States sought vainly to increase immigration quotas for Armenians.

Meanwhile, efforts toward Arab autonomy in the Empire had helped foster a rebellion which missionaries later defended. Americans, as discussed above, had aided the Arab cultural revival. Nationalism among Arabs had been developing before the war, even though few of these people changed their communal ways of thinking. A railroad between Damascus and Medina, completed in 1908, had improved communication between nomads and townsmen. New patriotic groups had sprung up — a literary club, a secret society among Arab officers in the Ottoman army, and a political movement (the Ottoman Decentralization party) led by Arabs in Cairo. An Arab congress met at Paris in 1913 and demanded autonomy within the Turkish Empire. After the Allied campaign in Gallipoli had stalled in 1915, the British high commissioner in Egypt, Henry McMahon, began sounding out Arab-British cooperation with the hereditary vassal of the Porte, the Sharif Husain, who ruled the areas in western Arabia adjacent to the Red Sea. As the McMahon-Husain correspondence continued, Husain's third son, the Emir Feisal, who knew of the Arab national ideas, joined a clandestine group. His father about the same time aspired out of traditional motives to lead the Arab movement (the elder man was opaque in the light of modern nationalism). After the British at last withdrew their troops from Gallipoli early in 1916, and McMahon promised an ambiguous freedom for the Arabs, Husain in June of the same year declared war on his surprised Turkish overlords. Helped by T. E. Lawrence of the British army, Feisal gave direction to the Arab Revolt and by December 1916 his men had occupied much of western Arabia.

The Arab uprising and the Armenian holocaust brought calamity and a massive surge of anguish upon Protestants in the Near East. Privation was widespread among mission schools and evangelical congregations in Syria. Cataclysm was the portion of the American Board, whose investment in the Turkish Empire of about twenty million dollars in property and one hundred fifty staff members had fallen by December 1915 to about half in financial value and personnel. Quite a few missionaries had died in epidemics. Interior schools had closed. Many of the Americans became intensely and righteously determined to salvage as much as they could from a century's labor, wanting to succor the Armenian remnant and to say "Amen" to punishment of the Turks.

NEARLY USELESS PETITIONS

Individuals from the United States, especially those in Constantinople, sought to alter Turkish policy toward the Armenians as soon as information had come of the troubles in the interior. Conversing with Young Turk leader Talaat on April 24, 1915, American Ambassador Henry Morgenthau, Sr., inquired about the minorities. Talaat said exertions of the Committee of Union and Progress were directed as much toward repressing revolution as fighting the Allies. Asked about the Armenians, Talaat admitted that the government was arresting many. Two days later two missionaries — Robert College's Caleb Gates and William W. Peet, local treasurer of the American Board — called on Morgenthau and discussed the Armenians.[12] Morgenthau, Gates, and Peet then worked to change the Ottoman solution of the Armenian dilemma.

Liaison between Morgenthau and the missionaries was not new. When in November 1913 Morgenthau first arrived in the Empire he had expected the Protestants to be sectarian and narrow. He discovered otherwise. "I found that . . . Christian missionaries in Turkey," he wrote in retrospect, "were carrying forward a magnificent work of social service, education, philanthropy, sanitation, medical healing, and moral uplift." During his early months in the Near East he increasingly believed that his duty was to encourage the missionaries whom he felt "exemplified the American spirit at its best." [13] He thought they were brave, intelligent, unselfish. The religionists liked Morgenthau. Gates related in his memoirs: "We were most fortunate in our ambassador. Mr. Morgenthau was . . . tireless in his efforts to protect American interests. . . . We became very good friends, and we used to ride [horseback] together several times a week;" educators at the Syrian Protestant College said in 1915: "We regard it as most fortunate that Mr. Morgenthau visited Syria last year. He has proved himself a staunch and able friend." [14]

A gregarious, self-confident Democrat, Morgenthau had boundless enthusiasm for public causes. Born in Mannheim, Germany, he had emigrated as a child to the United States. Graduating from Columbia College, he went into law and then business, and became rich. In the presidential race of 1912 he supported Woodrow Wilson and was financial chairman for the campaign. His reward was appointment to Constantinople.

Gates, a mission veteran, had come from the Midwest. After studying at Beloit College and the Chicago Theological Seminary, he had gone to the Turkish Empire for the American Board in 1881, and labored at Mardin. From 1894 to 1902 he was president of Euphrates College in Harput, a school with an Armenian clientele. At one commencement exercise during the period from 1894 to 1896, the students of Euphrates College interrupted the reading of a mild Armenophile statement which Gates had sanctioned, shouting: "Long live Armenia." In autumn 1895 Kurds and Turks sacked and plundered mission and Armenian areas in Harput, where one fifth of the twenty-five thousand people of the city lived. For three days Gates helped fight fires. At one point in the melee a Turk discharged a gun at a missionary; Gates said to the assailant, "God chastise you." Then the Turk fired at Gates. "He was a poor shot," the intended target remembered. When the frenzy ceased, missionaries at Harput cabled the American legation: "eight of our buildings . . . burned . . . special malice toward us; great religious pressure and terror; multitudes killed in vilayets; survivors destitute. Our loss probably one hundred thousand dollars." [15] Gates felt that the Archfiend of Hell had organized the onslaught. In 1903 he left Euphrates College to begin a long tenure as the third president of Robert College in Constantinople. (His successors, consecutively, at Euphrates were brothers Harry and Ernest Riggs, grandsons of Elias Riggs.) At Constantinople during the First World War Gates knew grief similar to that of the earlier disorders in the 1890s. An entry in his wife's diary for April 27, 1915, stated: "Sunday was again a wearing day. Cannonading in the A.M. was our breakfast accompaniment. A phone message told us of the arrest of 100 leading Armenians in this city. Among them Mr. Garabadian who was to have spoken to the boys [at the college] in the evening." [16]

William Peet was a sixty-three–year–old mission "statesman" (one might say), whose father had been a Congregational clergyman. As a young man of thirty residing in Omaha, Peet had turned from a promising future as an attorney with the Chicago, Burlington, and Quincy Railroad to accept the Near East treasurership of the American Board. Cyrus Hamlin's books had inspired him to seek mission service. Over the years after his arrival at Constantinople in 1881, he had schooled himself in Turkish law and international relations, as he ferried two hours each day between house and office at the Bible House. Incidentally, the Bible House was a six-story, Victorian structure which had served since the 1870s as headquarters for both the American Board and the American Bible Society. (See inset, Map 2, on p. 17.) By 1900 Peet had become a leading mediator among American mission institutions in Turkey, the diplomatic corps, and the Porte. An associate said that he had seen Washington dispatches to Constantinople in which "ambassadors were urged to consult Mr. Peet before taking important steps." The colleague continued: "I saw

Presidents Cleveland and Roosevelt personally thank Mr. Peet on behalf of the United States Government for the distinguished service he had rendered to the United States Embassy on behalf of American interests in Turkey."[17]

Morgenthau, Gates, and Peet — men of nearly the same age and of similar sympathy for Armenians — knew that much of the missionary structure in the Empire would fall if the Turks continued to eliminate the minority people. They decided that Washington should be notified of the persecutions. By summer Morgenthau had begun sending regular messages to Secretary of State Robert Lansing, who endorsed remonstrance with the Ottomans and with the German ambassador. At Gates' suggestion Morgenthau worked out a plan for moving Armenians to California. The Young Turks, though quite cold to this notion, were willing to consider it. When the American ambassador approached the State Department, it was unenthusiastic.

Morgenthau's pleas had little effect upon the Turks. In one long talk with Minister of Marine Djemal Pasha, the latter asked Morgenthau if Armenians were Americans. Realizing Djemal was stating that the domestic situation was none of his business, the ambassador replied that he was a friend of the Armenians, particularly since an old hand in the United States embassy, Arshag K. Schmavonian, was one. Djemal in his memoirs declared that constant intervention by the West in the Empire had caused Turks, Kurds, and Armenians to mistreat one another.[18]

Morgenthau also sought mercy for Armenians in discussions with Talaat. This Turkish official boasted that the Committee was doing more to answer the Armenian question within three short months than Abdul Hamid had done in thirty-three years. Talaat teased Morgenthau about his freshly shaved chin, saying that since the United States official had become young again he could no longer heed his advice. The ambassador rejoined that he had shaved because worrying about the Armenians had made his beard gray. Talaat declared the Young Turks were firm about finishing a job three quarters done, and justified their acts by several charges against the Armenians: the minority people had enriched themselves at the expense of Turks, had sought independence, and had helped the Russians.

Enver warned Morgenthau against American preference for minorities. This Young Turk felt that if Armenians allied with the enemy, as in the Van district, his government would have to quash them. Ottoman leaders in general ridiculed the ambassador, a Jew, for seeking to protect Christians. "I represent the United States," Morgenthau replied, "and 97 per cent of the people of my country are Christians and only 3 per cent are Jews. In this office I am 97 per cent Christian." [19]

While Morgenthau talked to the Young Turks, the picture at Constantinople from inside the Empire became grimmer. Censors tried to prevent specifics of the grisly doings from reaching Constantinople. Yet information got to the Bosporus: a missionary at Konya revealed that soldiers with bayonets had driven women and children out of town, and from Sivas came the story that around twenty-five thousand individuals had started a weary trek. Missionaries camouflaged some of their intelligence by jotting such references in the margins of their letters as the biblical passage in Hebrews 11:36–38, which says that men of faith (Armenians) "had trial of cruel mockings and scourgings, yea, moreover of bonds and imprisonment: they were stoned, they were sawn asunder, were tempted, were slain with the sword: they wandered about in sheepskins and goatskins; being destitute, afflicted, tormented . . . they wandered in deserts, and in mountains, and in dens and caves of the earth." Some of the American Board members from eastern Anatolia reached the Ottoman capital and the American embassy, where "with tears streaming down their faces," they told of the macabre scenes they had encountered.[20] Gates felt particularly helpless when the police took thirteen Armenian servants from Robert College and sent them into the interior.

Petitions by Americans to the Porte and to the United States Department of State were nearly useless. Armenians were disappearing constantly, and words could not stop the carnage.

JUST A GOOD BEGINNING

Peet outlined to American Board headquarters at Boston in August 1915 an idea which got by the censors. "The deportation of the Armenians," Peet wrote, "requires a pretty large expenditure in order to keep them alive, and this must be our first effort. They are sent generally either into the desert or into an unoccupied territory, or into absolutely new locations, where they will be needing everything, as they have left behind them everything they had in the world." [21]

Peet's plan indicated an American pattern. During the previous century, mission groups had led philanthropy abroad by being much more systematic than other public and private agencies and by orienting their countrymen to needs across the seas. After 1881 the American Red Cross had taken an increasingly important place in complementing the religionists. The government role throughout had been minor, since Congress had appropriated relief funds only once, and Washington infrequently had provided naval transport for gifts.[22]

Missionaries had developed philanthropy for the Near East in response to the killings from 1894 to 1896, as discussed; the National Armenian Relief Committee cooperated with the American Red Cross to lead in assisting the Armenians (see pp. 42 and 43). Peet had directed the distribution in Turkey of around $1,500,000 in relief, which probably saved about two hundred thousand orphans.[23]

Early in the First World War came benevolence for Arabs. When in 1914 the Ottoman authorities in Syria requisitioned food and animals, famine followed, bringing death to many people. The head of the Columbia University School of Journalism, Talcott Williams, and Stanley White, Syrian secretary of the Presbyterian Board, early in 1915 established the Syrian-Palestine Relief Fund.[24] (Born of missionaries in Turkey, Williams later became an outspoken supporter of the Protestants' political aims.) The Fund fared well; one of its sections alone reported in July 1915 that $155,000 had gone to the United States consul in Beirut.

Concurrently, the general secretary of the Presbyterian Board, Robert E. Speer, started a project similar to the Syrian-Palestine Relief Fund.[25] Speer heard of poor conditions among followers of Presbyterian missions at Urmia in Persia, issuing out of the Turkish-Russian conflict. He obtained some American Red Cross help. In March 1915 he decided that this means was insufficient and began the Persian War Relief Fund. Appealing to all Protestant denominations, Speer by July had raised several thousand dollars. During the summer, income began to taper off, so he turned to the Rockefeller Foundation.

Out of this tradition of fund-raising for the Near East arose Peet's scheme of August 1915. By then thousands had escaped Asia Minor, huddling in the Caucasus, Syria, and Mesopotamia where Americans could possibly aid them. An important call which arrived in the United States after the Peet letter was a confidential cable of September 3 from Morgenthau to the State Department. "Enver Pasha has promised," the ambassador related, "the departure of such Armenians to the United States whose immigration I vouch as bonafide. The destruction of the Armenian race in the Turkish Empire is progressing rapidly. . . . Will you please suggest to Charles Crane, Cleveland Dodge . . . and others to form Committee for the raising of funds and provide means to save some of the Armenians and to assist the poorer ones to emigrate and perhaps to enlist Oregon, California, and Washington to transport some of these people via Panama Canal direct to their shores."[26] The State Department on September 9 advised Cleveland H. Dodge, vice-president of the Phelps Dodge Corporation and father of two missionary educators in Turkey, of Morgenthau's message and asked him to set up a committee. Peet in Constantinople wrote James Barton, secretary of the American Board, urging him to solicit the Rockefeller Foundation; the Armenian story, he said, was "beyond words."[27]

Dodge brought together a group in his New York office on September 16. He induced American Board Secretary Barton to be chairman of this committee, believing him the best-qualified man in the nation for the position. The committee selected for its secretary Samuel Train Dutton, a Congregational church member who was board treasurer of Constantinople Woman's College, a leader in the American peace movement, and former executive of Teachers College, Columbia University.[28] In the meeting, Dodge pledged sixty thousand dollars for relief, and agreed to underwrite all overhead connected with funds received. The Dodge Relief Committee thereupon instructed Chairman Barton and an industrialist chosen its treasurer, Charles R. Crane, to visit the State Department for more information.[29]

Crane was an appropriate member of the Dodge Relief Committee to go to Washington, partly because of his connections there. Born in 1858 as the eldest son of the developer of Crane plumbing equipment, Charles had worked so hard during his youth that he showed chronic symptoms of nervous exhaustion. So, between nineteen and twenty-six years of age, he went to Asia and Europe instead of to college and thereby became interested in foreign affairs. After resuming work in 1884, he annually continued travel abroad, especially to Russia; usually he did not let duties in the family plumbing firm interrupt the overseas excursions. In 1900 he began to sponsor Slavic lecturers at the University of Chicago, including Thomaš Masaryk and Paul Milyukov, and in a few years endowed a chair in Russian culture there. Because of Crane's supposed expertness in Far East matters, President Taft chose him as minister to China. Actually, Crane understood no language other than English, and furthermore he possessed little more than a tourist's perception of the Far East. Owing to poor instruction procedures and his gaffe in a newspaper interview, the businessman resigned after he had gotten no nearer Peking than San Francisco's Chinatown. Crane thereafter expressed himself politically in the Progressive movement. When Robert M. La Follette's presidential aspirations ebbed, he turned to Woodrow Wilson and contributed fifty thousand dollars in the 1912 campaign. Wilson then offered the ambassadorship to Russia. Crane refused. A family quarrel over his father's will led him to leave his company's presidency in 1914 for full-time philanthropy and travel. Among recipients of the largess of this round-faced man with a short beard were Robert College and Constantinople Woman's College. In September 1915 he was a member of both schools' boards, chairman of the latter. His attraction to these Protestant institutions came out of his Christian idealism and his "personable sentimentalism" (he neglected regular participation in his family's Presbyterian church).[30]

Thus Crane, whose one son had become Secretary of State Lansing's personal secretary in May 1915, had several handles on machinery which could help the Armenians. Arriving in Washington on September 21, Crane and Barton received permission to consult confidential dispatches from the Near East. These messages confirmed their worst suspicions and showed more trouble than the few previously published pieces about the Armenian problem.

Ambassador Morgenthau soon learned that the Dodge Relief Committee was preparing to send between $50,000 and $100,000 to the Ottoman Empire and Persia. The Dodge Relief Committee advised him to dismiss the idea of mass emigration of Armenians because of insurmountable opposition in the United States. The ambassador replied that $100,000 was just a "good beginning." He "implored" the State Department to ask his friends to give liberally.[31] The United States consul in Aleppo currently reported over 150,000 refugees in the area, with hundreds dying daily. The consul recommended $150,000 a month to meet needs of that locality alone.

The Dodge Relief Committee proceeded to reinforce in the American mind the image of the unspeakable Turk. From data at the State Department, Barton and Crane prepared press dispatches and sent them to leading journalists throughout the United States. During the last two weeks of September 1915 headlines which made all Turks look like ogres appeared under nearly every dateline in the New York *Times* and in other newspapers and periodicals: "Mission Board told of Turkish Horrors, 10,000 Christians Drowned in Trebizond [Trabzon], Women Seized for Harems" and "Tales of Armenian Horrors Confirmed." In October the Dodge group released a cable from Morgenthau to Lansing and detailed accounts of disasters in Asia Minor.[32]

At the Bosporus, Morgenthau, Gates, and Peet continued as an Armenophile triumvirate. The three men could transfer funds from the United States. But they did not have approval of the Porte to distribute relief goods. Gates worked on Talaat, and the diplomat on Enver. Both Ottomans hesitated because they felt that large outside help would stimulate rebellion. The Young Turks angrily spurned attempts by the Americans to end the death marches or to plead a special dispensation for Protestant Armenians. Talaat said the government would not again allow the minority to pull in grasping foreign hands.

Since killing of Armenians was not to cease, and relief appeared a long-term proposition, the Syrian-Palestine Relief Fund, the Persian War Relief Fund, and the Dodge Relief Committee elected to join. The new agency, the American Committee for Armenian and Syrian Relief (ACASR), appeared on November 20, 1915. In 1918 and 1919 this movement changed its name twice, first to the American Committee for Relief in the Near East (ACRNE) and then, more simply, to Near East Relief. The ACASR board numbered about forty, representing nearly every American Protestant group in the Near East and including D. Stuart Dodge (Cleveland Dodge's uncle and board president of the Syrian Protestant College), Presbyterian Board Secretary Stanley White, Arthur Curtiss James (business associate of Cleveland Dodge and board member of the Syrian Protestant College), and Student Volunteer leader John R. Mott. Only four ACASR board members were either Jews or Catholics.

Leadership of the ACASR continued with three men from the former Dodge Relief Committee: Dodge, Crane as treasurer, Barton as chairman (of the three, the chairman was in some ways the most important). Barton spent his boyhood in a Quaker farm home in Vermont (many American Board missionaries came from rural New England). In 1881 he received his college diploma from Cyrus Hamlin, who currently was president of Middlebury. To pay debts, Barton traveled for a year as a covered buggy salesman in Illinois. Then he graduated from Hartford Theological Seminary, received ordination as a Congregational clergyman, and departed in 1885 under the American Board for Harput in the Armenian vilayets of

Anatolia. As a young man of thirty-eight, he became president of Euphrates College. The Board in 1892 called him from this position (in which Gates was his successor) to become a secretary in Boston. Barton soon was the dominant Board administrator. In the position of foreign secretary he gave priority to educational missions, becoming perhaps the outstanding American promoter of colleges abroad. He eventually assisted the start or development of twenty interdenominational Christian schools of higher learning in Spain, Greece, Bulgaria, Turkey, India, Ceylon, China, and Japan, helping them secure over thirty million dollars. In a constant dialogue with the United States government, Barton sought to guard Protestant institutions in Turkey and elsewhere. When he became captain of the newly launched ACASR, he was sixty years old.

With a regal bearing enhanced by a white Vandyke beard, Barton impressed those who knew him by a mastery of detail and a seriousness of purpose. Having concern for Armenians because of his years with them, he supervised with enormous energy. Staff people at American Board headquarters were aware of his presence, for they had considerably less to do when he was out of the office. Once, during a Barton trip, a colleague at Boston wrote: "Well, Old Fellow, . . . We miss you like a toothache when we get over it. I mean not as being so glad to have you gone but as being very conscious that you are gone."[33]

With Barton as ACASR head, missionaries felt that not all would be lost. After months of dismay, the Protestants to Turkey began to hope again.

A NATIONAL CRUSADE

Barton was an intense religious and philanthropic activist. As chairman of the American Committee for Armenian and Syrian Relief and American Board foreign secretary, he became many things to many people, whether officials or Sunday school children, so that he might save minorities and Protestant missions in the Near East. Using openings to the United States government helped by Dodge, Crane, and Morgenthau, Barton made repeated contacts with the Wilson administration and the American populace. What a promoter!

During the winter of ACASR's birth in 1915 and 1916, the missionaries' ally in Constantinople, Ambassador Morgenthau, left for home; Barton worried about a replacement. When Morgenthau reached New York City the executive committee of the ACASR met him at the docks. Barton soon got him to speak in Massachusetts, and to meet privately with the trustees of the American Board. In Boston the ambassador made nearly ecstatic remarks about the missionaries, and spoke of his abhorrence of the Turks. Ostensibly, he had come back for a vacation. But he had no intention of returning to the Empire. He desired to assist President Wilson's campaign for re-election. Together with Crane, he decided on a Jewish attorney, Abram I. Elkus, as his successor at the Porte. Wilson approved. Morgenthau assured Barton that Elkus would be "wholly sympathetic" to missions and relief. The Board secretary wanted to make sure that Elkus was "indoctrinated . . . to defend American institutions to the last."[34] Through Morgenthau and Dodge he arranged a long talk with Elkus. Barton sent many documents on the Protestant establishment in the Near East to the ambassador-designate. Just before Elkus' departure for Constantinople in August 1916, Barton sponsored a banquet at which representatives of the religious groups in Turkey were present. Satisfied, he wrote to Morgenthau: "I was very pleased with him and with his outlook to the work."[35] In relations with Peet and Gates during his short-lived, eight-month tenure at the embassy Elkus lived up to Barton's evaluation. Toiling at Constantinople partly out of faithfulness to the religionists, Elkus described his schedule: "I begin in the morning early and usually finish at ten o'clock at night or later; and it usually lasts seven days in the week."[36]

Barton also cultivated the prestigious Britisher, James Bryce, who had known many American Protestants in the Ottoman Empire for decades. Bryce had a wide repute as an attorney, sometime professor of law at Oxford, former member of the House of Commons and several British cabinets, author of the famous *American Commonwealth,* and ambassador to the United States from 1907 to 1913. The Englishman had gone to climb Ararat in 1876, beginning his fascination with the Armenians. In those days he felt independence for the minority premature.[37] By 1880 he had concluded that to expect the Turk to respect rights of minorities was useless. He became the principal Armenophile in Britain, and founder of an Armenophile society. During incidents from 1894 to 1896 he thought it intolerable that his government should watch the butcheries with folded arms. Bryce felt that the Armenians were one of the noblest races on earth, and the potential revitalizers of Asia Minor. In 1914 he visited Howard Bliss at the Syrian Protestant College; after the Armenian conflagration of 1915, he and Barton corresponded. Both Bryce and Barton sought to press their governments. The Englishman persistently tried in the House of Lords and other places to get British troops into Armenia, to block the Turks. But he always heard that London could not spare soldiers from other areas.[38]

Barton's chief effect in working with Bryce was a book edited by the Britisher and informally put together by the ACASR and a young scholar specializing in the history of the Ottoman Empire, Arnold J. Toynbee. Considerably over half the documents in the book, a 684-page volume, had come to the American and Presbyterian boards from Armenian refugees and other witnesses to the deportation. The purpose of this work, *The Treatment of Armenians in the Ottoman Empire, 1915–16,* was to attract favor for relief and for Armenian interests.[39] The American Board secretary in September 1916 ordered three thousand copies of *The Treatment* from Toynbee for influential personages. President Wilson and his adviser, Colonel Edward M. House, were among those who received the book. The New York *Times* on October 8, 1916, included three pages of extracts from *The Treatment.*

Lobbying for the ACASR, Barton obtained much support from the United States government. Beginning in 1915, Peet at the Bosporus used the diplomatic pouch to avoid censorship. This technique gave Barton almost as full information as Washington possessed. Through the State Department the mission director also received correspondence from American consuls at Tiflis, Tabriz, and Aleppo. He gave much of this specially received knowledge to the press; he also disseminated it through ACASR bulletins.[40] By mid-1916 local ACASR committees had been formed in thirty-eight cities in sixteen states, with each spreading information and raising money. To awaken the country's consciousness, Barton and his associates persuaded Congress to pass a resolution of compassion for Armenians and Syrians. Barton also recommended that the President of the United States appoint a special day in October 1916 for relief collections. The ACASR chairman appealed to Wilson: "Tens of thousands have miserably perished and still the assassin's hand is not withdrawn. I urgently trust that you will call upon all America sacrificially to remember this bleeding, stricken people."[41] The President complied. Copies of a White House proclamation, printed in red and black, reportedly went to every clergyman, governor, and mayor in the country. Many state and local figures issued similar statements.

The American Board head made ACASR propaganda a major factor in expanding the relief movement; public relations was this executive's forte.

While a student at Middlebury College, Barton had been a writer for the local newspaper and a correspondent for the Associated Press. As a resident in Turkey, he had regularly sent articles to United States periodicals. One of the first things he had done as Board secretary was to hire a press agent, a radical change for the staid mission. The World Missionary Conference in Edinburgh appointed him, the only American, to a committee charged to secure a larger place for missionary information in the secular press.

Barton in 1915 recruited a professor of church history at New York's Union Theological Seminary, William Walker Rockwell, to prepare several pieces on the Armenians. Rockwell studied carefully and in 1916 prepared several bulletins and three documentary booklets. Titles of the three booklets were *The Pitiful Plight of the Assyrian [Nestorian] Christians in Persia and Kurdistan, The Deportation of the Armenians* (an eyewitness account), and *Ravished Armenia: The Story of Aurora Mardigonian. Ravished Armenia* told of a fourteen-year-old girl who had become an unwilling concubine to a Turkish officer and who went through imprisonment, escape, recapture, and rape. Eventually the ACASR had rescued Aurora.[42]

These pieces were not good enough for the American Board publicist in Boston. Impatient with their dispassionate quality and with Rockwell's slowness, Barton also delegated pamphleteering to men who used such charged titles as *Atrocities—Talaat Bey Boasted that He Would Make the Armenians Pray for Massacre and He Has*. Enlarging on the idea of the terrible Turk which Americans had accepted since the 1890s, the ACASR aroused hostility against Turks as brutally inhuman, degenerate agents of German Huns; it glorified Armenians as responsible Christians victimized by Muslims. These astigmatic views portrayed religion as almost the exclusive problem in Asia Minor and ignored ethnic, economic, and political factors. Notions built up in this campaign would later militate against the understanding of Near East realities needed by the people and government of the United States to fulfil the missionaries' postwar desires.

One would have had to look endlessly for some American comment presenting the Turkish point of view. The closest to the Ottoman perspective was a concession that the Turkish peasant was not a bad sort; it was his leaders who were bad. Pages and columns of newspapers and magazines were full of such a Social Darwinist tone as the following in the *Independent* of October 18, 1915: "Intellectually and physically they [the Armenians] are vastly superior to the Turks. In education, enterprise, industry and love of home they surpass all the other races. Among all the peoples of Turkey they have been quickest to catch the spirit of modern education and twentieth century progress. . . . This ancient and proud-spirited race, conscious of its own innate superiority, ambitious to educate its children, Christian in its religion, and eager for progress, cherished the hope of an independent Armenia reestablished upon the ruins of its ancient kingdom. . . . We can hardly conceive of any power's favoring the perpetuation of Turkey in any form, after this ghastly exhibit [massacres] of Moslem incapacity to rule alien peoples or even Mohammedans." [43]

Feelings and instincts cultivated by writings like this, Americans responded with generosity to the ACASR. In addition to money, people gave jewelry, heirlooms, and wedding gifts. The Rockefeller Foundation in 1915 and 1916 gave over $300,000, and the proceeds of the Harvard-Yale football game of 1916 went to the ACASR. Dodge facilitated relief in the Near East by persuading the richest charitable group in the United States, the American Red Cross, to assist. The *Christian Herald* and the *Literary Digest* helped solicit. By the time the United States declared war on Germany, the ACASR had raised over $2,000,000 and had the second largest income of any American philanthropic institution.

"Relief for victims of war in the Near East became a kind of national crusade," psychologically not unlike the crusades of the Middle Ages.[44] Barton later wrote about what he believed was the major element in public support for the ACASR: "Religious leaders have from the first held foremost place in promoting and directing the organization. The movement arose from a religious impulse and has had the liberal support of all religious bodies." [45]

To meet increasing responsibility, the ACASR in 1916 employed many young men from the Layman's Missionary Movement. Charles V. Vickrey of this group became the chief paid administrator in spacious new ACASR quarters in New York City. Vickrey's duties subsumed many functions of part time Secretary Dutton, who had coordinated until then out of his own small private office. Continuing efforts begun earlier, Vickrey expanded the number of state and local committees throughout the United States.

In the Ottoman Empire, the Young Turks until 1916 did not permit relief goods to enter. Probably German missionaries to Turkey indirectly pressed the Porte through their government to allow food and clothing in the Empire. The United States government assisted in December 1916 by donating a collier to carry supplies to Syria. Barton helped influence the State Department to move the belligerents, including Turkey, to allow the collier through the Allied naval blockade. American missionaries, diplomats, and consuls distributed aid; mission properties became relief centers. The following individuals served on the local relief committee in Constantinople: Elkus, Lewis Heck (embassy official), Gates, Peet, Luther R. Fowle (Peet's assistant), and Elizabeth Huntington (Dodge's daughter and staff member at Robert College). Groups existed also in Beirut and Tiflis. In Persia, United States Minister J. L. Caldwell headed a committee of American residents there.

The relief goods went almost entirely to non-Turks. Muslims received about 2 per cent of relief; Armenian and Arab Christians obtained most of the rest. Constantinople was allotted 35 per cent, Tiflis 30 per cent, Beirut 13 per cent, and Tehran in Persia 20 per cent. Nestorian and Armenian displaced persons in Persia, wards of the Presbyterians, received most of Tehran's share.[46] Favoritism for Christian minorities did not promote goodwill with Muslims, many of whom also were destitute and pitiable.

What did relief accomplish? The ACASR, as noted, transferred funds and gave food, clothing, and medical assistance to "mutilated and pestilence-stricken refugees." It "set up workshops in which widows contributed to the support of themselves and children by spinning, weaving, and sewing. . . . 'homes' received the helpless aged and the abandoned orphans. Seeds were given to those whose land had been burned over. . . . What was done was, of course, small in relation to need. But in view of the gargantuan nature of the problem, the achievement was almost superhuman."[47]

Barton did not forget the American Board and other Protestant institutions as he pushed the ACASR. He tried by a letter in April 1916 to "instill a little more ginger" in Secretary of State Lansing, to get security for Americans and the forty million dollars invested over the years by the different evangelistic, educational, and medical mission groups in the Ottoman Empire. This gesture was like those in autumn 1914 when both Protestants and commercial interests in Turkey had requested warships to deter the Porte from acting against Americans and minorities (soon the *North Carolina* and the *Tennessee* were in the eastern Mediterranean). At that time, the Committee of Union and Progress formally sought to quiet United States fears, with Enver going so far as to enroll his brother and two sons in special classes at Robert College. The apprehension of Americans hardly disappeared over the first months of combat, because trade virtually ceased and several mission stations closed. In his worry of April 1916 Barton came out in the letter to Lansing with the exaggeration that no country other than the United States "has so extensive or long established financial interests in Turkey and the Balkans." [48] Barton listed the estimated worth of every mission organization. In reply, the Secretary of State assured him of protection of persons, not property.

Through the initial period of the ACASR, Barton and Dodge were not unmindful of how their concerns related to the Eastern Question. Barton hoped that philanthropy could affect American diplomacy with the Ottoman Empire. He wanted material which "newspapers will review, that promoters of the relief cause will use widely, and that will have influence in shaping thought with reference to the future of the Turkish empire." [49] On a sophisticated scale the ACASR practiced a conditional altruism not unlike that practiced by one untutored American contributor to the ACASR. This contributor wrote that since sending in his gift "i have thought i wold like to have one of the britest of the [Armenian] girls about 16 years old to live with me i would make a lady out of hire and when she is at a good age probley mirry her." [50] Former ambassador to the Porte, Oscar Straus, had noted as early as December 1914 in an article that mission endeavor in Turkey would be an "important factor" in the postwar development of the Ottoman Empire.[51] Barton and Dodge wanted a Turkish reconstruction which would advance missions.

Because of paroxyms involving Armenians and Arabs, American religionists in 1916 had altered emphases from evangelism and education to a "prelude to Point Four" (President Harry S. Truman's Point Four program began regular United States technical assistance overseas).[52] Both the Red Cross and the ACASR established philanthropic patterns to which Washington would add its contribution. Of course, the missionaries during the First World War were not trying to be intercultural frontiersmen for later efforts by their government. They wanted to conserve their commitments of nearly one hundred years in the Near East. Their pioneering was no less real because they were not conscious pathfinders.

Chapter 4

An Unofficial Cabinet

FORTUITOUS circumstances were necessary for the mission-directed American Committee for Armenian and Syrian Relief to make history move in its direction. No harm had come to its benevolent enterprise because Charles Crane and Henry Morgenthau were both close to the Protestants connected with Turkey and with the Wilson administration. The strongest personal factor helping the ACASR was the friendship of Cleveland H. Dodge and Woodrow Wilson. Until the Armistice of 1918, and beyond that time, Dodge was at the center of relief and governmental interaction with the Near East.

WILSON AND DODGE

To understand the preponderance of Dodge in Turkish-American affairs for what proved a decade, one needs to consider various aspects of Wilson's relation with Dodge — possibly the longest, deepening tie the President had with any male.

The Dodge-Wilson acquaintance (Dodge was the junior by two years) had begun in autumn 1875 and would end with Wilson's death in February 1924, nearly fifty years later. The New York *Times* obituary for Dodge in 1926 suggested him "to be the only early friend of President Wilson who remained his close friend to the end." [1] In 1911 Wilson stated to

Dodge that he was true to the core. At the beginning of the First World War, the Chief Executive recognized the large value of the attachment. "I know of no other friend like you. . . . Thank God that it is so, and that there is room somewhere for perfect trust!" [2] After the Versailles Treaty fight in 1920, Edith Bolling Wilson could say for her husband: "He asks me to give you his warm love and say that your friendship is one of the props that no matter how hard he leans on — never fails — never disappoints." [3] Just before his death, Wilson wrote: "Surely no other man was ever blessed with so true, so unselfish, so thoughtful, so helpful a friend as you are and always have been to me!" [4] When Mrs. Wilson was planning for Ray Stannard Baker to write her husband's biography, she told Dodge: "I wouldn't feel any biography of Woodrow complete that did not reflect your personality and long, true friendship." [5] Baker used the correspondence between the two men extensively, and concluded: "No one could have been more devoted to Wilson than Cleveland Dodge." [6]

Princeton was the initial interest that the comrades had in common. They shared the esprit of the class of 1879, but came away with no career commitment to each other. Young Cleveland after graduation went on to a master's degree, then in New York City began executive responsibility in the mining company started by his grandfather (it eventually became the Phelps Dodge Corporation). Young Thomas Woodrow studied law, practiced in Atlanta, and then turned to graduate study at the Johns Hopkins University and teaching at Bryn Mawr College and Wesleyan University. After Wilson became a professor at Princeton in the 1890s, Dodge along with other members of the class of 1879 raised a fund to supplement Wilson's salary to keep him at his alma mater. Dodge shared Wilson's reading tastes, Charles Dickens and Walter Bagehot, and appreciated the professor's published works. Dodge in 1902 joined fellow trustees of the school to elect Wilson the first nonclergyman president of Princeton. Wilson immediately sought a broader financial base for the college, and to assist him Dodge organized some of the wealthy alumni in the Committee of Fifty. His generosity in providing money for scientific and other projects caused Wilson to write: "As for your devotion to Princeton, it is her great asset!" [7] The industrialist also approved his friend's launching the preceptorial or tutorial system in 1905.

The Princeton controversy over establishing quadrangles with resident faculty, a system supposedly more educationally sound than the exclusive eating clubs, was a test of the Dodge-Wilson relation. Dodge was on a committee of trustees which helped lead the board in June 1907 to approve the quadrangle scheme. Soon a majority of alumni and a minority of faculty and board members showed opposition to the quadrangle idea. Hearing that critics had harassed Dodge, Wilson wrote: "I cannot bear to think of your being distressed in this way. I do not believe, my dear fellow, that you can know the affection and gratitude I feel for you." [8] Controversy became so heated that in October the trustees unanimously reversed their June action. To avoid humiliating Wilson, Dodge presented a motion, which passed, stating: "The Board fully recognizes that the President's convictions have not changed, and have no wish to hinder him in any way in his purpose to endeavor to convince the members of the Board and Princeton men that this plan is the true solution." [9] The promoter of the quadrangle notion, speaking to alumni groups, struggled so strenuously to win that he endangered his health. Alarmed, Dodge urged: "If a good solid rest is the best thing for you, you must take the medicine, not only because we love you but because we love Princeton and you are its best and biggest asset." [10] But by June 1908 it was clear Wilson had lost. This defeat included strained relations (particularly with Professor John Grier Hibben), alienated alumni, and a fragmented board. Amid the turmoil, Dodge's loyalty did not waver.

In another controversy, over the site and funding of a graduate school, Dodge with five or six other men conspicuously stood by Wilson. The Princeton president late in December 1909 wrote the already divided trustees defending central administration of a graduate school. "I am glad that you have at last taken the bull by the horns," Dodge stated in reply, "& forced the issue. . . . Anyhow rest assured that I am with you all the time." [11] Soon a subcommittee of five from the board, which included Dodge, unanimously presented to the full body a pro-Wilson report. When Dodge discussed this action in a message to his friend, Wilson's elation had almost no limit: "Thank you," he said to Dodge, "from the bottom of my heart for your letter. It went to the right place, and has sent my barometer up as high as it can go! . . . At last we are free to govern the University as our judgments and consciences dictate!" [12] The opposition trustees rallied and by June 1910 had buried Wilson's idea about a graduate school; Dodge was with him to the end.

Dodge had an important part in Wilson's move from Princeton to the governor's chair in Trenton, New Jersey. In June 1910 it was obvious that anti-Wilson members of the board had the upper hand; by October they would force Wilson to resign. In early summer the professor-president began to consider the Democratic nomination for governor. On June 29 he met until midnight in New York with Dodge, who had no reservation against his friend's acceptance. Dodge offered to help in every way he could. Next day Wilson received at his summer house in Connecticut a telegram from four Chicago members of the Wilson group among Princeton trustees, promising support for political ambitions he might have. This encouragement caused Wilson to write "My Dear Cleve": "I shall never forget that little visit or the impressions it made upon me! May God bless you. And for your letter, too, received this morning. It raises one's whole estimate of the world to be associated with such men!" [13] In the gubernatorial campaign of 1910 Dodge made substantial contributions. At the beginning of Wilson's governorship, he helped the new incumbent obtain a free hand in leading the state Democratic party. After Wilson forces upset the bid of old-style boss James Smith, Jr., for election to the United States Senate, Dodge deftly offered congratulations: "You poor scholar and amateur in politics! Why don't you get an expert like Smith to advise you?" [14]

The classmate of 1879 was no less important in the Wilson-for-President boom. As early as June 1911 he began providing most of the finances for an office in New York City to prepare Wilson's candidacy. For relaxation Wilson took a yachting trip with Dodge in the summer of 1911. During the contest for the party endorsement, Dodge gave larger amounts of money than anyone else, totaling about fifty thousand dollars. Finally, Wilson won the Democratic nomination in a wild convention at Baltimore on the forty-sixth ballot. "I am so happy," wrote Dodge, "I can hardly think." [15] To prepare his acceptance speech, Wilson retired to the Dodge yacht for six joyful days. Thanking his benefactor, the nominee wrote: "You are an ideal friend: you do everything in the best and most generous way. The speech is written, and I am at the same time refreshed and reinvigorated." [16] To power the president-making machine, Dodge then solicited donations and himself gave the largest contribution, coming to over a hundred thousand dollars.[17] For the election of 1916 Dodge again would give over a hundred thousand.

Refusing an appointment in the Wilson administration, Dodge contented himself with an informal relation with the White House. He helped prevent Zionist leader Louis D. Brandeis from becoming attorney general. Upon Wilson's request Dodge worked, unsuccessfully, to persuade John

R. Mott, head of the Young Men's Christian Association, to become minister to China (Dodge had made a practice of paying Mott's travel expenses). Dodge advised on the membership of the Federal Reserve Board. Responding to the President in 1914, Dodge gave twenty-five thousand dollars annually to supplement the salary of the American ambassador in London, Walter Hines Page (Dodge offered a twenty-five–thousand–dollar subsidy per year for Princeton mathematics professor Henry B. Fine as ambassador to Germany, but Fine refused the post). By February 1917 Wilson, ironically, had lost confidence in Page and asked his friend to consider being a replacement in Britain. Flabbergasted, Dodge said to the President that the "bloom" upon their relation would disappear "If you should offer me the richest plum you have to offer and I should accept it." [18]

It was to foreign more than domestic matters, at first Mexican and later Near East relations, that Dodge gave attention. He became involved in diplomacy with Mexico, in part because the seizure of the Mexican government by Victoriano Huerta early in 1913 threatened the Phelps Dodge Corporation, which had mining properties in Arizona and New Mexico, and in northern Mexico. As spokesman for Phelps Dodge and other American investors in Mexico, Judge Delbert J. Haff of Kansas City in mid-1913 prepared a plan calling for temporary recognition of Huerta, on condition of elections in Mexico. The Haff scheme had the approval of Dodge, who introduced Haff to the President. Wilson prepared a note to Mexico City in line with the Haff plan. Before the President sent the note, his business advisers presented a new idea, that Wilson offer mediation between Huerta and Constitutionalist forces. Again Wilson agreed. Then the President began hearing negative reports about Huerta (Wilson would later call him a brute), about the American ambassador in Mexico, and about United States firms there. "How far, after all, could he follow the advice of men who, however able, were far more concerned with the stability of their investments than with the welfare and good government of the Mexican people?" [19] So the White House decided it needed independent sources of information and sent investigators to Mexico.

In this crisis Dodge possibly came closer to endangering his friendship with Wilson than at any other time. Also, in 1913 there reportedly was a legal indictment against a munitions company owned by a relative of Dodge's for illegally selling arms to Mexicans. The case never came before a jury, apparently because the State and Treasury departments were making exceptions to the arms embargo for several companies.[20] Evidence is not easily available. Whatever the case, Dodge thereafter was careful. He cheered Wilson with such statements as: "I am rejoiced over . . . the better outlook in Mexico," [21] and, "I happen to know more about the Mexican situation . . . than most of the people who are howling against your policy in the present emergency." [22] In 1916 the Chief Executive obviously felt positively toward Dodge: "Your letter of January fourteenth came when my heart was pretty sad about the Mexican situation. It acted, therefore, like a ray of light in a dark place and I thank you for it with all my heart as well as with all my mind. Your approval in a matter which I am sure you understood to the utmost reassures me immensely." [23]

On a paramount issue of international affairs Dodge the next year, 1917, praised Wilson's diplomacy. After the message to Congress which led the United States into war with Germany, the President received Dodge's word that this document possibly was the greatest in American history. Wilson responded: "Your letter is just what my heart desired and I am delighted that you now have the opportunity of pointing out . . . that it was necessary for me by very slow stages indeed and with the most genuine purpose to avoid war to lead the country on to a single way of thinking. I thank God for the evidence that the task has been accomplished. I think that I never felt the responsibilities of office more profoundly than I feel them now, and yet there is a certain relief in having the task made concrete and definite." [24]

Through all these experiences of Princeton, Trenton, and Washington, Dodge and Wilson enjoyed many social occasions together. During Wilson's New Jersey days in higher education, the friends often had gotten together for an hour or so of entertaining, sometimes humorous storytelling at Dodge's small house in Princeton. After 1913 the industrialist occasionally stayed overnight at the White House and quite often had the President to his estate, Riverdale (on the Hudson a few miles north of Manhattan), to relax in a favorite chair. They had many discussions about the Near East at Riverdale.[25]

Wilson's professional advancement was perhaps the leading common interest of the two men. The industrialist and the politician usually suppressed negative feelings about each other, not analyzing their tie. Wilson often avoided direct identification of emotions. He usually liked feeling itself — often warmth toward trusted people and disdain toward antagonists — more than a scrutiny of feeling. Living in a prepsychological, melodramatic age, he and the New Yorker regularly affirmed devotion to each other. This intuitive style helped Wilson crusade for Christian idealism — of quite mature and of moralistic varieties — more than explore the emotional aspects of such associations as the one with Dodge. The educator's position on a graduate school, one of "conscience" and "great and noble principle" for Princeton, and the move for progress in New Jersey ("positively the right thing to do") were probably of more import to him than his link with Dodge.[26] In the battle of 1909 and 1910 when Wilson imagined his benefactor a "perfect friend and colleague" (Dodge was a magnetic person and a fine conversationalist), he hinted that the basic thing he liked about the philanthropist was backing for his ideas. One writer has stated that Wilson wanted men "to work for him, push him forward." [27] Dodge knew how to live with this ascendancy of Wilson's ambitions.

An ingredient in the friendship which helped the industrialist to influence the President about the Ottoman Empire was Protestant Christianity. Wilson's father had been a prominent Southern Presbyterian clergyman. Both his mother and his own first wife, Ellen Axson Wilson, were daughters of Presbyterian clergymen. Growing into manhood, Wilson never had a period of doubt when he openly questioned his orthodox training — he accepted or ignored it. As for Dodge, his heritage was Puritan. Members of his family had come to Salem, Massachusetts, in the 1600s. Cleveland's grandfather, William E. Dodge, Sr., an individual in the first family group to live in New York City, figured largely in many Christian organizations; he was vice-president of the American Board's trustees. Cleveland's father, William E. Dodge, Jr., gave himself mostly to business; he was also president of the national Young Men's Christian Association and took part in several Protestant movements. A Presbyterian, Cleveland had a style of religion much like Wilson's: much more pragmatic than theological and more ecumenical than denominational. Concentrating his Christian service on corporation and humanitarian projects, Dodge's philanthropies included giving over $1,000,000 to the American Red Cross and leading its coordination with relief in the Near East and with the government. He made large gifts to the national Young Men's Christian Association and the Young Women's Christian Association and was a board member of both. He invested time and money in the New York Public Library, the American Museum of Natural History, and the Carnegie Foundation for International Peace. After America entered the war (at the President's petition), he helped lead the United War Work Fund, which raised $170,000,000.

The Christianity of Wilson and Dodge was a mixture of living faith, culture-religion, and phrasemaking. Considerable genuineness on Wilson's part concerned his tenderness with women, generous financial assistance to relatives for their education, refusal to allow nepotism, avoidance of scandal in his presidency, and his prophetic role. Protestantism provided for Wilson a cosmic frame, helping the "higher realism" and the emphasis on principles which produced reform during each of his executive positions. For Dodge there was no small authenticity in his favorite wartime affirmation, "God moves in a mysterious way His wonders to perform," and prayer, "A thousand years in Thy sight are as but yesterday when it is past." [28] The two men accepted the pietistic evangelical ethos of their day. Dodge led in prayers and hymn singing at meetings of the ACASR; Wilson wore out many Bibles in family devotions.[29] References in their letters to reliance on God or expressions like "God bless you" were frequent. These exercises were both creative and ritualistic. Wilson and Dodge also used verbal religion as a cover for politics; they thought of the quadrangle plan at Princeton as a "scheme of salvation." [30] It is valid criticism that an adjunct to the Christian qualities helping bring Wilson a cornucopia of accomplishment were Pharisaism and bitterness toward opponents. These negative characteristics would harm missionary diplomacy with the Near East during the peace settlement after the First World War.

Other reasons for Wilson's tight bond with Dodge may be found in comparing it with the rapport between the President and his Texan adviser Colonel Edward House. Between 1912 and 1917 House was deliberately self-effacing, nonargumentative, and adulatory toward Wilson. The President and House had nearly the same political ideals, and the Texan believed that appeals to Wilson's vanity were necessary to exercise power vicariously.[31] The Chief Executive reveled in his relation with House, as he had with Professor John Grier Hibben, stating: "Mr. House is my second personality. He is my independent self. His thoughts and mine are one." To his adviser he rejoiced: "You are the only person in the world with whom I can discuss everything." [32] Not corrupt, but an adroit accommodater to different and sometimes contradictory forces, the wiry House would be the chief presidential adviser until the Paris Peace Conference. There, House, continuing a process begun earlier, moved out of the shadows. He tried to reveal who he was, to Wilson and to the world, by acting as conciliator between the American leader and the Allies. House overcompensated for his previous stance with Wilson, sometimes frustrating the President's direction of American diplomacy. If Wilson could have grappled with House's more honest style of friendship, he would have become a better person.

Dodge tested and confirmed his relation with Wilson in the Princeton difficulties before Trenton and Washington — experiences not shared by House. More nearly than House, Dodge had a type of Christianity like Wilson's. Because of larger business and philanthropic accomplishment than that of House, Dodge did not need Wilson to advance his own career. He could commit himself to the President, expecting few if any professional and political, as opposed to personal, rewards. Like House, he flattered Wilson, as when he said the President's war message was probably the greatest American State paper. Better than House, Dodge knew how to remain anonymous. He refused the ambassadorship in London, sensing that its glare could wither the relation with Wilson. Dodge studiously avoided attention in Near East matters, letting Barton, Morgenthau, and others carry open responsibility. Further, House was quite analytical (more so than Dodge), a manner sometimes irritating to the President.

Wilson's relation with the classmate of 1879 was something of a balance wheel on his emotional turbulence. The President once candidly described to the National Press Club his inner tumult: "If I were to interpret myself, I would say that my constant embarrassment is to restrain the emotions that are inside of me. You may not believe it, but I sometimes feel like a fire from a far from extinct volcano, and if the lava does not seem to spill over it is because you are not high enough to see into the basin and see the caldron boil." [33] Like the polar star, Dodge was a fairly fixed point for Wilson, whose private and public woes often correlated. The faithfulness of Dodge had a negative aspect, especially after House left the Wilson orbit; his dependability did not challenge Wilson's problem with inflexibility. The President's obstinacy would hurt missionary plans for Turkey greatly during 1919 and 1920.

In addition to ties with the White House, Dodge had family and Christian concerns attaching him to the Near East. His grandfather had figured in the founding of the Syrian Protestant College. His father was a trustee of this school, and his Presbyterian clergyman uncle D. Stuart Dodge was a leading advocate through his position from 1907 to 1921 as board president. Two of Dodge's four children, Elizabeth and Bayard, went as missionary educators to the Ottoman Empire. Elizabeth married George H.

Huntington, professor and vice-president at Robert College. Cleveland Dodge himself in 1909 became president of Robert College's board, a post he would hold until his death. His son Bayard married the daughter of Howard Bliss, the Syrian Protestant College's second president. In 1923 Bayard succeeded his father-in-law as the head of the school.

Family connections helped Dodge quietly invest in the relief enterprise in Turkey. A co-worker assessed Dodge's prominence in the ACASR: "There probably would have been no such organization . . . had it not been for Mr. Dodge; and there certainly would have been no such rapid and far reaching development of the organization had it not been for his inspiring leadership and financial generosity. . . . But vastly more important than all his large gifts of money, he gave himself." Dodge allegedly said after April 1917: "When this awful war broke out, I knew that we would all have to do our bit, and among other things I resolved that, whatever else happened, I would not allow myself and my estate to profit by it. Some people call us profiteers. We cannot help it. The government needs copper. The government fixes the price on copper, we don't. We profit at the price fixed by the government, *but I have resolved that not one red cent of this blood money shall stick to these fingers."* [34]

With all this background, it is apparent that Dodge was in a position to coach Wilson in Ottoman-American relations, a departure from the President's normal dominance in the friendship. Wilson generally led in the conduct of foreign policies.[35] When Secretary of State William Jennings Bryan took a course which Wilson felt might jeopardize his own control, he helped bring on Bryan's resignation. The President eventually sensed that Colonel House was not always faithful to Wilsonian ideas, and let their relation erode. If ambassadors became too independent, the President sent envoys or missions to establish his own lines of communication. But without any serious misunderstanding, Dodge would be able until 1921, together with James Barton, to guide Wilson in diplomacy with the Near East.

BUTTING IN ON STATE MATTERS

When in April 1917 Wilson submitted his war message to Congress, Dodge and Barton had figured in the President's neglecting to mention the Ottoman Empire. Wilson had not needed much convincing. The President feared for the safety of Americans in the Near East and had written Dodge two months before: "I have thought more than once of your dear ones in

Turkey with a pang of apprehension that was very deep. Fortunately, there is always one of our vessels there, inadequate though it may be, and I hope . . . there will be no real danger to the lives of our people abroad. Still, I know how very anxious you must be and my heart is with you." [36] Both Dodge and Barton had fretted that hostilities between the United States and Turkey would endanger American evangelistic, educational, and relief personnel and their activities.

Anticipating that some people would favor an Ottoman-American confrontation, Barton in February 1917 had prepared an argument for the State Department. For this paper the American Board secretary had obtained the support of Dodge, Morgenthau, and Crane. Barton listed five explanations why Turkish-American relations should be harmonious: The United States alone among nations did not have designs upon Ottoman territory. Next, German demands on Turkey would become more vocal if the Porte lost "friendship with the United States." Third, "Millions of dollars have gone from the United States to Turkey and have been expended there for the good and help of Turkey and her people and without even the suggestion that Turkish sovereignty should thereby be weakened or that American national control should be increased. . . . The philanthropy of American citizens is a genuine philanthropy by which Turkey is enriched." Barton declared that "if friendly relations are maintained, the scheme of unselfish philanthropy will continue to flow toward Turkey." Fourth, Constantinople needed the support of America's "great colleges and universities." Last, the United States after the peace would be in a better position than Germany to serve the Ottoman Empire, without imposing on the latter "conditions that will impair sovereignty." These points contained hyperbole. The relief chairman did not note that the ACASR had abetted minorities far more than the central government. He also glossed over his motive to safeguard the American Board. Concluding, Barton asked Secretary Lansing to let Elkus and the Turkish ambassador in Washington know about his ideas.[37]

The missionary's plea, though not unassailable, correlated with the United States government's official policy, though not with the government's attitude. Upon his first electoral triumph, Wilson had looked toward the end of the Ottoman Empire. At that time House suggested Morgenthau as ambassador to Turkey and the President-designate, reflecting on the recent loss to the Empire of Libya, responded: "There ain't going to be no Turkey." [38] House rejoined that they ought to send Morgenthau to hunt for the wounded bird anyway. As ambassador, Morgenthau received warnings from the Department of State to maintain a strict neutrality vis-à-vis Ottoman-Allied war. Concurrently, House and Wilson acquiesced to designs about the liquidation of the Turkish Empire in private conversations with the British. Still, when Barton addressed Lansing in February 1917, the formal policy of the United States toward Constantinople remained one of neutrality.

Barton's message to the State Department fit the Young Turk mood. Germany threatened to end assistance to the Porte if Turkey did not declare war on the United States. But Ambassador Elkus reported that Turkish officials were going out of their way to be generous. They hoped for American aid to offset the Germans if the latter would emerge ascendant in Europe or for reconstruction support if there would be an Allied victory.[39] Bending to German duress, the Turkish cabinet, by a one-vote majority, on April 20, 1917, cut diplomatic relations with the United States. When the American embassy closed, the missionary assistant to William Peet, Luther Fowle, represented United States concerns through the Swedish legation. Ottoman unwillingness to tangle with the United States indicated that, despite preference by the Protestants for disgruntled minorities in the Near East, the Turks felt attracted to the Western republic. This feeling consisted not so much of friendship, but of admiration for Yankee honesty and confidence in a government not aggressively playing the Sick-Man-of-Europe game. In times of crisis, individual Turks often had deposited money with the religionists without interest or security: "No bank had as high a reputation in Turkey as the treasury of the missions." [40]

After the diplomatic break, an argument over neutrality developed within the United States. Probably most Americans dismissed Turkey as a sideshow in comparison to Europe, but some people called for vengeance against Turkey. Opponents of this bellicosity echoed Barton's notions. The American Board of Commissioners for Foreign Missions at its annual meeting of 1917 feared that if the United States chose war, missions and the ACASR would fold, more minorities would die, and the Empire would seize all American property. Missionary insecurity increased in autumn when Turkophobes persuaded Congress to pass a bill which authorized the President to freeze assets of Ottoman citizens in the United States. Seeing that, if carried through, this measure would bring reciprocity, Barton sped a note to Wilson. He also urged Dodge to intercede with the President.[41]

91

Having a large respect for mission secretary Barton and glad to be an intermediary, Dodge acceded.[42] The industrialist decided to send the President a defense of the status quo between the United States and the two Central Powers in the Near East, Turkey and Bulgaria. Before writing, he had received unanimous approval of neutrality from the Protestant boards in the Ottoman Empire and former Ambassadors Elkus and Morgenthau. "I hesitate to butt in on matters of State," he began, "especially when I am biased by personal considerations, and . . . what I write may be unnecessary. Still I know you will forgive me and understand my motives. . . . war with Turkey would be a serious blow" to efforts there and would "jeopardize many American lives besides stopping the work we are doing in saving the lives of hundreds of thousands of natives. Nevertheless we all feel that our selfish interests should not stand in the way of what you think it best to do in carrying out your great purposes to end the war." In the long letter, Dodge asked that since there was heavy mission investment in Bulgaria, neutrality should persist in relations with that state.[43] (Bulgaria had joined the European conflagration as an ally of the strongest Central Power, chiefly because its royal family was German and because it desired to regain territory lost to pro-Allied neighbors in 1913 during the Second Balkan War.) The Sunday, December 2, on which Dodge wrote, he saw Elkus off to Washington. At the State Department, Elkus was to marshal the points Dodge had already made in his correspondence to Wilson.

The Chief Executive the next Tuesday showed endorsement of Dodge's letter. On that day there was no reference to action against the Porte in Wilson's annual message to Congress, which included a request for a declaration of war against what he called Germany's instrument, Austria-Hungary. The President in the message and elsewhere declared that Turkey and Bulgaria were tools of Berlin, yet not of enough leverage to hurt United States actions against the Central Powers.[44] Wilson stated that certain controlling reasons made a war with the Ottoman Empire undesirable. Concurrently, Democratic Senator William H. King from Utah introduced a resolution proposing hostilities against Constantinople and Sofia. Secretary Lansing soon informed the Senate Foreign Relations Committee that the administration could not start military operations against Turkey immediately. The primary result of passing the King Resolution, Lansing said, would be confiscation of church, school, and humanitarian institutions set up by American Protestants in the Near East.

The same week as the annual message Wilson replied to Dodge at Riverdale: "Just a line to say that I sympathize with every word of your letter . . . about war with Turkey and am trying to hold the Congress back from following its inclination to include all the allies of Germany in a declaration of a state of war. I hope with all my heart that I can succeed." [45] Barton received a copy of Wilson's comments to Dodge and exulted: "This quotation from the President's letter is worth everything." [46] The New Yorker then could relax as he penned to Wilson: "Just a line to thank you for your reassuring letter — that, coupled with the action of Congress, in not pushing the Turkish question, has made me very happy. It is needless for me to tell you how profoundly grateful I am for your wonderful message to Congress. Your little typewriter must have been inspired." [47]

But the American Board secretary apparently did not rest just because the President sanctioned Dodge's view. With what appears to be Wilson's approval, Barton attempted to convince Republican Senator Henry Cabot Lodge of Massachusetts that it was futile for Congress to try to override the administration's wishes on Turkey. Barton released in mid-December 1917 an open letter to Senator Lodge, repeating much of the rationale outlined to the Department of State in the previous February. ACASR chairman Barton hammered the proposition, with evidence, that Germany dominated Enver and his colleagues and that the Kaiser's government desperately wanted an Ottoman-American conflict. Barton said that it was unwise for the United States to give cause for the Young Turks to take American possessions in the Empire and to remove ACASR succor to the Armenians. He believed it would be absurd if the United States began a paper war. A novel notion had to do with what he considered a rising "tide of friendship between Turkey and America" (any growing Turkish friendliness with the United States probably issued from fear that Germany might lose the war).[48] Barton's analysis on this point, of course, was too happy in comparison with the ACASR's propaganda about cruel and corrupt Turks. Nor did Barton's thinking fit in with Washington's informal acceptance of the dismantling of the Ottoman Empire. Wilson and House then were considering a Turkey divided into autonomous regions along ethnic lines. Barton's open letter to Lodge, nevertheless, helped release a squall of mail on the Senate.

With foreboding about possible jeopardy, American Board leaders editorialized in the *Missionary Herald*: "Should the United States declare war against Turkey and Bulgaria? We say, unqualifiedly and emphatically,

'No.' It would be a tactical blunder, an outrage against humanity, and a moral crime." [49]

NEUTRALITY, WAR, AND MEDIATION

This editorial cry did not represent the ambivalence felt by both Barton and Wilson over American tactics toward the Ottoman Empire. Both men wanted to preserve Protestant investments in Turkey. This desire was clear. Barton and the President felt deeply about Ottoman matters, yet were not certain about methods.

Contending generally against Ottoman-American hostilities, the chairman of the American Committee for Armenian and Syrian Relief studied protection of missionary interests through United States military force against Turkey. In September 1917, Albert H. Lybyer, a Princeton-trained professor of Near East history at the University of Illinois and Presbyterian clergyman sympathetic to missionaries, had proposed to Dodge an American amphibious landing at the Gulf of Alexandretta in Cilicia to divide the Ottoman Empire. This inspiration had come to Lybyer after attending a national conference of the ACASR. The plan, he said, was a result of his impression "that if the war is prolonged, and conditions continue as now, nearly all of our effort and expense will be in vain, for most of the people will die." [50] At Lybyer's urging, Dodge promised to take up the notion in Washington even though he doubted its wisdom. In the autumn United States officials seriously considered sending the main body of American troops to Turkey rather than France, but soon discarded this idea.[51] Barton later instructed one of the missionaries in Asia Minor to spy out the land along the Gulf of Alexandretta. This field religionist replied that there was no Ottoman defense of the Berlin-to-Baghdad railway. Ghosting an editorial for an American newspaper, Barton in March 1918 recommended putting ashore at the Gulf of Alexandretta fifty thousand American troops who would snip the railway artery, with the result that the cutting probably would finish Turkey. Barton intended the proposal to test public reaction; not seeing a result, he let the scheme rest until summer.[52]

It is interesting that Field Marshal Paul von Hindenburg after the war declared that landing two Allied divisions on the Cilician coast would have forced Turkey to surrender. Hindenburg remarked that the Allies had no "reason to fear that in pushing east from the Gulf" they would be "treading on a hornet's nest. There were no hornets." Enver during the war told

Hindenburg: "My only hope is that the enemy has not discovered our weakness" at Alexandretta.[53]

Dispute over the merits of neutrality continued in America in the spring of 1918. Senator Lodge mustered a report that Turks and Bulgarians were on the Western front. Barton's reaction to Lodge by letter and informal discussion seemingly drove the Senator to a black-and-white view. Lodge declared that Constantinople and Sofia were "absolutely hostile" to the United States and that trying to separate them from Germany was a "perfect illusion." Ex-President Roosevelt spoke in Portland, Maine, asking for a declaration of war against Turkey.[54]

The Allies also challenged the mission-relief no-war stand, declaring to Secretary Lansing that a United States conflict against Turkey and that a mediation offer to Bulgaria would be advisable. Great Britain desired assistance for its dogged fight in the Near East. Even with Arab collaboration, the British had not broken Ottoman morale. General Edmund Allenby had inched ahead in Palestine during 1917 but only in December entered Jerusalem. Allenby's forces then languished in the barren hills north of the Holy City; a British column in the Tigris-Euphrates plains barely had proceeded beyond Baghdad. In the Caucasus, where Russians had withdrawn because of the Bolshevik Revolution, local Armenians and Georgians resisted the Turkish advance but needed the boost of a United States entry into the battles.

Barton and his backers in April 1918 determined to hold against the Allied appeal. They were still uncertain about protection of Protestants within Turkey if an Ottoman-American war began. They received information of European pressure on the State Department through James Bryce, who in turn showed Barton's correspondence to the British Foreign Office. Missionary William Peet, who had returned to the United States partly because his Armenianism had made him obnoxious to the Porte, lobbied in Washington. Peet sensed that Allied pleas were producing a shift in some United States officials. Charles Crane, who recently had come back to America after participation in the Elihu Root Mission to Russia, assisted Peet for a while. The secretary of the ACASR, Samuel Dutton, aided Peet by pressing for neutrality in the Senate.[55]

A Republican assault on mission-government policy occurred in May 1918. Opposition Senators in the Foreign Relations Committee stirred people against Turkey. Roosevelt helped these Senators in Boston on May Day by a speech which lashed Washington's nonmilitancy. The old Rough

95

Rider wanted America to charge into the Ottoman Empire. Roosevelt wrote Barton: "There is no question whatever in my mind that we are guilty of the greatest dereliction of duty in not going to war with Turkey; and that our conduct has been unpardonable in not declaring war against every ally of Germany just as soon as we declared war against Germany herself." [56]

Roosevelt's attitude toward Turkey, aside from its partisan aspects, had a rationale based on a mixture of moralism and tough-mindedness. In the 1890s he had begun wishing for the demise of what he believed was uncivilized Turkey, as noted earlier. In a book published in 1916, he stated: "If this nation had feared God it would have stood up for the Belgians and Armenians; if it had been able and willing to take its own part there would have been no murderous assault on the *Lusitania*, no outrages on our men and women in Mexico." In a letter to ACASR secretary Dutton he refused to participate in a pro-Armenian rally because the rally involved words, not action. Roosevelt declared to Dutton: "Let us realize that the words of the weakling and the coward, of the pacifist and the poltroon, are worthless to stop wrongdoing. Wrongdoing will only be stopped by men who are brave as well as just, . . . and who shrink from no hazard, not even the final hazard of war, if necessary in order to serve the great cause of righteousness." Both he and Lodge wanted an Ottoman-American fight so that the United States at a peace conference could help ensure the effacement of what they felt was Turkey's blot on history. [57]

Roosevelt explained to "Cleve" Dodge, whom he had known and corresponded with since boyhood, that sympathy for relatives in Turkey (he himself had relatives in Germany), for Robert College, and for Armenians was no basis for United States policy. Roosevelt claimed that only intervention could both rectify the Armenian massacres and prepare America for future service in the Near East. [58]

Dodge and Barton sought to parry Roosevelt's interventionist ideas, not his postwar goal. Dodge talked over the Republican threat with Lansing and House in New York. Writing President Wilson, Lansing said that many Senators as well as the Allies wanted United States troops in the Near East. But the Secretary disfavored this idea because "relief would come to an end, our missionaries will be expelled or interned and the great missionary properties will be confiscated." [59] Barton released a second open letter, addressed this time to Roosevelt. He set down five reasons for and ten against a conflict with Turkey and Bulgaria. Dodge sent House a copy of Barton's statement and asked that it be defended at the State Department. Dodge praised his Boston co-worker as one who "knows more about the situation in the Near East than almost anyone else." [60] When in mid-May 1918 Wilson and House met Dodge at Riverdale, the President still wanted concord with Turkey and believed that a war would lead to the extinction of the Turkish Armenians. He favored a contest with Bulgaria if necessary, though House did not feel the contingency would arise. The President recalled this visit with Dodge: "Your whole attitude at the meeting and everything that you said was admirable and delightful." [61]

House, one might note, for various reasons upheld mission and relief concerns in the Near East. One was his association with Dodge and Crane. Another was his acquaintance with George Washburn, physician son and namesake of the second president of Robert College; the younger Washburn lived a short way from House's summer place at Magnolia in Massachusetts. Since March 1918 American Board missionaries from Bulgaria had been visiting the President's adviser. Dodge wrote to the American Board secretary in late spring: "Whenever I begin to hope that the agitation for war with Turkey has died out, I get a new shock . . . I would therefore suggest that . . . you arrange for an appointment with Col. House." [62] Dodge thought of House as an auxiliary on Near East affairs. In a session at Magnolia Barton considered the eastern Mediterranean with the presidential aide. Of the ACASR chairman House recorded: "Our views do not materially differ. I regard him highly." [63]

All this missionary diplomacy helped Wilson advocate to the Senate Committee on Foreign Relations that there be no change in United States policy toward Turkey and Bulgaria. A journalist in June 1918 described this private lobby: "Some weeks ago Senator King introduced a resolution calling for a declaration of war on Turkey. He was vigorously supported by Senator Lodge and by a considerable section of influential opinion. But there was no declaration of war. The President quietly said no. . . . From such events the average citizen gets an impression of vast, silent power somewhere, capable of giving to President Wilson the Olympian confidence with which he squelches the suggestions of distinguished statesmen. . . . It is the silent, unofficial Cabinet [Dodge, Barton, and Elkus] which buttresses this confidence." [64]

Busily working in the "silent cabinet" for neutrality, Barton also wondered about a secret American commission to the Near East. He knew that if the United States were not a belligerent or a mediator, it might not have much say in an armistice and peace treaty with Sofia or Constantinople. In summer 1918 American military action did not seem the best option for him to promote. So he developed the idea of a commission which would attempt to detach Bulgaria or Turkey from the Central Powers.

Mediation had first been attempted the year before. Believing then that the Young Turks would be sympathetic both to Zionism and to negotiation with the Allies, Henry Morgenthau in June 1917 had received approval from the Wilson administration to go to Europe and Cairo. Publicly Morgenthau's goal was to investigate conditions of Jews in the Near East; secretly it was to explore possibilities for getting the Ottoman Empire out of the war.[65] Morgenthau's mission stalled on July 4 at Gibraltar, where with British connivance, such Zionists as Chaim Weizmann convinced Morgenthau his effort was futile. Zionists told Morgenthau that the forthcoming British offensive could better work for Jewish interests in Palestine and for Armenian interests than could peace efforts. Morgenthau meanwhile talked too much and embarrassed Washington, helping turn his mission into a fiasco.

American Board secretary Barton decided on an attempt like Morgenthau's but more in line with previous Allied advice to Lansing. A catalyst was the Bulgarian minister to the United States, Stepan Panaretoff. This man had graduated from Robert College, taught there for over forty years, and "knew well" Dodge and the younger George Washburn. Panaretoff had been aiding missionaries maintain Bulgarian-American neutrality. Theodore Roosevelt lambasted Panaretoff, calling him a spy; Dodge countered by telling Wilson that he would vouch for the Bulgarian's integrity. With Panaretoff's approval, Barton and others during July and August 1918 planned to send Washburn to Bulgaria along with Edward C. Moore, trustee president of the American Board, clergyman, and professor at Harvard University. Ostensibly Red Cross observers, Washburn and Moore were to offer Bulgaria President Wilson's mediation of tangled boundary issues in the Balkans. Sensitive to its territorial losses in 1913, Bulgaria probably would respond favorably — so Barton and his associates believed. If things did not go amiss, events would isolate Turkey from Germany and force the Porte to give up (every Balkan neighbor of Bulgaria had inclined toward the Allies, and Sofia was on the main route for supplies between Berlin and Constantinople). Barton expected that the Young Turks would open the Dardanelles to the American fleet, bringing a new atmosphere in the Near East.[66]

House and the Department of State reportedly endorsed the Washburn-Moore Commission, but this project was not high on the agendas either of House or Lansing. Attention in late summer 1918 was on Germany's withdrawal of men and munitions from the Eastern front and an Allied expedition's push north from Salonika to cut off the Berlin-to-Baghdad railway. The Bulgarian Army was close to collapse. Allenby counted a triumph against the Ottoman Empire near the hill town of Nazareth in mid-September and his forces marched on north. During the first week of October, Beirut and Damascus fell to British and Arab soldiers, and in Mesopotamia Allied troops reached the outskirts of Mosul. The United States contented itself with asking for information from the Allies about the Near East. Washburn and Moore understandably hesitated to depart on their mission.

Deciding meanwhile that the Washburn-Moore Commission was still-born, Barton revived the notion of an Ottoman-American war. The missionary wanted to get the United States squarely into the Eastern Question before an armistice. He thought it might be wise for American forces to make a quick attack on Constantinople. Barton felt that United States soldiers were needed for America to take part in the Ottoman settlement. On this point the American Board secretary and Roosevelt agreed. Roosevelt described his view to Lodge: "Let us dictate peace [with Germany] by the hammering of guns and not chat about peace to the accompaniment of the clicking of typewriters. . . . We ought to declare war on Turkey without an hour's delay. The failure to do so hitherto has caused the talk about making the world safe for democracy, to look unpleasantly like insincere rhetoric. While the Turk is left in Europe and permitted to tyrannize over the subject peoples, the world is thoroly unsafe for democracy." [67]

Wilson and House took up the prospect of intervention on September 22, 1918. Wilson was willing to ask Congress for war, but "disliked to do so at this time when the Bulgarians were in full flight. He thought it might look as if we had waited until they were beaten." [68] House disagreed and determined to return to the problem later. Circumstances soon eliminated this contingency.

Because Barton had not obtained mediation or a last-minute American belligerency, the United States was in a difficult position to be a senior partner with the Allies in allotting territory of the Ottoman Empire. The ACASR chairman would have in the days ahead a less well-prepared public

99

opinion and a weaker government than he would like for political help in reversing Protestant fortunes in Turkey.

ADOPTING AN INFANT OR DOTARD

While assisting United States neutrality toward the Empire, the unofficial cabinet of religionists and philanthropists had been getting ready for postwar configurations in Turkey.

A factor in much of the preparation was American emotion about the Armenians. In 1916 when Morgenthau discussed the massacres with Wilson, the stunned President momentarily had felt the United States should fight Turkey for humanity's sake. Reading cables from Constantinople about the Armenians a few months later, the President became "sick at heart." [69] It is difficult to overstress the sorrow experienced for this minority people by citizens of the United States and by the President. Yet in acting upon America's grief, Wilson could not think of anything the government could do beyond facilitating relief.

In spite of the President's hesitancy, Barton in 1917 had begun to plan especially for a United States adoption of an infant Armenia. Or possibly for an adoption of the dotard-like Ottoman Empire. It was hard for this missionary, who knew the Armeno-Turkish language and who temporarily sheltered in his Boston house escapees from the massacres, to foresee anything other than a free Armenia. His desire to have Turkey punished for its sins — perhaps even rubbed off the map — helped him neglect thinking about postwar American aid to Turkey. His anti-Turk impulses and those of his fellow Americans too often reveled in Armenianism and denied concern for the whole, complicated Ottoman Empire.

It was a coterie at the top of the American Board and the ACASR which led the promotion for an American involvement in the Near East. Some individuals connected to missions and relief knew little about its lobbying for specific designs. Bayard Dodge has recollected that in the First World War he regarded a United States protection of Armenia "most unreasonable. I never remember hearing my father say anything in favor of it, or got into discussion about it with him." [70] The important thing then, however, was that the Armenianism of both followers and leaders was crucial. Some Congregationalists and Presbyterians who made negative comments about Protestants' busybodying in politics usually liked the goal of some United States help for Armenians. The critics often disliked religionists' becoming embroiled in the process.

100

To ready a possible future American assistance in the Near East, Barton and his associates had a kaleidoscope of proposals. One involved Ambassador Elkus, who early in 1917 had still been at his post, striving to increase the Porte's trust in the United States. William Peet then had reported that several members of the Committee of Union and Progress felt American favor after the war would be useful. Barton urged Secretary Lansing to give Elkus higher entertainment allowances — the way to a Turk's heart, Barton advised, was through the stomach, and through Corona cigars. In another procedure, the American Board asked the State Department to appoint a commissioner for the conference which would settle hostilities with Turkey. Barton also issued statements on the incapacity of the Turks to rule anyone. "I want," he declared, "to create a sentiment that will be overwhelmingly on that side of the question." Such remarks went out of Boston and New York to wire services and editors. Copies of James Bryce's book on the Armenian atrocities by mid-1917 were on the desks of every Congressman and many other framers of public outlook.[71]

Interacting with Armenian spokesmen, the ACASR chairman introduced to Washington officials Mihran Sevasly, head of a federation which brought together several Armenian-American institutions. Barton helped tone down extravagant statements about Armenian freedom made by Sevasly's federation. The American Board secretary contributed to the State Department's hiring of Arshag Schmavonian, formerly a staff member in the United States embassy at Constantinople and an Armenian familiar to Peet and Morgenthau. Schmavonian became a consultant on Turkish affairs; for several years he would be a confidant of Barton and Dodge. (One returned missionary from Turkey, Charles Trowbridge Riggs, regularly translated Greek newspapers for Schmavonian.) Also, the mission executive corresponded with Boghos Nubar Pasha, wealthy Armenian chairman of the railway directorate of Egypt and son of a prime minister there. After the European conflict began, Boghos Nubar had gone to Paris to defend Turkish-Armenian interests. Boghos promised France to recruit Armenian troops for the Western front in exchange for an autonomous Armenia under French suzerainty.[72]

Barton's earliest exertions about a Turkish peace settlement made less of an impression in Washington than did Allied ambitions. Beginning in 1915 and continuing in the Sykes-Picot Agreement of April and May 1916, Russia, Britain, and France had defined spoils in the Ottoman Empire. Italy then joined the imperial arrangements through the St. Jean de Maurienne Agreement. These secret treaties promised Constantinople and four vilayets of Turkish Armenia (Trabzon, Erzurum, Bitlis, Van) to Tsarist Russia (the Bolsheviks later renounced and revealed these pacts to the world); two vilayets of Turkish Armenia (Mamuret Ul-Aziz and Diyarbakir), Cilicia, and Syria to France; part of western Anatolia to Italy; and Mesopotamia to Britain. Palestine was to be an international zone.[73] (See Map 3, p. 52, and Map 4, p. 103.) Wilson and House reviewed these documents in 1917, reading copies and privately talking about them with Allied spokesmen. The United States leaders agreed with the Europeans that the Ottoman Empire needed an overhaul, but would not officially acknowledge the existence of the treaties. Wilson and House desired to preserve American initiative to help a settlement benefiting the Near Easterners as well as the imperial powers. Wilson publicly condemned war aims seeking an acquisitive dismemberment of empires; away from newsmen's pens he explicitly criticized aims proposing to split Asia Minor.[74]

In the latter part of 1917 the Protestant lobby began to press the government through The Inquiry, the commission organized after Wilson had instructed House to collect information for the peace negotiations. House delegated most duties for The Inquiry to his brother-in-law, Sidney E. Mezes, president of the City College of New York and philosopher of religion. The commission eventually included one hundred and fifty experts who wrote or collected about two thousand documents and over a thousand maps. (The secretary of The Inquiry was Walter Lippmann.) Former Ambassador Elkus sent to Mezes ACASR bulletins on the future of Armenia. Morgenthau introduced House to William H. Hall, professor at the Syrian Protestant College and secretary of an ACASR committee appointed by Barton to put together data on reconstruction of the Ottoman Empire; Hall became an official assistant to The Inquiry. Consulting with Boghos and Bryce, Barton favored an American protectorate over a free Armenia and passed this idea to the Hall Committee.[75]

In contrast, Mezes and Morgenthau thought of autonomy for the Armenians and declared to Hall and Barton that the Ottoman Empire might remain as a loose federation. For the Empire there should be a guidance by one of the Western nations, preferably the United States, toward the goal of self-government. Mezes hoped to resist the secret treaties.[76] Seeing that the inclinations of Mezes and Morgenthau were not necessarily inimi-

102

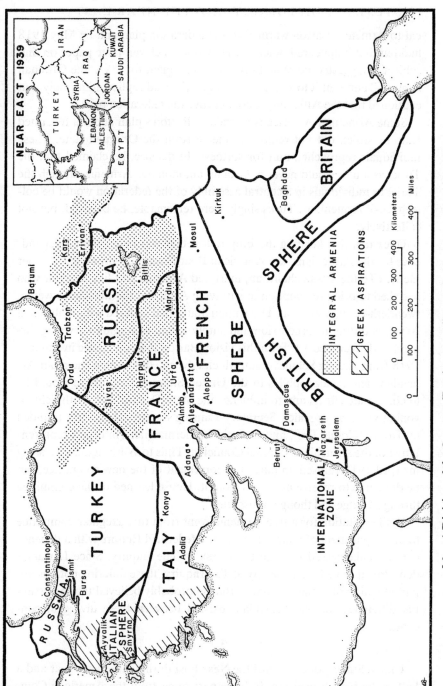

Map 4. Division of the Ottoman Empire according to the secret treaties, 1915–1917

cal to Armenia, Barton warmed to the federation plan and by May 1918 had felt that it appeared practical. He wrote an eleven-page paper on that subject, "Suggested Possible Form of Government for . . . the Ottoman Empire," and sent it to Mezes. The Inquiry's head replied admiringly, but cautioned that the Allies might not approve the federation plan.[77]

Some Armenian Americans learned of Barton's plan about a federated Empire, which did not remove Armenia from the Ottoman state. These individuals reproached him for softness. In defense, he claimed that the Turks as a unit would never control an autonomous Armenia, though the Turks as individuals in a central assembly of the federation would be colleagues of Armenians. Turks singly were reformable, he believed, but not collectively.

Uncertain that keeping the Empire together was better than independence for the Armenians, the American Board secretary promoted another tactic. (To the ACASR chairman, martyred Armenia was like a savior who had died to bring redemption to surviving Armenia; the massacres were a twentieth-century passion. The United States had suffered with maltreated Armenia during its crucifixion and surely would champion surviving Armenia's deliverance.) [78] With this vision Barton took up advice in January 1918 from Arshag Schmavonian which advocated grouping the main Armenians and Armenophiles in the United States. The purpose would be to coordinate efforts and to influence the State Department. With Schmavonian working to solicit Secretary Lansing's approval, Barton rounded up Dodge, Crane, Peet, and Garegin Pasdermadjian (informal representative of the Armenian National Council at Tiflis to Washington). Lansing in April 1918 refused an official endorsement of the new committee, but he did agree to receive materials from it. House learned of the committee through Dodge and thought it useful.[79]

While agitation for a free Armenia went from this irregular committee to the Department of State, support for a federated Empire with a dependent Armenia passed through the ACASR to The Inquiry. Since Lansing's department linked inadequately to The Inquiry, these differing notions apparently did not bother anyone.[80] Barton probably believed that no essential difference for the Armenians existed between these divergent concepts.

◄ ►

United States policy toward the Near East during America's year and a half in the First World War in large part came from the American Committee for Armenian and Syrian Relief and from the American Board. For a century, one surprise after another had startled missionaries to Turkey. They had withstood these shocks. But the hell of the Armenian situation from 1915 onward had been too much. Operating out of an American milieu which had never separated society and Protestantism, Barton felt a moral imperative to seek what he believed was a political advancement of divine justice and mercy, and public events appeared to reinforce his efforts. Political moves were untypical of previous missionaries during the decades since Parsons and Fisk. But given the massacres, politics was indeed a logical extension of the religionists' evangelism, education, and philanthropy.

Chapter 5

Transatlantic Visions and Doings

AN IMPORTANT part of mission-relief strength by 1918 was going into an effort to make America's internationalism in the Near East political as well as cultural. Old restraints against involvement in foreign policy were weakening. With Armenians moving toward freedom, it looked to many United States religionists as if God favored "Christian" America and Armenia more than "Muslim" Turkey. They deduced that God's will must encompass some connection between Allied military superiority and an official task for the "Protestant" United States in the Ottoman Empire. Armenianism was more intoxicating to them than the view that the Creator is no respecter of persons.

DEBTORS TO A NATION

During the last months of the First World War, Barton received encouragement because contemporary circumstances had allowed a certain liberty to Russian Armenians. Amid near-anarchy wrought out of the deaths of millions and vast economic disruption, Russia had relaxed control over its restless nationalities. The Armenian National Council of Tiflis in September 1917 became the Armenian National Assembly. After the Bolshevik Revolution, Vladimir I. Lenin recognized the Russian Armenians' right to freedom. Lenin believed this act would have little adverse effect on the Bolshevik infiltration within the Caucasus which had been going on for over a decade. His government negotiated a peace treaty with Germany at Brest-Litovsk in March 1918 which gave to Berlin's ally, Turkey, a strip of the Caucasus including the cities of Kars and Batumi. Armenians, Georgians, and Azerbaijanis lived there; together they sought unsuccessfully to prevent the Porte's troops from taking over. These three nationalities in April 1918 formed at Tiflis the Transcaucasian Federal Democratic Republic. Within weeks the new government disintegrated, partly because Turkey tried to occupy areas beyond the Brest-Litovsk line. Receiving German support against these Turkish pressures, Georgia saw larger security in an independence buttressed by Germany than in a federation without such aid. (Wanting oil, Germany competed with Turkey for control of the Caucasus.) Georgia declared its independence on May 26. Azerbaijan and the Erivan (Yerevan) Armenian Republic declared their freedom two days later. In June 1918 Germany sought to gain access to Caucasian oil sources by sending a contingent from its forces occupying western Russia to Tiflis. The British had anticipated this German move when Russian troops pulled out of the Caucasus late in 1917. From then on Britain's request for the United States to fight the Turks concerned its desire to prevent German intervention in the Caucasus.

A response to the British was Barton's urging Secretary Lansing to promote an Allied entry into the Ararat region to help Armenians. Dodge, seeing in March 1918 that the State Department was not responding, approached House. Apparently none of these attempts brought United States diplomacy to make appeals to the Allies. The British were already pushing against the Turkish flank in Mesopotamia to reach Baku in Azerbaijan, the leading oil city in the Caucasus. In Baku, besieged Armenian volunteers, in cooperation with the Erivan Republic, held out against the Turks until mid-September 1918, thereby helping deny Turkey and Germany the oil they needed until it was too late. Viewing a British slowness in driving the Ottomans out of the Caucasus, Barton asked the United States to grant a loan of twenty million dollars to the struggling Erivan Republic. William Peet worked to this end in Washington, but obtained no commitment.[1]

With British entrance into the Caucasus in prospect, Barton in October 1918 labored for an "integral" Armenia. This kind of Armenia was to include not only the Erivan Republic, with border claims equivalent to the

Russian-Armenian provinces of Kars and Erivan, but four to eight Turkish-Armenian vilayets as well. (See inset of Map 7 on p. 229.) The plan for an integral Armenia was balanced on shaky legs. Before the First World War, Armenians had exceeded 50 per cent of the population in only one Turkish-Armenian vilayet (Bitlis) and averaged 30 per cent throughout the six vilayets having the highest percentage of Armenians. Massacres and deportation had left only a remnant. For Barton to ask for an independent, extensive Armenia nearly empty of Armenians was a gamble against the Turkish majority in eastern Anatolia.

Other realities with which the American Board secretary had to contend as he labored for an integral Armenia were factionalism and scarcity of leadership among Armenians. Turkish police had sought to annihilate educated and prestigious men among the minority people. Potential statesmen were in ghettos throughout the Near East. Poorly patched differences in the Armenian Gregorian Church involved three religious heads. There were two Patriarchs in Turkey, the legally recognized one in Constantinople and the other in Cilicia. There was the head of the Gregorian movement in the Caucasus whose reputation Russians had polished since the 1820s to counter the Constantinople Patriarch. The Erivan Republic was weak, threatened by Georgians, Azerbaijanis, Turks, undermined by Bolsheviks. At least half of its estimated six hundred thousand residents were displaced persons; its income was probably ten times less than its expenditures.

The gravest schism among Armenians was between the Dashnaktsuthiun and the Ramgavar party. The Ramgavar group had begun in 1908 at Alexandria in Egypt, originally had no revolutionary goal, and represented primarily clerics and middle-class individuals in Cilicia and Egypt. One of its founders was Boghos Nubar, who also started a large relief, philanthropic, and cultural organization with branches throughout the West, the Armenian General Benevolent Union. Boghos and the Ramgavars had a liaison with the Patriarch in Constantinople and controlled the Armenian National Delegation in Paris. A Ramgavar plan was to establish an autonomous community for Armenians, preferably in Cilicia and northern Syria. About eight hundred Ramgavar volunteers had fought with the French Foreign Legion in Europe; all but forty had perished. The Dashnaktsuthiun had directed approximately one hundred fifty thousand volunteers in the Caucasus during the war. But in contrast to the Ramgavars, the Dashnaktsuthiun had forged an independent state.[2] A victory of Dashnak regiments against the Turks in May 1918 made the Erivan Republic possible. This party represented primarily peasants and a few intelligentsia in eastern Turkey and Russia.

In the United States misunderstanding existed. There was poor communication between Gregorian Christians (in their churches and in the Armenian General Benevolent Union) and the Armenian Missionary Association, the denomination established by the American Board for evangelical refugees. To end this disjointedness, seven Armenian-American bodies, including a Dashnaktsuthiun group, set up a twenty-one member committee, the Armenian National Union, led by Mihran Sevasly of Boston. Still, there was rivalry and jealousy. Sevasly worked with Boghos Nubar in Paris, whereas in Washington the Dashnaktsuthiun hero, Garegin Pasdermadjian, represented the Erivan Republic. Amid this confusion Barton had brought both Sevasly and Pasdermadjian into the unofficial committee advising the State Department, known by October 1918 as the Armenian-American Committee.

Using the Armenian-American Committee, Barton sought to influence the State Department in view of the approaching end of hostilities with Turkey. He asked that an armistice give civil and military authority in the Ottoman Empire to an international commission and permit troops in sections where there were Armenians. Then on October 25, 1918, members of the Armenian-American Committee completed a memorandum asking for a Western administration of Turkey. They argued for independence of an Armenia whose territory was to include two Russian provinces (Kars and Erivan) and part or all of eight Turkish vilayets (the six so-called Turkish-Armenian ones, plus Adana and Trabzon), including ports on the Black and Mediterranean seas. (See Map 3 on p. 52.) A reason for such a large territory was Barton's faith in his favorite people's ingenuity: "Give the Armenian capital and a righteous government and he will turn the whole of Turkey into a Garden of Eden in ten years." [3] Another reason for an inflated Armenia was that Ramgavar leaders desired Cilicia. Pasdermadjian and others also felt that Armenia strategically needed access to both seas, even though demographic evidence did not support this; committee members knew that the numbers of Turkish Armenians in the Ottoman Empire or as refugees elsewhere had dipped to around a million (there were a million Russian Armenians). The memorandum recommended emigration of Turks and Kurds from an integral Armenia so that Armenians would be a majority in each vilayet and suggested moving the Nestorians along the border of Persia and Turkey to southeastern Armenia. For a guardian of the proposed country, Barton and his colleagues wanted a great and disinterested nation, such as the United States.[4]

The State Department did not persuade Britain to include the ideas of the Armenian-American Committee in the armistice signed on a British vessel off the island of Mudros on October 30, 1918. One difficulty may have been that the Committee's recommendation arrived on Secretary Lansing's desk too late, although he no doubt had known its contents before he got it. The main problem was that Lansing sought to take no part in the armistice negotiations, even though the Porte tried to get America to take initiative in these talks. The Mudros armistice agreed to stationing French and British troops throughout Arab portions of the Ottoman Empire and to placing Western officials in Constantinople and the Straits. For the most part, British units occupied Syria; there were also token French troops along the coast from Sidon to Alexandretta. The Allies dissented on Anatolia, for which Greece, Italy, and France had claims. Therefore the victors did not dispatch more than a few officers as observers into Asia Minor, although the armistice gave the right of occupation. (See Map 7 on p. 229.) An independent Turkish administration continued in Anatolia. Knowing the meaning for Armenians of an Anatolia untended by the West, Boghos Nubar in mid-November asked for United States troops there, to no avail.

Dissatisfied with post-Mudros developments, Barton took several steps before President Wilson embarked for Europe early in December 1918. Knowing that both the ACASR and the Armenian-American Committee had political weaknesses, Barton helped develop a lobbying group, the American Committee for the Independence of Armenia (ACIA). Leaders of its executive body included James W. Gerard, recent ambassador to Germany, and Cleveland Dodge. An Armenian American named Vahan Cardashian was administrative secretary. The chairman of the new group was Gerard, New York attorney and strong-willed individual who until the 1930s was to be eminent among Armenophiles in the United States. Cardashian was an extremist who later wrote indiscriminately about people who disagreed with him, and became a sort of evil genius within the ACIA. Others on the executive body of the ACIA included Republicans Henry Cabot Lodge, Charles Evans Hughes, and Elihu Root.[5] Barton was a member of the ACIA, but not prominent in its activity. With this fresh movement, the Armenian-American Committee lapsed.

In correspondence with Cardashian, Barton considered possible members of a cabinet for an integral Armenia. The two men agreed, as had the periodical of the American Board, that missionaries might serve in the cabinet.[6] With this idea, the thinking of the Board had broadened from evangelizing and educating to governing.

The chairman of the American Committee for Armenian and Syrian Relief at the same time implored Secretary Lansing. Barton wanted him to go beyond such previous statements as the Fourteen Points of January 1918, which backed autonomous development of subject nationalities in Turkey, and to endorse Armenian freedom. Barton sent a statement Lansing could use for this endorsement, adding: "I hope I have not appeared to intrude on matters that are not within my sphere of action, but I feel deeply upon this subject and I know I voice the sentiment of the entire country in what I have written." [7] The President reportedly approved Barton's stand, but believed that a public declaration was not necessary before the question came up at the Peace Conference.[8]

Barton and the ACIA sought to press Wilson by tutoring American opinion. They assisted in publication of a short book, *Why Armenia Should Be Free*, written by Garegin Pasdermadjian.[9] The author came from Erzurum, where as a boy he had learned of American Board missionaries. For his education he had gone to Europe, and there in the 1880s helped organize the Dashnaktsuthiun. He had coordinated the volunteer program in 1914, commanded the second Armenian battalion for a few months, and directed rescue operations during the deportation. In the spring of 1917 he went to Petrograd to negotiate with the Tsarist government. In the summer he left for the United States where he served on the Armenian-American Committee. Pasdermadjian's book interpreted the Armenian cause in a way which made an integral state appear just. He claimed that if Armenians had chosen to fight alongside the Turks and Germans no mass killings of Armenians would have occurred and Russia would have lost the Caucasus within a few months. Persia and Afghanistan, already pro-German, might have joined the Holy War. The Allies would have responded, Pasdermadjian wrote, by moving troops from Europe to the Near East. Neither Italy nor Rumania then would have joined the Allies, and the Central Powers would have won on land by 1916. He claimed that Armenians, not the Allies had borne the brunt of Turkish arms. He believed that the Western countries were debtors to a people of which nearly half had died; survivors deserved emancipation.

111

Avetis Aharonian, Pasdermadjian's associate and President of the Erivan Republic, set forth in poetry his image of Armenia, published in the periodical of the Boston-centered Armenian National Union: [10]

Sons of Armenia, to you I speak.

Thousands and thousands of hidden hands are eagerly digging a ditch, on thy hill of Golgotha, to erect a cross of thy new and final sacrifice; the mother earth is shaking under the blows of enemy's arms, the dust rises in sheets to heavens, but thy cross shall not be erected, and thy Golgotha shall groan under the heels of thy militant sons.

Let death knell roar resoundingly and furiously; it is the sigh of those who were crushed beneath the heels of barbarism, like pilgrims, and whose grief and blood boil and seethe from our mother earth. And that earth shall bring forth new blossoms.

Let death knell roar with bluster and tumult, let the cursed bronze sob over our alert souls. Justice and Freedom shall finally triumph in our sorrow-laden land.

Barton's British correspondent, James Bryce, and the latter's protégé, Arnold Toynbee, added their skills to make as sure as possible that the Armenian knell would sound eventual triumph for Aharonian's cause. The eighty-year-old Bryce, a thin, alert man with bushy white eyebrows, was giving undiminished energy to his beloved Armenia. Since the beginning of the war he had been writing such Americans as House and President A. Lawrence Lowell of Harvard. Bryce had corresponded about British coordination with the United States on various issues, particularly a league of nations, but also on Armenia. One letter to Theodore Roosevelt was a plea for American aid to Armenian freedom.[11] He led the Armenophile lobby in Britain partly because of his Christian idealism. Bryce prepared public arguments for sending Western soldiers into Asia Minor to carry out the Mudros armistice, to rescue women in Turkish harems, and to resettle emigrants. Feeling that the Ottoman government was incurably ill when it came to ruling subject people, Bryce wanted a liberated Armenia helped by the United States. The Britisher believed American missionaries best knew the area. Toynbee had remarked similar views in a booklet, titled by a quotation from an Allied document, *The Murderous Tyranny of the Turks*.[12] Prime Minister David Lloyd George's eager advocacy of an American mandate over Armenia at the Peace Conference would result partly from this propaganda.

The United States and the West, aroused by missionaries and their friends, by the end of the year 1918 nominally had sided with the Armenian cause. As noted, the Wilson administration supported autonomy. Roosevelt at the New York City Hall in September 1918 declared that "Armenia must be freed." [13] Henry Cabot Lodge of the ACIA in December introduced a resolution in the Senate, which would languish in the legislative hopper, favoring independence for six vilayets of Turkish Armenia. In Europe some pro-Turkish expressions continued to circulate, as they had for decades, along with Armenophile attitudes. The Premier of France purportedly gave Boghos Nubar a promise to settle the fate of the Near East minority according to the supreme laws of humanity. The Foreign Secretary of Great Britain told Boghos that the liberation of Armenia was one of the war aims of the Allies. Generally, French and British official policy sought the elimination of the Porte's dominion over non-Turkish peoples. Yet both Paris and London made vague comments about freedom for oppressed groups in the Ottoman Empire so as to permit much of the secret treaties. In December Boghos declared the independence of integral Armenia and called for supervision by the United States. The Italian Parliament concurrently approved a statement on freedom for the Armenians.[14]

ISOLATION DAYS, GONE FOREVER

Love for Armenia in the United States held forth the prospect of ending the isolation of the United States from a direct part in transatlantic power struggles. After America withdrew from the French alliance in the year 1800, it had remained aloof from high politics in the Old World. Hiding behind an Atlantic moat, having weak neighbors, and having Canada as a kind of hostage after 1815 to forestall another war with Britain, the United States took advantage of European distresses for its own expansion to the Pacific Ocean. It could do so since European affairs did not menace American security. The United States retreated from the relatively strong Old World to control Latin American areas, Hawaii, and the Philippines. In the First World War the United States not only entered the conflict, but Washington determined to lead in establishing peace and democracy overseas. Missionaries and philanthropists involved with the Ottoman Empire liked this shift.

A global perspective, seemingly so new in contrast to frontier-mindedness and isolationist dogmas, actually was implicit in the export of America's way of life, which had been increasing for a century and more. Private individuals and groups — missionaries and humanitarian agencies like the ACASR and the American Red Cross — had made firmer, earlier commitments to various regions of the world than had the United States government. On the North American continent (for example, in Texas), squatters and settlers regularly had preceded the flag. In Hawaii, merchants and particularly American Board Puritans had Americanized religion, education, and public affairs by the 1850s, long before annexation. Missionaries to the Turkish Empire were acculturating people there in a pattern similar to the Hawaiian one.[15] The industrial revolution, helped by oceanic steamers and cables, sent Yankee salesmen knocking at all kinds of portals abroad. The nation and its citizens from the American Revolution onward proclaimed ideals of liberty and prosperity to the inhabitants of lands around the earth.[16] Formal policies and programs — the Monroe Doctrine and its interventionist corollaries, the steel navy of the 1880s, the imperialism of the 1890s, the Open Door doctrine — in many ways resulted from overseas interests of private individuals and institutions. Other results were President Roosevelt's strutting in the Caribbean and President Taft's Dollar Diplomacy. In short, public internationalism grew out of unofficial internationalism.

A basic factor impelling Americans to act with and think about foreigners was the Protestant mission. The religion of Jesus had an ardor for universial evangelism from its origin, vitalized by the economic expansion and Second Great Awakening in the United States during midnineteenth century. In the next decades, such forces as post-Civil War nationalism, Social Darwinism, the Social Gospel, and premillennialism helped an American missionary growth possibly unmatched in the history of missions (incidentally, the Congregational constituency of the American Board led Protestant denominations in application of the Social Gospel). Along with endeavor in China and India, the Near East ministry of the American and Presbyterian boards was at the fore of this expansion. The devout President McKinley politically fused many of these forces when he decided that the United States should annex the Philippines by God's grace and uplift and "Christianize" their Roman Catholic inhabitants. Conscious of many millions of souls passing to an eternity without a Protestant revelation, missions reached ever higher points from the year 1900 onward. John Mott published *The Evangelization of the World in This Generation,* and thousands of young men and women were recruited for this evangelism by the Mott-directed Student Volunteer Movement. Roman Catholics also founded their first organization dedicated to overseas missions, the Mary-knoll Society. An optimistic cry of religious America in 1918, including the voice of James Barton, was to civilize savagery, to Christianize the nations, to back Wilson's internationalism.[17]

There was at the end of the First World War an American Board publication which blended nationalism and Protestantism. It was a work by Cornelius Patton, Barton's friend and home secretary of the Board, entitled *World Facts and America's Responsibility*. Patton set out ten "facts." One of them was that Islam, Hinduism, and Buddhism were decadent, chiefly because Western colonialists had dominated their followers. Another was that Christianity was extending itself because the Allies had defeated the Turks. Patton claimed that the "indescribable woe" of the war had helped wonderfully to establish "the Kingdom of love, joy, and peace. . . . a new world unity emerges, and a basis for brotherhood and permanent peace is being laid." America was the model for nations, and he quoted a Chinese official's prayer: "Oh God, make China like the United States." Realizing that commercial greed and mob lynchings were not the cheeriest examples for foreigners, he nevertheless believed that God had used the hostilities to prepare the Christian United States to reorganize international affairs, particularly in the Near East. "At last America knows herself and her world. The days of our isolation . . . are gone forever. The transformation was sudden, radical, permanent." The United States had become a missionary country to help minorities in the Ottoman Empire. In facts six and seven, Patton noted that Anglo-Saxons controlled half the world's trade and that in 1917 they gave twenty-eight of thirty million dollars for Protestant missions in Asia, Africa, and elsewhere. These statistics were proof that American and British democracy would gain world supremacy. Acknowledging that he wrote like one who had a "shortcut to the millennium," he justified his ideas as practical idealism. In a final fact, he called for Christians to lead America in the coming domination of the earth. For this future, he urged that news of the Kingdom of God take equal space with other news, all to the exaltation of the risen, conquering Christ.[18]

Patton's thinking in many ways was the same as the American Board's since its beginning. Through the nineteenth century it had been using messianic phrases, as noted previously. A pamphlet of 1849, *The Hand of God in History*, claimed that the Anglo-Saxon race was to extend an all-controlling influence over the earth. An annual meeting of the American

Board (1860) predicted that missionaries were "to lead the van of Immanuel's army for the conquest of the world." The president of the Board's trustees in 1892 declared that America's discovery had been planned by God specifically to advance Christian missions.[19]

Barton published material similar to Patton's, returning to ideas of Parsons, Fisk, and Jessup. Frustrated by the Protestants' inability to penetrate Islam, Barton proposed the evangelization of Muslims by international and interdenominational coordination. He saw Islam's Holy War crushed as Allied armies rolled over the Near East. "What the Christian world has been unable to accomplish among Moslems during the last hundred years of missionary endeavor, is now being achieved by the army of Christian heroes, heroines and martyrs backed by the great Christian heart of America and England." Barton felt that Islam was inadequate because its founder was an immoral character, because of its ritualism, polygamy, permission of slavery, and fatalism. He saw Muslim conversions to Protestantism in the Dutch East Indies and British Egypt as heartening signs. Christian evangelists, he thought, should stress the unity of an omnipotent God, the miracles of Christ, and Jesus' doing what he taught; these ideas would have more appeal to Muslims than the divinity and resurrection of Christ. For the invasion of Islam, Barton believed there should be emphasis on Bible translation, Christian schools, hospitals, and social clubs (such as the Lions). He concluded: "the war has prepared Islam for the Christian approach, and we hope and pray that it is preparing the church of Christ to fall into step with God . . . and overcome all the evil forces of Islam and enthrone Christ as Lord of all."[20]

Barton probably thought a great crusade against Islam could develop out of Wilson's support. The American Board leader quoted the President as having said during wartime: "I think it would be a real misfortune . . . if the missionary program for the world should be interrupted . . . that the work undertaken should be . . . at its full force, seems to me of capital necessity." [21]

The "missionary program for the world" that Wilson remarked had to do with rather fixed connotations in public opinion. Protestant churchmen for decades had seen America as favored by God with an advantageous geographic position, an advanced religion (Protestantism) and race (Anglo-Saxon), a special task in history. Missionaries provided content for this task, institutionalizing means by which intelligence from abroad came to American attention. Congregational clergyman Josiah Strong in

Our Country (1885), a bestseller which sold nearly two hundred thousand copies, prescribed his view. Strong asked Americans, whom he believed were superior in culture, wealth, aggressiveness, democracy, and Christianity, to impress their ways upon mankind. The editor of the *Missionary Review of the World,* Arthur Tappan Pierson, in 1896 said that since Christianity had made America the great nation it was, the nation owed Christianity a debt, namely, "proper and lawful endeavors to reconstruct all other governments upon the basis of the Christian religion," including displacement of pagan fetishes, Buddhist prayer wheels, Turkish crescents, and Romanist crucifixes. Pierson did not think it proper, though, that gunboats should coerce an opening for the Gospel; gunboats should protect only missionaries who had already entered foreign lands. Most Protestant leaders pointed out that their primary goals were church building, not United States prestige, extension of Christianity, not United States expansion. The motive for America's Protestant diplomacy, in missionary minds, was Christian more than national.[22]

American Progressivism complemented the missionary program for the world. Reform drives in United States history, containing both Christian and Jeffersonian elements, had brought more rapid change than usual toward social justice. In the early twentieth century the heritage of rural Populism and of equalitarianism helped nurture changes—civic renovation, regulation of business, woman suffrage. Promoters of this change were middle-class people with swollen consciences, from Massachusetts Bay to Puget Sound. Protestant morality was a large ingredient in Progressivism: indications of its strength were the publicists' muckraking, the battle against alcohol, the Social Gospel. Along with domestic improvement early in Wilson's presidency, the spirit of renewal turned to people beyond United States borders, beginning with the Mexicans. Having had since colonial times a Promised Land self-image in contrast to a presumably corrupt Old World, America in 1918 generally saw Europe as well as Mexico as a place in need of impartial discipline. This duty, it seemed, was a part of a refurbished, purified Manifest Destiny, above and beyond the earlier continental absorption and the Caribbean and Pacific imperialism. Observer William Leuchtenberg has written that Progressive America believed repression of evil abroad comparable to wiping out slums, and justified killing overseas as doing battle for the Lord. The United States determined to impose virtue on the world.[23]

Martial tempos as well as Progressivism were helping Americans con-

117

centrate on wickedness abroad. The Chief Executive in his war message of April 1917 had asked his countrymen to put away excited revenge against the German people. He did not restrain feelings by his call for vindicating right principles and creating a world safe for democracy. He undercut his remark about revenge by stating that with God's help the United States would spend its blood with pride and dedication; drownings caused by German submarine sinkings had stirred it deeply. So with national piety unloosed, Americans began singing:

> Over there, over there,
> Send the word, send the word, over there
> That the Yanks are coming, the Yanks are coming,
> The drums rum-tumming everywhere.

Editorialists began writing enflaming phrases, such as the following from the *Cosmopolitan:* "The Kaiser has wagered his crown and sixty million subjects that ideals do not pay. If he wins, we lose two thousand years of ethical growth, and every conquered domain shall become a Teuton harem. This war must decide whether Force or Faith shall inherit progress. Morally, mentally, and officially, Germany has declared for paganism. The infamous repudiations of the empire, the unbridled savagery of officers and men, the profanation of Christian altars, the abandonment of civilized usage, the elevation of prostitution to patriotism, the decoration of assassins, the sterilization of Armenia, the sack of Belgium proclaim that Berlin has deliberately canceled the Decalogue. We are fighting God's enemy—facing the supreme menace of earth."[24]

Playing upon the country's self-righteousness were religious officials. In a manner unparalleled during any of the United States' earlier wars, clergymen began talking about good and evil on a cosmic scale. Minutes of one conference of the Methodist Church read: "We see the trembling [Allied] lines . . . the hellish Hunnish hordes beat against them to seize the panting throat of the world. We hear the cry, 'Hurry up, America,' and we go with fierce passion for world freedom." Newell Dwight Hillis of the Plymouth Congregational Church in Brooklyn thought that United States doughboys could die no fairer deaths as God's soldiers than in French trenches. Hillis gave virulent anti-German lectures in over one hundred fifty cities. With the House of Representatives listening, Billy Sunday addressed the divine Presence: "Thou knowest, O Lord, that no nation [Germany] so infamous, vile, greedy, sensuous, blood-thirsty, ever disgraced the pages of history. Make bare thy mighty arm, O Lord, and smite the

118

hungry, wolfish Hun, whose fangs drip with blood, and we will forever raise our voice to thy praise." Congressmen applauded. Sunday believed that if "you turn hell upside down, you will find 'Made in Germany' stamped on the bottom." These words, probably meeting favor with men much more than God, showed a devil theory about the war. Some religionists, like the secretary of the Presbyterian Board of Missions, Robert Speer, warned against such hymns of hate. But counter to churchmen's caution about and opposition to Vietnam policy a half-century later, almost no pulpits protested the American intervention of 1917. Among the few dozen clergymen who did, some lost their posts. For others there was beating or tarring and feathering. Sociologist Ray H. Abrams has stated that clergymen, behaving like tribal religionists, demonstrated lines from Miles Standish: [25]

> War is a terrible trade;
> But in the cause that is righteous
> Sweet is the smell of powder.

The pulpit and American society generally oversimplified information to fit an enemy image. Extremely nationalistic perceptions dehumanized Germans. Conflict and guilt felt by Americans toward one another helped find aggressive expression against overseas groups. As a concession to modern word-consciousness, propaganda rather than the war dance developed illusions necessary for violence in Europe. The government led the propaganda, distributing exhibits for state fairs, movies (*Pershing's Crusaders*), two hundred thousand slides, seventy-five million copies of booklets, and over a thousand different kinds of posters.[26]

In this climate of opinion isolationism was retreating, and Wilson's missionary diplomacy was going forward. The President carefully had built before 1917 a consensus about involvement in the war. Yet, being somewhat naive, he tried to hold to a legalistic neutrality amid the industrializing, economically integrating nations of the early twentieth century. This policy had not survived a test one hundred years earlier. During the French Revolution young America, being mostly agricultural and commercial, was then far more self-sufficient but nevertheless unable to avoid the European conflict. Wilson's attempts at mediation did not stop the fighting as Americans became financial creditors to Europeans for the first time. Wilson not only did not gain concord by his neutrality stance, but turned to United States hostilities rationalized by a vision of international stability. He recognized only occasionally that the Central Powers were

119

tipping the equilibrium of forces in Europe so much that the United States might no longer be able to assume that the British Navy would be a shield in the Atlantic against threats to the Monroe Doctrine. In many minds the machine-gunning and gassing of Western youth was part of the Armageddon which would banish war. Hamilton Holt, editor of the *Independent*, and other individuals in the League to Enforce Peace supplied most Americans—including Republican leaders, historians, and the President —with a method to carry out an apocalyptic dream. One observer has noted that approval of a league of nations was so hearty that the unanimity was what one would expect for the League to Enforce Not Kicking Your Grandmother. Progressives saw a league of nations performing internationally the same functions as the Federal Trade Commission or Interstate Commerce Commission domestically.[27]

Protestant clergymen had a large part in shaping pro-league sentiment. More than three thousand of them joined the League to Enforce Peace. They also helped establish the National Committee on the Churches and the Moral Aims of the War. One of the National Committee's directors was Talcott Williams, son of missionaries to Turkey. Composed of representatives from three interdenominational organizations and from the League to Enforce Peace, the National Committee became a prominent lobbying group for American entrance into an association of nations; it sponsored meetings for over seven hundred thousand people (including thirty-three thousand clergymen). Spokesmen published books entitled *Christian Internationalism* and *Marks of a World Christian,* which equated supporting a league with an obligation of the Christian life. Clergymen believed that a league would apply Jesus' teachings worldwide, move toward peace on earth, provide the United States with its best opportunity for Christian stewardship, and aid missions. Enthusiastic religionists viewed Wilson, whose Fourteen Points of January 1918 concentrated on a league of nations, as the "Ambassador of God." [28]

The Fourteen Points were a masterstroke giving the United States more initiative than European nations in peace planning. But the President overstated his ideas, partly because of American optimism and partly because settings across the Atlantic seemed to call for such exaggeration. Groups in Europe for some months before the Fourteen Points had been increasingly confident that many people would favor a new diplomacy. The new dispensation would include nonannexation and self-determination rather than the old diplomacy's secret treaties which often ignored public opinion. Lenin and the Bolsheviks late in 1917 came forward as sponsors of the new diplomacy when they published the secret treaties of the Allies. They endorsed a peace of self-determination in negotiations with Germany at Brest-Litovsk. Spokesmen of the old diplomacy became unnerved by the appeal to forward-looking movements in their own countries and in areas sought as possessions by them. After Lloyd George answered the Russian summons, Wilson outdid the Welshman and Lenin with his Fourteen Points. Advocating a world community through a league of nations, open diplomacy, free trade, and self-determination, Wilson wisely gave the West something larger than myopic nationalism. The President weakened the threat of the "Red peril" to Europe. At the same time he also became a savior figure of such magnified proportions that much of the populace began expecting his Fourteen Points to be the final salve for man's wounds. Many Allied officials felt, as Walter Lippmann noted, that before beginning a foreign policy statement they had to take a kind of immunity bath by prefacing their remarks with a pledge to Wilson's ideas. Quite a few leaders of the old diplomacy determined to salvage something of the secret treaties and turned to Edward House as "the Human Intercessor, the Comforter, the Virgin Mary" between themselves and the President. They wanted House's advice because it was presumably "a little nearer this world than the President's and a good deal nearer heaven" than that of the cynics.[29]

Barton, Dodge, and their associates came under the spell of both Wilson's Fourteen Points and the current Christian internationalism. One postwar goal, as Dodge phrased it to his White House friend, related to "permanent peace" in the Near East.[30] Barton on October 1, 1918, wrote to the New York industrialist: "We are now in a position to do more in cleaning up that Eastern question and in getting Turkey and Bulgaria set right than we could possibly have done had we been classified among the belligerents. I think the United States is now in a position to take the lead in the reorganizing of the entire Near East and that its lead will be gladly recognized by both Bulgaria and Turkey." [31] Wilson and House on October 11 lunched at Dodge's estate and discussed protection of Christian ethnic groups in the eastern Mediterranean.[32] When Barton heard of this meeting at Riverdale he declared: "I pull myself up over and over again upon that absolute confidence that I have in the President in his wide grasp of the whole great subject and in his determination to have this miserable affair settled right for time and for eternity. It does seem as if the

Lord of Lords and the King of Kings is working out a mighty plan even beyond the power of our finite minds to grasp and that He is using President Wilson as His agent and mouthpiece." [33] The miserable affair the American Board secretary especially wanted terminated was the political insecurity of the Armenians. On that subject the Chief Executive promised in November to read aloud to his wife a book crammed with the most graphic details of the Armenian massacres, *Ambassador Morgenthau's Story*.[34]

United States expectations for the peace were thus too intuitive and grandiose at the close of 1918. To a considerable degree Wilson became a captive to his prophecies about a collective security for the nations primarily through moral suasion. He was disgusted with European schemes for reparations and land-grabbing. Wilson reportedly stated that he was "heartily sick of the balance of power," the old diplomacy's maneuvering for allies and territory in the Western state system.[35] His feeling was practical insofar as it rejected narrowness and conserved the best in Western culture. Together with Dodge and Barton who used such words as *permanent, set right, absolute*, and *settled for time and eternity*, the President was also impractical. Rather than a Utopia promised by Americans who had known no destruction on their soil, people in Europe and the Near East wanted concrete compensation for terrible losses during the war. In the United States, internationalist promoters had glossed strategic, military, and economic obligations the United States would have to undertake in a stable peace. Americans generally masked their self-interest with an idealism highly susceptible to disillusion.[36]

If not with the best wisdom, Wilson and the Protestants interested in Turkey sensed that isolationism and colonialism were not the strong movements of the twentieth century, that their country, notwithstanding Thomas Jefferson's dictum against entangling alliances, needed steady responsibilities in transatlantic matters.

MISGIVINGS ABOUT PEACE AIMS

If missionaries were sanguine about United States internationalism broadly, they wondered about an American tutelage in the Ottoman Empire when in December 1918 the President journeyed across the ocean on the *George Washington*. Wilson and the American Commission to Negotiate Peace (eventually totaling about a hundred individuals, one third of whom formerly had been a part of The Inquiry) met tumultuous crowds in Europe which momentarily forgot the horrors of the war. A new dawn was brightening; its heralds had arrived. Frenchmen cried: "Vive Vilson!" and Italians hailed Voovro Veelson. When the American leader failed to make one scheduled appearance in Rome, women wept and men tore their hair. Armenians and religionists to Turkey shared the Europeans' feeling but fretted about the specific United States role in the Near East peace. They were glad that Wilson had put America squarely into consideration of the Eastern Question for the first time. Yet they were uncertain what Washington would do.

The public statements of the Wilson administration on the Ottoman Empire had been abstract, open to several kinds of application. The President wanted a flexible position at the Paris Conference. Self-determination did not easily fit both the overlapping ethnic populations of Turkey and the imperial designs of the Allies. It was the twelfth of Wilson's Fourteen Points which set out formal policy: "The Turkish portions of the present Ottoman Empire should be assured a secure sovereignty, but the other nationalities which are now under Turkish rule should be assured an undoubted security of life and an absolutely unmolested opportunity of autonomous development, and the Dardanelles should be permanently opened as a free passage to the ships and commerce of all nations under international guarantees." [37] This declaration had issued out of a memorandum prepared by The Inquiry in December 1917. The memorandum spoke of autonomy for Armenia, Western protection of Palestine, Syria, Mesopotamia, and Arabia, and a new start for Turkish sectors of the Empire.

Files of the American Peace Commission, which included papers of The Inquiry, contained amplifications of Point Twelve. There was the extended version of the Fourteen Points drawn up in October 1918 by Frank I. Cobb, editor of the New York *World*, and Walter Lippmann. This explanation dealt explicitly with the Ottoman Empire, stating that the Straits and Constantinople should be under an international commission or a mandate. Turks should control western Anatolia except perhaps for a Greek mandate where Greeks predominated, and Armenia should probably be under France or Great Britain. France should receive a mandate over Syria, and Britain over Palestine, Mesopotamia, and Arabia. To give unity, the anticipated League of Nations should establish a code binding on all mandates. Wilson's reaction to the Cobb-Lippmann Memorandum,

123

reported by House, was that it was fine on principles and illustrative and unofficial on specifics. Then another interpretation came from the leader of the Western Asia Section of the American Peace Commission, William L. Westermann, professor of ancient history at the University of Wisconsin. In his "Report on Just and Practical Boundaries for the Turkish Empire," Westermann asked for an Empire in divisions like those in the Cobb-Lippmann framework. He hesitated to name Western guides for the various areas and omitted mention of mandates. Soon after getting to Paris, the Peace Commission prepared further studies on the Near East. Two important modifications of the Cobb-Lippmann Memorandum emerged: no designation of Western mentors for mandate regions and strong opposition to a Greek responsibility in Asia Minor.[38]

The secret treaties had affected these views of Point Twelve, especially in their earliest forms. One can see a reason in the thinking of a young American in Cairo, William Yale. Before the First World War Yale had worked with Standard Oil in Egypt, and after April 1917 became an agent of the State Department; during the Peace Conference he would join the King-Crane Commission (an American investigation in the Near East). He had told The Inquiry that Syrians in Cairo indicated that Christians and Muslims in their homeland agreed to sponsorship by the United States, but not by France. Syrians intended to ask the Paris conclave to allow a plebiscite to frustrate French designs. He felt that France would overcome Arab opposition and control Syria. In contrast to Yale's idea, one report to The Inquiry by a Presbyterian missionary from Beirut, Franklin E. Hoskins, thought there was hope for British or American control of Syria. Hoskins' notion prefigured the recommendation of the King-Crane Commission.[39]

The most comprehensive settlement for the Near East among American Peace Commission papers was James Barton's plan for a federated Turkey (for its origin, see pp. 102–104). Sidney Mezes defended to Lippmann an essential element in Barton's notion: "Undoubtedly Turkey should be continued as a unit. . . . to agree to a severance of such an organic unity would be to lay one's self open to the rebuke Solomon administered to the false mother." [40] In Britain, James Bryce, who was in contact with the Foreign Office there, favored the federation scheme.

The Barton proposal related to the report of the ACASR-appointed committee headed by William Hall, whose members mostly were professors at missionary colleges in Turkey. The published report of the Hall Committee dealt with Turkey's political history, ethnology, religion, education, public health, and economy. The Hall Committee recommended that a Western supervisor of Turkey use such procedures as the United States had established in the Philippine Islands and Puerto Rico. Pointing out that railway routes were artificial in the land of the Porte because European investors had an imperial purpose, the Hall findings concluded that a Western power not interested in colonial ventures should receive responsibility for Turkey. The relief organization sent the Hall report to the Peace Commission.[41]

In documents to The Inquiry, Barton, supported by the Hall Committee, offered considerable detail about a federated Ottoman Empire, which he hoped would be led by the United States. A unified Empire would prevent Balkanization of the Near East, Barton wrote. He asked that a Western nation watch over each of six sections — Georgia, Armenia, Syria (including Lebanon and Mesopotamia), a Jewish area around Jerusalem, Turkish Anatolia, and a Greek enclave around Smyrna. For Constantinople he advised an international commission. He said that no European state would permit another nation to dominate the Black and Mediterranean seas. Only America, which had no sphere of influence in the Near East, could take over. The United States also had the best qualifications, he thought, because of its spiritual and relief investment, its financial ability, and its attraction to peoples of the Ottoman Empire. Barton contended that the Peace Conference should itself select a Western mentor, instead of undertaking a plebiscite which would only show differences among races and religions. The protectorate should include a governor general and cabinet, positions filled by nationals of the Western tutor. After a period of separate government in each section of the federation, there should emerge a central assembly. At first courts of justice should follow the old millet system, but as Western education spread, Barton believed that a legal pattern based on Christian values would evolve. The American Board secretary's remarks hinted at his call for a crusade against Islam. As for costs, he said the Hall Committee report had demonstrated that after a short time the mineral wealth in Turkey would pay for the protectorate.[42]

In addition to materials by Barton, Cobb, Lippmann, and Westermann, there were many other statements on the Near East in Peace Commission files. Mission and relief workers had prepared for The Inquiry several accounts of Armenian atrocities and defenses of Protestant rights in Turkey.

The Inquiry alone, not to mention the State Department, contributed dozens of papers to the Commission. Generally, missionaries, attorneys, and ancient historians prepared records. These data often were lacking in expertness and in relevance to American diplomacy.

Agreeing substantially with the later Peace Commission versions of Point Twelve, Wilson had differing emphases and emotions. Probably he was more pro-Greek than his experts, as indicated by his subsequent blessing upon the Greek occupation of Smyrna. On Palestine, the President in 1917 privately had endorsed issuance of Britain's pro-Zionist Balfour Declaration — which dismayed Lansing. Wilson withheld public approval until the end of the war. Lansing and House were nervous that a Jewish homeland implied the rejection of Wilsonian self-determination concerning Arabs.[43] For Armenians, the President had deep sympathy. Dodge in November 1918 reminded his friend of their recent discussion at Riverdale and said the way was open for the "rehabilitation and reconstruction of the Christian races in Asia Minor." (Albert Lybyer, the individual who in 1917 promoted landing American troops at Alexandretta, observed that Wilson had "deep personal interest in forwarding the regeneration of the Near East.") [44] Mostly because of the mission-relief lobby, Wilson had more concern for Armenia and the Barton-promoted notion of an important place for the United States in the Turkish settlement than shown in the Cobb-Lippmann Memorandum and its corollaries. The Chief Executive also, out of his growing desire to use the proposed League of Nations to reply to the Eastern Question, was less willing than his aides to bend to the secret treaties.

While Wilson and his Peace Commission were getting ready for negotiations at Paris, missionary spokesmen made two moves designed to increase the probability of a secure Armenia and a commitment by their government east of the Bosporus. From the United States Barton wired Bryce: "Intense feeling here that troops should occupy Turkey, especially Armenia, Transcaucasia and Cilicia as only possibility Christian population escaping destruction." [45] This attempt to influence London failed; Bryce apparently had inadequate leverage. From Robert College, Gates sent a design for Turkey to Dodge. The Gates plan did not differ markedly from the Barton federation plan except that it was against separating Turks from Armenians. Gates felt that harmony between them would come better in one administrative unit. "I presume that the peace conference will stop short of a radical solution," he concluded to Dodge, "and leave an unsolved problem . . . but I do hope that it will act soon, for conditions grow worse and worse. The British and French intrigue against each other." [46]

So the mission-relief establishment, with fears exemplified by Barton and Gates, was waiting for bargaining to begin at Paris. Protestants had misgivings about the absence of Allied troops in Asia Minor, about Western disagreement on the disposition of Turkey, and about America not acknowledging publicly a possible United States assistance to Armenia and the larger Near East.

"BIG BUSINESS OF THE WORLD"

Partly to make certain a United States involvement in the Ottoman Empire, the missionary "state department" in Boston prepared a relief expedition.[47] Chairman Barton of the American Committee for Relief in the Near East (ACRNE), the name of the ACASR after June 1918, organized a commission to go to Europe and the Near East. Plans developed at the time that he and Dodge had given up on the Washburn-Moore Commission and on an American declaration of war on Turkey. Through a relief expedition, the ACRNE chairman proposed to get over a hundred missionaries of the American and Presbyterian boards back into the Ottoman Empire as relief workers. They were to occupy the mission stations, to distribute aid, and to advance a United States protectorate. Missionary physician Frederick W. MacCallum, on leave as director of Central Turkey College's theological school in Marash, coordinated preparation for the return of the religionists from relief headquarters in New York (after Turks in 1895 burned the American Board college at Marash, MacCallum had begun his first venture in relief).[48]

Barton could postulate success for his goals because the ACRNE had become a powerful institution. Many Protestant congregations in America included someone on a relief committee. The ACRNE had prepared over a dozen types of material for churches, backed the Sunday School War Council drive which raised one million dollars for relief during Christmas 1917, and outlined Sunday school lessons about Armenian "Heroes of the Cross." (The author's parents recall how as children in rural Midwestern churches they heard about destitute Christians in the Ottoman Empire.) An ACRNE handbook gave detailed instructions for local committees about publicity techniques: letters to the editor, posters, leaflets, book-

127

seller displays, speakers' bureaus, slides in theatres, public proclamations by governors and mayors, and house-to-house canvasses. An appeal by President Wilson for funds had become an annual event, with former Ambassadors Elkus and Morgenthau, consuls, and Congressional resolutions complementing the call from the White House. Rallies in every state heard such speakers as Rabbi Stephen S. Wise of New York, who said to one audience that nothing among German crimes was worse than acquiescence to the murder of the Armenian nation. The ACRNE was making it almost as impossible for Americans to forget Armenia as for later generations to forget Pearl Harbor. (See Illustration 7.)

Money came in from April 1917 through October 1918 at an average of half a million dollars a month. The ACRNE in this period alone handled over eight million dollars, nearly half as much as the estimated value of all American Board property in Turkey. The total raised by the ACRNE from its beginning until October 1918 was eleven million dollars. The organization hired a certified public accountant, began publishing financial reports, and sought a Congressional charter. Paying administrative expenses as well as contributing to the general fund, Dodge also had replaced Crane as treasurer when the latter left on the Elihu Root Mission to Russia in 1917. Dodge helped get two million dollars in 1918 from the Red Cross, and facilitated joint Red Cross–ACRNE committees and projects. The Red Cross and the ACRNE cooperated on a program in Palestine – a program which became solely ACRNE's in mid-1919 (the Palestine work had such a leader as educator John H. Finley, who toured the Near East under YMCA and Red Cross auspices in 1918 and in 1921 became an editor of the New York *Times*).[49]

Many among returned missionaries from the Near East were spokesmen for the ACRNE. An example was Charles Riggs, a third generation missionary, born in Sivas, grandson of Elias Riggs, and one of six brothers and sisters who were Protestants to Turkey. He graduated from Princeton in 1893, taught at Robert College, trained at Auburn Theological Seminary, and served at Anatolia College from 1900 to 1903; he then became Near East secretary of the American Board and editor of the *Orient*, one of the Board's periodicals. Operating out of Northampton, Massachusetts during 1918, Riggs wrote articles for national periodicals (*Outlook, Moslem World, Missionary Herald*) and local newspapers. Giving illustrated lectures on Christian internationalism and reconstruction of Armenia and Turkey to dozens of churches, colleges, and other organizations

128

throughout New England, he raised several thousand dollars for the ACRNE. He also prepared maps and pamphlets for relief publications and for the Hall Committee.[50]

In the Near East the ACRNE functioned fairly well. At Constantinople there were three orphanages, a hospital, and many soup kitchens (feeding 161,000 individuals in June 1918). Alexander MacLachlan headed the relief program in Smyrna, channeling funds impartially through the city administration. Bayard Dodge, United States Consul J. B. Jackson at Aleppo, and others in Syria helped sustain at least 150,000 Armenian refugees. The Syrian ACRNE program also treated needs among local Catholic and Orthodox people so well that traditional hostility between American Protestants and indigenous Christians abated. At Tiflis Consul F. Willoughby Smith and missionary Ernest Yarrow set up spinning and knitting facilities and provided three thousand water buffalo and oxen for resettlement purposes among more than 300,000 refugees in the Caucasus. Disorders related to the Bolshevik Revolution threatened relief in the Caucasus when Smith, Yarrow, and all but two Americans in Tiflis fled to Vladivostok. The two people who remained — YMCA men — continued philanthropic activity. In Persia, local committees ministered at the same sites as Presbyterian stations.[51]

Through the months in which the United States fought Germany, the ACRNE riveted familiar Armenophile, anti-Turk ideas to America's mind. Pages of relief material attached adjectives to Turks like *brutal, genocidal, rapacious.* Publicists ignored evidence that Armenians also had murdered Turks. (When Russian troops captured Erzurum and Bitlis in 1916, Armenian irregulars had hacked, abused, and burned thousands of Turkish men, women, and children, and had destroyed many Muslim villages.) Barton recognized this deception when he wrote to Boghos Nubar: "There is no danger of any propaganda making the Americans feel that the Armenians are maltreating the Turks. The idea is universally established here in this country that the Armenians are the worst sinned against of any on the face of the earth, and that the chief of sinners is the Turk, backed by the Teuton." [52] In an article for the *Red Cross Magazine*, Morgenthau, who worked closely with the ACRNE, called Germans and Turks "diabolically" guilty and uncivilized, whereas he referred to Armenians as "fine, old, civilized Christian peoples" caught in the "fangs of the Turk." [53] And in *Ambassador Morgenthau's Story*, he gave five chapters to the deportation of Armenians, including many stories about tortures and killings by Turks and Kurds. Morgenthau concluded that the "whole history of the human race contains no such horrible episode as this." [54]

Armenophile information intimated that the United States should stabilize the Near East. Relief officers believed that this contingency would end the massacre, publicity, money, relief, and further massacre. Barton in March 1918 declared to Bryce that the relief movement "and its extensive propaganda has everywhere revealed the incompetence and cruelty of the Turkish Government. I think you can rest assured that there is no thought on the part of the President or anyone in the State Department contrary to this point of view." [55] Thus, in September 1918 Barton anticipated that an expedition to the Near East might help larger involvement by America in the Eastern Question.

The Wilson administration gave indispensable assistance to the relief commission. Missionary Peet at Washington in early November 1918 sought State Department support. The Department offered every cooperation and induced the War Department to release a ship without charge to carry goods and supplies. With backing by Dodge and the State Department, Barton requested help from the head of the American Relief Administration, Herbert Hoover. Hoping to get between one hundred to two hundred trucks from Army supplies in France, Hoover asked the ACRNE to move into Asia Minor in the same sense that the American Relief Administration was going into Europe. Peet and Morgenthau took care of details between the two relief organizations. Secretary Lansing on November 20 declared that the expedition plan "enjoys complete approbation of this Government." [56] Seeing that a large-scale commission to the Near East would need much public aid, Morgenthau and Dodge asked Wilson to endorse a drive to raise several million dollars. Dodge reminded the President that a relief group to Turkey was to be a link in reconstructing Christian races in Asia Minor: "Your sympathy and cooperation in the past three years . . . has been the largest single factor in enabling us to secure the generous amounts which the American people have given." [57] The President assented. In a proclamation Wilson sought thirty million dollars for those who through no fault of their own had been left in starving and shelterless conditions in the Near East.

The main body of the ACRNE commission prepared to leave on the *Mauretania* early in January 1919: Chairman James Barton, William Peet, George Washburn, Edward Moore, Dodge's business associate Arthur Curtiss James (also board vice-president of the Syrian Protestant College), J. H. T. Main (president of Congregational Grinnell College in Iowa), and Harold A. Hatch (businessman board member of Constantinople Woman's College and co-editor with William Hall of the publication on reconstruction of the Ottoman Empire sent to the American Peace Commission). Three other members of the ACRNE commission were to steam soon after the *Mauretania*: Stanley White of the Presbyterian Board, Walter George Smith (prominent Roman Catholic attorney from Philadelphia who in 1918 had been president of the American Bar Association), and Rabbi Aaron Teitlebaum (representative of the Jewish Joint Distribution Committee). Barton concurrently wrote to Bryce: "America is dead in earnest in its endeavor to save the Christian populations . . . from complete annihilation and I am confident that by urging this relief work we are creating a sentiment that will later favor if desired . . . the political reorganization of Armenia at least." [58] Typically, this veteran of eastern Anatolia had Armenia in his thoughts. (See Illustration 12.)

As the Barton group crossed the Atlantic, the ACRNE was distributing to clergymen throughout the United States a handbook, *Practicing Bible Precepts in Bible Lands*. This booklet was to gear them and their churches for the effort to raise thirty million dollars. Included in the handbook was an estimate that missionaries were ministering angels, a description of starving children stripping flesh off dead camels, and an endorsement of the thirty-million dollar effort by Theodore Roosevelt, given just before his death ("With all my heart I wish you Godspeed in the work of relief you have undertaken for the Christians in Western Asia"). There were also lyrics for the tune of "America the Beautiful": [59]

> Oh! beautiful for martyr feet —
> Whose weary, bleeding stress
> A line of life in death hath beat
> Across the wilderness!
> Armenia! Armenia!
> To God thy dead arise
> And low at even songs of heaven
> Acclaim thy sacrifice.
>
> Then let us take our lighter Cross
> With hearts and courage high,
> And give until we feel the loss, —
> Our faces to the sky!
> Armenia! Armenia!
> We share our best with thee

> Our hearts and hands, our harvest-lands,
> Our Christianity!

But the financial campaign encountered difficulty. Fund raising began soon after Wilson had asked one hundred million dollars from Congress for the American Relief Administration. Dodge cabled the President in Europe that many people interpreted his action to mean that the ACRNE's solicitation was unnecessary. If ACRNE was to press on, Dodge said, an urgent message for the public from him was vital. Wilson gave the statement to his friend by return cable. The relief organization then publicized both Wilson's response and Dodge's donation of four hundred thousand dollars to the ACRNE drive for thirty million dollars.[60]

Primarily because of intercession by Washington, the Barton Relief Commission [61] received help from officials in Allied capitals. Through Bryce and the American ambassador in London, the British Foreign Office cut tape on travel arrangements. In Paris, Barton mentioned to House that the United States government had agreed to provide three ships for the relief expedition. The French also promised transport to and about Turkey for Barton and his party and for others coming later. In France, United States Army physicians and nurses joined the relief group.[62]

Parenthetically, Barton had met people in London on a mission jointly sponsored by the ACRNE and the State Department, which under President Harry Pratt Judson of the University of Chicago was returning from Mesopotamia and Persia. Judson and Barton discussed this Persian Commission's reports to the American peace delegates about conditions in the Near East.

While the American Board secretary promoted the Relief Commission, he also thought about inclusion of missionary rights in the peace settlement. He desired to revive Protestant labor in the Ottoman Empire which, as noted, had dwindled to a low point. The numbers of American Board personnel within Turkey late in 1918 had dipped with loss of about 75 per cent of staff to 36, the mid-nineteenth–century level. During the fighting, around twenty of those religionists who had stayed at their posts to combat epidemics and give succor died of typhus, cholera, smallpox, or pneumonia. Only two hundred of over a thousand former local clergymen were alive. Mission activity often had ceased as compounds became refuges for Armenians. Estimated damage to mission property throughout Syria and Asia Minor, which before the conflagration was valued at over forty million dollars, ran as high as twenty million dollars.

Events had gone somewhat better for the educational work, although many schools in the interior had disintegrated. Robert College, Constantinople Woman's College, and the Syrian Protestant College had difficulty getting supplies and went into debt. Germany had urged nationalization of all United States educational institutions. The Young Turks, who closed French and British schools, refrained from doing so with centers of American higher education, partly because the latter provided medical services for Ottoman troops. The Syrian Protestant College did stop operations briefly in April 1917 when Turkey broke relations with the United States. Enrollments dropped, perhaps least seriously at the Syrian Protestant College where figures went from 970 to 770. Not the smallest problem for the staff at Robert College was making corset stays for Mrs. Caleb Gates out of discarded hacksaw blades. The staff also assisted in surgery upon wounded Turkish soldiers (one American teacher fainted while helping remove an eye). Other difficulties included seeking to avoid Allied shrapnel in air raids, constructing a mill to grind flour for bread, and looking disappointedly for mail which often did not come through from America. One letter of October 1917 from Dodge to Gates safely arrived several months late with a pledge for fifty thousand dollars to make up the Robert College deficit for the year. "When I read your report," Dodge wrote, "the tears came to my eyes and a gulp to my throat as I realized all that you have gone through during the last three years." [63]

At Paris in January 1919 Barton and his associates prepared documents on missionary privileges for the American Peace Commission. They urged that in the coming treaty with the Ottoman Empire the citizens of the United States should receive permission to give religious instruction, be tax exempt, enjoy customs immunities, receive public aid for medical schools, and extend physical facilities. The Protestants, with a hope that Christian faith helped give them, shunned futility by looking forward to rebuilding in Turkey. An American Board official wrote that the Lord was working out a mighty plan for that great blood-stained, sin-cursed country. The official believed the sacrifices of the war could never be in vain; in the Kingdom of Heaven there was no waste. [64]

When the Barton Relief Commission was about ready to go to Constantinople, its chairman reflected that the ACRNE was getting more government undergirding than ever before. He undoubtedly remembered comments at the last annual meeting of the American Board in October 1918, where he heard complaints that the Board was "mixed up in politics too

133

much." Sensing a certain accuracy in the charges, he had stated defensively: "Missionary enterprise is the Big Business of the World. . . . If democracies are not based on the principles of the Gospels, then God pity this world." [65] Barton also had written in an article: "Protestant missionaries . . . have always been warned against entangling alliances in national or international affairs. They have never been political. With the rarest exceptions have they been implicated in government questions." But in many instances "missionaries have been the confidential advisors of ambassadors, ministers and consuls. . . . under the revelations of the war, we are discovering that foreign missions hold a position in the East never before recognized, but which has vital relations to the future peace of the world." [66]

The ACRNE surely was "Big Business," considering everything it was and symbolized about the mission-relief place in United States ties with the Near East. The slogan of the World Missionary Conference, "Christianize the nations," seemed to be coming to pass in such efforts as the Barton Relief Commission. Evangelism in its new interpretation included relief and politics as well as individual redemption, church-forming, education, and hospitals. Barton probably was taking as broadly as possible Saint Paul's explanation of his strategy: "I am made all things to all men, that I might by all means save some." [67]

Transatlantic visions and doings of American religionists toward Turkey during the Great War had been unusual. Their concern, especially for Armenia, had advanced what appeared to be a turn away from the hallowed national policy of isolation from Old World entanglements. Their humanitarianism had channeled American aid in unprecedented amounts to Near Easterners. Their losses in lives and property in Anatolia proportionately had been as costly as those of the United States Army in the Meuse-Argonne fighting in northern France. Their determination to take the American Dream into the Ottoman Empire had been as dizzying as Wilsonianism generally.

Chapter 6

The Nestorian Kettle

WHEN in January 1919 Barton met Harry Pratt Judson of the ACRNE-sponsored Persian Commission in London, the two men talked not only of relief but also of a Western nation's sponsorship of Nestorian Christians. Barton desired political security for the Nestorians, not the least because the Presbyterians had fashioned among them before 1914 their model station in Asia. With the World War, military swirls on the neutral soil of the Shah had swept the Nestorians into their vortex. Presbyterian missionaries, like colleagues helping Armenians, had sought to avert tribulation for the Nestorians.

A LEVER ON A FULCRUM

Protestant work among the Nestorians had begun with nineteenth-century American Board missionaries Eli Smith, Harrison Dwight, and Justin Perkins. Before the year 1800 New Englanders had known nothing about Nestorians. Then notes on Nestorians, published in the 1820s by a chaplain of the British embassy in Constantinople, circulated in the eastern United States. Smith and Dwight, on the trip into Turkey's interior discussed earlier, received instructions from Boston to visit the Nestorians. Attracted by the lush vegetation in the Urmia (later Rezaieh) valley of northwest Persia, the two men zealously reported that an American Board lever on a Christian fulcrum there could overturn the Muslim "delusion" among Persians, Kurds, and Arabs. Upon this overoptimistic recommendation, the American Board in 1833 sent Justin Perkins to Persia.[1] Going over strange land from Trabzon in Turkey to Urmia and staying nights in a tent, he and his young wife met one bizarre and harrowing circumstance after another. Mrs. Perkins, pregnant, barely survived childbirth at the new mission site, at which there was no medical aid. To be a religionist away from the coasts at that time, as later during the First World War, was no easy experience.

Perkins had settled in an ethnic group with a curious history. After the year 1500, Nestorian Christians had become known in the West variously as Chaldeans, Syrians, Assyrians, or Nestorians. Such names arose because some of these people resided in Mesopotamia and appeared to be descendants of the ancient Chaldeans, because they were a remnant of Syriac-speaking peoples connected to the historic church of Antioch, because some observers thought they derived racially from Assyrians, and because they adhered to doctrines of a fifth-century churchman named Nestorius.[2] From the Islamic invasions until about a thousand years later, the Nestorians, under a hereditary Patriarch, lived largely in seclusion from Western Christendom. Literacy nearly disappeared, and only parts of the Christian Scriptures were extant among them. During the sixteenth century Roman Catholics got in touch with them and induced a schism. Nestorians living around Mosul in the Ottoman Empire gave allegiance to the Pope. Mountain Nestorians southeast of Van in Turkey and plains Nestorians around Urmia in Persia remained faithful to their Patriarch. (See Map 1, p. 16.)

The presence of American Protestants among the Nestorians soon helped a desire for protection by the West, which resulted in violence. When in the 1840s the Anglican Church Missionary Society attempted to establish a station among Kurds and mountain Nestorians, an early missionary physician of the American Board in the Near East, Asahel Grant, endeavored to prevent this British competition. Putting theological loyalties above discipleship to Christ and not understanding the political implications of religious disputes, Anglican missionaries (they apparently bore the larger responsibility) and Grant augmented a petty feud between Kurd and Nestorian leaders. The feud grew into open conflict for attention from foreigners and then into a veritable war. Over ten thousand Nestorians had perished by 1846 in what was the worst bloodshed among this people since the thirteenth century. The Anglicans and Americans withdrew, but not until five of eight missionaries from the United States, including Grant, died in an epidemic among refugees.[3] The calamity showed an effect of Westernization upon millet-ridden culture in the East and was a microcosm of the later Armenian massacres.

After this debacle among mountain Nestorians in Turkey, American Board missionaries concentrated on their enterprise in Urmia. They translated the Christian Scriptures from classical Syriac into the modern dialect spoken at Urmia, which they had reduced to writing. They started schools, developed a hospital from a private dispensary, and established evangelical groups. Although at first trying to reform the Orthodox Nestorian Church, missionaries in 1862 established a Protestant organization, as their associates in the Ottoman Empire had done. In 1870 the work in Persia came under the Presbyterian Board. Many Roman Catholic and Orthodox Nestorians meanwhile resisted Protestant aggressiveness. Seeing followers defect to the Americans, the Papacy around the year 1840 sent French Lazarites to Urmia. Patriarchal leaders threatened their constituents: "We will excommunicate you, your fingernails shall be torn out; we will hunt you from village to village and kill you if we can." Amid such vulgarities and rivalry, the mission from the United States at Urmia expanded until it became the liveliest Christian institution among the Nestorians.

The Presbyterians often had political troubles; thus the American government came into formal relations with Persia. Great Britain and Russia in the 1870s both agitated the Kurds and struggled for spheres of influence in the lands of the weak Shah. In 1880 Ottoman Kurds attacked Persians and briefly occupied Urmia. Amid these upheavals a Presbyterian missionary asked his brother-in-law, a Congressman from Ohio, to approach the State Department for assistance. Washington at the time had no diplomatic representatives in Persia. Therefore, the State Department in 1883 appointed a son of missionaries to Turkey, S. G. W. Benjamin, the first minister of the United States accredited to the Shah's government. For the next two decades, American interests concerned almost exclusively the Presbyterians, notwithstanding attempts by several officials at the United States legation to involve America in strategic and commercial adventures.[4]

Soon after the turn of the century unfortunate events like those of the

1840s came upon the religionists. A Presbyterian missionary, Benjamin W. Labaree, died in 1904 at the hands of Kurds, a retaliation after American and British missionaries urged punishment of the Kurds who had killed a British subject. The Presbyterians were unsatisfied with a liberal indemnity of thirty thousand dollars by the Persian administration and the arrest of a Kurd involved in Labaree's death. They persuaded the United States to consider sending warships to press Persia to punish the accomplices in the murder. Finally, the central government sent troops against a Kurd tribe responsible for the deed. When the tribe easily escaped into the Ottoman Empire, Persian and Turkish soldiers clashed at the border. In the melee the Turks uprooted mountain Nestorians and occupied Persian territory.

This confused Labaree episode, enlarged by missionary demands, did not end for several years and overlapped with another inopportune commotion. During a revolution in Persia from 1906 to 1909, which resulted in a constitutional monarchy, some American Protestants rejected instructions from Washington. The State Department had forbidden food and shelter for homeless rebels. Then a romantic twenty-one-year-old Princetonian employed by the Presbyterian Board, Howard C. Baskerville, fired by sparks of liberty among Persians, joined revolutionaries at Tabriz, the center of the disruption. At the request of the State Department, missionaries asked for Baskerville's resignation. Not long after leaving the Board, the young man lost his life at the front of an assault on old-guard Royalists.[5]

The Baskerville and Labaree incidents represented Americans' increasing entanglement in political turbulence. Partly to withstand the Protestants from the United States, Patriarchal Nestorians for decades had invited European nations to intervene in Persian affairs; Orthodox officials often sought Western guardianship through whichever mission wielded the biggest club. The Patriarch late in the 1860s asked the Anglican Church to resume activity among Nestorians. Remembering the war of the 1840s, Anglicans in 1877 came to Urmia without vigorous backing by London. The disappointed Orthodox Nestorians turned to Russia, which in the 1820s had occupied Urmia during combat with Persia and then had annexed much of Azerbaijan. The Patriarchal leader at Urmia in 1897 obtained a union of his bishopric with the Russian Orthodox Church. The Tsarist Army followed its religious group into northwest Persia after the British and the Russians in 1907 signed an agreement on spheres in Persia. Civil administration of Urmia passed to the Tsarist consul, and "Russian Orthodox" Nestorians enjoyed preferential treatment. At first the Presbyterians trembled; but Russian proselyting was ineffective. Non-Orthodox missions continued to expand. Also, between 1905 and 1914, at least ten new religious organizations arrived in Urmia from the West.

Presbyterian enterprise in Persia early in the twentieth century was robust, notwithstanding political and religious turmoil. Around fifty missionaries were in the Shah's domain, most of them in Urmia. Of forty thousand Nestorians on the Urmia plain and sixty thousand in the mountains, about three thousand were Protestant Nestorians. The Urmia station was the pride of Presbyterians in Asia, for nationals there helped open centers throughout Persia — Tehran (1871), Tabriz (1873), Hamadan (1881), Rasht (1906), Kermanshah (1910). (See Map 2 on p. 17.) Attending to Muslims and Jews in these cities, the Americans and Nestorians confronted laws and traditions which made progress among these non-Christians painstaking. The nationals in Urmia also sent clergymen to the United States, Russia, and Turkey. In the overall Presbyterian structure in Persia, there were around one hundred fifty congregations, seventy-five local clergymen and evangelists, nearly one hundred schools, and two thousand students. Urmia College and Fiske Seminary excelled among academic institutions in Persia. Giving initiative to local Protestants was Nestorian insistence that the Americans could not subsidize them beyond certain limits. There were more self-supporting churches among Nestorians than the Presbyterians had in India.[6]

The United States missionary movement south of the Caspian Sea resembled the Protestant movement in Turkey. Both were the chief concern of their country's diplomacy with Persia and the Ottoman Empire; both were giving increasing priority to education. Both aided national feeling among Christian minorities, contributed indirectly to internecine fighting, and helped interference by outside powers. In neither case had the original idea worked — the idea of using a missionary lever on a local Christian fulcrum to overthrow the Muslim "delusion."

NO ONE ON EARTH TO HELP

Then came a crisis for Presbyterians similar both to the Armenian deportation and American Board reaction. After hostilities began between the Porte and Russia, Turkish soldiers late in 1914 approached the Russian sector of neutral Persia and on the way uprooted mountain and plains Nestorians. Arriving at Urmia, Nestorians asked foreigners to protect them. The Turks in January 1915 occupied the city after the Tsar's soldiers had left. A missionary wife described Nestorians surging into missionary schools, hospitals, and homes: "every hallway, washhouse, cellar and closet was packed full, not lying-down but sitting-up. . . . As the refugees continued to pour into our yards by the thousands and as our buildings filled up, we took the surrounding yards, all of which belonged to Syrians [Nestorians], who were eager to connect their yards with ours by cutting holes through the walls. . . . During the first weeks there were fifteen thousand or more crowded into our own and adjoining yards." [7]

Relief for refugees then began. In the United States the general secretary of the Presbyterian Board, Robert Speer, organized the Persian War Relief Fund mentioned above, which soon merged into the ACASR.[8] The product of a home in eastern Pennsylvania known for its Christian witness and political interests (his father served in Congress from 1871 to 1875), Speer already was receiving the recognition which would make him a giant among missionary statesmen; he would lead the Presbyterian Board for forty-nine years. A reason for the Relief Fund was Speer's closeness to the Presbyterian director in Urmia, William A. Shedd. Since 1890 during student days at Princeton Seminary, the two men had felt like brothers. Writing about the Urmia resident, Speer noted Shedd's "peaceableness, his courage, his quiet power . . . his prudence." [9] Shedd was a man whose grandparents had been missionaries to Indians in Ohio and whose parents had been with the Presbyterian Board in Persia.

At Urmia in 1915 the food and medical aid, although saving thousands, was not enough to prevent serious reverses. Among people crowded like animals, disease spread rapidly, deaths multiplied. Thirteen of eighteen missionaries developed high fevers from either typhoid or typhus. One missionary prayed a dozen times a day, "Oh, Lord, how long?" Missionary physician E. W. McDowell by May 1915 supervised burial of three thousand bodies, including those of his wife and Shedd's wife. Before the Russians returned to Urmia late in May 1915, about eight thousand Nestorians tried to reach Russian lines to the north. Shedd believed that only half of them survived.

Missionaries relied upon the ACASR and Speer's concern to preserve their program, and received altogether during the war years assistance worth more than one and a half million dollars. The Presbyterian Board and the ACASR distributed in the United States *The War Journal of a Missionary in Persia,* which gave details of the misery in Urmia from January through June 1915. American diplomacy made representations at Constantinople on behalf of the Nestorians; nothing came of these contacts. In the two years after May 1915 that the Tsar's soldiers held Urmia, more than one Nestorian left for New York City to work with the ACASR and to lobby for Western favor. In the interval, something of normal ways returned. Shedd in the spring of 1917 was planning an extension of the mission.[10]

Then the Bolshevik Revolution caused Russian troops to leave Urmia late in 1917, a move which initiated fresh havoc. A few Tsarist officers remained and helped arm many of the mountain Nestorians. Along with Armenians, mountain Nestorians held much of the long front against the Ottomans. With these weapons fierce mountain Nestorians not only repulsed the Porte's regiments, but despoiled the 1917 harvests and many Persian and Turk villages. This wantonness diminished the food supply, and during the winter thousands of people starved. At Urmia, the patience of Muslim Persians with the mountain Nestorians waned. William Shedd at one point in February 1918 got Muslim Persians and Nestorians together at a meeting where they promised not to attack each other. Within an hour a fracas began which went on for two days and which the Nestorians won. The defeated people appealed to the mountain Kurds for vengeance, and together they devised a plot. On an appointed day, March 16, a Kurd chief and the Nestorian Patriarch held a supposedly friendly conference and pledged good will. After the two leaders kissed, Kurdish aides assassinated the Patriarch. Mountain Nestorians retaliated by killing every adult and child in several Kurdish areas. At the same time in Urmia tension was rising, and a watchword reportedly was circulating: "He who has no rifle, sell his wife and get one."

Problems for Presbyterians increased. In the Ottoman Empire the city of Van fell to Enver Pasha during April 1918. Over twenty thousand Armenians left Van to join mountain Nestorians. Together they sacked Muslim villages as they drew back toward the Persian frontier, pursued by Turks and Kurds. The retreat finally became a headlong flight, and one night in June about thirty-five thousand Armenians and Nestorians funnelled tumultuously through the last mountain pass separating them from Urmia.

This new emergency overwhelmed the courageous Shedd, who by then was both mission head in Urmia and an American vice consul. With the Persian government ineffective or absent, Shedd's house before this point had been a place of safety for contending leaders to meet secretly, or for Shedd to arbitrate. When the Armenian-Nestorian volunteers surged into Urmia, they cut communication with the outside and disrupted the inter-communal city council which Shedd had established only weeks before. As Turks and Kurds nearly surrounded Urmia, a majority among the fifty thousand Nestorians inside linked with the newcomers. Ottoman troops in June rammed the city's barricades, but could not breach them. A British airplane from the Mesopotamian front came to Urmia on July 8 and left word that if the defendants would hold on, the British in two weeks would meet an Armenian-Nestorian detachment several days' march to the south and give them rapid-firing guns, ammunition, and money. To some of the besieged people the plane appeared as an other-worldly messenger. Yet their officials and Shedd had misgivings. They remembered that when the Russians left Urmia in 1917, British attachés with the Russian troops had not found a way to carry out a promise — a promise to provide military help in a few weeks to the Armenian-Nestorian volunteers if the latter would withstand the pan-Islamic aspirations of Turkey.

Shedd was wary of British ability to make their word good. Sensing Armenian-Nestorian defeat if supplies were not forthcoming, he used the credit of the local relief committee to purchase munitions from some adventurers who controlled an abandoned Russian depot in the area. He understood the illegality of his act. During the previous winter Muslim Persians repeatedly had accused him of giving guns to the Nestorians. When the American minister in Tehran heard this rumor, he had insisted to the Shah's government that Shedd was not guilty. At the same time he had warned Shedd against actions as vice consul other than protection of United States property and personnel. The missionary director in July 1918 disobeyed his superior because of the intense situation. The missionary also thought the British had an obligation to make right their broken commitment of 1917 to the Armenians and Nestorians, who had kept their part of the bargain. Shedd looked upon himself as a proxy for the British who would later repay the relief fund.[11] Rifles replenished, Armenians and Nestorians continued to repel outside attack. About two weeks after the Allied plane had flown over, they sent by night two thousand men toward the appointed rendezvous with the British. This group got in touch with Britishers, and together they prepared to lift the siege of Urmia.

Meanwhile the American vice consul and other leaders were losing control in the beleaguered center. A rumor spread that the Turks had ambushed the detachment sent to the south, and with Allied support only days away, the people stampeded. Shedd, with his deep-set eyes and with argument, pleaded with them to remain steady. Nevertheless, streets became clogged with animals and humans. A hectic exodus of Nestorians and Armenians began on the last day of July 1918, heading for the British lines. Shedd, a physician, and his wife (he had remarried), elected to join the evacuees and care for the sick and wounded. Turks and Kurds harassed the seventy thousand persons in the slow-moving caravan which departed from the barricades, especially its mounted troops at the end, among whom Shedd rode. The missionary, feverish with cholera, worked day and night amid bullets to advise soldiers and succor the ill. Then the third day out of Urmia, as the rear guard at dusk was approaching a British outpost, he died. His wife described the pathos among the people as they continued toward the main British army: "The news of Dr. Shedd's death swept along that line of suffering humanity like a wave of black despair. . . . as I rode along on my horse, I was greeted by grief-stricken faces and the despairing cry, 'What shall we do? Our father is gone, our back is broken; there is no one left on earth to help us. Would that half our nation had died and he had lived!' As they mingled their tears with mine and the moan of my own heart found ten thousand echoes in theirs, I became one of them, and we all knew that the worst had come to us." "The worst" was also happening in Urmia to the six thousand Nestorians and several missionaries who had stayed. After the exodus Turks and Kurds took the city, looted it, and shot an American Presbyterian. Ottoman officers eventually ordered to Tabriz every remaining United States citizen and all but a thousand Nestorians. Late in 1918, Robert Speer in the United States, with no message from Urmia since July, did not know whether any mission buildings were standing or Nestorians were alive.[12]

A missionary physician and recent graduate of Princeton, Edward M. Dodd, had conserved his wit through all these trials. His post was Dilman, a Muslim-Persian city north of Urmia, from which he administered relief to Nestorians. In spring 1918 Nestorian-Armenian volunteers from Turkey approached Dilman, intending to destroy it. The frightened city council turned to Dodd. Describing a frantic council meeting, he recalled: "At last someone said: 'Write it on a white flag that we are surrendered.' " Dodd could not write in Syriac or Armeno-Turkish, only in English. But council members insisted. "Finally more to pacify them than anything I sat down to it. Someone placed a healthy-sized white cloth and a bottle of red ink in front of me. Here was where the Princeton preceptorial system fell down. What should one as an educated man write in surrendering a Persian City? None of Woodrow Wilson's courses at Princeton had brought this in, so far as I knew! And none of the 'fifty stiffs' who worked us students night and day had passed out any dope on it. I hastily wrote in flaring red ink: 'This city is surrendered and should be respected as such. Edward M. Dodd.' " Fortunately for Princeton's reputation, the inscribed flag was not put to the test. Dodd's Nestorian assistant meantime had decided on his own to meet the volunteers; he talked them out of an attack. Situated in Urmia after Turks and Kurds had captured it, Dodd narrowly missed being killed. Through August and September 1918 he and other missionaries, along with four hundred Nestorian refugees, were Turkish "prisoners" on the Presbyterian compound at Urmia; all the American Presbyterians were seriously ill at one time (one died of malaria) and half the Nestorians perished. Concurrently Dodd edited an intermittent periodical, the *Weakly Squeak*, which dealt with "imaginary foreign news and exaggerated local news, very local." One edition had the readers laughing till they cried. After the Turks sent the religionists to Tabriz, he immediately organized an understaffed, undersupplied hospital. His light touch there came out at a party where he played the bride in a mock wedding.[13]

Among causes of the ruin which hurt the enterprise of Dodd and his colleagues were, of course, the First World War and the millet system under Western stress. Specifically, missionaries deserved some responsibility for showing preferential treatment to Nestorians. Before the Armenian-Nestorian volunteers entered Urmia in 1918, Shedd had recognized that the barbaric mountain Nestorians were a poor risk for relief. He had stated that he wished he could deal only with Protestant Nestorians. "While in our native Church, there have been lamentable lapses, a very large proportion are living up to the high ideals of Christian conduct, toward enemies as well as toward neighbors." He had deplored his enmeshment in political affairs and said he never wanted the post of vice consul, only taking it to safeguard possessions and lives. (Missionaries traditionally had taken mediating roles in communal politics; Shedd's activities imitated the style of a former leader in the Presbyterian group at Urmia, missionary physician Joseph Plumb Cochran.) "In a good deal of this," Shedd had declared, "I can only rest on the belief that we have earnestly desired and prayed to be guided, and that to doubt guidance in the past is as wrong as to doubt that we shall be guided in the future." Departing Urmia, he intimated that the gamble of supporting the mountain Nestorians had been too great. Two days before he died he saw mountain Nestorians robbing each other, and Muslims. Shedd reportedly had written that when his current mission with the mountain Nestorians ended, he hoped never to see them again.[14]

According to a survey some years afterward by the Presbyterian Board, the disorders of 1918 brought "persecution, massacre, pestilence, famine, deportation, flights, death and destruction." [15] Conflict had damaged or demolished all mission property at Urmia, killed over a third (about thirty thousand) of the Nestorians, ended the lives of several missionaries, scattered the remainder, and apparently finished the mission station. The pride of the Presbyterians in Asia was a mangled heap.

The plight of the Protestants in Urmia indicated how American and Presbyterian boards had emphasized minorities and inextricably tied themselves to national movements, government affairs, and, ultimately, the use of force. It was saddening that no tough-minded leader had arisen among the missionaries to show that the large cultural and legal barriers between Muslims and Christians made it unlikely that United States institutions would ever be free from politics. If over the previous half-century the Americans deliberately had been developing nonsectarian schools and hospitals for both Muslims and Christians, there might have been a possibility that the First World War would have been less disastrous to the Protestants.

THE PERSIAN COMMISSION

When early in 1918 reports of conditions at Van and Urmia reached Boston, Barton had redoubled efforts to guard relief and missions in eastern Anatolia and northwestern Persia. After Russia's pullout from Urmia in 1917, Britain had sought to prevent Persia from joining Turkey in the Holy War and had asked for American aid. Barton and Peet then tried unavailingly to nudge the State Department to act, short of an Ottoman-American war. Dodge in March 1918 consulted House. When a Turkish offense against Armenians at Van soon began, the ACASR chairman together with Dodge, House, and Mezes decided to send a relief expedition to Persia, and to approach the State Department about backing.[16]

The Inquiry's leader, Mezes, suggested that his fellow academician,

Harry Pratt Judson, president of the University of Chicago and former professor of history, should guide the proposed commission. Barton and Dodge endorsed the advice, although apparently they did not know Judson. Crane, Chicago resident and friend of all these men, figured in this selection. At the American Board secretary's request, Mezes on May 7 telegraphed Judson and inquired if he would be willing to lead the envisioned ACASR group. By then the commission idea had the semiofficial consent of the State Department. During the same week the Department and Dodge, again after a proposal by Mezes, approved the choice of an assistant for Judson, A. V. W. Jackson, a specialist on Persia at Columbia University and member of The Inquiry.[17]

Judson, a serious-minded man past seventy years, did not quickly accept the offer of the ACASR and State Department, partly because of his age and partly because he did not understand the purpose of the Persian Commission. In the initial query to Judson, Mezes had mentioned philanthropic and political functions. In reply, Judson assumed that the first object was to get relief to the Armenians and Nestorians who had left Turkey for Persia. He said frankly that his main interest was neutral Persia's place in the war. Further thinking on the aim of the Commission came late in May 1918, when Judson traveled to Washington and New York. In the capital Peet conducted him to interviews at the British Embassy and at the State Department, including a talk with Secretary Lansing. Each of these conversations approved both humanitarian and government goals. After discussion in New York with Dodge and Mezes, in which he was led to believe that if he "got back alive" from Persia he might be an adviser at peace negotiations "on that neck of the woods," Judson promised on June 1 to go with the Persian Commission.[18] The university president almost retracted this commitment. In two weeks he was "thunderstruck" when the New York *Tribune* exposed the political side of the project. The lead for the *Tribune*, Judson was to discover, had come through the New York City office of the ACASR. The newspaper said the Commission's end was to oppose German moves to fill the void left by Russia's withdrawal from Persia, and to develop Persia's confidence in America. Claiming that this disclosure might hinder his efforts, he questioned continued service. With careful State Department reassurance, he resumed preparation for the trip.[19]

Meanwhile, other matters irked Judson. He had come to feel that missionaries would circumscribe his freedom. He did not oppose working under ACASR auspices or participation by missionaries on the expedition. But he had wanted other concerns represented. Judson regarded the Commission as a "great business enterprise with humanitarian ends." [20] Having temporized through May 1918 about his inclusion, he had not taken part in choosing such members of the advance party of eleven men as Jackson of Columbia and five Presbyterian missionaries. This Jackson-led party at the end of May set out from Seattle for India. After deciding to go with the Commission, Judson selected two people: a University of Chicago physician and Maurice Wertheim, New York businessman and son-in-law of Henry Morgenthau. The ACASR finally gave Judson full authority on July 12. Next day he and his two companions sailed for London.[21]

For some months thereafter, the Judson unit in London and the Jackson party in Bombay made travel and distribution arrangements with the British government, which regulated much of southern Persia. While they planned, life worsened among Nestorians, Armenians, and Muslim Persians. Missionaries on the scene said that typhus and typhoid were taking much of the population. People were not only sick, they wrote, but famished and eating "dogs, dead animals, grass, and even human beings." [22] Fortunately, the Persian Commission included three Presbyterian physicians in addition to Judson's university colleague. With them were ten tons of medicine including serum for fifty thousand people and quinine for two hundred fifty thousand.

While the Persian Commission negotiated with the British in India and England, its political purpose became clearer. Barton confidently expected that the venture under Judson and Jackson would do much in combatting German influence in Persia, replenish missionary and relief personnel, and save the destitute. He hoped it would strengthen the Caucasian republics, whose instability was hindering the ACRNE (new name of the ACASR). In two reports, members of the Jackson section decided that they should labor mainly among refugees, principally Christian. They also should seek to prevent Persia from falling into unfriendly hands. An official of the Shah declared with poignancy: "The heart of Persia rests in the hand of America." [23]

Tehran's touching feeling about the Commission stemmed from a desire for help against imperial Europe, an ideal view of the United States partly because of Wilsonianism, and an earlier American technical mission (the Shuster Mission) to Persia. In 1911 a group of financial experts under W. Morgan Shuster, prompted by the same kind of needs that pro-

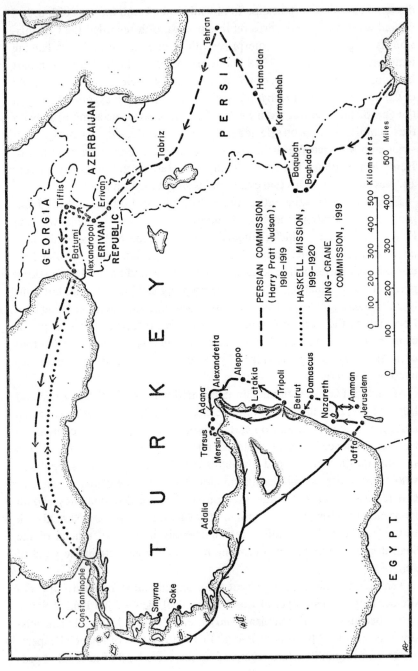

Map 5. Routes of Persian and King-Crane commissions and Haskell Mission, 1918–1920

- - - PERSIAN COMMISSION
(Harry Pratt Judson),
1918–1919

········ HASKELL MISSION,
1919–1920

—— KING-CRANE
COMMISSION, 1919

0   100   200   300   400   500 Kilometers
0   100   200   300   400   500 Miles

duced Judson's expedition, had developed the first nonmissionary incident of import in Persian relations with the United States. Having no formal State Department acceptance, the able Shuster (a Washington attorney with experience in Cuba and the Philippines) had received a mandate from the Shah's government to modernize fiscal policies. Persia wanted to lessen its dependence on Russia and Britain. Russia soon reacted negatively to Shuster's sweeping with a wide broom and sent an ultimatum to Persia which helped drive him out of the country. A legacy of this Yankee was that many Persians made him an idol.[24]

About to carry on in the Shuster tradition, the Persian Commission ministered first in British-controlled Mesopotamia. The Jackson party early in September 1918 went from Bombay to Baghdad where they joined the recently arrived Judson group. United for the first time, the Americans spent nearly three weeks there with refugees, most of them Nestorians. Numbering about thirty thousand, the Nestorians were barely subsisting at Baqubah in a desert camp set up by the British thirty miles north of Baghdad. (See Map 5 on p. 148.) These pitiable creatures were the main body of survivors out of the seventy thousand Nestorians and Armenians who had fled Urmia nearly two months before. When in mid-October Judson's circle departed Baqubah for Persia, it left behind Presbyterian physician E. W. McDowell, Shedd's colleague during the siege at Urmia.[25]

At last the Persian Commission was on the Iranian plateau. The United States team set up five committees under the chairmanship of four Presbyterian religionists and American Consul Gordon Paddock. In Tehran the Judson group reinforced an already existing organization under United States Minister J. L. Caldwell. Concurrently, missionaries on the expedition and Paddock gave consideration to the Urmia riddle. They asked Judson to urge the British to occupy Urmia so as to permit the return of Nestorians and American Presbyterians. Judson discussed the idea with local Allied leaders, who claimed they could not comply since their resources were inadequate to push out the Kurds who dominated Urmia. (It was not until April 1919 that one missionary, without military protection, went back to Urmia. Soon the irascible Kurds killed about two hundred of the remaining Nestorians in the city. The missionary and the tiny remnant of Nestorians did not stir until rescued in a daring effort by Paddock and three missionaries, including Edward Dodd.) Judson also took up with the British the use by Shedd of relief credit in arming the mountain Nestorians. After study, Judson decided that the missionary martyr should

149

not receive criticism for his course, and that Shedd's unpaid debts were a moral obligation of the British government and not the responsibility of the ACRNE.

Judson wrote from Tehran late in November 1918: "We have succeeded, I think, in accomplishing all that we set out to do." [26] As for military aspects, he exaggerated. The Persian Commission had done little to prevent a German or Turkish penetration of the Shah's realm. British troops had reduced this peril before the Americans arrived. As for both philanthropy and Persian–United States friendship, Judson was accurate. Finding Tehran eager for enlarged commercial and political ties with the United States, he had encouraged this avidity. Long smothered by Russia and Britain and as enamored with Wilsonian self-determination ideas as earlier with Shuster, businessmen and officials there wanted Washington to counter Great Britain. The British were plotting a hegemony over Persia. Tehran hoped that the United States would become an adviser and defend its integrity and independence. The Persian government wrote the State Department that the Persian Commission had brought Persians and Americans "closer together than ever before." A relief official in Persia stated that Judson's diplomacy and Jackson's scholarship had made America's name magical.[27]

Missionaries remaining in Persia, the expedition was then off for Paris. On the way at Tiflis, Judson helped reorganize the ACRNE in the Caucasus under an American Board missionary. After a short visit with Gates at Constantinople, the expedition proceeded to France, where Judson on January 8, 1919, submitted statements to House and Mezes. At Paris, Judson got permission for Persia to send observers to the Peace Conference.

He recommended to the American Peace Commission a continued British presence in Mesopotamia, Persia, and the Caucasus until the conference made a final settlement. Unlike Gates and Barton in their plan of a federated Turkey, Judson advised a separate protectorate by Britain over Mesopotamia. Regarding Persia, he thought the expected League of Nations should appoint a trustee to reconstitute the government and reorganize finances. For this help he said that the Persians "preferred the United States." During negotiations at Paris later, America made several moves to introduce the Persian question in Supreme Council meetings, only to have Britain brush them aside. Judson in his reports did not mention autonomy for Nestorians, notwithstanding such a request earlier by missionary McDowell. Probably Judson refrained, believing that his proposal for

150

a trusteeship over Persia, if accepted, would satisfy concerns of the Presbyterians and Nestorians.[28]

Mezes agreed with Judson about Persia, and asked him to increase dedication among people in the United States to overseas duties. After contacting the Barton Relief Commission in London and orienting it to current problems in the Ottoman Empire, Judson returned to New York. His fellow commissioner, Maurice Wertheim, soon had an interview with the New York *Evening Post* in which he said that Near Easterners were "yearning for aid and counsel from the United States." Wertheim asked: "Are we to allow injustice to be done to smaller nations and the seeds of war sown; then come forward after wars have begun and sacrifice our men to set things right again? Would it not be the part of wisdom for us to assert ourselves at first, take part in the management of world affairs, according to our own ideals of right and justice, and thereby do something to prevent future wars?"[29]

Thus, another example of mission-ACRNE influence! The Barton-Dodge group had done it again; the United States government was implicated in Near East dilemmas in both Turkey and Persia.

THE FUTURE OF A FAVORED MINORITY

When Judson returned to his university, Presbyterian Board leaders welcomed data he could give about the future of a favored minority of theirs. He stated that there probably would be guarantees for Turkish Nestorians in the Ottoman treaty, perhaps along the lines of a Barton notion that they become part of an integral Armenia. Feeling there was not a chance for a protectorate solely for Nestorians, he believed that Urmia Nestorians would and should not withdraw from Persia, but seek British assistance for indemnities from the Porte and for a resettlement.[30]

Usually acceding to Judson's idea that no good would arise from putting halos on minorities, Robert Speer sent pro-Nestorian correspondence to the United States government. Together with such individuals as Dodge and Morgenthau he asked in February and March 1919 for "repatriation, protection, indemnity and the return of captives" in messages to Mezes, Wilson, and the State Department. Speer wrote that his wish to see "full security" for the Nestorians was "very deep." He said that if outside policing over northwest Persia would not be expedient, the Peace Conference should charge consular agents to guard non-Muslim peoples from "persecution and all illegal molestation." Speer enclosed long statements on the Nestorians by McDowell and other Urmia missionaries. Mezes in April answered from Paris in sympathetic but noncommittal terms: "there are so many larger things here to be dealt with before matters as far afield as those affecting the Syrians [Nestorians] can be reached, that I am still unable to do more than assure you that there is every desire on the part of our delegates to do full justice to them." [31]

A method that Secretary Speer of the Presbyterian Board used was collaboration with James Bryce and with the Archbishop of Canterbury. These Britishers liked the Nestorians because the English Church Missionary Society since 1877 had maintained a mission in Urmia. Petitioning in London, Bryce and the Archbishop helped maintain a British supervision of the Baqubah camp and a British shield for Nestorians in Persia.

Another tactic related to the coordination which Speer gave to Nestorians in the United States and the Near East. To his office came representatives of Patriarchal, Church Missionary Society, and Presbyterian Nestorians of Urmia, as well as officers of Nestorian-American societies and communities. Speer usually discouraged excessive demands like those of the ambitious Nestorians in the Chicago colony, which numbered from two to three thousand. These immigrants resolved that Turkish and Persian Nestorians should receive independence and a mandate, preferably by their new country. Speer had little contact with an outspoken group, the Assyrian (Nestorian) National Association, which favored autonomy for Nestorians and since 1916 had published *New Assyria*. Speer most trusted such leaders of another institution, the Assyrian Central Committee, as Anglican-Nestorian Abraham Yohannan, Patriarchal Nestorian Paul Shimmon, and Isaac Yonan, moderator of the Presbyterian Synod of Urmia. The ACRNE's New York City office had employed Yonan and Shimmon during the war. At the same time, Shimmon had promoted the cause of the Nestorians; he received in 1918 one thousand dollars and encouragement from ex-President Roosevelt. Speer tried unsuccessfully through the State Department and the American Peace Commission to get Yonan and Shimmon to Paris as delegates of the Assyrian Central Committee. [32]

Presbyterian Secretary Speer in February 1919 turned to a former member of The Inquiry, Abraham Yohannan, as a possible representative of the Assyrian Central Committee to the Peace Conference. Yohannan was both a professor of oriental languages at Columbia (a colleague of the

Persian Commission's A. V. W. Jackson) and a clergyman trained by the Church Missionary Society at Urmia. In 1916 he had published *The Death of a Nation or the Ever Persecuted Nestorian or Assyrian Christians*. In 1918 he had filed with The Inquiry a request that Wilsonian principles be applied to the Nestorians, who should receive a free state under guarantee of a great power.[33] With State Department permission, Speer saw Yohannan off for London to confer with Bryce and others. The Nestorian then went to Paris, where he joined countrymen from Urmia who represented the Persian branch of the Assyrian Central Committee. Persian Nestorians earlier had presented a formal petition to the Peace Conference. Yohannan edited a second one with help from members of the American Peace Commission, repeating Speer's pleas to Wilson and Mezes and muting his own Inquiry request. "By the nature of their situation," he declared, "the Assyrians have had neither political or territorial centers through which they could preserve their national integrity. . . . The Assyrians are desirous of being placed under the protectorate of a friendly power . . . so that, unhampered and unembarrassed, they may rise to the proper level of self determination." [34]

While Yohannan lobbied, the Persian Minister of Foreign Affairs at Paris sought American support of Persia's attempt to be free from British influence. At a Persian-American dinner the Minister praised the United States for the Commission led by Judson "which saved many of my country men from death and thus further increased the already good relations." [35] He asked America to facilitate Persia's liberty and progress. Secretary Lansing pledged nothing except an airy helpfulness.

Since the Supreme Council put off a decision on Nestorians, Yohannan had time to dream. He wrote Speer about the old image recently redrawn by Barton, formerly painted by Parsons, Fisk, Smith, Dwight, and Jessup. Yohannan said that the Peace Conference's anticipated act for Nestorians would prepare the way for the Kingdom of God, and that soon a great opportunity would arise to carry the news of Christ to Kurds, Turks, and the entire Muslim world. What was the devastation of Urmia, he exclaimed, "compared with the reparation, which I believe shall be made some day, in the salvation of millions of immortal souls." [36]

◄ ►

In distinction to Yohannan's idea there was the new identity of Arabs, Turks, and Persians. Turkish soldiers had attacked Armenians and were still unshackled. Arabs had revolted successfully against Ottoman rule. Persians were waiting for a chance to remove British control. There was much evidence in 1919 that no Christian community surrounded by a Muslim society was strong enough to win freedom from an encircling majority. Further, neither Western mission group nor Western government had been able over the years to put a cover on the boiling Nestorian kettle — or the Armenian one for that matter. It seemed possible that ethnic Christianity would continue to decline, as it had since North African churches disappeared in the seventh century.

Chapter 7

Missionary Internationalism

THE incongruity between Yohannan's reverie and Persian and Turkish nationalism was one manifestation of the polarities with which Speer, Barton, and their colleagues had to live. Another polarity was a clattering of gunfire in Eastern Europe and Western Asia during the "Peace" Conference as Armenians, Arabs, and Nestorians waited impatiently for the Paris parleys to produce miracles. The negotiators ranged confusedly between the new and old diplomacy, between moralistic internationalism and narrow patriotism. As some typewriters set out utopian aspirations, certain others demanded petty aggrandizements. Leaders of Britain, France, and Greece saw themselves partly as helpers to people in Western Asia. But many Near Easterners, along with the American Protestants, felt that it was unfair to have imperialists masquerading as benefactors. They wished that the United States would save the Near East from Allied saviors.

A TEST CASE

An area to deliver was Syria, where missionaries had become involved in the problem of independence. Both President Wilson's friend, Cleveland Dodge, and the head of the Arab Revolt, the Emir Feisal, contributed to a discussion of the Syrian question at Paris. Dodge early in January

1919 cabled his son's father-in-law, Howard Bliss of the Syrian Protestant College, to go to France. Dodge sought to strengthen the American influence upon the Arab future.[1] About the time Bliss arrived, Feisal and T. E. Lawrence were pleading for Syrian independence at Paris. The Arab personage eventually visited Woodrow Wilson, Edward House, William Westermann, and William Yale. Concerning House's conversation with Feisal, House wrote: "I soothed him as best I could. . . . I have a kindly feeling for the Arabs and my influence will be thrown in their direction whenever they are right." [2]

Bliss, one might note, was a thin, dedicated, well-trained educator who had succeeded his father as president of the Syrian Protestant College in 1902. The younger Bliss had attended Amherst College and the universities of Oxford, Göttingen, and Berlin; he had been a Congregational clergyman in the Brooklyn church Henry Ward Beecher made famous. At Paris in 1919, Bliss labored so hard for American aid to Arabs and for missions that he later became seriously ill.[3]

While in France, Bliss helped guide the United States out of the open spaces of broad Wilsonian principles into the thickets of Western Asian politics. He had this role, not because Syria was vital to American policy but because this place brought forth the first clash at the Peace Conference between Asian nationalism and European colonialism. The United States President did not believe he could let the secret treaties about the Ottoman Empire go unchallenged without returning to the old diplomacy and neglecting Point Twelve. Syria was a test case.

Wilsonian and other factors had already facilitated a certain trimming of the secret imperial treaties about Turkey. Russia had renounced all claims; the Balfour Declaration had mentioned a Jewish homeland instead of an internationally sponsored Palestine; the Anglo-French Declaration of November 1918 had made a gesture about Arab freedom. The Fourteen Points generally had liberalized colonialism. Thus, Feisal could say about Syria even before the Conference opened: "England, France and I are now like merchants in front of a merchandise which has no owner. Is it not logical that each of us should try to appropriate it before the others?" [4]

The Arab prince recognized that the "merchants" would shove to get the "merchandise." The French Foreign Office, the Quai d'Orsay, was not happy because thousands of British soldiers occupied the Syrian territory specified for France in the secret treaties, except along the Mediterranean coast; Feisal was a British underling and military governor in interior Syria. (See occupation areas in Map 7 on p. 229.) The Quai d'Orsay also disliked it that mercurial Lloyd George had persuaded French Premier Georges Clemenceau to give both the oil-rich Mosul area (allotted formerly to the French sphere of influence) and Palestine to London. Though Lloyd George had made compensation elsewhere, the Quai d'Orsay was jumpy about its weakness on Syria and about the American government's vulnerability to self-determination missives from Feisal and others. The Syrian leader sought to improve his position by an understanding with the Zionists.

Then came the issue of an investigation in Syria. United States diplomatic agent William Yale had told The Inquiry that many Arabs intended "to demand at the Peace Conference the right to choose the country which is to direct the destiny of Syria, and . . . to request the United States to assume this responsibility." [5] Bliss had been aware of and perhaps encouraged this design.[6] Certain it was that the Hall Committee, set up under the ACRNE in 1918 and chaired by Professor Hall of the Syrian Protestant College, had favored an inquiry.

Pro-American feeling among Syrians impelled the idea of an inquiry. This feeling had arisen out of the long identity of the Presbyterian missionaries with the Arabs. Wartime was the catalyst for Americanism to swell larger than pro-European sympathy. Early in the fighting there came massive shocks to Syria: requisitioning of food and animals for the Turkish Army, an Allied blockade which cut most Western commerce, locust plagues, epidemics. Disease and starvation eventually killed over six hundred thousand Syrians (about 30 per cent of the population). Into this catastrophe stepped the missionaries. Since the Allies were enemies of Turkey, neutral America was the only Western nation able to provide systematic relief. Presbyterian religionists and mission educators often became consuls or vice consuls, devoting much of their energy to philanthropy. At the end of the war Presbyterian missionary James H. Nicol directed the relief program, at first primarily under Red Cross, later ACRNE auspices. Hundreds of thousands of dollars in goods and credits went to impoverished people. The missionaries distributed their aid so impartially to local Christians in the traditional churches (Orthodox, Catholic, and Maronite), that the hostility toward Protestants which local ecclesiastics had maintained for decades nearly melted away. Relief, coupled with Wilson's idea of self-determination, swung majority opinion from Anglophile or pro-French thinking to support for an American mandate.[7]

Missionaries had attitudes which permitted both religious and political appropriation of this shift of opinion. Two books by Presbyterian missionary William S. Nelson in 1913 and 1914 presented a "life and death struggle" between Syrian "superstition" and American Protestant "progress," between the Muslim muezzin and the church bell.[8] As European hostilities began, Nelson's supervisor, Stanley White, longed to "impress" Christian principles upon Syria after the "cataclysmic" war. When General Allenby entered Beirut, one missionary believed that the British victory was a "dream" which would lead to the substitution of the "bloody cross" for the "Turkish crescent"; he urged his fellows to follow the "bugle-call" forward with "grim determination to occupy the whole land for our King."[9] Such imagery (*struggle, impress, occupy*) implied an aggressive part for Western governments in facilitating Protestant advance. Syrian Protestant College and Presbyterian missionaries through the war strongly preferred "Anglican" Britain to "Roman Catholic" France for a mandate. It was largely Bliss and Hall of the college and Presbyterian missionaries Franklin Hoskins and C. A. Dana who actively sought both to transfer religious imagery to politics and to respond openly to the Syrians' Americanism. Unlike Barton, Presbyterian Secretary White was not oriented toward public affairs. White was surprised by the opportunity of the United States for a mandate in Syria and content to let other individuals do the lobbying for it (he was primarily concerned with mission expansion).[10]

Some missionaries to Syria hesitated about politics, but many people among the American community of about a hundred thousand Syrians in the United States did not. A spokesman for Syrian Americans, Protestant clergyman A. H. Rihbany, published *America, Save the Near East*. Asking Washington to redeem Syria "not only from Turkish misrule, but from European complication," he remarked: "Being in the large majority the products of English and American missionary schools," Syrian evangelicals "prefer to have an English-speaking Protestant Power act as their country's deliverer." (Rihbany went to Paris and cooperated with missionaries.) Syrian-American H. I. Katibah, a graduate of Harvard Divinity School, filled one issue of the *Syrian National Bulletin* with his article "Syria for the Syrians under the Guardianship of the United States." He felt that reference to the Monroe Doctrine was not an argument against an American adoption of Syria. In future European wars there would be no place for neutrals; an American presence in the Near East would prevent future conflicts. He summed the platform approved by the Syrian National

Society, the New Syria National League of New York, and the Syrian-American Club of Boston: a solution to European contention for the "golden apple" of Syria would come by the "fairest of all nations" (the United States) receiving the "apple." [11]

Thus the context within which Bliss agitated at Paris. On January 28, 1919, he saw Secretary of State Lansing and asked that the Peace Conference appoint an international investigating commission for Syria. He believed the Arabs would want first the United States and then Great Britain for a supervisor.[12]

As the Syrian Protestant College president talked about a field study, Wilson was gaining a victory for the new diplomacy. The Chief Executive had wanted to give the United States the mobility to overleap the secret treaties. The way over, he believed, would be to assign authority for such areas as the former German colonies to the proposed League of Nations and to mandates assigned by that organization. He felt democratic nationalism was a better omen of the years ahead than imperialism. At Paris both the American President and Jan Christian Smuts of South Africa pushed these mandate ideas. At the same time Barton urged using the new notion on mandates for the Ottoman Empire. Although the Quai d'Orsay and the New Zealand government resisted Wilson and Smuts and desired outright annexation of prizes in Turkey and the Pacific, the United States President adhered to mandate views with skill and tenacity. The Supreme Council on January 30 provisionally accepted the mandate scheme and applied it to several areas, including Syria, Armenia, Mesopotamia, Palestine, and Arabia; the Council did not name supervisors for Turkish mandate regions. At the same momentous meeting Wilson said his nation might assume a mandate in the Ottoman Empire.[13]

The United States delegation then developed an inquiry for the Near East. Lansing informed the President on January 31 that he and House recommended mission executive Barton to head a solely American study; Lansing failed to mention Bliss' concern that the investigation be international. The Secretary praised Barton as "the man best equipped by experience for this service." [14]A day or two before Barton had talked with Lansing and held a long conference with House, who had told of plans for the American Board head to assist an inquiry in Syria. House told him to "go to Turkey at once." [15] On February 1 Wilson wrote Barton: "I am very happy to think you are going as our Commissioner." In Italy Barton soon received a telegram formally putting him in charge of an American group to Syria. The message stated that Frederic C. Howe, commissioner of immigration on Ellis Island and unofficial observer at Paris, would join him in Constantinople. Barton in Rome informed his Boston headquarters that associates at Paris "were unanimous in believing that my investigation for the Government would be equally valuable for our relief work and that I could hardly afford to lose the opportunity to learn at first hand the conditions in the interior of Turkey . . . and so influence affairs by seeing that the real facts were put into the possession of the Peace Conference." [16]

Barton's fellow appointee, Howe, soon withdrew from the inquiry. This impulsive Progressive had been a student of Wilson's, a reform figure in the city of Cleveland, and during the war had written idealistic letters to the President about the Ottoman Empire. Howe believed that the source of international disorder was the Near East and that a peace treaty should eliminate imperial grubbing there. At Paris he heard that Syrians preferred a Turkish hell to a French heaven. That view fitted his theory moderately well, but European cynicism about Arab self-determination upset him. He developed chills standing on a crowded train to Brindisi in Italy, where he was to meet Barton. There the missionary was nowhere to be found. A cab driver led Howe around in a cold rain for several hours hunting a room and taking the miserable man through tenements filled with drunken sailors and refuse. Finally the American found a bed. But alternating between shivers and fever, Howe succumbed to pessimism. He got up and returned to Paris to tell House that the Barton Inquiry[17] was too small an effort to fight the secret treaties.[18] Hearing of Howe's abrupt act and having no consuming concern for Arab nationalism, Barton in Constantinople on February 18 wrote the American Peace Commission that he wanted a release from the investigation so he could get on with relief. The delegates acceded. They asked Barton to assist any commissioners who would go to the Near East later, which he did with the King-Crane Commission and the Harbord and Haskell missions. The Americans in Paris then wondered about a replacement for the Barton Inquiry.[19]

It was unfortunate that the Barton Inquiry had disintegrated. Such a venture might have done less to exacerbate European jealousy over Turkey and postpone an Ottoman settlement than did later Supreme Council discussions and efforts of the King-Crane Commission.

Agitation for an international, as opposed to American study, had continued in Paris while the Barton Inquiry was falling apart. In white robes, Feisal and Lawrence of Arabia had appeared before the Supreme Council on February 6. They appealed for freedom and unity for all Arabs. The Syrian spokesman also requested the Council to dispatch an international inquiry (as Bliss had suggested) to his land. A couple days thereafter, Bliss wrote to Barton that the still-alive Barton Inquiry was wonderful news; he should use the people at the Syrian Protestant College.[20] But Bliss also stated contemporarily to President Wilson that his own and Feisal's thought about an international commission would show the Peace Conference more clearly than could a United States investigation that Arabs distrusted France as a possible mandate country for Syria. "If America should be indicated as the Power desired," he declared to Wilson, "I earnestly hope that she will not decline."[21] The President replied that he was anxious for the missionary educator to speak to the Supreme Council. Bliss on February 13 addressed this body. He urged the Peace Conference to give Syrians an opportunity through an international commission to express in an "untrammelled way their wishes and aspirations." He declared: "My plan is based upon the ground that the 12th point of President Wilson's 14 points and the declarations made by France and Great Britain in November 1918 have committed the Allies and the United States to the granting of . . . self-expression to the people freed from the Turkish yoke. . . . Such an opportunity . . . has not as yet been given."[22] Wilson soon departed France for a short stay in the United States, and the Council did not act on Bliss' recommendation.

Bliss next talked to the assembled American delegates, a session of February 26. Secretary Lansing in the session stated that he had proposed an international group to the French, who had refused to consider it. Small wonder, for Clemenceau soon told House that his nation intended to control Syria because France had been a preponderant European power there since the Middle Ages. Great Britain, having somewhat contradictory agreements with the French and with Feisal, tried to find a course between the secret treaties and promises of independence to the Arabs. In the midst of these ambiguities Secretary Lansing assured Bliss that the matter of an international study would not end by default. Bliss agreed to another effort by an American commission to Syria if the international idea proved impossible.[23]

The United States government thus determined to become involved in the Syrian muddle. Most Americans at Paris favored the Bliss idea that the Peace Conference should take Arab desires into account. The Syrian Protestant College president sent the American Peace Commission an outline of excerpts from Western state documents which said that the will of a community must be a consideration in selection of a mandate state. A few experts opposed an inquiry in the eastern Mediterranean because they felt there was enough information in France. An investigation might prolong unrest and embolden the Arabs. Notwithstanding Bliss' preference, and partly because Wilson's departure had left the Americans rudderless, the delegation went ahead with preparations for a replacement of the Barton Inquiry. On March 20 it sanctioned an investigation led by Leon Dominian, an Armenian American who had studied at Robert College and who knew several Near East languages. Dominian had served on The Inquiry. Included in his team were William Yale and Harold B. Hoskins (son of Presbyterian missionary Franklin Hoskins). The elder Hoskins in an Inquiry report, noted above, had held out for British or American guidance of Syria.

Meanwhile, mission and ACRNE individuals had been interacting with the Wilson government. In the United States, Dodge reviewed his goals for the Ottoman Empire with the President. (Dodge apparently had proposed the younger Hoskins for the Dominian Inquiry.) [24] In Syria, missionaries Franklin Hoskins and C. A. Dana assembled a statement for the State Department which claimed that the subject of an American protection for Syria "has swept the country with a wave of enthusiasm," and declared that only the United States could prevent Arab disunity. The statement ended: Syrians "demand only the opportunity to make their voice heard and . . . at least 85% have but one thought in their minds, the leadership of the United States." [25] Concurrently, Charles Crane was lobbying in Paris. The former treasurer of the ACRNE had been in the Far East and in February 1919 had gone to France where his business associate, Walter S. Rogers, was chief of the American Peace Commission's news bureau. Crane urged Protestant aims upon House, and cabled Dodge in New York to confer with the President.[26] Crane did these things after talking with Bliss, who early in March left for the United States.

Wilson returned to the Peace Conference after a month's absence. Bolstered by contact with Dodge, the President thrust the United States further into the Near East tangle. While Wilson was away, House had come closer to acquiescence to a French takeover of Syria. Lloyd George had warned Clemenceau that France could not subdue Syria and Cilicia without warfare. Then in a Supreme Council meeting of March 20, Wilson listened to French and British representatives debate the secret treaties.

No longer able to remain silent, the President countered with the self-determination principle which Bliss had been using. He pressed the Allies to accept an international inquiry to Syria. Clemenceau finally assented, on condition that such a group should give attention to the whole Ottoman Empire.[27] The President thus gained an investigation. This decision came not only because of Bliss and Feisal but because General Allenby had reported to the same meeting that a Franco-Arab conflict probably would begin if the French obtained a Syrian mandate. The Supreme Council decision made it appear that the new diplomacy might bypass colonialism and that the United States might lead in reorganizing the Near East.

The purpose and the personnel of the so-called International Commission on Mandates in Turkey then took shape. On March 24 House talked to the President concerning American members. Next day the Council endorsed two commissioners each for Britain, France, Italy, and the United States. The Council also stated that this inquiry should acquaint itself with Near East opinion and suggest mandates for the entire Ottoman Empire. Wilson chose as American commissioners two men who were close to Barton — Crane and Henry Churchill King. A Congregational clergyman, the president of Oberlin College, and a promoter of Christian internationalism, King at the time of his appointment was vigorously supervising the program of the Young Men's Christian Association among United States soldiers in France.[28] House and Wilson briefly had thought of men other than King and Crane. The President had not designated any previously chosen members of the Dominian Inquiry, mostly because he knew little or nothing of this group's existence. Exemplifying communication difficulties within the American Peace Commission, the Dominian Inquiry (without its chairman, who had resigned) as late as March 31 was still expecting to go to the Near East.[29]

King and Crane selected, the United States had initiated a salvation of sorts for Syria. But the International Commission on Mandates in Turkey was primarily a paper recognition of Wilsonian principles. It was a delaying move to ensure that the United States had an important part in the Ottoman peace. This Commission was the President's tactic to challenge the secret treaties. Yet the American idealist had overreached himself. What alternative did he have to French suzerainty in Syria? He was sure that the Arabs liked the United States and Britain more than France, that Lloyd George had no intent of Britain's taking Syria, and that there had been no readying of United States attitudes for a mandate in Syria. The

President had said to the Supreme Council on March 20 that he intended to try to get the United States to take a task in the Ottoman Empire. But Wilson noted that Americans had a large antipathy to such a duty, and even felt the Philippine Islands were a bit hot in the hand and would like to drop them.[30] Given these circumstances, his policy of an investigation was a poor one.

A PLAY IN BARTON'S GAME

While Paris deliberated about Syria, the American Committee for Relief in the Near East was achieving considerable financial success in its effort to erect a new Near East. Its campaign to raise thirty million dollars had fallen short. But it distributed goods worth nine million dollars in the first half of 1919 and dispensed much of ten million dollars in grain and other commodities Hoover's American Relief Administration had allocated.

Its progaganda increased in sophistication and intensity. The monthly *News Bulletin* received editorial help from Talcott Williams of Columbia University's journalism faculty. The ACRNE sent a team to Turkey to prepare a movie version of *Ravished Armenia,* the story of Aurora Mardigonian. After conducting previews for prominent figures, the relief group showed the movie at theaters in fifty cities. Announcements portrayed a scantily clad Aurora with hands behind her back, dragged by a stallion. Scenes in the movie included a flogging of girls who refused to enter Turkish harems, a nailing of twelve Armenian maidens to crosses. As to ACRNE rallies, ex-President Taft declared in Pittsburgh that the Armenians had made Near East valleys bloom like the rose. Morgenthau (chairman of the ACRNE finance committee) stated elsewhere that unless the United States aided Armenians the "race will die." A newspaper article with the headline, "War's End Brings No Relief from Outrage to Armenians and Syrians in Persia," mentioned such phrases as fanatical Muslims, five hundred women forced to accept Islam, and "absolutely destitute Christians in most abject misery." A full-page ACRNE advertisement in the New York *Times,* reprinted from *Literary Digest,* presented two pictures: the first was four million Armenian and Syrian Christians living in lands made luminous by the footprints of Jesus, the second was Christ-led Americans rescuing needy Near Easteners.[31]

Meanwhile at the beginning of the Peace Conference, Barton had considered with Colonel House the relation of the ACRNE to the Eastern Question. Seeking a quick commitment by the Supreme Council on the Otto-man Empire, the American Board secretary told House that efficient relief and resettlement of Armenian refugees depended on the Council's conclu-sion about Turkey. The ACRNE chairman also stated: "I know how the Turkish situation weighs upon your heart, and if I can do anything to help clear that up I want you to know that I am at your service as well as every member of our commission." [32] Several members of the Barton Relief Commission argued one night that its head should stay in Paris to assist House and the American Peace Commission in Turkish reconstruction while the rest of the group went on to Asia. House settled this point. "His decision was that I go to Turkey at once," Barton wrote his wife, "get in touch with the situation there just as quickly as possible, and, at the same time, keep in touch with him in Paris. He said he might call me out, by wire, for final decisions in the Conference." [33]

The Barton Relief Commission left early in February 1919 for Con-stantinople. Dodge's business associate, Arthur James, remained in Paris as a liaison; James arranged for the passage of what was eventually several hundred relief workers from France to Turkey. In the Ottoman Empire the Commission received red-carpet treatment. British authorities fur-nished storage and ordered their troops to guard relief supplies; the French and Italians helped. Americans aided the most. Hoover sent a man to Asia Minor to coordinate the American Relief Administration with the ACRNE, especially controlling wheat speculators. Hoover allowed Relief Adminis-tration grain to go through the ACRNE, particularly for the Caucasus. His agency soon was delivering cereal at the rate of five thousand tons a month. This relief helped make known the American Board — it prompted Georgians to ask for missionaries in their nation. The first of three ships provided by the United States Navy, the *Mercurius,* docked in Constanti-nople on February 12 with over a million dollars' worth of goods, includ-ing 2,000 tons of flour, 2,500 cases of canned foods, 500 cases of con-densed milk, 18 trucks, 20 ambulances, 500 sewing machines, 200 oil stoves, 1,750,000 yards of cloth, 50,000 blankets, 800 hospital cots, 26 tents, 78 X-ray machines, and 200 tons of coal. The ACRNE stored these and American Relief Administration supplies in warehouses near the sta-tion of the Baghdad railway, across the Bosporus from Robert and Con-stantinople Woman's colleges. (See inset of Map 2 on p. 17.) At the same time other vessels with goods valued at several million dollars — the *Pensacola* and the *Leviathan* — were ready for the trip to the East. On the

Leviathan, which left New York February 16, were 240 mission and relief personnel, including 30 physicians and 60 nurses.[34]

Missionary Charles Riggs was in the *Leviathan* party. His group took a United States Army train from Brest to Marseilles and a British transport across the Mediterranean. Landing at Constantinople early in March 1919, Riggs immediately became local treasurer of the Barton Relief Commission; co-passenger George White of Anatolia College became director of personnel.[35]

The Barton-led expedition got every assistance from Mark L. Bristol, a rear admiral who was the agent of the American Peace Commission and the United States Navy at the Porte. Bristol met daily with the Barton Relief Commission, centered in the American consulate. The admiral put destroyers at its disposal, and was the "spokesman wherever necessary in dealing with the Turkish Government, as well as with the officials of European Governments residing in Constantinople." [36]

A solid-jowled career officer, Bristol shared with a State Department commissioner United States representation to Turkey. In August 1919 he would take over the State Department function. He had close ties with missionary educators in Constantinople, visiting often in their homes, residing weekends at the Constantinople Woman's College (also, receiving an honorary degree from that institution), and presiding at functions of the American schools. An able, friendly, straightforward man who attempted to treat each of the ethnic communities in the Ottoman Empire equally, he had a reputation for verbosity. His letters and dispatches often went on for pages, and a co-worker once declared: "When I try to milk the admiral's intellectual capacity . . . all four teats run at once." [37]

With help from Bristol, J. H. T. Main of the Barton Relief Commission late in February 1919 led a contingent across the Black Sea to the Caucasus. Walter George Smith later joined Main. This pioneer party took "over 5,000 tons of flour — 1,000 cases of milk — 1 hospital unit; 5,000 prs. shoes . . . 50 sewing machines." [38] Main reported to ACRNE headquarters in New York: "On the streets of Alexandropol on the day of my arrival 192 corpses were picked up. This is far below the average per day." In a message signed both by the United States consul in Tiflis and the State Department representative in Constantinople, Main wrote: "Should our Government delay in reaching out a helping hand to these suffering people? The question of political expediency ought to be forgotten in the presence of this world catastrophe. These people look to America. Our Gov-

166

ernment is under moral obligation to respond." [39] This message appeared in American periodicals. Supported by the Erivan Republic and Georgia, the Main unit established stations in Alexandropol (later Leninakan), Tiflis, and Erivan. From the Caucasus such statements as the following went to the ACRNE at home: "Saw Refugee Women stripping flesh from dead horse with bare hands today. . . . Another week will score ten thousand lives lost. For heaven's sake hurry." [40] Missionary Ernest Yarrow succeeded Main when in May 1919 the latter went back to the United States.

Groups similar to the Main contingent went by train or United States destroyer to various parts of the Empire. George Washburn led a party to Konya, Harold Hatch to Samsun, Stanley White and Aaron Teitlebaum to Syria and Palestine. Other leaders took workers to such places as Smyrna, Adana, and Bursa.[41]

Directed by American Board secretary Barton and accompanied by Caleb Gates and Gates' son, a twenty-two–car relief train set out on the Baghdad railway, headed straight into evidence about the Armenian massacres. (See Map 6 on p. 168.) The Protestants on the train discovered that the deported minority of Asia Minor usually had not dared to try to repossess its seized property. From Aintab the elder Gates winced: "We have heard many sad, sad tales here." At Urfa young Moore Gates came up with rather stupefying data: only twelve out of four thousand houses were intact in the Armenian Quarter, no more than five hundred of twenty thousand former inhabitants of the Quarter were left (Urfa in 1914 had about eighty thousand total population), fewer than five hundred Armenian children were in orphanages there, and the Protestant church building was empty. Turks had killed all Armenians connected with the American Board. The missionary who had been in charge at Urfa during the killings, being threatened, overworked, and driven beyond his emotional limits amid cannonading, had taken poison.[42]

This information was fuel for Barton's Armenianism. It heated his conscience; he thought it wrong that no Western armies were occupying Anatolia in 1919 to provide security for Armenian survivors to find their broken houses and start afresh. He therefore left his group at Aleppo to go to Cairo for a few days, where early in April he sought to persuade General Allenby to send British regiments into Asia Minor. Allenby did not fulfill Barton's burning desire. Without protection of Allied soldiers, the mission executive and his colleagues in April and May nevertheless moved

167

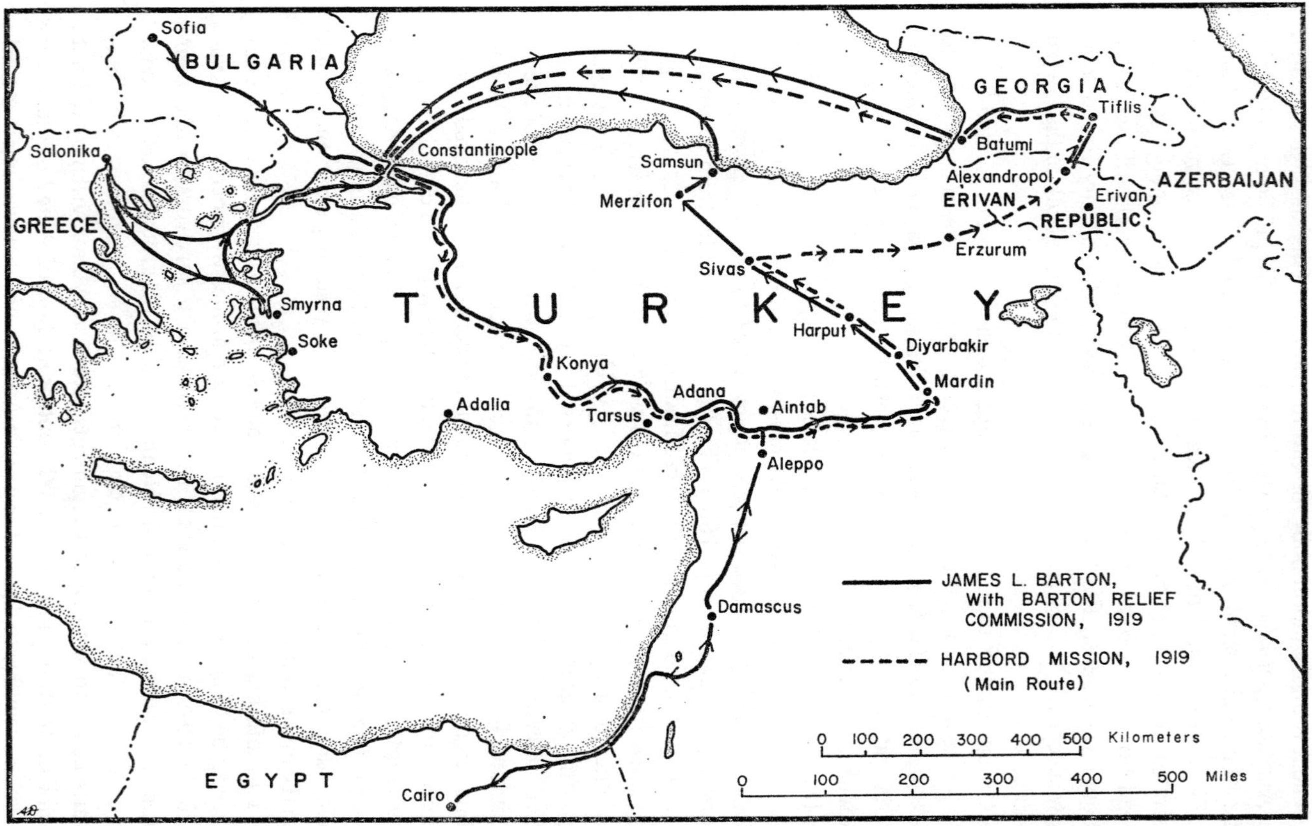

Map 6. Routes of Barton Relief Commission and Harbord Mission, 1919

north by auto from Mardin across the Armenian vilayets of Turkey. Group members were among the earliest Western visitors since the war. They saw devastation everywhere, and in damaged mission compounds came upon a few, isolated American Board heroines still at their posts. They established relief centers at compounds and prepared to reopen mission schools.

President Gates had left the relief train at Aleppo and retraced his way to Robert College. There he made a speech, called a "bombshell" by one missionary, which warned against hope for a final enlightenment of the Muslim-Christian enigma. Less of an Armenophile and farther-seeing than the ACRNE chairman, Gates felt that any treaty setting up a separate Armenia would be unwise. Unless the Peace Conference regarded Armenian and Turkish disputes within a single frame — preferably a mandate by the United States — strife between Muslims and Christians would persist. The missionary believed that Turks would adjust to this mandate if the Allies acted quickly. In his last comments Gates said: "I have been astonished at the ardor and unanimity with which the peoples of Asia Minor, both Turks and Christians, express their desire for an American protectorate." [43] Gates' evenhandedness so upset Armenian workers at Robert College that they planned a strike. Some Armenians in Constantinople were angry enough to think of seeking Gates' removal as head of the missionary school. With endorsement from Admiral Bristol, Gates departed the Bosporus on April 24 to present his view at Paris.

As the Robert College leader journeyed to France, Barton was completing his trip within Anatolia. The mission secretary late in May 1919 took a destroyer from Samsun to Constantinople. Estimating that he had covered over five thousand miles, the ACRNE chairman reported to Boston: "everywhere we took up the question of the condition of the Armenians. . . . I found nowhere on the part of the Turk any sense of guilt growing out of their treatment of the Armenians. There is no desire on their part as a whole to give justice. . . . The mandatory of this area will have much to do in getting the refugees back." [44] Not waiting for a mandate choice, Barton corresponded with Arthur James in Paris. The mission secretary obtained United States military personnel led by Major Davis G. Arnold to bolster the ACRNE in the Near East.

Some observers regarded the Barton Relief Commissioners as frontiersmen for the coming Near East. The editor of the *Missionary Herald*, W. E. Strong, writing earlier from Massachusetts to Barton had mused: "Why don't you take Woodrow [Wilson] along with you to Turkey? Many think we can get along without him here, as we are doing, and he might be quite a card for you to play over there." When the American Peace Commission had established the ill-fated Barton Inquiry to Syria, Strong had quipped to the ACRNE chairman: "I salute you as an appointed officer of the Peace Conference, Plenipotentiary and Extraordinary. You will have to get another uniform now and pad up your traveling account to correspond with the dignity of your position." After the Barton Relief Commission was in Turkey, the *Herald* editor exuberated: "it is the biggest advertisement of particular Christian altruism that the world has ever had. The men that are in it are making a demonstration that will never be blotted out of history's page. How's that for rhetoric?" [45]

How large would be the political factor in this exhibition no one knew. Rumor in Paris was that members of the Barton Relief Commission were to be part of the future administration of Turkey. The jests of Strong were not hiding the factor that a unique demonstration of Christian altruism was a play in Barton's game. The American Board leader wanted to get an ace, the Woodrow card, on the Near East table. [46]

What were the odds of the American Board secretary's winning his goal? Favorable signs were Hoover's aid, the presence of American military men in the Near East through Major Arnold and his staff, and Gates' move to the Peace Conference. A poor sign was Barton's own unwillingness to give credence to Turkish as well as Armenian nationalism, as the Robert College head had done in his speech at Constantinople. There was no small irony in that for a period of several days in May 1919, two symbolic individuals — Barton, the West's chief Armenophile, and Mustafa Kemal Pasha, the future "father" of Turkey — were in the Samsun-Sivas region and did not speak with each other. The ACRNE chairman coddled Armenians and scarcely communicated with leaders of the Turkish ethnic group, by then the overwhelmingly majority people of eastern Anatolia.

THE MORGENTHAU MEMORANDUM

Barton was one among many mission-relief workers and their friends who during the Paris Conference had prepared designs for a United States place in the Ottoman Empire. Although agreeing that America belonged in the postwar Near East, his and other plans failed to concur on the kind of involvement. With the Empire virtually ended, what the Protestant establishment lacked was a coordinated, specific program.

Peripatetic Barton had the capability not only to mastermind philanthropy but to compose memoranda and other documents indefatigably. He vacillated in 1919 between dealing with the entire Empire and dealing with Armenia (as he had done in papers submitted to The Inquiry and the State Department before the Armistice of Mudros). This vacillation was partly owing to his changing environment. At Paris, under Boghos Nubar's pleadings, he had given attention to Armenia. Boghos insisted with good intuition, but without success, that he needed Barton's guidance in France. The American Board secretary was the principal person to tie mission-relief strategy — and the only way he could avoid squandering much of his effect on politics was to remain in Paris. But, as noted, he left. While there, he was active for Boghos' cause: "We have spent much time with the Peace Comm.," he wrote. "I think we will be able to do a good thing for Armenia." [47] In the name of the ACRNE, its chairman sent the United States delegates a nine-point outline emphasizing that only America qualified as a mandate for Armenia, and should not shirk the responsibility. Traveling in the Empire with Gates, Barton during February and March shifted his emphasis in dispatches to American officials. The Supreme Council should put a single mandate, preferably by the United States, over the entire country. Evaluating local opinion about a mandate by Washington, Barton stated to the American Peace Commission in Paris that Armenians seemed unanimous and Arabs positive by more than three fourths. In an article for the *Missionary Herald*, he remarked that leading Muslims were speaking freely of the United States and not Europe as the ideal: "The Turks honor and respect the American missionaries, their character, integrity, and fairness. . . . They know America only as they have learned it through the American missionaries. . . . with astonishing unanimity they turn as officials to America to help them in this time of their extreme need. . . . We must not hesitate to respond." [48] Removed from Gates' counsel by April, Barton in his messages thereafter dropped references to a single mandate for all of Turkey. Fresh from hearing sorrowful stories among the ethnic group to which he had given much of his life, he cabled House and others that the Armenians at once should have a guaranteed independence. He begged for a strong mandate immediately: "The Turkish Government is not preventing new atrocities to the Armenians." [49]

Barton's intimates in the American Board also advertised a United States role in the Near East. A *Missionary Herald* editorial in March 1919

171

said that Turkey, because of Protestant education and humanitarianism there, should fall to America. The editorial argued that it would be craven for the United States to urge at Paris a regard for the fortunes of oppressed states and then refuse to take any part in a practical rescue. The *Herald* castigated a selfish United States kneeling behind the Monroe Doctrine, and glorified a stalwart America walking out into the world. Echoing Barton's idea of federation, a missionary in Turkey with the ACRNE wrote that a stable Empire guided by the West and holding together the different sections of the country for some years to come could give tranquility. The furloughed assistant treasurer to William Peet, Luther Fowle, strongly advocated in an interview with the Boston *Herald* that the United States take a mandate for Armenia. The Armenian Missionary Association, a group that the American Board had helped organize in America, resolved its deep appreciation to Barton for his acts on behalf of its countrymen overseas. The Armenian Missionary Association requested the Board to facilitate aspirations of Armenia for independence under a United States wing.[50]

Important nonreligious periodicals in America aided mission-relief promotion. The New York *Times* discussed a notion attributed to Cleveland Dodge which asked for a mandate over Armenia by the United States. Talcott Williams wrote for the *Independent* on America's duty in Turkey. Articles by Williams and by Henry W. Jessup, another missionary son, set out similar ideas in an issue of the *Annals of the American Academy of Political and Social Science*. Williams believed that a Balkanization of the Ottoman Empire would be foolish, and urged a United States mandate over the whole nation. He thought that spending five billion dollars on such a venture was necessary for world order and much better than losing tens of billions in the whirlpool of some future war which would unavoidably pull in America.[51]

The words of Dodge and Williams about an obligation by Washington in the Near East were similar to the contentions of three presidents of mission colleges in Turkey. The president of International College in Smyrna, Alexander MacLachlan, responded to a request from the American Peace Commission for his view on a Greek occupation of Smyrna. "Of all the possible solutions of the Near East end of the peace settlement," he wrote, "the one proposed is the worst. It cannot fail to be disastrous for both Turkey and Greece. Turkey will never submit to Greek domination. So long as a Greek armed force remains in Asia Minor we who are domiciled here will be doomed to live under bitter war conditions." His analysis could not

172

have been more accurate. On June 6 he appeared before the United States delegation in Paris. He had left International College about two weeks after the Supreme Council endorsed the Greek occupation of Smyrna. MacLachlan said he and many other observers in his area were against the Greek takeover. He believed a healing could come to Turkey if Allied troops would replace Greek and if the Council would end its scheme of sovereignty by Athens over southwestern Anatolia: "the country can only be saved from ruin under protection of a British or an American mandate." [52] To headquarters in Boston the president of Central Turkey College, John Merrill, said that the best solution for Cilicia — corroborated, he claimed, by sober-minded Christians and Muslims — was an American or British suzerainty in his region. The head of Constantinople Woman's College, Mary Patrick, went to the French capital at the end of June and there prepared an article imitating the Fourteen Points: "Fourteen Reasons for an American Mandatory over Turkey." Point one on the distaff side argued that "All the people of the Near East would welcome an American mandatory." [53] Armenians, Greeks, and Turks would prefer the United States, Miss Patrick said in her other points, because they felt it would be more democratic than other nations, would promote harmony among ethnic groups, introduce a superior educational system, not exploit the country commercially, and not stay forever.

The American Committee for the Independence of Armenia (ACIA), the institution whose founding Dodge and Barton had aided late in 1918, neglected all Ottoman peoples except Armenians. Cooperating with Mihran Sevasly's Armenian National Union, James Gerard and Vahan Cardashian of the ACIA distributed widely a booklet, *Should America Accept Mandate for Armenia?* The booklet gave an affirmative response to its title: "the mandate that America will be expected to exercise in Armenia will be chiefly an extension of the noble relief and educational work which the brave men and women from America — the missionaries — are now carrying on in that historic land." Gerard and Senator Lodge in February telegraphed President Wilson, pressing for freedom of integral Armenia. The ACIA sent two petitions to the President asking the same goal; twenty thousand clergymen reportedly had signed one petition, and forty governors and two hundred fifty college presidents the other.[54]

In contrast to the ACIA, Caleb Gates upheld the unity of Asia Minor and showed a considerable objectivity about minorities there. Writing a member of the American Peace Commission, he said: "I think that the crux of the Near East Question is not the Armenians but the Turks. The attention of the Peace Conference should be centered upon giving the Turks a good government rather than upon delivering the Armenians and Greeks from the Turkish government. Because it will be of little profit to establish an Armenia, more than half of whose people will be Turks, if alongside of this new State there remains a Turkey of the old type. . . . To save the Armenians and Greeks you must save the Turks also." [55] Wilson read this statement of Gates and said it was interesting and important. In Paris, the Robert College president opposed Greek control of Smyrna, broad territorial claims by Armenians, and the International Commission on Mandates in Turkey. He had little respect for the international investigation because he felt that there was sufficient evidence available in France. He felt, further, that the inquiry would postpone a settlement, and procrastination would bring fighting.

Edgar J. Fisher, acting president of Robert College in summer 1919 during the absence of Gates and Vice President George Huntington, viewed the Eastern Question quite objectively. He had completed a doctoral program in history at Columbia University in 1911. Fisher felt truth vindicated when both extremist Armenians and Turks reacted negatively to an article in *Outlook* based on his ideas. He desired, like Gates, a united Empire, and believed an American mandate over it a "wonderful opportunity." [56]

Mark Bristol shared much of Gates' outlook. The admiral wrote that the Greek landing at Smyrna and other factors pointed to the absolute need of combining all of the Ottoman Empire under one mandate. Turks were leaning toward America as a mentor. After trips into Asia Minor, Bristol stated that Greece's possession of Smyrna had antagonized Turks tremendously and would make an Ottoman treaty difficult. Seeking to point out from the Greek abuse of Turks at Smyrna that the ethnic peoples in the Near East were alike, Bristol claimed that if someone would put all the races "in a bag and shake them up you could not predict which one would come out first as being the best one." [57] The admiral disapproved of excessive pro-Greek and pro-Armenian propaganda in the United States. He believed it encouraged an American idea about the Empire which would create a new Balkan mess. For the sake of stability in the Near East and around the world, he wanted the United States to accept a mandate over the whole of Turkey.

Henry Morgenthau combined the best views of Bristol, Gates, and Bar-

174

ton. Using an invitation to help the International Red Cross as an excuse to get to France, the finance chairman of the ACRNE on the first day of arrival, in March 1919, had conversations with Wilson, House, and Hoover. Concern with European problems prevented him, until May, from agitating for the Near East. Then helped by several others (including Gates), and invited by the American Peace Commission, he prepared a memorandum for Wilson: "The Future Government of Asia Minor." [58] The Morgenthau Memorandum advocated that one nation, the United States or else Britain, supervise each of three mandates: Constantinople, Turkish Anatolia, and Armenia.

The Morgenthau Memorandum was a useful, even revolutionary document. It included much from the overlapping views about Turkey held by people in or related closely to the Protestant lobby. Coming out of the new diplomacy, it stressed public opinion in the Empire, which had preference for British or American mandates. Realistically, it ignored the cries about one mandate for the whole country. It therefore bypassed some Americans' ethereal yearning over Syria, recognizing that a United States mandate over the Arabs was not a viable option. The paper rejected a totally independent Armenia. It took into account the prediction that such an entity with its mixed population would not easily escape hostilities with Turks. (The ACIA felt that the Morgenthau Memorandum's failure to approve unqualified freedom for Armenia was immoral.) It was most importantly an unorthodox policy proposal, capitalizing Wilson's prescription of a mandate system for Turkey, overriding the secret treaties, disregarding the Cobb-Lippmann and other explanations of Point Twelve, admitting a long-term United States embroilment in the Old World.

But the Morgenthau Memorandum had important weaknesses. It came late in the Peace Conference. Further, the American public had little or no conditioning to the idea of a United States mandate, an idea which probably required the experience in mission-relief-government coordination developed by Barton during the years since 1915, and the American Board secretary was nearly inaccessible to Paris, having left a command post there for scouting in Asia Minor.

TORTUOUS EVENTS

The Morgenthau Memorandum of May 1919 came at a critical juncture in the struggle between new and traditional diplomacy, between self-determination and colonialism. Since the origin of the International Commission on Mandates in Turkey two months before, Henry King and Charles Crane had remained in Paris, caught in tortuous events connected to the Near East.

The day before Wilson and House had chosen King and Crane for the International Commission, misgivings about the inquiry were prevalent. In a six-hour informal meeting that evening (March 25), French and British specialists had reached a substantial accord: France should seek to conciliate Feisal and be ready to allow him considerable leadership among Arabs; it was better to decide the Syrian matter in Paris rather than through an investigation which would upset conditions in the Near East. Differing with these Europeans, Feisal in an interview with House said that the International Commission was the "best thing he had ever heard of in his life." [59] The Arab prince sensed that Franco-British ties were stronger than his own with London, and asked for an American mandate. Having minutes of the Allied experts' meeting, House told Feisal that a United States mandate was doubtful. Whereas House did not oppose an investigation, such members of the American Peace Commission as the head of the Western Asia Section, William Westermann (who had sent the above-mentioned minutes to House), felt the inquiry had developed too tardily.

Perhaps it was mission-minded Professor Albert Lybyer of the University of Illinois who kept the International Commission from expiring. Lybyer had taught for seven years (until 1906) at Robert College. Partly because of this experience, he had been able to write a book on Turkey, one of the best by Americans on Ottoman affairs. He had been one of the activists in the ACRNE. In Paris since December 1918, a specialist on the Balkans within the United States delegation, he had worked easily with Crane, Bliss, Gates, Barton, and Peet for American sponsorship of Armenians and Syrians. He also had contacts with such missionary professors visiting Paris as Lynn Scipio and Abraham der Hagopian of Robert College. An ambitious man, he had sought to influence beyond his duties as a technician, and was dismissed from his post late in March. Depressed, he turned to his friend Henry King (Lybyer had taught at Oberlin); King told him about the Commission to Turkey. Lybyer waited all of five hours to apply for a post on the Commission and soon received an appointment. King took this former associate into his confidence, and together they settled on the selection of such assistants as William Yale (a member of the disbanded Dominian Inquiry) and George R. Montgomery (a son of missionaries to Armenia). King and Lybyer then moved out against the current pessimism about the Commission. Lybyer stated privately early in April that "King and I decided to push it. He pressed upward toward the President, and I ran around among our people . . . [and] among the British, French and Italians." [60] From Allied nationals being considered for the Commission, Lybyer encountered dilatory tactics. Jean Gout and Robert de Caix, possible French appointees, said to him that the international investigation should agree on mandates in Paris and fill out details in the Near East. At one point, Gout accused the American missionaries of using ACRNE philanthropy as a bid for United States territorial control of part of the Ottoman Empire; Lybyer protested moralistically.

William Westermann assessed the situation of April 1919: "Lybyer's chest expands daily; he is with King morning, noon and night. . . . My merriment is unabated." [61] To the busy, serious Lybyer, the times did not call for laughter. History was to be made, and he and King were making it.

Next came a showdown. Clemenceau, the Tiger of France, on April 14 told House that the French government was willing to give up Cilicia if the United States took a mandate over Armenia. Clemenceau would allow an inquiry, but slyly advised against its beginning right away. Simultaneously, the French Premier was negotiating with Lloyd George and Feisal. Clemenceau wanted an agreement in Paris for a French mandate in Syria and for replacement of British troops by French in the Damascus area (France's soldiers were only along the Syrian coast). Robert de Caix on April 17 "accidentally" lost a document in the American-occupied Hotel Crillon. Apparently a secret memorandum for use only by the Quai d'Orsay, the de Caix Note stated that the British feared an investigation would encourage fighting in the Near East and that the French intended to have Syria regardless. The fraudulent de Caix Note, accepted as authentic by the United States Peace Commission, led the Americans next day to decide that the Ottoman Empire was the great loot of the war and that the International Commission would be senseless. Other voices helping in this capitulation to the old diplomacy were those of the United States Zionists. The Zionists had seen that polling Arabs in Palestine was not the best way to create sentiment for a Jewish homeland and had been importuning Wilson and House with their anxieties. Lybyer and Crane thereupon planned a private trip to Constantinople, and King made reservations to return to Oberlin.[62]

For years the American Zionist movement had been growing, but its competition with missionary diplomacy had not become clear until the

Peace Conference. Some United States ministers and consuls to Turkey in the late nineteenth century had taken an active interest in Jewish immigration to Palestine. Many American Protestants, like Presbyterian clergyman William E. Blackstone, had supported Zionism. Blackstone in 1891 led a group of prominent personages to petition the United States Department of State for a Jewish homeland in Palestine. During the early months of the First World War, the Wilson administration cooperated with Zionists to help prevent the deportation of a hundred thousand Ottoman Jews. Throughout the war, the United States government aided American Jewish relief enterprise in Palestine like it aided the ACRNE. At the same time, public opinion favoring a homeland became quite strong. In 1916 the Presbyterian General Assembly passed a resolution, sponsored by Blackstone, which endorsed a Jewish homeland. Wilson's daily Bible reading aided his assumption that since Jews and Armenians were peoples of the Bible they were certain to be reborn politically after the war. In 1919 pro-Arab missionaries like Bliss did not feel the same as Wilson and Blackstone about Zionism. These missionaries sensed the strife inherent between Arab nationalism and Zionism; they were not as much anti-Zionist as pro-Arab.[63]

Felix Frankfurter, a spokesman for American Zionists at Paris, sought to counter what seemed to him the anti-Zionist Protestant diplomacy. He wrote Wilson that the appointment of the International Commission had brought the "deepest disquietude" to world Jewry. The President's reply to Frankfurter neglected the threat of the inquiry to a Jewish homeland: "I never dreamed that it was necessary to give you any renewed assurance of my adhesion to the Balfour Declaration, and so far I have found no one who is seriously opposing the purpose which it embodies." [64]

Bliss' plan for an investigation was not laid to rest by Zionist or French disquietude. An expert with the British peace delegation, Arnold Toynbee, on Saturday, April 19, stimulated Lybyer's imagination. Toynbee informed him that Lloyd George had selected Henry McMahon (former high commissioner in Egypt), the scholar David Hogarth, and Toynbee himself for the British section of the International Commission. Concurrently, bases for a Franco-Arab understanding in Paris were cracking. The next Monday, just before departing for the Near East, Feisal saw a way to retain his authority among his countrymen, who had high expectations for the announced investigation. He visited House and "insisted that the . . . Commission should go as soon as possible. If it did not, he would not be

178

1. Robert College, fortress of Rumeli Hisar on left, looking
across Bosporus to Asia Minor, c. 1925

2. Daniel Bliss (center, first row) with the faculty of
Syrian Protestant College, 1872

3. Cyrus Hamlin, 1875

4. Howard S. Bliss with graduating
nurses of the Syrian
Protestant College, c. 1918

5. John R. Mott (left), Caleb F. Gates, and Bayard Dodge, 1924

Edwin M. Bliss, *Turkey and the Armenian Atrocities* (Boston: H. L. Hastings, 1896), 306

6. Slaughter of
   Armenians at
   Sassun, 1894

7. ACASR poster
   for 1917

9. Cleveland H. Dodge, 1916

8. Cleveland H. Dodge and Woodrow Wilson
in First World War parade

10. Cleveland H. Dodge
and Charles V. Vickrey, after
Dodge conducted farewell service
on relief ship, *Newport News*,
on April 22, 1919

11. James L. Barton with nurse, inspecting flour
to be carried on relief ship

12. George Washburn (left), James L. Barton, and William W. Peet embarking on
January 4, 1919, on the *Mauretania* with the Barton Relief Commission

13. Henry Morgenthau, Sr., 1913

14. Mark L. Bristol, 1928

15. Charles R. Crane, 1920

16. Harry Pratt Judson, c. 1918

17. Russian-Armenian Patriarch Mesrob and General James G. Harbord
in the Caucasus

18. Ahmed Djemal Pasha (front) and Halidé Edib (right)
at Syrian Protestant College, 1916

19. Orphans with toys at Sidon, c. 1920

20. Checking children for trachoma in the Near East
Relief clinic at Ghazir, Lebanon, c. 1920

21. Armenian boys in relief orphanage at Marash, c. 1919

responsible for the peace." [65] House sat down and wrote Wilson, asking him to stop King from sailing back to America. About the same time, word from General Allenby in Cairo helped convince Westermann that only the inquiry could satisfy Syrian desires and quell disturbances. President Wilson then told King and Crane on Tuesday, April 22, that they should again prepare to go to Turkey.[66]

Lybyer was elated, though not for long. By talking self-determination, America had stirred Arab emotions in Beirut, Damascus, Jerusalem, and their environs. The United States could hardly forsake its lofty principle, no matter what the Quai d'Orsay determined for the Near East. But Wilson and House were cautious in their delicate stance between Syrians infatuated with Bliss' notion, on one side, and French colonialists on the other. The result of the inquiry could be a boiling of Arab passion, with no possible refrigerant available but a French mandate, which might make things hotter. House actually went quite far toward the old order. He implied that the International Commission would not have to traverse the Mediterranean if Lloyd George and Clemenceau could agree on a French presence in Syria which treated the Arabs fairly. Stalling by the Quai d'Orsay continued. King, Crane, and Lybyer remained in Paris, perturbed at the postponement.

One reason the United States was not assertive about an investigation related to Armenia. For months the assumption among the Allies in Paris had been that the United States should take mandates for Armenia and Constantinople. Lloyd George and Clemenceau desired American obligations in Turkey because each leader had mistrusted the other country's gaining an edge in the Asia Minor settlement. Both were willing to let the United States assume the portions allotted to Russia in the nefarious secret treaties (see Map 4 on p. 103). Lloyd George especially liked the stability the presence of the United States could give to the Near East. Both he and Clemenceau were aware that if America accepted a mandate in Turkey, the New World nation would not look radically unlike the secret treaty spoilsmen in Syria and Mesopotamia. In all this talk, no one urged a field study in eastern Anatolia. The massacres had depleted the Armenians there so much that nowhere were they a majority of the population. Since it seemed best to resolve the Armenian matter at Paris without an investigation, Wilson and House could see how the French felt about Syria.

On the subject of a United States mandate in eastern Asia Minor, it was Wilson, Dodge, and Barton among Americans who had forged a tie between

179

the United States and Armenia during the Paris deliberations. One section of the American Peace Commission on January 21 had recommended a United States mandate for the ethnic group of eastern Anatolia. The President thereupon wrote Dodge: "You need not doubt my advocacy of the utmost autonomy and protection for the Armenians and I am sure you do not." [67] Barton's nine-point plan for an integral Armenia under United States tutelage, noted above, went to the Peace Commission on January 28. At Supreme Council sessions two days later, Wilson hinted about a United States duty in Turkey. Lloyd George, influenced by James Bryce and other British Armenophiles, said the duty should be in Armenia. On February 8 the President wrote his Secretary of War, asking if it was legal to dispatch American soldiers to Armenia and Constantinople. He got an affirmative opinion, with the caution that bring-the-boys-home demands were increasing. Then the New York Federation of Churches cabled Wilson asking British or American supervision for the Armenians in Asia Minor. To Gerard of the ACIA the President soon said that Armenianism struck a stirring chord in his heart. In London and Paris, Barton's comrade Bryce concurrently insisted that the United States, because of its beneficence to the Near East, should have Armenia. [68]

And so it went. Disembarking in Boston after recrossing the Atlantic, Wilson in a speech of February 24 orated there: "Have you thought of the sufferings of Armenia? You poured out your money to help succor the Armenians. . . . Now set your strength so they shall never suffer again." Bostonian Mihran Sevasly of the Armenian National Union inquired of the State Department for instructions on how to carry out the President's advice to "set strength." Wilson suggested that the State Department tell Sevasly that if and when the Supreme Council asked the United States to take an Armenian mandate, he considered Dodge a leading candidate to guide a propaganda campaign for American acceptance. [69] At a White House dinner for Congressmen on February 26, the President said he hoped his country would be prominent in the policing of Armenia. [70] Two days later he declared to the Democratic National Committee that the Allies were pushing United States mandates for Armenia and Constantinople; he believed the Democrats ought to urge the nation to agree. ACIA member Senator Lodge was aware of this presidential thinking through Peace Commissioner Henry White in Paris. Lodge sympathized with Wilson's view, though he wanted nothing to do with America's appearing to help what he believed were tyrannical Turks. [71]

At the French capital an image which bridged Armenia and the United States soon became clearer. President Avetis Aharonian of the Erivan Republic and Boghos Nubar addressed the Supreme Council late in February and petitioned for the freedom of an integral Armenia. They sought a mandate by Britain or the United States. From London came word that Bryce's British Armenia Committee had formally adopted a resolution asking the United States to take an Armenian mandate. House then told Lloyd George and Clemenceau that his government would probably accept mandates for Armenia and Constantinople. On March 20 Wilson tentatively approved House's statement. ACRNE finance chairman Morgenthau at this time indicated in his diary the probability of a United States mandate over Armenia.[72]

Unexpectedly, it was Italy's avarice for Adalia in southwestern Anatolia, not United States assent to a separate Armenian mandate or French cupidity for Syria, which first produced a dramatic display of the West's intent toward Turkey. Italian Premier Vittorio Orlando was a nineteenth-century imperialist guided by an excited feeling in his country that the promises of Adalia in Anatolia and other spoils to Italy by Britain and France at St. Jean de Maurienne in 1917 and in other secret agreements were sacred. Then Wilson on April 24, 1919, showed in the Supreme Council and in a press release an indomitable opposition to Italy's violating the Fourteen Points by seeking to annex the Slavic-speaking city of Fiume. Orlando thereupon left Paris and from Rome planned a retaliation. Within a week, the Italian government sent warships to Fiume across the Adriatic Sea and to Adalia (Antalya). Soon Italians were ashore at points on the Turkish coast and moving inland. An occupation of Smyrna seemed imminent.[73] (See Map 7 on p. 229.)

As news of Italy's actions reached Paris, consternation arose, not least within missionary Caleb Gates, who had arrived at the French capital early in May. This Robert College educator had said for months that procrastination over the Ottoman settlement would lead to the use of force. Consulting the American Peace Commission, Gates advocated a quick Supreme Council decision on the Ottoman Empire. He desired a United States mandate over Turkey down to the Arab-speaking line. Negative about Bliss' project, the International Commission, he felt it would add to the wierd confusion about the Near East. As for Armenians, he believed only Western troops in Asia Minor could save them. To proclaim a sep-

181

arate Armenia without Allied soldiers in the area would cause a massacre.[74]

The Supreme Council finally discussed the complicated situation. Lloyd George perceived that the best way to block Italy's unilateral moves was an overall revision of the status of Western troops in Turkey. On May 5 he urged United States garrisons for Armenia and Constantinople, French garrisons in Syria, and Greek in Smyrna. His last suggestion came partly out of his own Philhellenism and out of Greek Premier Eleutherios Venizelos' eloquent misapplication of self-determination to the Greek minority in the Smyrna region. Lloyd George hoped that Athens could become an ally of London and a bulwark against possible Russian expansion. That day and the next, the Big Three considered Lloyd George's revision-of-status notion, and also Gates' idea of an American mandate over all of Asia Minor. In these discussions Wilson balked. He feared anti-Turkish opinion at home (including that of Senator Lodge) and was unsure of political backing for sending soldiers into Anatolia since his nation had not been a belligerent against the Porte. He was afraid to order the United States Army into Turkey, in spite of his Secretary of War's opinion that such a move would be legal. Indeed, the Terrible Turk picture, mostly developed by the ACRNE, was a boomerang. The anti-Turk stereotype was returning to strike the missionaries' desires for American protection of Armenia. Unwilling to obligate the United States in Asia Minor yet piqued by Italy's bitter reaction to his view on Fiume, Wilson went along with Lloyd George's wish to have Greeks land regulars at Smyrna; he did not bring into play his earlier private statements against splitting Anatolia. The tired President had an inadequate touch with his experts. They were vociferously against a region around Smyrna under Athens' control. Wilson apparently was familiar with missionary MacLachlan's statement against a Greek occupation, but he possibly did not realize that Greece and Turkey had been fratricidal enemies for a century, as Italy and Turkey had not been. To throw Greek liquid on the Italian flame in southwestern Anatolia was to add gasoline rather than water.[75]

Gates raced to help define an Asia Minor policy for the American Peace Commission before the West divided Anatolia. Strongly pressing House to back a unified Asia Minor under the United States, Gates made known very freely his idea. He told House that if the Allies insisted on dismemberment, they should not announce the policy until they occupied Anatolia. Hearing of Gates' proposal for a unified Asia Minor, Gerard of the

ACIA cabled House, irresponsibly charging Gates with being more interested in converting Muslims than in defending Armenia. Gerard said the United States under no conditions would accept a mandate which included horrible Turks. To buttress his contention he cited editorials in the New York *Times* and *World*, and Senator Lodge's attitude. Boghos Nubar soon expressed similar shock to House. The loose confederation of educators, philanthropists, evangelists, Armenians, and Armenophiles which Barton and Dodge had so laboriously put together in 1918 had begun to come apart.[76]

In conclaves of government heads, momentum toward splitting Anatolia continued, and tension and complexity increased. Thus, it was not unusual that on May 13 Wilson demurred when Lloyd George said that the United States should take Armenia and Constantinople, but a few minutes later seemed to reverse himself. Using Gates' idea and saying there was real advantage to Turks' belonging within a single mandate for all of Asia Minor, the President announced that the United States might assume such a task. By the next day, May 14, Wilson must have sensed he had neither battalions ready nor support at home to hold out for a unified Anatolia. Also, of course, he had given his blessing for a Greek army at Smyrna. So the weary man bowed to the imperialists, even to Italian leader Orlando, and endorsed resolutions tentatively assigning mandates for Smyrna to Greece, Adalia to Italy, and central Anatolia and Cilicia to France. Subject to confirmation by the Senate, the United States was to have Armenia and Constantinople.[77]

Divisions in Paris immediately produced the concrete violence familiar to Asia Minor. Within twenty-four hours the Greek military, escorted by an Allied squadron, landed at Smyrna. The Greek invaders then ripped fezzes and robes off Turks, and forced them to cheer the Greek premier: "Long live Venizelos." According to eyewitness Alexander MacLachlan of International College, Greeks killed over five hundred Muslims in acts "absolutely barbaric" and "equal to the worst that the Turks have ever done."[78] This was an auspicious way for the West to civilize the Turks. A few days after the Greek intrusion the infuriated Turkish general, Mustafa Kemal, took a self-appointed lead in organizing a Turkish movement in eastern Anatolia to protect Asia Minor from the European protectors. Soon the frail Erivan Republic on its first birthday (May 28), proclaimed the annexation of six Turkish-Armenian vilayets and increased the anger of Kemalist Turks. Gates' prescience about conflict if the Allies sundered Anatolia was becoming a reality.

Edgar Fisher at Robert College sensed the foolishness of the Greek occupation. In his diary during the week after the landing, he labeled it a blundersome, untimely mess bound to bring unfortunate consequences. The reasoning of the Peace Conference leaders, he believed, was "inexplicable, unless they are acting on the policy of stirring up as much discontent as possible." Turkish mass protests and sniping at Greeks soon occurred in Constantinople. As to the Smyrna hinterland where Greeks began devastating Muslim villages, a Turkish graduate of Robert College told Fisher that he was helping organize Turkish volunteers to resist.[79]

Meanwhile, in Paris such associates of the missionaries as Washburn, Morgenthau, and Bryce were rushing to help Gates' program. After service with the Barton Relief Commission, Washburn had taken up with Lybyer and others the cause of Gates (who had left for New York where he promoted Asia Minor's unity under an American mandate). Washburn stated: "Of what use is it to save thousands from starvation and disease if they are . . . subjected to the same dangers again? If the American people could once see the conditions of existence in Asia Minor, they would surely be roused to act vigorously and unselfishly for the permanent care of this plagued spot." [80] James Bryce was trying through Secretary of State Lansing to end the current partitioning ideas of the Allies. Bryce particularly did not want the French to detach Armenians in Cilicia from an integral Armenia under an American mandate. On May 21 Morgenthau sent to Wilson his paper already discussed, "The Future Government of Asia Minor," a document supported by many of the United States delegates. The Morgenthau Memorandum insisted that the secret treaties had no place in the Anatolian settlement. Under no circumstances should Greeks and Italians receive any part of that area. "Only a comprehensive, self-contained scheme" such as a tripartite protection of the whole of northern Turkey "can overcome the strong prejudices of the American people against accepting any mandate." [81]

The same day the Morgenthau Memorandum was submitted, the British in the Supreme Council indicated a fear that Greek and Italian military measures might renew war in the Near East. Conscious of the Muslim outcry in India against severity toward the Sultan's government, the British Prime Minister that day advocated the theme of Morgenthau, Washburn, and Gates. Not mellowed by his eighty years, Clemenceau retorted angrily; the wrinkled French Premier, wearing his black skull cap, suspected an Anglo-American collaboration to lock France out of the Near East. After Clemenceau's outburst, Wilson calmly said he felt that it would be better not to divide Anatolia, yet was uncertain whether the Republicans would permit a United States mandate over Asia Minor. But he was unequivocable about Armenia according to the official interpreter at the session: "I will examine the question [of a mandate over Asia Minor]; but it seems impossible that America will accept this mandate. But she will take the Armenian mandate for humanitarian reasons. Americans have already sent missionaries, money, and relief to Armenia. American opinion is interested in Armenia." [82] (Colonel House had asked Hoover about becoming Armenia's governor.) On the morrow House, in a message to the President, did not incorporate Morgenthau's theory and showed that both he and Wilson had had some ideal desires taken out of them in regard to the Ottoman Empire. House presumed Greece in Smyrna, Italy in Adalia, France in Cilicia and Syria, and Britain in Mesopotamia and Palestine. As for Armenia, Constantinople, and a Nestorian region in southeastern Asia Minor, he left open the naming of mandate powers. [83]

◄ ►

Setting up a Near East of "permanent peace," to use Dodge's phrase, was not turning out to be so simple that waving the Fourteen Points would get the job done. Instead of missionaries seeing Heaven, they were smelling Hell. Not serenity but confusion was reigning in Paris; peacemakers suffered trauma as old and new orders butted each other. Both the American Peace Commission and the Protestant contingent found that a speedy, united approach to the Near East was ephemeral.

Chapter 8

Commissions amid Conflicts

THE month of May 1919 was a pivotal time in the missionary effort for American mandates over peoples in the Near East. Before this month the Protestants had not had one reversal of import in their ever-enlarging philanthropic and government enterprises. Then they discovered they could not brake and redirect inertia from the past century as much as they had thought. Usually optimistic, they became baffled as their opponents advanced old-style imperialism. They wondered as never before if their goals would be possible. Yet there were things to come which encouraged them: the King-Crane Commission and two other commissions to Turkey led by Americans, the Harbord and Haskell missions.

CAESAR AND GOD

A reason why the mission leaders could not deal easily with forces arrayed against them was their awkwardness over being in public affairs. The month of May 1919 might not have been so deflating to their ambitions if they could have acted during the Paris Conference without scruples about separation of Church and State.

A feeling of maladroitness appeared in remarks of W. E. Strong, editor of the *Missionary Herald*. In a letter to Barton in January 1919, he had said: "Don't allow yourself to get mixed up in politics or diplomacy, but if you do, make sure that the American Board gets a place in the sun." And again: "Now that Kaiser Bill has been dethroned from his lordship over the Ottoman Empire, how would Woodrow do for a successor? Mrs. Wilson might be glad to consort with the Sultan and his ladies at Constantinople and Woodrow certainly would be interested in the missionary side of the case." [1] The question, as Strong well knew, was serious. Realizing that the First World War had brought a unique American Board–government connection, he maintained in the *Missionary Herald* that the attitude of the Board toward international relations was aloofness. He protested that the Board had never gotten into the mud of intrigue but had kept to moral tasks. Public matters, the *Herald* said, were outside the Board's province. Yet the American Board was quick to recognize that when military moves disturbed boundaries of mankind, the missionary and his influence were often brought out into the light. [2]

The *Herald* admitted that reports had circulated about the Board's meddling in politics. The periodical probably was alluding to negative talk in Congregational churches about three missionaries who, during the Peace Conference, had sought a United States defense of Bulgarian and Albanian interests. One of the individuals had become an official Albanian representative to the Paris deliberations. Prompted by constituents' alarm over disclosure of this behavior, the Board executive committee in May 1919 disciplined the three missionaries. At the same time the committee advised Barton in Turkey that it was hesitant about openly promoting Armenian freedom. [3]

Declaring that the Board was trying to be neutral about territory where its personnel were, the *Missionary Herald* simultaneously acknowledged that the task was not easy. The editorialist at this point undoubtedly was thinking of the Ottoman Empire, and his ambivalence was clear. He insisted that foreign missions and world politics were unlike, but nevertheless were mutually dependent, since Christianity had a bearing upon national and international life.

Political uncertainty and inspirational certainty. Fluctuations between these emotions bothered Barton and his mission associates. Preserving thousands among Christian minorities through relief allowed their consciences to say *yes* about being in politics. Using the American Committee for Relief in the Near East to request United States mandates in Turkey was a cultural and religious imperialism which probably prompted their

187

consciences to say *maybe* as well as *yes*. Recompensing the Armenian massacres: yes. Hating Turkish officialdom: maybe. For nonprofessional Christians like Wilson, Dodge, Crane, and Judson to have prominence in public matters was right; for American and Presbyterian board executives to do the same things was not so proper.

Jesus' enigmatic "Render therefore unto Caesar the things which are Caesar's and to God the things which are God's" was a reason for the Protestants' imprecise line between Christianity and public activity. That there should be two different types of institutions — one giving priority to the civil and the other to the religious area — had never been in doubt either in theory or in practice within most of Western civilization since Saint Augustine. Ambiguity had of course arisen over trying to identify the function of each type; this imprecision had nurtured various methods for relating Christ and culture, from a Pope's forcing a Holy Roman Emperor in rags to demonstrate penitence by standing in the snow for several days, to an Emperor's incarcerating a Holy Father. In the English New World colonies there had been some contention between Church and State, but probably more friction between tax-bolstered Puritans or Anglicans and the independent sects. During the decades from George Whitefield in the Great Awakening to Charles Finney in the Second Awakening, the sects converted many people to an evangelical faith of revivalism and social reform.[4] Revivalists helped overthrow legal but advocated cultural establishmentarianism. European nations in the nineteenth century witnessed a decline of active participation by baptized adherents within state churches. The United States at the same time witnessed increasing numbers of people voluntarily becoming active members within a plethora of free, revivalistic churches.

The conditioning of the missionaries to the Near East contained values of an unofficial, fluid denominationalism and of a Protestant society (the second aim dated from the Massachusetts Bay Colony's design for a Puritan Zion). Informally, American churchmen and their denominations had influenced the government process through religious sanction of public decisions and through creation of expectations which the government helped fulfil (the Social Gospel was a major element in the Progressivism of Presidents Roosevelt, Taft, and Wilson). These expectations led to such matters as tax-paid chaplains, religious oaths in court, and establishment of the Thanksgiving holiday. Basically, what majority Christian sentiment had done was to create the idea of a Protestant America.[5]

188

Yet in the writings of Barton and other religionists the line between Caesar and God never disappeared. For them the free Church, not the State, was most important. Protestant leaders were never advocates of a formal national religion. They wanted a supranational Christian community. Further, they did not forget, although sometimes repressed, that Protestant America was a mixed culture from which evil (American Board Secretary Cornelius Patton's recognition of lynchings and commercial greed) as well as good radiated to the world. It simply happened that in the early twentieth century missionary and national interests overlapped considerably.[6]

Tugs within missionaries during the First World War toward overtness in politics became stronger, aided by a general American blurring of God and country. Social Gospel theology in 1912 put forth *Christianizing the Social Order*, by Walter Rauschenbusch. It was not a long step from Rauschenbusch's theme to Patton's view that a world transformation was about to start through a Christian America which had revoked isolationism. Protestants previously had established sanctuaries and classrooms throughout the American frontier and had attacked Demon Rum. There was a heady idealism that foreign "devils" (Islamic practicers) as well as domestic demon rum were candidates for exorcism. A resurgent nativism shouted slogans about 100 per cent Americanism. These slogans were a way to slow immigration of non-Protestant peoples and to solidify an Anglo-Saxon United States. Native-born Protestants were finding it almost impossible to assimilate Roman Catholic ghettoes in the cities. Clergymen, partly out of guilt because of schisms in their ranks before and during the Civil War, injected a divine sanction into this nationalism during the years 1917 and 1918; they made America's cause into God's cause, as detailed earlier. Extreme Protestant nativists so vilified Huns that at least one German-born resident of the United States was lynched; German Americans erased many of their place names (New Berlin in Ohio became North Canton) and watched helplessly as propagandists changed sauerkraut to liberty cabbage. Impulses of patriotism and Christianity were nearly synonymous. Little wonder that the missionaries did not find it too uncomfortable pressing the government about the Ottoman Empire.[7]

In what was almost a national revival campaign, Barton and his companions put aside their normal hesitation about pushing Washington. Two factors, in addition to those discussed, helped them to let down their restraint. They linked ideas of suffering, Christian Armenia and co-redemp-

189

tive America. Choosing these theological rather than secular terms helped reduce the wall between Church and State. Also, the Wilson-Dodge friendship made no sharp distinction between the Progressive cry about battling for the Lord and the forays of politicians. In their letters biblical and public-affairs words intertwined.

With so many incentives pulling toward matters of State, mission and relief individuals facilitated a series of developments: Ottoman-American neutrality, the Armenian-American Committee and the ACIA, the Barton federation plan sent to The Inquiry, the Judson-directed Persian Commission, the Barton Relief Commission, the Bliss plan leading to the short-lived Barton Inquiry to Syria and to the International Commission on Mandates in Turkey, the scheme of Gates for a United States mandate over Asia Minor, the Morgenthau Memorandum, and the willingness of Wilson and House for the United States to take mandates over Armenia and Constantinople.

Traditional hesitations about politics deterred the missionaries and philanthropists from contesting unabashedly in public. (Barton often had to work through Morgenthau and Bryce.) Typically these people demonstrated nervousness about being in politics. Their standard, defensive phraseology was that mission and relief activities were strictly neutral and nonpolitical, not tainted with ulterior motives or territorial ambitions.[8]

Realizing large handicaps, as compared to aspirations, Barton thought he could best affect a Peace Conference decision on the Near East by going abroad in January 1919. His naiveté did not reckon with the old order and the lethargy of the Supreme Council. By leaving both Boston headquarters and then Paris, Barton removed one of the best possibilities the Protestant interests had to correlate their strategy. Such missionaries as Bliss, Gates, and MacLachlan and such accomplices as Crane, Morgenthau, Bryce, Lybyer, and Washburn were at the Peace Conference at staggered times, did faulty planning together, often conflicted. Disagreement among Armenophiles even became nasty in the way the ACIA's Gerard castigated Gates' notion about Asia Minor. Gates noted that pro-Armenian Americans denounced him for being pro-Turk. The Morgenthau Memorandum implied that a consensus about Asia Minor among people backing both the ACIA and Gates was imperative for the Protestant future in Turkey: "The large missionary and educational interests of the United States in Anatolia must be protected, and it is illusory to imagine that this can be done if Anatolia is subjected to Greek, French, or Italian sovereignty." [9]

By May 1919 the chance for close identity among evangelistic, educational, relief, and Armenian-American groups had become slight. Successful politics possibly was a load heavier than the mission-relief groups could carry.

PROCRASTINATING CONFERENCES

Another problem for the mission-ACRNE people had been the Supreme Council's continual postponement of the Near East settlement. The Protestants had agonized over the slow pace of peacemaking. Bliss in February 1919 had requested that the Council should lose no time in sending an international inquiry. Equally urgent and contrary to Bliss, Gates in retrospect wrote that the Peace Conference drug things by proposing an investigation, which would take at least three months. From Turkey, Barton begged Paris to take the initiative. In late March he appealed to House for early action in France because each class in Turkey desired it and because Turkish conditions were deteriorating. A few days later Barton reported that there was a universal feeling that Paris would have to deal soon with the Ottoman Empire to avoid a bad situation. Sensing the explosiveness of a hundred thousand or so Armenian refugees in Syria, he insisted that all ethnic groups wanted a quick definition of Allied terms. In his last message to House before Wilson left the Conference, he pleaded for drastic, immediate decisions to prevent dangerous complications.[10]

There were broad tensions which militated against the speedy negotiation sought by missionaries. Europe was declining in relative importance. The United States and Soviet Russia — agreeing on the need for a new diplomacy but diverging sharply between plans for a confederation of democratic states and a Communist International — were rising toward world dominance. These two nations represented the large, emerging confrontation between have and have-not societies. Further, the Allied and Associated Powers at great risk forbade Germany and Russia to attend the Conference (at the end of the Napoleonic wars, France had joined in the Congress of Vienna after completion of its preliminary treaty and had taken responsibility for a European peace which lasted without major reorganization for a century). Traditional institutions had been unable to control social and political results of the nineteenth century's technological and imaginal revolutions. This lack of control had made possible history's first total war and had shattered the German, Austro-Hungarian, Russian, and Ottoman dynastic relics from a medieval past. Widespread violence in

Central and Eastern Europe during the "Peace" Conference was a symbol of the world's tensions. (An observer at Paris said it was fitting that the number of "wars" in the spring of 1919 which used cannon had grown to fourteen, one for each of Wilson's Fourteen Points.) All these conflicts were amplified by a world press.

Another factor prolonging deliberation was disagreement about how the Fourteen Points fitted Europe's needs. Great Britain wanted primarily to keep a balance of power on the continent so that no strong state could challenge its domination of the seas and its Empire. France desired a Franco-Anglo-American alliance to ensure against another war with Germany. Implicit in these Allied ideas was Britain's soft and France's hard line toward Germany, a gap making difficult an understanding among the victors. In regard to clashes with President Wilson over Paris' aims, Clemenceau reportedly remarked testily that "The Almighty gave us Ten Commandments, but Wilson has given us Fourteen," and that Wilson thought he was "Jesus Christ come upon the earth to reform men." [11] Recognizing some truth in these comments, House believed the President was stubborn and unreasonable. (Wilson's adherence to principle and over-simplified approach to economic matters irritated some people.) House often overlooked the parochialness of Clemenceau and Lloyd George. Impelled by an extravagant nationalism producing votes of confidence before the Peace Conference, the Allied leaders demanded Carthaginian peace features (unreasonable reparations). Prophetically, Wilson resisted. The President bucked the old diplomacy so well that he assisted a closer resemblance between ethnographic and political maps than had existed in modern history.

Deliberation on all these issues was terribly slow, helping Wilson become violently ill in the first week of April. He had severe coughing spasms, a temperature of one hundred three, diarrhea, and what probably was a mild stroke. Earlier in 1906 he had temporarily lost the sight of his left eye as a result of hypertension and an apparent attack of arteriosclerosis.[12]

It appears that Wilson's passion for Point Fourteen (on the league idea) had a direct bearing both on decreasing his resistance to illness and on deferring answers to the Eastern Question. From arrival at Paris until mid-February 1919, he worked triumphantly to write the Covenant and to see its inclusion in each of the peace treaties. At the same time he altered the secret treaties by the mandate scheme. Then he was jolted by the Round Robin, circulated among Republican Senators in America with whom he had not been communicating. The Round Robin declared that the Covenant was unacceptable as proposed; Wilson obtained revisions, such as one safeguarding the Monroe Doctrine. To him a Senatorial approval of the League and its mandate system was the route to United States mandates in Armenia and Constantinople. He believed the League of prime import and Near East matters secondary.

Wilson's insistence on the precedence of the untried League was too inflexible. His approach stressed political reform at the top of the traditional state structure. He neglected harmful economic competition in the West, and regional security arrangements. Admittedly, the President helped anticipate the North Atlantic Treaty Organization by grudgingly signing a guarantee treaty with Clemenceau which promised American intervention in case of an unprovoked German aggression and which was to remain in effect until superseded by League of Nations' decisions. Senator Lodge and other Republicans inclined to favor such a pact. (Wilson would so tardily submit the Guarantee Treaty to the Senate that it would not have a chance to pass during the heated ratification debates about the Covenant.) The League goal probably would have been better as equal to rather than paramount above a Western alliance system, tariff reductions, domestic reforms in Western nations, and speedy adjustment of the Near East.[18]

Both an agenda for the Conference and a preliminary treaty could have accelerated decisions. Wilson's stress upon the League helped prevent these procedures. The President disdained a preliminary treaty because he felt that this traditional tactic would help the Allies violate his principles. Also, he had not used the large applause from Western audiences to push an agenda. His prestige in December 1918 was at its height. The Fourteen Points were the agreed basis among Allies and their enemies for peace talks. There was as yet almost no tarnish on his diplomatic armor. With both the opportunity and duty for this kind of leadership in negotiation, he did not press for what was probably the best means for bargaining. The Conference of some thirty nations, fifty commissions, a thousand delegates and experts, stumbled along with no clear agenda, no preliminary peace, no groups which dealt with overall affairs. The Supreme Council, having to pound out compromise in ad hoc fashion as one unrelated topic after another came to it, engaged in ponderous discussion. The Council became a fantastic bottleneck and put an almost inhuman strain on its members.

Another factor contributing to procrastination was disunity among Wilson, Lansing, and House. On the *George Washington* steaming to Europe, the President and his Secretary of State held only one session together. Lansing did not "worship" the League "idol" which Wilson was sculpturing. Nor did Lansing get excited about an Armenian mandate. Wanting a quick preliminary treaty before fashioning the League Covenant, the Secretary prepared a skeleton document and claimed that Wilson did not even glance at it; Lansing felt like resigning.[14] Pre-Conference lack of communication between The Inquiry and the State Department reflected itself at Paris. Through Sidney Mezes and a private staff, House operated independently of the American Peace Commission; he became an increasingly less loyal presidential aide by attempting to be a mediator between Wilson and the Allies. Bemoaning a lack of openness within the Peace Commission, its secretary Joseph Grew stated: "Our right hand does not know what the left is doing. Colonel House never attends the daily meetings of the Commissioners [led by Lansing] and his office frequently takes action unknown to them."[15] Wilson aggravated disorganization by rarely taking the commissioners into his confidence (he did, however, consult many of his technicians). During one period of ten days he did not speak to Lansing. He found it hard to take counsel on substantive issues. These muddled conditions helped Wilson put off many decisions, including those concerning the Ottoman Empire.

Semi-isolated from his commissioners, Wilson assisted in a blunder of Olympian proportions for both the Protestants to Turkey and himself through his failure to resist the Greek landing at Smyrna. And as late as the President's departure from France in June, American technician William Westermann still did not understand the President's program for the Near East. Westermann then wanted specific guidance on the United States part in the Turkish treaty.[16]

Although House did much to hurt efficient work among Americans, he realized that delay was harming the cause of the missionaries in the Ottoman Empire. In March he began trying to push completion of all the treaties at once. Soon he noted that King and Crane had been appointed to the International Commission and were awaiting an explanation of their task. "There is no one to give the word, and so it is with innumerable other matters," he told his diary. "It could be done so easily that it is maddening to see the days go by and nothing decided."[17] At the end of May he regarded it nearly impossible to prevent foreboding events in Turkey and elsewhere that were issuing from procrastination.

A query lingers. Why did Wilson put off the Ottoman settlement, partic-

ularly since Lansing, House, the experts, and mission and relief spokesmen all agreed on a speedy transaction? To repeat, concern for the League
Covenant absorbed the President. Then, too, the Big Three assumed that
the German treaty should come first and the Ottoman and other treaties
second, even though there were ample signs that Turkey with its unoccupied Anatolia needed a solution. Another factor which for a while did not
detract from the President's slowness, was Lloyd George's crafty toying
with Clemenceau about French troops replacing British in Syria. London
and Paris had been aggressive colonial competitors for decades. The Prime
Minister used the edge provided by thousands of British soldiers encamped
in the Near East to make Britain the arbiter between France and the
United States. But the Prime Minister during the Adalia and Smyrna crises
became serious. He repeatedly asked Wilson to accept mandates in Anatolia and often pushed for a comprehensive solution in the Ottoman Empire. The President hedged, saying that these choices should not "be settled in a hurry." [18]

Possibly the largest reason for Wilson's hesitation related to his political
situation at home. He frankly told the Supreme Council that his uncertainty concerned the imponderables of anti-Turkish opinion and Republican
opposition. Well should he have been uneasy, for in a sense he was attempting to speak at Paris for an America which had repudiated him in the
Congressional elections of November 1918. He had compounded this
weakening of his position by refusing to have Republican Senators represented at France, by not keeping the Senate informed, and by implying
publicly that this body's desire to amend his Covenant was ignorant and
selfish. Probably he feared that individuals irreconcilably against the
League and against other transatlantic duties would use a formal presidential agreement to take an Armenian mandate to blast the Covenant. He
waited, therefore, thinking that when he returned to the United States he
could rally the citizenry to a Near East duty after the Senate had consented
to the League Treaty.[19]

There was evidence among his countrymen that such a postponement
on an Armenian mandate might not work. The wind of chauvinism (including Turkophobia) which had helped the ACRNE and its Armenianism
zoom upward was changing directions. Lyrics in this new, less-crusading
sentiment were being sung by the doughboys in Europe: [20]

> We drove the Boche across the Rhine,
> The Kaiser from his throne,

> Oh, Lafayette, we've paid our debt,
> For Christ's sake, send us home.

Republican Senator William E. Borah of Idaho stepped to the same cadence as the returning soldiers. Leader of a small band of fifteen Senators, Borah was a more-than-100-per-cent American. He fervently preached that his ocean-guarded land should build a wall around its Eden, to make it secure from the gnashing of teeth outside. He was ready to offer his life to assail what he believed was the treasonable, unpatriotic Covenant. Borah also was the most important supporter of Senator Lodge's method of delaying a Senate judgment about the Covenant, for whose passage the President was waiting before pushing a mandate. On the side of Borah's battalion in the Senate was isolationism, one of America's most long-established beliefs. Wilson apparently did not see that battles between imperial and nationalist forces in Turkey could stir American isolationists to oppose rigidly any American embroilment in Old World machinations.

Hindsight indicates that the month of May 1919 was probably the best period for Wilson to have moved toward his desire for American mandates. Occupation of Armenia and Constantinople by United States soldiers would not have met a crystallized Turkish nationalism. Precedents for such an act were Wilson's sending the Army into Mexico and into Russia. Senator Lodge, who was to become Wilson's arch protagonist, had not yet shut the door to a mandate over Armenia. A tangible, properly publicized duty by the United States in Asia Minor, as well as the intangible League responsibility, could have advanced pro-Covenant ranks more than retarded them in the ratification controversy to come.

The Greeks' disembarkment at Smyrna on May 15 and the attendant violence gave the impression to missionaries and other observers that force might prevail over prolonged talk. The leading feminist among Turks, Halidé Edib, was nearly in a trance after the Greek attack upon her co-nationals. She delivered speech after speech to stunned, indignant crowds looking for a way to express their revulsion with Allied methods. Robert College's Gates believed excessive Armenian claims, let alone Greek ones, were so exasperating to Turks as to make imminent the extermination of all Christians. Barton felt that deliberators in Paris were losing out to events in Asia Minor. He reported to United States officials that the weak Ottoman government was not halting atrocities to the Armenians and was content to have refugees remain in exile. In sympathy with cowed and terror-smitten Armenians, he said the future of Anatolia would be as the

Turks desired unless the Conference acted. Barton felt that the enemy of Armenia was not so much the Turks as postponement.

Delay, increased by conflict between the ideal and the possible, gradually brought disillusion on many who had expected clear skies in a new Near East and indeed a world safe for democracy. When the Supreme Council accepted the Covenant, letdown had not yet come for Barton. He had exulted: "Wilson's ideas are beginning to walk on the ground." [21] Soon Albert Lybyer experienced disgust at the seething intrigues in Paris; disputing for territory in Turkey, the West appeared to be entering upon a peace to end peace. Charles Crane felt man's helpless inadequacy to reach conclusions by rational processes while in the cauldron of political revolution. Peace seemed impossible to many delegates, no matter how many clauses they wrote. An American expert believed pessimism was rampant everywhere. Seeing the peoples of Europe and the Near East shedding tears for bread, Secretary Lansing said the Conference was giving them the League stone instead. House did not feel that the German treaty was a good one. Gates said in his memoirs that the Paris situation left him heartsick. He felt like praying: Good Lord, deliver us from wars and procrastinating peace conferences. An observer captured the prevalent mood by the following declaration: God is making His own treaty.[22]

DARK AND LIGHT MEAT

Some sunlight penetrated the delay. Advocates of the Bliss-initiated International Commission on Mandates in Turkey had not given up after King and Crane were stalled by Clemenceau, Gates, Westermann, and the Zionists. On May 20, House both talked with King, who felt like disbanding the investigation, and received a letter from Feisal's delegation. The letter said that the Supreme Council's honor would be at stake if it did not send the inquiry. The same day House "told the President it was something of a scandal that this commission had not already gone to Syria as promised the Arabs. . . . I then suggested that he set Monday as the time when our commission would start regardless of the French and English. He adopted the suggestion and said he would tell Clemenceau and Lloyd George tomorrow." [23]

The subject came up in the Council. Allied leaders countered Wilson's request for the inquiry to depart by a circumlocution. Lloyd George agreed that the investigation leave at once, but not until the French appointed commissioners. Clemenceau refused to name commissioners until French troops took the place of British in Syria. Lloyd George did not intend to withdraw British soldiers, yet he wanted the inquiry to go.[24]

Impatient with this circular artifice (House once compared Lloyd George to a weathervane) and stimulated by a cable from Feisal, Wilson determined on a solely American investigation. King and Crane on May 22 went to the President for instructions. King properly felt that the Peace Conference had reached a point where it should make selections of mandates in the Turkish Empire and discontinue the International Commission. The inquiry should go, King believed, only if it could do something that the Supreme Council had not decided or would not do before he and Crane had finished their study. Wilson replied that he desired direct information about the preferences of people, declaring that data uncovered could change mandates if necessary.

The President's longings had overcome him. His tentative acceptance of the partitioning of Anatolia on May 14, and the Smyrna affair, were probably impossible to undo. He knew that a King-Crane inquiry would encourage Syrians, Armenians, and other ethnic communities to expect American protection and that United States opinion was ill-prepared for that wish. He apparently hoped that an investigation would increase support for his principles and restrain a colonial adjustment of the Ottoman problem.[25]

Lybyer heard about the President's ideas within minutes after the end of the King-Crane-Wilson session and cried "Electrification!" The former Robert College professor had been an irrepressible promoter of the inquiry for weeks and had written most of King's memoranda. Lybyer's excitement came partly because he wanted to be an administrator in a mandate in Anatolia.

Satisfied that an American commission would have an important part in answering the Eastern Question, King sat down with House. The two men discussed "the dark meat and the light meat of the Turkey." [26] The Oberlin president talked about a note on the Ottoman Empire he had left with Wilson the day before. Lybyer had prepared this note, and the King-Crane group had expressed much of its content to Wilson over three weeks earlier. Gates, perhaps more than any other person, had shaped its propositions, which paralleled the Morgenthau Memorandum. The note urged a United States policy toward the Near East which included no European splitting of Anatolia but an American fourfold mandate over the non-

Arabic portion of Turkey (Armenia, Turkish Asia Minor, Smyrna, and Constantinople); British mandates in Mesopotamia, Palestine, Arabia; a French mandate in Syria.

Long after the demise of the Barton Inquiry and Bliss' appearance before the Supreme Council, members of the King-Crane section of the International Commission finally were ready for their odyssey. From the Bosporus Admiral Bristol cabled the United States delegation in France that the inquiry would be a safeguard against bloodshed. He stated that Turks and Americans in the Ottoman Empire almost unanimously favored a mandate by the United States over the entire country. As the investigation was about to leave Paris for Constantinople, Morgenthau intimated to the press that the King-Crane expedition would lead to an American mandate in Asia Minor. He hinted to friends that he might seek a mandate post.

After King and his companions departed with Wilson's "God-speed" sounding in their ears, the Big Four continued to discuss the International Commission. With British designates still thinking of joining the American group, the Supreme Council on May 31 remained deadlocked over French occupation of Syria. Lloyd George, afraid of appearing to be an anti-French conspirator, then dropped the idea of sending his representatives. The touchy Clemenceau had never formally appointed French commissioners and smiled over his obstruction of an international inquiry.

Of the nine individuals on the King-Crane Commission, all but two had an important relation to the Protestant enterprise in the Near East. Five were Congregational or Presbyterian clergymen — Henry King, Albert Lybyer (general technical adviser), George Montgomery (technical adviser for the northern regions of the Empire), Laurence Moore, and Donald Brodie (secretary). Brodie was a former student of King's. Moore had taught at Robert College from 1904 to 1908. Montgomery was a son of missionaries to Turkey. Lybyer had many connections with the ACRNE and the missionaries. Congregationalist King had, at Oberlin College two years before, conferred an honorary degree upon Barton and knew much about the American Board program in Asia Minor.[27] Sami Haddad, a physician and instructor at the Syrian Protestant College, was the Arabic interpreter. Charles Crane, the philanthropist who liked missionary educators and served as president of the board for Constantinople Woman's College, departed France early for commencement at this mission school. Incidentally, Crane had been instrumental in the Fourteen Points' advo-

199

cating autonomy within the Austro-Hungarian Empire, partly because he was a financial backer of the Czech leader, Tomaš Masaryk (a son of Masaryk's married Crane's daughter). Crane would be minister to China in 1920 and 1921. In his latter years he extended his mark upon international relations by founding the Institute of Current World Affairs with a two-million-dollar endowment, out of which came the American Universities Field Staff. The two men on the King-Crane Commission without close ties to missionaries were William Yale (technical adviser for the southern regions of the Empire) and Paul Toren.

The inquiry spent a few days at the mission colleges and the American embassy in Constantinople. Walter George Smith of the Barton Relief Commission talked with Crane. Writing in his journal, Smith noted that the investigation would recommend a "plan for maintaining the integrity of the Empire as advocated by Dr. Gates and others." [28]

From June 10 to July 21 the group went to nearly forty cities, from Jaffa and Jerusalem in the south to Tarsus and Adana in the north, from Amman and Damascus in the east to Beirut along the coast. Using eight "mechanical camels" (Ford cars) secured from the ACRNE and the British Army, the Americans jolted over more than a thousand miles of rocks and sand. They visited such people as General Allenby (who liked the idea of a United States mandate over greater Syria, which included Palestine), the Emir Feisal, local officials, American relief workers in Adana. (The relief workers were succoring twenty thousand returned Armenians while being bothered by swarms of mosquitoes.) Although receiving 1,863 petitions from over fifteen hundred locations and meeting hundreds of delegations, commission members also had time for visiting mosques and bazaars, seeing a sword dance, and riding some wild Bedouin steeds into Amman (in the mad gallop Lybyer lost his helmet and glasses). (See Map 5 on page 148.)

Crane sentimentally wrote that it was dramatic to hear the Arabs' Americanism: "it will be tragic to disappoint them in any material degree." [29] Of course, he knew that parties were maneuvering for advantage. Feisal and other Arab nationalists early in July held at Damascus what they called the Syrian Congress, which adopted a statement demanding Arab independence under Feisal as king, condemning the Allied secret treaties and the Balfour Declaration, rejecting a mandate by any nation (especially France), asking assistance from Britain or the United States. The Arab prince, growingly anti-French and wary of the British, pathetically cabled Wilson: "I earnestly beg you not to leave me between the paws of the devourers." [30] Clemenceau's government squirmed because of the Syrian Congress, using suppressive tactics in Lebanon to give the appearance of a pro-French attitude there. William Yale would later write that it was inevitable that the sending of the King-Crane Commission would "foster sectarian animosities, intensify antagonisms, and increase the friction between French and Arabs, and between French and British." [31] Actions by the French in Lebanon, among other factors, made Yale and George Montgomery feel it was unrealistic to reject a French mandate. They reacted this way despite evidence that most Arabs trusted America because of ACRNE aid, the Syrian Protestant College, reports from Arab immigrants in the United States, and Wilson's principles. Other commission members felt as Crane did and disagreed with Yale and Montgomery.

Lybyer believed an American mandate over a greater Syria, which would not include a Jewish homeland, might be the one reasonable solution. The King-Crane group on July 10 sent a preliminary report to Wilson along the lines of Lybyer's idea. The United States was genuinely the first choice for a mandate of most people interviewed, the message stated. Allied officers believed that the unity of Arabs along the eastern Mediterranean was desirable. Crane sent a separate letter to the President which showed the tie of the inquiry to missionaries: there was in Syria better "raw material" than the United States had in the Philippine Islands twenty years earlier, he wrote, and asked Wilson to check with Bliss to see if the educator's conclusions tallied with the Commission's. [32]

Back on the Bosporus late in July and housed at Constantinople Woman's College, the King-Crane Commission met with Barton. The American Board secretary advised the Commission, as instructed by the American peace delegation at the time of the Barton Inquiry's demise. (Barton after the relief trip to Armenia had been sick with dysentery on a United States hospital ship at Constantinople during late May and June; then he had been in Bulgaria for a week early in July. Using a destroyer provided by Bristol, Barton next had visited relief personnel and missionaries in Smyrna and various parts of Greece.) Arriving in the Turkish capital about the same time as King and Crane, the mission secretary telegraphically summarized a discussion with the commissioners about Syria: "Syrians oppose French . . . supporting R.C.'s. [Catholics] abroad for purely political motives. . . . Superficial Ed. without character bldg. French irreligious and immoral literature. . . . Bribery worse than under the Turk. Financial exploitation of colonies." [33] Barton's note implied that a part of the motive for Bliss' diplomacy in Paris had been fear of French Catholic educational competition to the Syrian Protestant College (such fear had been common in the history of ecclesiastical rivalry between American Protestants and French Catholics). Eager for suggestions, King and Crane on August 3 had a long conference with Barton and Peet. These two missionaries urged the Commission to recommend guarantees for integral Armenia. Crane felt this and other counsel was wise; King and Crane then announced to the Turkish press that the Supreme Council in Paris had resolved Armenia should be separate from Turkey. Lybyer noted that Barton thought the Commission had the power to settle the fate of the Ottoman Empire. In the American Board secretary's mind, the fate would assuredly involve the United States. [34]

Barton and Peet soon left the Straits for the Caucasus; the King-Crane inquiry remained and received testimony from other Protestants. All these religionists wanted American internationalism in the Ottoman Empire to be governmental as well as missionary and philanthropic. Gates' proposals circulated in Turkey at the time although their author was in the United States. From Paris Mary Patrick of Constantinople Woman's College sent instructions to her college personnel to do everything possible to please the board chairman, Crane. Miss Patrick sent to the commission her fourteen reasons for an American mandate over Turkey. One of her reasons was that a United States mandate would produce an outstanding school system. Sympathetic to this notion as an exuberant financial backer of education in the Near East, Crane during the inquiry's time on the Woman's College campus promised to subsidize the expenses of several Albanian girls. He also told Edgar Fisher of Robert College that he would continue to aid Albanian students there. Then a missionary alumna of King's Oberlin College, Miss Mary Graffam, who had remained in the interior through the war, testified about the impossibility of keeping Armenians and Turks together peacefully. Miss Graffam noted that only ten to twenty thousand Armenians had come back to the Sivas region out of a former population of eighty thousand. The president of the American Board's Anatolia College at Merzifon, George White, appeared before the Commission. White spoke out against Turkish independence anywhere, saying Ottoman officialdom had been incapable of anything but exploitation. Having just met Mustafa Kemal, he believed the Turkish mentor was instigating his countrymen to battle Armenians and Greeks. White desired a United States mandate over a free Armenia without delay, over Constantinople and the rest of Asia Minor if possible.[35]

These missionary words of midsummer 1919 showed well both the consensus and divergence among the Protestants in Turkey. There was agreement that an American mandate in Anatolia was good and that procrastination was bad, but disagreement on a territorial stress. Barton, Peet, White, and Miss Graffam, who had worked almost exclusively with Christian minorities, thought a free Armenia was almost a God-sanctioned end. Miss Patrick and Gates, who served Turks and Albanians as well as Armenians and Greeks, saw the justice of an Asia Minor of mixed peoples remaining intact. The educational view from the Bosporus differed from the relief perspective in central and eastern Asia Minor.

Nonmissionary Americans talked with King and Crane. Bristol, by then United States high commissioner at the Porte, thought the Greek landing at Smyrna had been a large error, giving initiative to Turkish hotheads, and that Greeks and Italians deserved no part of Anatolia. He believed the United States should take a mandate over the entire Ottoman Empire and should educate its scrambled masses in self-rule for the sake of peace there and throughout the world. This broad scheme, advocated as well by American Consul General Gabriel Bie Ravndal, was much like the Barton federation plan.

During the first two weeks of August, the King-Crane Commission received a hodgepodge of ethnic delegations whose ambitions conflicted extremely. Greek groups desired sovereignty for Greece around Smyrna; radicals among them asked for Constantinople. Both Nestorians and Kurds wanted separate nationhood in the same region of eastern Anatolia. Armenians generally sought an integral nation with American tutelage, also in eastern Anatolia.

The Turks, the largest in numbers throughout Asia Minor, did not concur with any of the other groups. The Turkish leaders who spoke before King and Crane — usually Westernized ex-government officials, journalists, and professors residing in the capital — feared European imperialism. They liked Wilson's Point Twelve, which mentioned self-determination for the Turks. Willingly acknowledging the Ottoman Empire's sound defeat in the war, they wanted foreign help. Probably three fourths of them preferred a mandate by the United States, some liked a British mandate, none wanted a French, Greek, or Italian mandate. Among these

Turks were members of the Wilsonian League. Professor Hussein Bey of Robert College was a Wilsonian League founder and an agitator for an American mandate (Hussein, one of the first Muslim graduates of Robert, later became its vice-president). Some groups speaking to the Commission wanted to maintain the full Ottoman Empire (as had compatriots who had appeared on June 17 before the Supreme Council at Paris). Most of them, though, approved the severance of Arab-speaking areas. A few admitted that a free Armenia was proper compensation for the massacres. Many either desired to keep Armenia small and close to the Russian border, since they believed an integral Armenia would be a violation of Wilsonian self-determination, or wanted no free Armenia since the Christian minority no longer included more than twenty per cent of the population anywhere.

The famous alumna of Constantinople Woman's College, Halidé Edib (a member of the Wilsonian League), translated for several Turkish delegations, learning to know King and Crane. Previously, as noted, she had addressed crowds of her countrymen and captured their nearly religious, fervid belief that Greek occupation of Smyrna had violated Wilson's Point Twelve. She felt shame about the Armenian massacres, yet excused them as military necessity. Writing Kemal, she stated that an American mandate might be the "least harmful solution" to Turkey's problems; she used Crane's argument that the United States could do in Turkey what it had already done in the Philippines.[36]

King and Crane showed understanding of the emotion which had swayed Turks after the Smyrna incident. But like other Westerners, they dimly perceived the Kemalist form of this emotion. During the Commission's trip to Syria in June and July, the movement under Kemal had become the most cohesive expression of Turkish nationalism. The Kemalists had conducted a congress from July 23 to August 17 in an unpretentious schoolroom in Erzurum. A Kemalist delegation talked to King and Crane at the Bosporus and asked for a United States mandate over the entire Ottoman Empire. Many individuals at the Erzurum Congress desired an American mandate (one called it the "gilded pill of the moment"). At the same time Kemal and most of his colleagues were leary of the Armenianism of both the United States government and the missionary-led ACRNE. Kemal occasionally sent instructions to followers in Constantinople to talk there about an American mandate. This probably was a ploy to gain time to offset Allied power. The most Kemal apparently wanted from the

United States was aid. The Erzurum Congress eventually resolved an independent, unpartitioned Turkish Empire with no millets, no mandates. The Sultan's government at the Porte tried to slow down the nationalist movement in Asia Minor, first by ordering Kemal's return to Constantinople, then by ordering his arrest. Administrators receiving the arrest order were Kemalists themselves. Dominated by the British and disobeyed in most areas outside the Straits region, the Porte was a bystander to the crucial events in central Asia Minor. The King-Crane sampling of Turkish opinion came mostly from the Bosporus area, where the Allied presence colored attitudes. The Turkish government in Constantinople preferred a British to an American mandate, but was not eager for either.[37]

Crane, with a genuine trust in Wilsonian self-determination, tried to penetrate the Turkish spirit in the interior. Following Halidé Edib's suggestion, he persuaded Louis E. Browne of the Chicago *Daily News* to write a series of dispatches from mid-Anatolia. Despite this gesture, Crane, along with Bristol and most missionaries, underestimated Kemalist strength. A centuries-long freedom and a nationalism learned from the West were helping Turks resist subjection to any local group, Armenians or Greeks, or to any foreign government.

As the King-Crane Commission was writing its reports, Bristol was becoming alarmed by rumors of increasing violence between Kemalists and Armenians. For months, he and other American representatives at the Porte had been sending dispatches to the United States delegation at Paris about instability within Anatolia. Courts-martial of Turks responsible for massacres had been a farce. The Constantinople government could not keep a grip on conditions. Asia Minor was full of Turkish soldiers who had not demobilized and who were more concerned about disturbing than maintaining order. Armenians could not return to their homes. The Allies were at loggerheads. After the Turkish protest following the Smyrna debacle, Bristol had asked vainly for Western occupation of Asia Minor to rectify the damage. The Admiral believed in mid-August that the Kemalists were favoring a United States mandate while setting up a de facto government against Armenians and Greeks. He asserted to Americans at Paris that the only way to curb the unruliness in Turkey was for the United States to take a mandate for all of the Ottoman Empire. He rejected a separate mandate over Armenia, which he thought would only reinforce partitioning and increase Turkish resentment.

The King-Crane members then completed their report. Lybyer had

205

worked on historical background, Brodie on tables, King on recommendations. Donating remaining supplies of coffee, cocoa, and jam to the Constantinople Woman's College, the Commission left by ship for Venice on August 21. A few days later in Paris the investigation presented its proposal on Asia Minor to the American delegates: a tripartite mandate by the United States over Anatolia. King and Crane's study among Turks, minorities, and missionaries thus agreed with the Gates view and the Morgenthau Memorandum.

The King-Crane report generally recommended that all of Turkey, except Mesopotamia, be under a United States mandate. This idea was almost identical with the maximum hopes of the Protestants, put forth over a year earlier in the Barton federation plan.

MORE RHETORIC THAN OUTPUT

A fundamental factor about the King-Crane report was the uncertainty about United States willingness to act upon it. An observer could have asked: how much evidence did the Wilson government need before it would do something more than moralize, study, and aid the ACRNE? What would it take for the President to sense that he was helping tension more than calm within Turkey? How large and disruptive would the post-Smyrna crisis have to become before the Washington administration realized that words and inquiries were no substitute for hard decisions?

Questions like these nagged the missionaries and their friends ever since King and Crane had begun their circuit in Syria. On June 15 Barton sent Relief Commission member Walter Smith and missionary Clarence Ussher to Paris with the task of maintaining ACRNE control of relief in the Caucasus, getting American military personnel into integral Armenia, and securing Supreme Council approval of Ussher's scheme for repatriation of Turkish Armenians. Barton then cabled House on June 21: "Confident Turkey would accept orders from Paris for immediate allied military occupation." [38] (The American Board secretary previously had stated to Bristol that only by giving Armenia a safe government could the ACRNE prosecute its job; the Christians in Turkey were in danger of elimination, Barton felt.) The day after the ACRNE chairman's message to House, the American Committee for the Independence of Armenia (ACIA) — prompted by Cleveland Dodge — sent a cable signed by Senator Lodge, Charles Evans Hughes, and other prominent Americans importuning the

206

President. The ACIA wanted United States or Allied food and munitions sufficient for fifty thousand Armenians to occupy integral Armenia.[39]

Using these statements in Paris, Morgenthau, Smith, and Ussher worked for endorsement of a military commission to the Caucasus. They met with House, Lansing, Hoover, and other leaders of the American Peace Commission. By June 27 the mission-relief lobby had talked Hoover into approving a letter to Wilson requesting permission for an Allied high commissioner to Armenia. Morgenthau at the same time obtained permission from the American peace delegation to search for an individual to fill the proposed post and approached Major General James G. Harbord, chief-of-staff under General John J. Pershing. Noting that relief was not adequate to solve the Armenian problem, Morgenthau offered Harbord not only the office of commissioner, but the directorship of the ACRNE in the Caucasus and the likelihood of becoming an administrator in an anticipated American mandate over Asia Minor.[40]

The Supreme Council concurrently took up the Near East. Lloyd George on June 25 asked for a skeletal peace treaty with Turkey. His government wanted to find a method to bind the United States to an obligation in Turkey (the British Foreign Office met with missionary Alexander MacLachlan and urged him to press the American Peace Commission about a United States mandate). President Wilson again postponed a treaty, saying he needed two months' delay. For the next two days the Council went over the tangled Turkish issues and tugged at strings leading nowhere. What was to be done with Italians in Adalia and Greeks in Smyrna? Uncertainty. Should Western troops occupy central Anatolia? Uncertainty. Wilson, Clemenceau, and Lloyd George were exhausted after the negotiations on the German treaty. They could find no way to unsnarl matters all entwined with the obscure place of the United States in the Ottoman future.

Limply, the tired men agreed that negotiation on the Turkish treaty would have to wait until the President could test American sentiment about mandates in Armenia and Constantinople. Trying to mitigate the effects of postponement, Wilson outside the Council instructed Morgenthau and Hoover to prepare a memorandum about an Allied high commissioner to Armenia. At a news conference the President indicated that the United States might assume mandates in Asia Minor. Then, on June 28 (the day plenipotentiaries signed the German treaty in the Hall of Mirrors at Versailles and Wilson's last day in Paris), the Council approved the

207

high commissioner idea. According to Morgenthau, the Council did so with the positive expectation that the United States would accept the mandate for Armenia.[41]

Next, a commissioner had to be gotten. General Harbord declined the position, fearing inadequate Allied backing. On July 1 the American delegation discussed the high commission scheme and related matters. Hoover, who had been hearing about the Caucasus from one of his Relief Administration men attached to the ACRNE there, felt cold about a mandate in Armenia. He thought costs to pacify and build a viable nation — fifty to a hundred thousand soldiers and at least three hundred million dollars — would be too high. But Hoover was willing to go along with the high commissioner plan. Soon he and Morgenthau reported to the ACIA on current developments, including Hoover's negative thoughts about Armenia. On July 3 Morgenthau and Smith completed arrangements for a former member of the American Relief Administration staff in Rumania, Colonel William H. Haskell, to take the office of commissioner, subject to Barton's approval. The Council of Heads of Delegations, successor to the Big Four but often called the Supreme Council, in two days appointed Haskell high commissioner and gave him authority to head the relief program in Caucasian Armenia. Later the Council added Georgia and Azerbaijan to Haskell's jurisdiction. Accompanied by a sixty-five–member mission composed mainly of United States military men, Haskell set out for Constantinople in mid-July. Barton skillfully fought Hoover to tie Haskell more closely to the ACRNE than the American Relief Administration.[42]

Morgenthau envisioned methods, in addition to Haskell's group, to deepen the United States commitment to Armenia. Reporting to Dodge, Morgenthau asked the New York industrialist to get backing by the ACIA for a measure not unlike the King-Crane Commission — an inquiry into Armenia to be led by General Harbord. By July 5 Morgenthau had persuaded the American Peace Commission to ask President Wilson for a Harbord investigation. To Dodge, Morgenthau stated that its purpose would be to estimate the Congressional appropriation and military force required for a quieting of Armenia's turmoil. The ACRNE finance chairman also mentioned to Dodge another goal: "the Armenian refugees can only be saved by a determined effort of the American government." [43]

For some weeks the notion of a Harbord inquiry remained in the background. Kurdish and Azerbaijani irregulars reportedly preyed on Armenians. Georgian authorities slowed the transport of relief goods on the railroad from Batumi in Georgia to Erivan, feeling that the ACRNE slighted their needs. In the Erivan Republic, large numbers of refugees starved. Two British officers whom the Kemalists had imprisoned for a time in Erzurum told Americans in Paris that no integral Armenia was possible without foreign troops.

Disorganization prevailed among missionary-relief interests. Morgenthau's leadership in France ended in mid-July when he went to Poland on a Peace Conference mission to study the Jewish situation there. Barton concurrently tried to brighten the view of the Turk in America. Writing for the *Missionary Herald,* he stated that Turkish spokesmen were entertaining hope that the United States would soon become the savior of their turbulent country. In contrast, Gerard of the ACIA declared to Secretary Lansing that the Paris Conference probably had lost its opportunity to establish a mandate over Armenia, let alone Asia Minor. Gerard proposed that the United States help the Erivan government help itself, giving de facto recognition and sending munitions for fifty thousand men.

Among American officials there was continued hesitancy. Wilson wrote the delegation in Paris that there would be quite a delay before he would know about mandates in Anatolia. But he reiterated his wish for an American presence in Armenia and Constantinople. Under Secretary of State Frank L. Polk, the official who had become head of the Peace Commission at Paris by the end of July, reported to Lansing that the "situation in Asia Minor, to my mind, is hopeless. England is going to withdraw [from the Caucasus], and the French and British . . . are 'between the devil and deep sea.' They cannot act intelligently until they know what our plans are and Asia Minor cannot wait until we have made up our minds. Is there any possible way of having the question settled?" [44]

At the time of Polk's plaintive query, urgent cries seemed to sound everywhere. The American consul at Tiflis cabled Paris that the Armenian situation was deteriorating; it would become disastrous unless the United States did something. One of Hoover's agents in the Caucasus warned that a massacre of Armenians was imminent. The President of the Erivan Republic formally requested American troops and arms. In Paris, missionary educator Mary Patrick lobbied for a Harbord mission and an American mandate over Asia Minor. The Peace Commission in France believed Congress should be told that the immediate sending to Armenia of at least ten thousand American soldiers was the only remedy for the emergency there. Dispatching Harbord would remove danger temporarily.[45]

The pressure got to Wilson; on August 1 he accepted the plan for a Harbord inquiry. Harbord gathered some twenty men for his mission, most of them Army officers. In mid-August he received final instructions from Frank Polk to investigate possible American responsibilities in eastern Anatolia. (Harbord has described himself as "one born in the Middle West, whose boyhood was passed on the Western prairies, whose early manhood was spent under the fiery suns of the great Southwest, with twelve years of middle life in our tropical isles of the Eastern Seas [the Philippines]." [46]) The Harbord Mission spent several weeks during September and October in Asia Minor and the Caucasus, interviewing representatives of many ethnic groups and of missionary and relief organizations.

After the President's approval of the Harbord Mission, a new unrest arose. Britain declared its intent to withdraw its twenty thousand troops guarding the Batumi-Baku railroad in the Caucasus. The Lloyd George government was trying to husband its resources and to persuade Wilson to send American soldiers to Armenia. The President hesitated to order contingents to the Caucasus other than the token military personnel in the Haskell and Harbord missions. Puzzled, Wilson stated to Lansing: "I fear that it would be most unwise to put before Congress just at this stage of its discussion of the Covenant either a proposal to promise to assume the Mandate for Armenia or a proposal to send American troops there to replace the British and assume the temporary protection of the population; and yet will our own public opinion tolerate our doing, or at least our attempting, nothing?" [47] Cleveland Dodge did not challenge Wilson's hesitancy, stating to the President that he hoped Britain would prevent the catastrophe which would result if it withdrew its troops. Wilson then instructed Lansing and Polk to inform the Allies that the domestic situation prevented America from sending soldiers at the time to Armenia and to request that Britain retain its forces in the Caucasus. The President on August 14 outlined to Dodge his strategy for Asia Minor: "It is manifestly impossible for us . . . in the present temper of the Congress, to send American troops there, much as I should like to do so, and I am making every effort . . . to induce the British to change their military plans in that quarter, but I must say the outlook is not hopeful, and we are at our wits' end what to do." [48]

The ACRNE concurrently pressed the British government to main its troops in the Caucasus. Dodge in the United States and Walter Smith in Paris initiated this effort, and Colonel Haskell sent Major Arnold of the relief staff in Constantinople to assist at Paris. Smith saw Lloyd George's private secretary, Philip Kerr, who declared that unless Wilson promised to secure an American mandate over Armenia, the British decision to withdraw troops was irrevocable. Going to London, Smith worked with James Bryce and with the United States ambassador; he also wrote articles for American periodicals. On August 17 Smith had a session with Foreign Minister George Curzon, who complained of Wilson's procrastination on the Turkish settlement. Smith stressed to Curzon that the American public needed more education on the Near East and "told him of the vast interests at stake; the wide interest in our relief work and the 100 years of missionary effort"; the threat to Armenians and peace in the Near East; the dependence of world order upon British-American cordiality; the negative reaction in American opinion if the British withdrew. Curzon was skeptical, partly because a British diplomat in Washington reported that there were no preparations by the United States War Department to send forces to Armenia and that missionaries, the main backers of a mandate, probably would not be strong enough to "turn the scale." The British diplomat in the United States noted that Wilson had not prepared the public for a mandate and that Lansing opposed it. The most Smith could get from Curzon on August 17 was that the British would temporarily keep some regulars at Batumi.[49]

American officials continued talking. The President warned the Porte to prevent attacks on Armenians. (This message to the tottering Constantinople government rather than to the de facto one at Erzurum showed how out of touch Wilson was. The gap was as large as the one that led to his mistake on Smyrna.) The Porte replied that ever since Greek atrocities had begun at Smyrna, it had been unable to control Anatolia; the only way to prevent insecurity in the interior was an early peace treaty. Wilson also wrote Democratic Senator John Sharp Williams of Mississippi: "I have found it impossible to hold my spirits steady enough" to read of outrages in Armenia. "I wish with all of my heart that Congress and the country could assent to our assuming the trusteeship for Armenia." [50] Amid countless drains upon his emotions, the unnerved President said he felt he was leaving something undone for the Near East (he had received a letter from Senator Williams, who hoped America would send munitions to Armenia but concluded lamely that things just might have to be left in the laps of the gods). Contrary to Wilson's evaluation of his domestic foes, such Republicans as Lodge, Hughes, and Root reportedly (through Gerard) did not object to the administration's ordering United States soldiers to Armenia.[51]

Near East Relief, the new name of the American Committee for Relief in the Near East (ACRNE), at the same time sought a larger political weight than it had. A Congressional charter, granted on August 6, helped draw to the relief board of trustees such men as Hoover and Franklin D. Roosevelt (the latter assisted by donating legal services). Ex-President Taft had joined a year earlier. In Asia Minor, the Barton Relief Commission linked with the Haskell group. After giving a dinner for Haskell in Constantinople, Barton felt he could work perfectly with the Allied high commissioner to Armenia. Haskell and Barton journeyed together to the Caucasus, arriving in mid-August, and began an assessment of means to alleviate the terrible suffering there.[52] (See Maps 5 and 6 on pp. 148 and 168.)

With a strengthened Near East Relief, Barton and Peet (advised by Haskell) sent a telegram to Dodge. Armenians needed ten thousand United States rifles, the missionaries said, and one hundred machine guns. American forces of one reinforced brigade and one squadron of reconnaissance planes should be in the Caucasus within a month. The two men stated that unless Washington followed their recommendations, relief might cease among twenty thousand orphans and three hundred thousand Turkish-Armenian expatriates. Barton and Peet urged Dodge to see Wilson right away, for the President alone could redeem a condition which threatened to become a "world menace." [53] Aware of the Chief Executive's reluctance to act determinedly in Armenia, Dodge probably did not discuss the pleas of his Near East Relief associates with Wilson; Dodge sent their telegram to the State Department.

August was as critical a month as May had been. Wilson had fought a good fight on the level of principles, from January through April, ensuring that Near East opinion and the mandate idea would blunt some of the edges of colonialism. But the summer days were almost the last in which he could expect to maintain a large American place in the Ottoman negotiations. Since early May circumstances had been weighing American diplomacy in the balance and finding it wanting. More than generalship, there had been the trips of King, Crane, Haskell, and Harbord. More than output, rhetoric. Instead of cooperating in May and June with Lloyd George on a quick treaty, Wilson had deferred to the Italian and Greek imperial forces, and to the Turkish nationalists. Wilson also would not send the United States Army to a disorderly portion of the world. All the while, he sought to give the appearance that he had not retreated.

Missionary and relief individuals found that tough antagonisms were thwarting their aspirations: Republican Senators against an increasingly enervated President, Gerard's views versus Gates', spreading strife opposite diminished stability in Anatolia and the Caucasus. These confrontations helped produce the vacuum of delay which the King-Crane and other commissions were not filling. The missionaries' own special tension about Church-State relations was not aiding them to be forceful. The Protestants obviously were having large difficulties in transmuting their cultural internationalism into American mandates.

Chapter 9

The Isolationist Revival

BARTON by August 1919 had been asking futilely, since the end of the war, for the United States to commit itself to the Near East. He watched disconsolately as the Wilson administration passed one opportunity after another at Paris. Further disappointment came when his and Peet's cable to Dodge from the Caucasus had brought no United States soldiers. More frustrations were to follow, because the President assumed, notwithstanding his unabashed concern for Armenia, that Senatorial consent to the League Covenant had to come before the mandate question. Waiting was to make mission-relief people ever more anxious, because the tempestuous Senate debate over the League was to last for months.

THE MANDATE SHIP

The debate, which restrained missionary plans for Armenia, got its strength from reviving isolationism in the United States. Many people in America no longer wanted soldiers "over there" for, after all, the war had been won; the United States had finished its job across the ocean. Senators Lodge and Borah felt that they could use this emotion and the tradition about abstention from transatlantic entanglements. They helped convert many internationalists in their party to the idea that the Covenant needed conditions.

214

Aspects of the current isolationism stemmed from Near East sources as well as internal. Under Secretary of State Polk in Paris sensed late in August 1919 that Clemenceau's offer to answer calls for troops in Armenia with ten thousand French soldiers was probably to carry out the secret treaties in Cilicia, rather than bolster the Erivan Republic. Upset by the "grand free-for-all scramble" over Turkey, Polk manifested a typically American sentiment. He wrote Colonel House in London that he yearned to escape negotiation of the Ottoman treaty. In the United States the same untidy image of Asia Minor which bothered Polk was arousing the New York *Sun*'s ire; it declared that the Peace Conference was trying to saddle America with the plagued area of Armenia.[1]

"The isolationist impulse," remarked by historian Selig Adler, hurt the Protestant hopes for Turkey through the way Republicans and Democrats related this impulse to the Covenant. American citizens had tired of the Wilson administration's neglecting injustice in the United States while uttering ideals about peoples abroad. Inequities at home included restrictions on civil liberties and a cost-of-living increase about 75 per cent above prewar levels — an increase which hit hard the 90 per cent of the people who owned less than half the nation's wealth. There were disruptive labor strikes and race riots. Social discontent found its most conspicuous, although often indirect, expression in the institutional and personal turmoil over the League Covenant between the Democratic President and Republican Senate Majority Leader Lodge.

In the League fracas, Lodge and the irreconcilables exploited both narrow nationalism and an exhausted President. Lodge tabbed real and exaggerated faults of Wilson: the President's including no Republican regulars or Senators in the delegation to France (William McKinley had appointed three Senators, one of them a Democrat, to the commission to make peace with Spain) and maneuvering the Senate out of prerogatives to allow Democrats to claim success in peace as well as war. Saying he favored the League of Nations, Lodge apparently believed Wilson's Covenant dangerously extended far larger privilege to the American Chief Executive and to the new international organization than the Constitution permitted. Lodge since May 1919 almost certainly had not intended to assure passage of the Covenant. He had intended to keep the Republican party united no matter how far it had to stretch to include pro-League William Howard Taft and League-hater Borah. Helping to hold the majority leader fairly close to the irreconcilable position, Borah vowed he

215

would not vote for what he believed was the Covenant's sterilization of nationalism if the Saviour of men revisited earth and declared for it. Borah was a likable individual, but on principles he was so intransigent that Washingtonians never quite understood how on his daily horseback rides in Rock Creek Park he could consent to go in the same direction as his horse. Rejecting Wilson's concessions in response to the Round Robin, Lodge packed the Foreign Relations Committee with Senators like Borah. After the President presented the League document to the Senate on July 10, Lodge took two valuable weeks to read aloud the Versailles Treaty (Covenant included) to snoozing Senators or to empty chairs. He conducted long hearings, which allowed internationalist enthusiasm to subside while Borah organized isolationists throughout the country. Lodge and his colleagues strapped the Covenant with amendments and reservations, including one requiring Senatorial approval of any American mandate.[2]

Confronting the Lodge forces, Wilson was becoming less capable of coping with them and with the missionary program for the Ottoman Empire. His coughing spasms at Paris had been a sign of physical and emotional strain. What Wilson called his hot-lava interior was beginning to erupt, helping his tendency when under intense pressure toward single-track thinking. Months of hard and often brilliant concentration upon world issues had placed him increasingly in that frame of reference and had shut out things which to him were secondary. His communication with associates like Secretary Lansing and with Congressmen had lessened. Wilson also became increasingly suspicious of House, a disengagement not slowed by Edith Bolling Wilson.

House had foreseen in May 1919 how Wilson, not renowned for turning the other cheek, could tangle with his political opponents. "One of the great defects of the President's character is his prejudice and self-will. . . . The manner in which he has antagonized the Republicans in Congress is an instance of this. He has steadily built up a fire there which is now beginning to scorch him and it will became worse and worse as his term wanes. It was all so useless . . . and will probably hamper him in the exercise of the Treaty provisions." Just as Wilson was about to depart from France for the United States, House urged him to meet the Senate in a considerate way. Anglo-Saxon civilization, House said, was built on compromise. The President retorted: "House, I have found one can never get anything in this life that is worth while without fighting for it."[3]

Cleveland Dodge and other close friends of the President had not been near enough while Wilson was developing this unbending streak in France. Upon the President's return, Dodge kept within his usual supportive role and did not counter Wilson's expanding self-righteousness. Castigating Republicans, Dodge exclaimed: "confound their politics. You are showing the patience of a Saint and are going to win out, but how you can stand your awful burden I cannot see. We all think of you constantly and if fervent prayers do any good you ought to be helped." [4] Dodge did not perceive that Wilson could not stand his burden; prayer was not necessarily going to stop a breakdown. What friendship at that point called for from Dodge was a mixture of petitions to God and gentle instruction to Wilson about Christian understanding toward enemies. Of course, Dodge had not practiced that advice previously, and he did not do so in this trial. The President also expected so much from the Covenant that he put off addressing himself to Dodge's projects in the Near East.

Wilson was abetting rising isolationism and its threat to the missionary goal in Turkey because he did not have the strength either to conciliate or outflank the Senate. He was as psychologically irreconcilable as Borah, when in July 1919 he had returned to the United States. He then told a Democratic Senator he would crush the Republicans and boasted to another individual that the Senate would have to swallow his medicine (the Covenant). In a speech to Congress he was abstract and moralistic. An architect of the President's first presidential election victory, George Harvey, editorialized on this address: "The Senate of the United States had no need . . . of exhortations to seek the good, the true, and the beautiful. . . . What it wanted, what it was entitled to, was an explicit and practical report upon the President's extraordinary mission, and it did not get it. . . . It wanted facts: it got 'words, words, words.' " [5] Harvey's mood was like that in a poem Senator Lodge once wrote to satirize the President: [6]

> It's wiser being good than bad;
> It's safer being meek than fierce:
> It's fitter being sane than mad.

Some Republican Senators dismissed the presidential address as anti-American, soap-bubble oratory.

Then on August 19 the President kept his temper under three grueling hours of hostile questioning before Lodge's Committee; but he also got lost in rather meaningless semantics when discussing the Covenant's Article Ten (about each League member upholding the others' integrity and independence). Wilson argued for no formal reservations and amendments to this article and other sections of the Covenant; he was willing to have informal reservations. His testimony made it appear that the League would control the United States and deny America its independence. Republican leaders did not like that implication or take up Wilson's willingness to compromise through informal reservations. Combative Lodge three weeks later finally made a statement for the Foreign Relations Committee to the Senate which approved ratification but with forty-five crippling amendments and four reservations. Lodge's statement was full of sarcasm.

What the nation and its leaders needed was a sense of humor. One reason the country had made it through the late 1890s without a partisan deadlock was because decision-makers at that time read and enjoyed the Mr. Dooley column, created by Irish-American journalist Finley Peter Dunne. During debate on the treaty to end the Spanish-American War, Dunne wrote a column in which Dooley is talking about "larning" the Filipinos a lesson. A companion of Dooley's responds, "We have a thing or two to larn oursilves." Dooley declares, "But it isn't f'r thim to larn us. 'Tis not f'r thim wretched an' degraded crathers, without a mind or a shirt iv their own, f'r to give lessons in politeness an' liberty to a nation that mannyfacthers more dhressed beef thin anny other imperyal nation in th' wurruld. We say to thim: we'll larn ye our language, because 'tis aisier to larn ye ours thin to larn oursilves ye'ers, an' we'll give ye clothes if ye pay f'r thim, an' if ye don't ye can go without. . . . We can't give ye anny votes because we haven't more thin enough to go around now, but we'll threat ye th' way a father shud threat his childher if we have to break ivry bone in ye'er bodies. So come to our arms, says we." Unfortunately, Finley Dunne was so depressed by the First World War that from 1915 to 1919 he did not have the desire to write the Dooley column; Dooley could have offered some comic relief to the postwar settlement.[7]

Nearly all of Wilson's waning energy went into striking at Republican shortsightedness, so he had almost no time for the Near East. At the August 19 hearing on the League, Wilson almost resignedly agreed with Lodge that public opinion did not seem to favor a mandate over Armenia. The absence of a large public approval for a mandate was mostly the President's responsibility. Near East Relief had put down the foundation for popular support through its publicity; he had not put up the building. When Mihran Sevasly in February 1919 had asked about propaganda on a mandate, Wilson had said, "Not yet." Nevertheless, in Paris the President had hobbled the Turkish settlement and kept the Allies waiting for an American judgment without speaking forcefully to newspapermen on Armenia. How could be deceive himself that allowing Armenianism to wilt was the way to gain a mandate? Why did he think Americans might rally behind a duty in Armenia without himself carrying a sign toward that end? Probably he had become so tied up with the League that inconsistency between what he was saying about Armenia in the Supreme Council and not doing in the American press did not become evident. Lodge, less inclined toward a mandate than he used to be and influenced partly by reports from Hoover and Bristol, had not missed this discrepancy. Lodge wrote to Peace Commissioner Henry White in Paris the same day as the August 19 hearing: "Do not think I do not feel badly about Armenia. I do, but I think there is a limit to what they [the Allies] have the right to put off on us." [8]

Wilson's one-way thinking had been harming his own and the missionary cause for a long time. He had not responded to the King-Crane messages of July 10 from Syria. In Paris, Crane on August 31 cabled the President a summary of recommendations that America should take mandates for Syria and for all Asia Minor (Constantinople, Anatolia, Armenia). In muted tones, King and Crane announced this view to the press. Sensing Wilson's engrossment with the League, Crane stated to the President that the King-Crane report was not in harmony with many things the Allies were doing: "I believe it would help your campaign" for a Covenant without reservations to have the report published.[9] Wilson did not follow this counsel. He also gave little or no thought to Colonel Haskell in Armenia or to General Harbord, who on September 2 arrived in Constantinople.

At the same time the President went to the stump instead of to the large bloc of mild reservationists in the Senate, to convince a weary populace that Lodge's amendments were disabling to the League. Against the pleadings of Secretary Lansing and physician Cary Grayson, Wilson began an eight-thousand-mile trip through the hinterland after the Foreign Relations Committee had spurned his offer to accept clarifying reservations. House from London observed in his diary that no matter how incorrect the Lodge people were, Wilson was making Senatorial approval of the League as difficult rather than as certain as possible.[10] In September the President gave forty-some ethereal speeches, not marked by goodwill toward the Republicans. Only once, at Salt Lake City, did the President ask for an Armenian mandate.

Back in Washington the majority of Senate comments, untutored by data such as those in the King-Crane research, reflected growing negativeness in the United States about an Armenian mandate: Armenia had no mineral resources. A mandate was unconstitutional and against the Monroe Doctrine. Americans once burned on the Philippine insurrection were twice-shy about Armenia.[11]

As Wilson's tour moved toward its climax, a highly fatigued President muffed a chance to please Barton and Peet in the Caucasus. This setback to missionary wishes and to the President's own romantic Armenianism arose out of a resolution introduced by Senator John Sharp Williams on September 8. The Williams Resolution endorsed a free integral Armenia; the sending of American soldiers, arms, and money to Asia Minor; the allowance for Armenians in the United States to raise money and volunteers for the Erivan Republic. The Williams Resolution did not mention a mandate. Senator Lodge and other Republican leaders in the American Committee for the Independence of Armenia (ACIA) liked the Christian minority in Turkey; Gerard reported to the State Department that Lodge, Hughes, and Root favored the Williams Resolution and wanted an international military force for Armenia. From California, Wilson telegraphed his reaction to the Williams Resolution: "I am heartily in favor of such a course if the Congress will authorize it, but of course am still willing to defer to the French . . . or to join them if . . . we get the authority of Congress." [12]

Despite some evidence that Republicans wanted the administration to be resolute about Armenia and to work through the Supreme Council for an international military contingent in Armenia, Wilson did not act. This temporizing played into the hands of Clemenceau, who in response to pleas of Haskell and Barton had been offering French soldiers to Armenia for several weeks. Because of several factors — Clemenceau's willingness, the opposition of irreconcilables to the Williams Resolution, and Wilson's indecision — Senator Williams by September 20 had decided to strike the provision in his resolution for United States forces in Armenia. Assistant Secretary of State William Phillips then appeared before a Foreign Relations subcommittee, stressing the danger of an Armenian massacre and reporting that Near East Relief spokesmen urged the immediate dispatch of American troops to Armenia.[13] Polk cabled from Paris that Clemenceau did not plan to move troops into the Caucasus but only into Cilicia to fulfill the secret treaties. The French soon replaced the few British soldiers in south-central Asia Minor, an area far from the Erivan Republic.

Meanwhile, the chairman of the Foreign Relations subcommittee holding hearings on the Williams Resolution, Warren G. Harding, exemplified American nearsightedness in an oration of September 11: "Ours is truly an expanded influence and a world interest, but there is yet for us a splendid isolation. . . . It is very appealing to portray the woes, the outrages, the massacres, the awakening hopes of Armenia, and visualize the doubts and distresses and sacrificed lives while 'the Senate waits.' I know the appeal that touches the heart of Christian America in its concern and sympathy for Armenia. It easily may be made to seem as if the sympathetic Son of God had turned to the Omnipotent Father to send this twentieth-century defender of the New Testament [the United States] to succor those stricken believers in the great Trinity. But the big, warning truth is little proclaimed. . . . A hundred thousand soldiers are needed. [The number probably came from Hoover through the ACIA.] More American soldiers for Armenia than we heretofore maintained under the flag in any of the years of peace. Answer the call, and we station this American Army at the gateway between Orient and Occident, to become involved in every conflict in the Old World, and our splendid isolation becomes a memory and our boasted peace a mockery. This is not the way to peace. This is the avenue to unending war. Mr. President, I am not insensible to the sufferings of Armenia, nor am I deaf to the wails forced by the cruelties of barbarity wherever our ideals of civilization are not maintained. But I am thinking of America first. Safety, as well as charity, begins at home. Selfishness? No. It is self-preservation." [14]

Borah's speeches throughout the country were like Harding's. At the Chicago coliseum on September 10 Borah asked the audience: "Do you want to go into a league you can't get out of?" "No," shouted the crowd. "Do you want foreign nations to say where and when the Monroe Doctrine should apply?" "No," the people again shouted. He told them: "England has suggested that we send 100,000 men to Constantinople." They retorted: "Don't let 'em go." [15]

Then came disaster. The man whom missionaries and philanthropists saw as a savior was throbbing with tensions, augmented by such things as Borah's and Harding's addresses. He could not save himself, let alone minorities in the Ottoman Empire. Wilson had been suffering for days before the evening of September 25 at Pueblo, Colorado, where he stooped to his knees trying to carry the Covenant; face twitching, head racked with aches, sleepless, Wilson had to return to Washington without completing his engagements. On October 2 he fell unconscious, victim of a cerebral blood clot which paralyzed one side of his body and which was a nearly fatal sequel to the illness earlier in Paris. The President was left with speech thickened, emotions permanently unstable (Lloyd George later said the only faculty unchanged by the thrombosis was Wilson's stubbornness), and matters of State often ignored or decided by an overprotective wife. (Mrs. Wilson had no training in public affairs and almost no formal education.) Wilson would not be able to take minimal responsibilities of the Presidency for six weeks or to meet with his cabinet for six months.[16]

Even though Wilson's condition was grave, mission-relief circles continued to feel that America would have prominence in Asia Minor's future. William Peet in Constantinople trusted that King and Crane's recommendations would brighten prospects. Haskell tried to use the idea of protecting relief to get two thousand troops. Polk wrote Bristol that after seeing Europeans try to "carve up the Turkish Empire and present us with the claws," he wondered if America should not keep the Empire together.[17] Barton reached New York early in October, and stated that his recent expedition forbade the United States from so "selfish, cowardly, and irresponsible a course as to pull out and leave Turkey to another and yet more unbridled orgy of massacre, lust, and loot." [18] A Near East Relief convention petitioned Congress for assistance to one hundred thousand women and children in harems in the Ottoman Empire. The American Board in annual meeting at Grand Rapids, Michigan, featured such speakers as Barton, Howard Bliss, and Alexander MacLachlan. The gathering asked the President and Senate for action such as that contemplated in the Williams Resolution. The Board established a committee, including Barton and Henry King, to get Congregational churches to petition Congress about Armenia. After the expected ratification of the League Treaty, the Congregational Committee was to educate the public for a United States mandate over Armenia. Some members of the Wilson administration reportedly favored this effort and believed the Congregational Committee would bring pressure on Congress. The British ambassador to Washington, Edward Grey, saw indications that the administration intended eventually to dispatch troops to Armenia. About the same time, Barton suggested that Bryce in England should send a British delegation of Armenophiles to assist the Congregational Committee on Armenia. As the American Board planned, the press kept presenting Armenianism.[19]

The National Committee on the Churches and the Moral Aims of the War, perhaps the leading lobby for the Covenant, climaxed its drive in October 1919. Having spent more than one hundred thousand dollars in its campaign, the National Committee presented a pro-League petition to the Senate. Over sixteen thousand clergymen reportedly had signed the petition.[20]

That long-time associate of Barton and Dodge, Morgenthau, sought to defend missionary internationalism before the Senate had spoken on the Covenant. In the New York *Times* of November 9 he stated that unless the United States took a responsibility in Asia Minor, civilization would be in peril. Having spent forty billion dollars for war, the United States should spend at least four billion for the establishment of right. The former ambassador said that Lloyd George and other statesmen in Europe believed the United States was the only power which could stabilize Anatolia.

Finally, voting on the Covenant. After the Senate turned down the Foreign Relations Committee's forty-five amendments, Lodge rewrote most of the amendments' content into fourteen reservations (the number fourteen was mocking). Secluded by solicitous Edith Wilson, the President clung to a Covenant without Lodge's reservations, which he felt nullified the Treaty. It was an irony that before his speaking tour, Wilson had given to Senate Democratic Minority Leader Gilbert M. Hitchcock four formal reservations he would accept. These reservations were almost identical with Lodge's on Article Ten. But neither Wilson nor Hitchcock had revealed this move. Hitchcock eventually became one of the few individuals to see the isolated Chief Executive. The minority leader kindly told the President, who had a white beard covering part of his twisted face, that he might well hold out the olive branch to the Republicans (even Edith Wilson said the same thing). The tearful, sick man snapped: "Let Lodge hold out the olive branch." [21] On November 19 just before the final voting, Lodge found himself crying during Borah's closing speech. Then two groups of odd companions – pro-League Democrats and the Borah-led battalion – defeated the Covenant with the fourteen Lodge reservations. In another motion, the Republicans, many of them pro-League, rejected the Covenant without reservations. Myopic irreconcilables and Lodge had been better parliamentarians than Hitchcock, Wilson, and other internationalists. Ex-President Taft wrote an epitaph for the situation: Lodge and

Wilson "exalt their personal prestige and the saving of their ugly faces above the welfare of the country and the world." [22]

Thus, the mandate ship for Armenia remained at the ratification pier. One reservation which passed during the Senate voting required Congressional approval of a mandate. Lodge commented that "Congress would never assent to take a mandate for Armenia, Anatolia, and Constantinople. It cannot be done. The only way to help Armenia is by direct help." [23]

A WEIRD JUXTAPOSITION

While Senate and President were deadlocking over the Covenant, they were squandering the pro-American sentiment in the Near East which the Protestants and the commissions to Turkey had been accumulating. The din producing the impasse was so noisy that the Wilson administration could hardly hear what the Barton Relief Commission, the King-Crane Commission, and the Harbord Mission were saying.

Despite the incapacity of the American government, the head of the Barton Relief Commission, after spending seven months in the Near East, was optimistic. Barton was sure that the United States could draw upon its pro-American account in the eastern Mediterranean. Using a white-man's-burden style, he maintained privately that one could divide the nations of the world into three classes: those able to govern themselves and other peoples, those able to govern only themselves, and those able to do neither. The entire Turkish Empire fell into the third class and the United States into the first. America therefore should take a mandate for peoples in the Ottoman territories. When in Europe on his way to New York, he sought unsuccessfully to advance this rationale. He also tried, for what must have seemed to him the hundredth time, to get Western troops into Asia Minor.[24]

An outcome of Barton's and United States officials' imploring for soldiers in Anatolia was a widening cleavage between Russian and Cilician Armenians. In the early days of the Paris Peace Conference, two rival Armenian delegations — one led by the Dashnak president of the Erivan Republic, Avetis Aharonian, and the other by Boghos Nubar of the Ramgavar party — had agreed to elect a contingent to represent all Armenians. Although Dashnak people won a majority in the new combination, the united body elected Boghos as its head. Aharonian and Boghos at first worked together for an American or British mandate over integral Armenia. As the West dallied, the Ramgavar group did not like it that the Erivan Republic in its proclamation of May 28 annexing six Turkish-Armenian vilayets failed to consider Ramgavar concerns in Cilicia. Resentment by Ramgavars grew when their attempts through negotiation with the Dashnaktsuthiun to control or have a large part in the Erivan Republic did not work. Ramgavars withdrew from general elections in the Republic, which the bloody-flag Dashnaktsuthiun swept. The Ramgavars decided to cooperate with France for a place of their own in Cilicia. It was sad how Wilson and Lansing in September welcomed Clemenceau's offer of soldiers for Armenia as a way of helping the Erivan Republic. This ineptness indirectly helped split Armenians, and assisted European imperialism. Western Armenophiles then had the new dilemma of thinking about two widely separated territories, neither viable without powerful outside aid.[25]

The attempt of American Armenophiles to get Western military force into the Erivan Republic was as clumsily unhelpful to Armenians as the King-Crane Commission was to Arabs. Since America was a magic word and the Fourteen Points a Magna Carta to many Syrians, around 60 per cent of some eighteen hundred petitions received by the King-Crane Commission selected the United States as first choice for a mandate power. King and Crane took Arab feelings too literally. Winston Churchill later wrote that the American inquiry roved around searching for truth in the powder magazines of the Near East, with a notebook in one hand and a cigarette in the other. The investigation made things worse.[26]

While President Wilson during September barely thought about the dry-tinder setting that King and Crane had helped create in Syria, the Emir Feisal and the Allies were worrying about the consequences of American neglect. Not that the Allies were without fault. France through the summer had pursued the secret treaties in Syria, imitating what Britain had accomplished in Mesopotamia. The British had been doing a remarkably thorough job for years of making a mess with a series of overlapping, imprecise promises: freedom for the Arabs to Feisal's father, an imperial domain among Arabs to France, a Jewish homeland on Arab territory to European Zionists, and an inquiry into Arab opinion about mandates to Wilson and Feisal. Lloyd George finally realized that the Allies could not count on the United States to take any responsibility for the Arabs. On September 13 he asked his country's ally, France, to replace British soldiers in Syria and Cilicia by November. He also requested that such interior cities as Damascus remain under solely Arab garrisons. Clemenceau agreed – and used this understanding as well as the American requests for Western troops as an excuse to move into Cilicia. In Paris and London, Barton (still in Europe in September), Crane, William Yale, General Allenby, and the Emir Feisal tried to use the King-Crane research to modify the troop-exchange scheme. The Arab prince frantically sought in talks with Polk and other Americans to get the United States government to follow through on its King-Crane activities. Feisal even gave a blank check to these Americans: he would approve any Wilson declaration on Western military occupation of Syria. Since the President was desperately ill after early October, the government in Washington was deaf to Peace Commission cables about this offer. With French troops moving inland from the Mediterranean by mid-November, and Arabs resisting, Feisal much too late decided that maybe no salvation was to come from the New World. The distressed prince later joined his fighting comrades, who coordinated strategy with the Turkish nationalists and carried out several attacks on the French in Syria and the British in Mesopotamia.[27]

The Arabs might have done better to have copied the Kemalist model much earlier than to wait on the slow, increasingly fainthearted application of American missionary diplomacy to the Syrian test case. The Bliss-induced inquiry led to war rather than to peace. After implying to the Syrians by a strong emphasis on self-determination and on an inquiry that the United States would check France's colonialism, Wilson simply did nothing.

Parenthetically, while fighting was commencing in Syria, Western statesmen had a chance to reclaim some of the initiative lost by the Smyrna debacle. A Supreme Council–appointed international commission, which included Caleb Gates' friend Mark Bristol, held sessions from August 12 through October 15 to investigate the Greek occupation of western Asia Minor. The commission concluded that Greek sovereignty over Smyrna was not justifiable because Greeks there were in a minority and the invasion had upset rather than maintained order. Bristol and his colleagues asked for what missionaries and the King-Crane Commission generally had recommended: supplanting of Greek soldiers by a small Allied contingent, and restoration of Turkish administration. Lloyd George in the late autumn nevertheless determined to continue Supreme Council support for the Athens government. He led the way in shelving the commission's report; the United States again did nothing. So a course which missionaries and other Americans in Turkey lucidly saw as suicidal to Wilsonian interests was perpetuated.[28]

As for the Harbord Mission, it had begun at Constantinople in the company of mission-relief people. The study group disembarked from the *Martha Washington* early in September (the ex-transport ship smelled badly and had rats and cockroaches, leading one mission member to announce that George Washington had married beneath him). Mary Patrick soon gave a party for the Harbord investigation at the Constantinople Woman's College. Both Hussein Bey of Robert College and an Armenian-born United States Army officer joined the mission there as translators. Having secured the services of Hussein for the investigation, Edgar Fisher gave several interviews to Harbord group members; the missionary educator supported American involvement in the Turkish settlement. Bristol let Harbord read his dispatches, which emphasized Gates' idea of a unified approach to Asia Minor. Having just returned from the Caucasus and about ready to leave for the United States via Europe, Barton helped plan Harbord's itinerary in the interior. The American inquirers also talked to Turkish-Armenian spokesmen.[29]

Then, as Wilson and the Senate headed toward a standoff, part of the Harbord group went to Batumi on the *Martha Washington*; the main section under Harbord, accompanied by Charles Vickrey of Near East Relief, started across Anatolia. The main section used trains, autos, and horses and followed the same route the Barton Relief Commission had used months before. (See Map 6 on p. 168.) At Adana in Cilicia Harbord saw a missionary-run Near East Relief orphanage caring for six hundred Armenian children and a girl's school teaching rug-making and embroidering. Many of the young women had blue tatoos on cheeks, chin, and brow, indicating they had belonged to a harem. As Harbord and his associates pushed through one city after another to Mardin, they stayed at missionary compounds. They urged Turkish officials to treat the Protestant emissaries to their land with respect.[30]

At Sivas Harbord group members divided their time between missionaries and Turkish nationalists. Among seventeen American Board personnel engaged in relief there was Miss Graffam. Fluent in four languages, she had walked over one hundred miles with Armenians during the deportations. Returning to Sivas after this trek, she had given relief to Armenians throughout the war (even though Turks threatened to kill her and three of her companions died of typhus). She was the only American at

Sivas when the Barton Relief Commission appeared in summer 1919. Harbord gave her a great tribute: "Her experiences have never been duplicated in the story of womankind." [31]

Harbord met for over two hours with Mustafa Kemal, chairman of the recently adjourned Sivas Congress, which had assembled the week of September 4 and approved the platform of the earlier Erzurum Congress. The Sivas Congress had considered passing a resolution asking for a United States mandate over Turkey. Deciding that American acceptance would be doubtful and fearing loss of prestige by a rejection, the Kemalist meeting instead had sent a telegram to the United States Senate requesting its own investigation in Asia Minor. Harbord heard Kemal outline nationalist aims and blame the Young Turks and foreign intrigue for the Armenian massacres. At one point the Turk jerked a string of prayer beads around his neck, with beads spilling on the floor. Slowly he picked them up, saying that the nationalists intended to unify the pieces of their country. Harbord got the impression that Kemal wanted a United States mandate.[32]

As Wilson's thrombosis came upon him, the observers from the United States continued to the Caucasus. Erivan Republic representatives, guided by the new president, Alexander Khatissian, hoped the Washington government would heed the beckoning of Armenians. Gregorian ecclesiastics felt the same way. At the Republic's capital, the Khatissian administration poignantly proclaimed a national holiday in Harbord's honor and covered the city gates with flowers; crowds of hungry refugees cheered the Harbord Mission members as modern messiahs. Colonel Haskell asked his countrymen to propose the military aid necessary to get three hundred thousand Turkish-Armenian refugees back to their homes (they were still on a less-than-subsistence level in Near East Relief camps he was supervising). The Harbord group decided that necine killings among Azerbaijanis, Kurds, Armenians, and Georgians were undermining the landlocked Erivan Republic more than the Kemalists. Returned to the Bosporus by October 11, the mission assembled material based on interviews with diverse ethnic groups in the many areas visited and with Westerners, especially American missionaries. (See Illustration 17.)

The Harbord Mission soon completed a report and sent it to Washington. In a document enlivened by ninety-four photographs, there was evidence supporting the ideas of Gates, Morgenthau, Bristol, King, and Crane. The Harbord statement set forth a federated, five-part mandate over Anatolia and the Caucasus. (See Map 7, including inset, on p. 229.)

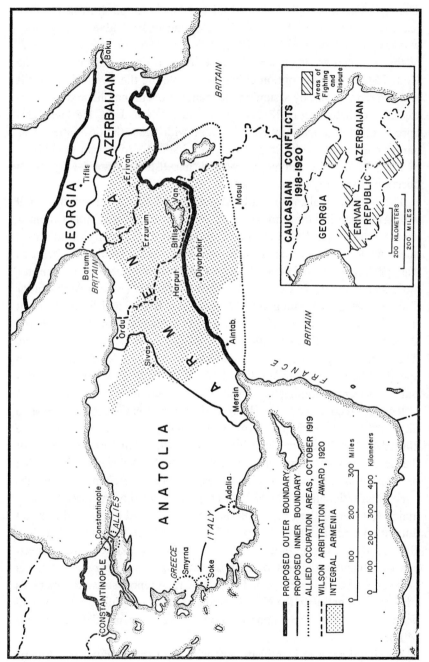

Map 7. Five-part American mandate proposed in the Harbord report, October 1919

The report mechanically balanced thirteen positive and thirteen negative reasons for and against America's accepting this mandate. Acceptance would cost an estimated $756,104,000 for the first five years. At the end of the balanced arguments Harbord set forth a ringing exhortation: the United States had the option either of completing the tasks for which it had entered the war, by assuming the mandate over Anatolia and the Caucasus, or of betraying millions of people in the Near East. He later reminisced that American nonentanglement with transatlantic matters was hardly compatible with the motive which had sent American doughboys to Europe. Nor was it compatible with a satisfactory answer to Cain's question, "Am I my brother's keeper?" [33]

The internationalism of Harbord juxtaposed weirdly in autumn 1919 with American isolationism. In agreement with the King-Crane Commission and the Barton Relief Commission, Harbord was saying yes to Cain's query while irreconcilables at home were crying no. While Morgenthau was speaking of using Harbord's report to produce a surge of idealism for American mandates in Constantinople and Armenia (British Ambassador Grey reported to London that Morgenthau, Elkus, and Smith thought that Americans could be aroused to accept a mandate for Armenia), the Wilson administration was floundering miserably on its Near East policy. The Harbord report was including a declaration that it would be better to spend millions for a mandate than billions for a future war while the Republicans were swaddling the Covenant in restrictions. [34]

Why did recommendations by American observers to the Near East so disregard the increasingly narrow views among their countrymen in the United States? The American inquirers felt that Senatorial approval of the League in some form was inevitable. They also believed the Wilsonian peace program required a territorial responsibility more tangible than abstract internationalism. The Harbord report included a statement that as a major founder of the League of Nations, the United States had a moral duty to take a mandate and start healing the world in the war-ridden Near East. King and Crane thought similarly, although, like the other American investigators, they often minimized strategic and economic factors in defending a possible mandate. The King-Crane report stressed America's Christian obligation in the Near East and claimed the United States would demonstrate "absolutely honest unselfishness" in a mandate over Asia Minor. [35]

The inquirers also identified more with the overwhelming pro-Americanism before their eyes than with the isolationism at home, partly because their experiences overseas had exposed them to a broader view than the average American held. Both Barton and Harbord said that sentiment in Turkey was practically unanimous in admiring the United States. The climate was so friendly that nearly every American in the Ottoman Empire came under its spell — not only commission members and missionaries, but diplomatic and consular officials.[36] Yale and Montgomery, in relation to Syria, and one person on the Harbord Mission, in relation to Anatolia and the Caucasus, were almost the only individuals to resist openly the notion that love for America should bring a mandate or mandates.

The investigators believed that an America with no colonial record in the Near East could solve the Eastern riddle more peacefully than the imperial nations of Europe. King and Crane realized that Arab territories artificially divided by the French and British or by a Jewish homeland would stimulate a belligerent Arab nationalism sooner or later. All of the American inquirers felt that a partition of Anatolia by Greece or Italy was impractical.

King, Crane, and Harbord wanted to advance the cause of the Protestant internationalists in Turkey. The large place of mission-relief endeavor in the minds of the commissioners manifested itself both inside and outside the reports. Believing that Constantinople Woman's College had remade the womanhood of the Near East, Crane discussed this notion with Feisal. The Arab prince declared to what must have been an incredulous Crane that he would like an American woman's school at Mecca, the pilgrim center of Islam. The official King-Crane document to Wilson quoted a statement by a European: "I firmly believe that Robert College has done more to render possible a safe solution of the 'Eastern Question' in Turkey than all the Ambassadors of all the European Powers." [37] King and Crane said that Arabs preferred the United States among Western states because the spirit of such American educational institutions as the Syrian Protestant College had constantly encouraged Arab nationalism. Proud to belong to the same country as the religionists, Harbord believed their philanthropy and devotion had no historic equal. In his report he said that America's interest in the Near East was due partly to "missionary and educational influence exerted for a century." [38] A reason for a mandate, the Harbord report declared, was to protect "our missions and colleges." [39]

The large missionary influence on the investigations had resulted partly because American Protestants in Turkey were quite closely knit. Despite increasing diversification, the Protestant movement to Turkey in 1919 had a considerable homogeneity. Mission and relief figures at Constantinople participated in and interchanged responsibility for worship exercises, prayer meetings, YMCA activities, commencements, receptions, and parties, which occurred at the Bible House, the colleges, houses, and other locations. Often a particular individual had religious, teaching, and philanthropic duties simultaneously or sequentially. The diaries of Edgar Fisher and Charles Riggs, among other evidence, show that American Board and Presbyterian personnel, relief men, educators, and political leaders regularly worked together and visited. Fisher, besides serving as dean and professor of history at Robert College, presided at the organ in Protestant meetings, taught a voluntary Bible class, assisted the YMCA, and played in a tennis club involving American Board and college people. He symbolized both the consensus missionary view that America needed a role in Turkey's future and the view's dissemination among United States officials. During 1919 he talked to every important missionary, diplomat, and military man among his countrymen who lived in or visited the Ottoman Empire.[40]

Perceptions held by the Harbord and other inquiries added to little more than zero because Wilson's personal diplomacy had amounted to little more. Wilson developed his Near East policies pretty much apart from the American Peace Commission and the United States press, whereas Clemenceau all along was coordinating his Syrian policy with the Quai d'Orsay and French newspapers. A fault of the President's personal more than institutional approach was that he did not have the peace commissioners, the Senate, or informed American opinion in close touch to bolster or enlighten him. He stood almost alone as the governments of France, Italy, and Greece took advantage of his weakness. Further, he turned increasingly to an absorption with the League contest as the means to United States mandates in Armenia and Constantinople. This priority made him the prisoner of the irreconcilables. Wilson became psychologically immobile on Ottoman matters, then physically disabled.

America slowly withdrew from the Near East settlement. Because of his illness the President did not see or read the King-Crane report. The State Department told Crane that there was probably no possibility that the Senate would assent to its conclusions. The Harbord Mission findings got no better recognition in Washington. After the Senate in November declined to consent to the Covenant, Wilson ordered the Peace Commission at Paris to disband. He also told the Allies, who were anxious to negotiate the Turkish treaty, that he would again have to postpone a decision on America's involvement. Such an ignominious contrast — all this — to the President's leadership in Europe months earlier.[41]

"PUT UP OR SHUT UP"

The second winter of peace presented American Board Secretary Barton with troubling questions. Should he stress a United States mandate, or favorable reconsideration of the Covenant by the Senate? How much emphasis should go to relief as opposed to a mandate?

Waiting for a second Senate vote on the League Treaty, he took pleasure in the philanthropy of Near East Relief. In the fiscal year ending in 1920 the organization collected $12,000,000, bringing the total since its founding to over $40,000,000. After his return from Anatolia, Barton helped persuade Congress to authorize a United States Grain Corporation grant to the Erivan Republic of 35,000 tons of flour, worth nearly $5,000,000. Haskell during his first year in the Caucasus distributed goods valued at over $20,000,000 (including around 100,000 tons of flour) to 338 communities, and established 40 hospitals and 17 orphanages. At one point in this period Haskell was feeding approximately 300,000 people daily. Throughout the Near East the relief staff of about 400 Americans supervised nearly 200 orphanages as well as 20 houses for women rescued from harems.[42]

Humanitarian activity in Marash, Constantinople, and the Beirut region exemplified aspects of relief. In Marash, a city of eighty thousand people, there were five orphanages and a hospital. In Constantinople there were orphanages serving over fifteen thousand children, a recreation program with athletic competition between orphanages, a six-week institute for teachers (orphanages taught academic subjects as well as shoemaking, baking, farming, sewing, and weaving), tuberculosis and trachoma facilities, and day nurseries for widows. In the Beirut area, under missionary James Nicol's direction, there were over six hundred workers (including some forty Americans), nine hospitals, fourteen orphanages, two nurseries, and an employment bureau; over twenty motor vehicles and forty horses provided transport.[43] (See Illustrations 19–21.)

It was not philanthropy but safeguards for philanthropy and missions which most concerned the Near East Relief chairman. Writing Bryce in November 1919, Barton said that he and his associates had not agitated for a mandate, for fear of hindering ratification of the League Treaty. He fretted to the Britisher that party squabbles in the United States were making it hard to do anything with the Harbord and King-Crane reports. He hoped the documents would soon become public. Barton during the Christmas season decided to push for ratification of the Covenant through a committee of three people. The committee members, one of whom was President Gates of Robert College, were to communicate with the Senate Foreign Relations Committee. While the Gates group was obtaining discouraging results, the League of Nations officially came into being, and the Allies began negotiating on the Ottoman treaty without waiting for America. Meanwhile, Bryce from England begged Barton to insist through Near East Relief that the United States take a part in the Turkish settlement. The American Board secretary hardly knew what to do. There were so many dead ends. Although an idealist with increasing frustrations, Barton was not a quitter. Believing that the relief institution with its enormous mailing list could urge America's duty to assume a mandate, he agonized to Bryce late in January 1920: "Our people are sick at heart over the dilatoriness of Congress and the obstinacy of the President in reaching common ground on the Treaty. I have never felt such a spirit of indignation before." [44] Not only Barton but thousands of observers were angry. Members of the National Committee on the Churches and the Moral Aims of the War, blaming either Wilson or Lodge for nonpassage of the Covenant, failed to agree on a strategy; the National Committee eventually lost its unity. Barton thought his country disgraced before the world. He decided it was right to mobilize sentiment for a mandate whether the Senate approved the League or not.

Professor Fisher of Robert College, on furlough from autumn 1919 through summer 1920, represented attitudes and activity of the missionaries in the United States. Meeting with Gates and Dodge two days after disembarkment in New York, Fisher thereafter began a heavy schedule related as much to America's postwar stance as to education in Turkey. Based in his hometown of Rochester, New York, he lectured there and through the East and Midwest at colleges, churches, service organizations, and relief rallies. He spoke on "Why Help Turkey," "America and Near East Mandates," "The Call of Armenia," and "The Influence of Christian

America in Turkey." For two months he assisted Near East Relief, which scheduled a tour for him involving as many as six speeches a day. He also gave an interview to the Associated Press and wrote an article for the New York *Times*.

Nonpropagandistic ("It is my constant prayer that I shall maintain a just and impartial point of view"), Fisher thought the United States should couple action with talk about world order. Like missionaries generally, he became disillusioned. His *Times* article declared that as the Peace Conference delayed a settlement and the United States refused to decide whether it would "lend a hand," conditions in Constantinople had gone from bad to worse (fires, often started because of communal hatreds, had destroyed at least twenty thousand houses). He expressed himself in his diary: "Cursed be the politicians." [45]

All this time the interests related to Barton were showing a certain practical internationalism. Remembering that the King-Crane report had stated that a mandate in Asia Minor would help save the United States from a reaction to the high aims in the war and would make a reality of the League of Nations, Henry King stated such ideas to Senator Harding; King wondered if the nation would not respond more readily to a mandate than a theoretical Covenant. Fisher declared in his diary about Americans: "how dilatory we have proved to be in accepting and shouldering our international obligations. . . . The Americans stand aloof, but criticize. . . . Our part of the job in Europe was not finished with the cessation of formal hostilities, but we should carry on in the era of reconstruction." Missionaries and their friends believed that the United States, as a leading status quo power, needed a tough duty at the center of the international balance of power. They foresaw that a United States politically and militarily connected with Europe could possibly avert another world conflict or at least develop realistic experience. Using material from the Harbord report, Morgenthau in his New York *Times* article warned that if Americans rejected an Asia Minor mandate, "we shall become responsible for another world conflagration." [46] (Implicit in mission-relief thinking was a paternalistic idea about America's acting as the world's policeman.)

The methods of missionaries for mandates lacked realism. In a book published early in 1920, William Hall of the Syrian Protestant College challenged his government to shepherd a Near East flock as a Christian obligation: "Who knoweth but thou art come to the Kingdom for such a time as this?" Barton wrote the last chapter of the Hall volume, asking the United States to take mandates over Asia Minor and Syria, to demonstrate "a piece of disinterested internationalism which would go down in history as an example of what one great nation can do for weak and defenseless peoples in putting them on the high road to prosperity and self-government." [47] Gates lectured at the Army's General Staff College and the University of Chicago; Fisher spoke at the Naval Academy in Annapolis. But Barton and associates did not arouse military and business people to support mandates for strategic and economic as well as for humanitarian and religious reasons. There was a contradiction between the Protestant goal of mandates and the appeal to disinterest. No one willingly does anything in which he does not have interest. Nations act out of self-interest, at best out of enlightened self-interest. Noted as a student of American society, Bryce made a mistake when he told Barton that mandates would come from mission boards stirring the Christian sympathy of people.

What kind of mandate or mandates? The Near East Relief chairman on occasion talked of mandates over the entire Turkish Empire, Asia Minor, Armenia, and Syria. His stance was usually between the positions of Admiral Bristol and James Gerard. Convinced that the Near East was like a mass of jelly with tremors in one part shaking the whole, Bristol maintained that militarily and politically a mandate over Armenia was indefensible unless it accompanied a mandate for the Ottoman Empire. He tried to get Barton to slight pro-Armenian propaganda so that Americans would see Turkey in his own perspective. Bristol was not necessarily anti-Armenian. He declared that if the United States did not answer the Armenian question by a mandate over all of Turkey "it would be the greatest crime of the last 100 years." [48] Gerard criticized the American Board secretary for proposing any mandate. The chairman of the American Committee for the Independence of Armenia (ACIA) insisted, at times obnoxiously, that the only program for the United States in the Near East was assistance and de facto recognition to the Erivan Republic (the Supreme Council gave such recognition in January 1920). The ACIA executive committee (without Dodge's support) petitioned Wilson for aid to Armenia and put out a fifty-two-page booklet attacking a mandate.[49]

One area marginal to Barton's ideas was Syria. A Presbyterian Board official in November 1919 wrote an article on the opportunity in a Syrian mandate: "If America heeds this call, it will be her strength and glory to find that in her Missionary Colleges and Schools . . . she has an asset well nigh invaluable and the Missionary in turn will face an opportunity for establishing the principles of righteousness, justice and truth in one of the great strategic centers of the World." After the United States Senate rejected the Covenant, missionary William Jessup sent a letter to his brother in America which was negative about the King-Crane Commission: "The people now are exasperated at such treatment. Men who are the salt of the earth and who worked hard to have a clear expression given for America now look at me askance and say, 'What did America mean by sending that Commission? Why are we put in such a predicament? Are Americans ruthless and cruel like the others?' " Jessup stated that if bloodshed occurred in Syria, the United States would be responsible; he asked his brother to do something to clear America's name in Syria.[50] Margaret McGilvary, niece of missionary C. A. Dana and herself a relief worker in Beirut, early in 1920 published *Dawn of a New Era in Syria*. She thought that a United States mandate would benefit the world. "If Syria turns to America with a prayer for assistance shall we lend a deaf ear? Shall we condemn her to exploitation by unscrupulous Powers who have no interest in her welfare?" [51]

Soon dealing with her questions in a second book (published by the Presbyterian Board), Miss McGilvary noted that the United States had refused to follow up the political advantage gained by relief activities during the war. She remarked that the Wilson administration had neglected Feisal. (When in March 1920 the Arab prince declared the independence of greater Syria and crowned himself king, he continued to hold an unfounded, childlike confidence in the aloof American President; Washington did not even bother to answer Feisal's messages.) The Presbyterian Board complained that the United States was closing a providential door by not rescuing Syria and lamented the darkness as France tightened control over the Arabs. The Syrian Protestant College's Bliss resigned himself to a French mandate.[52]

The missionaries' reversals in Syria were like those in regard to Nestorians. The Nestorian cause had languished ever since Robert Speer had sent Abraham Yohannan to Europe. Receiving little encouragement, Yohannan and others of his countrymen labored at the French capital. Yohannan explained to Speer in November 1919 that there was nothing more he could do in Paris or London, though the Nestorians had no security. Yet Speer by late winter had seen more promise ahead for the Nestorians than "the poor Armenians." [53]

In postwar Persia, Britain had countered the Judson-led Persian Commission's prestige, preventing American technical assistance to the Tehran government. The British secretly framed the Anglo-Persian Agreement of August 1919 which virtually made the Shah's domain a protectorate. Secretary Lansing had protested the British imperial policy for Persia — an act which eventually helped the Persian legislature reject the Anglo-Persian Agreement. So it was that the mission-inspired Judson Commission contributed to the strength of modern nationalism in what later became Iran.

No matter how much Persians, Arabs, or Turks deserved or wanted the political resources of Protestant diplomacy, an American mandate for Armenians was Barton's first hope among possible United States mandates.[54] For a while he used the Congregational Committee on Armenia. Through the secretaryship of missionary Ernest W. Riggs (Charles Riggs' brother), the committee widely distributed a pamphlet, *Save the Armenians*. Then, because of rebukes from American Board constituents who disliked its political activity, the Committee collapsed in January 1920. Barton and Riggs soon got together such people as Gerard, Morgenthau, and A. der Hagopian (a representative of Boghos Nubar and former professor at Robert College) to consider a new organization for the Armenian cause. One reason Barton wanted another start was that he found it hard to coordinate with Gerard's ACIA, which had come under the domination of Armenian Americans whom Barton could not control. At the same time Morgenthau wrote in the *Independent*, "To hundred and fifty thousand children, orphaned by the unspeakable Turks, are calling in the only English they know: 'Bread, Uncle Sam.' " [55] Morgenthau insisted that America must free the Armenians from such pitiful circumstances.

In February 1920 a phrase came to Barton's office in Boston, a gruesome phrase used so often since the 1890s. Massacres of Armenians. This time it was Marash, located at the center of the medieval Armenian kingdom. Mabel E. Elliott of Near East Relief, who had gone to Marash with the Barton Relief Commission, was an eyewitness. Everything had developed quite well in the Marash hospital where Miss Elliott worked — until French troops took over from the British in autumn 1919. Many of the incoming "French" soldiers were Ramgavar Armenians in the Legion d'Orient. Incidents occurred between these Armenians and local Turks.

There is evidence that French-led soldiers destroyed some Turkish villages. When France began to interfere with Turkish administration in Cilicia, the Kemalists decided to resist. Mustafa Kemal's movement was robust by that time; the Turkish nationalists had received recognition from the Porte and elected a majority in the Turkish legislature, which endorsed the resolutions of the Erzurum and Sivas congresses. At the end of January 1920, as the Kemalists began a siege of Marash, murders and exchanges of fire in and around Miss Elliott's hospital became frequent. Miss Elliott later said that Armenians panicked on February 12: "they were sobbing and screaming. Thousands of them, screaming! They had relied on us, on the promises of the great, powerful Allies. They had come back to Marash, to their wrecked homes and lives, under our protection. Now they were being left to the Turks." [56] Amid a bitter winter night, frantic parents picked up children at the hospital. By morning there was a disorderly withdrawal of French officers, relief workers, missionaries, and Armenians toward the town of Islahiye some distance to the south. Swirling snows came upon the people in the mountains. Miss Elliott saw at least fifty children freeze on the bent backs of often barefoot mothers. Hardly able to keep walking herself, she had to step many times over bodies. About three thousand people perished in the mountains. Back at Marash, the Turks killed hundreds of Armenians who had stayed behind.

The Marash episode seemed to double Barton's energy for a mandate over Armenia. At first Barton asked Dodge if there was anything the two could do to get the United States Army into Cilicia. A contact at the State Department did not hearten the relief chairman. Gates restated to Barton his long-held view that only a mandate over all of Asia Minor could deal with tensions there. The Robert College president mentioned the resentment missionaries felt about the postponement on mandates: "The United States ought either to put up or to shut up." [57] The indomitable Barton could not tolerate America's doing anything other than putting up. He ignored Gates' notion on a unified Anatolia, and wrote Lodge, Bryce, and others about a "protectorate" over integral Armenia. Senator Lodge replied spiritlessly and said the place to turn was the White House. Probably relying on Bryce's communication with the British government, the American Board secretary wrote to Wilson that if the President needed a formal Allied request for the United States to protect Armenia, "I feel sure that I could bring that about." [58]

THE SAME AS PONTIUS PILATE

Barton was a brash man. He thought he could get the Allies to invite the United States to accept a duty in Armenia whether or not America joined the League. Just as he was starting to agitate this matter, the Senate was nearing a second vote on the Covenant.

Through the winter, the mandate ship for Armenia had remained at the ratification pier, at least in the President's mind. During the same period, isolationism had grown. The important voices of William Howard Taft, William Jennings Bryan, and Herbert Hoover had urged Wilson to bend and deal with this traditional force. House, who had not seen the President since June 1919, wrote advising him to state publicly that he would prefer no reservations to the Treaty and would take no responsibility for alterations if the Senate insisted on them. House suggested that this course would assure passage. Because Mrs. Wilson was jealous of House, the President possibly never saw this recommendation. Dodge made some unproductive efforts to get House together with Wilson. Feeling that Mrs. Wilson was hampering both the cause of the League and a mandate, Dodge at one point muttered to House: "damn the women." The President's illness had hardened his attitude toward Senator Lodge. Wilson reportedly said he "would see both the Treaty and Lodge in Hades before he would give Lodge the satisfaction of having Article 10 labeled with his name." [59] The President looked to the coming presidential election as a referendum on an unrestricted Covenant. Apparently he was not going to accept a League treaty with fourteen reservations attached to it whether it passed the Senate or not, or even if the Allies said they could stand a covenant quite severely qualified by United States reservations. So the Chief Executive asked Democratic Senators to defeat a treaty tied to Lodge's terms. With more Democratic mavericks voting for a covenant with reservations than the previous autumn, the decision of March 19, 1920, still fell seven votes shy of the needed two thirds. This decision nearly sank a mandate.

Dodge and Barton made what protests they could. Dodge helped start a group whose plan was for Wilson to resubmit the Treaty, accept all points on which the Senate could agree, and put the remaining points to a national referendum. The President's intransigence prevented the group from getting anywhere. A Near East Relief pamphlet declared that if the Senate action meant that the United States was washing its hands of supervision of Near Easterners currently undergoing crucifixion, America was in the same class as Pontius Pilate.[60]

Then a strange surprise. Wilson tried to go back to the May 1919 situation, as if little had happened in the interim. Like Barton, he decided to ask for an Armenian mandate even though the Senate had not consented to the League. An observer could have asked Wilson: "Why did you reverse a position which was so rigid? How could you for a year watch the Ottoman Empire deteriorate into violence while you waged a domestic struggle on the Covenant? How could you wait to turn to a mandate in Asia Minor until after both the Near East and the United States were in a political shambles?" A possible reply could have been: "I only had the fortitude to fight one battle at a time. The end of the tussle with the Senate freed me from my emotional loads enough to do something again about my devotion to Armenia." Wilson also may have believed that defeat of the mandate was inevitable, but wanted to make at least a token effort to support commitments he had made to the Allies about Armenia.[61]

The President late in March 1920 had Secretary Lansing's successor, Bainbridge Colby, write a long letter to the Allies, who were negotiating the Turkish treaty. The letter expressed interest in the Open Door (equal opportunity for American oil companies) and interest in Armenia. The President explained his desire to his friend Dodge: "I have set my heart on seeing this Government accept the mandate for Armenia. You and those associated with you in Armenian relief know the most effective channels of public opinion with regard to this matter and I would be very much pleased to see some kind of legitimate propaganda started which would have the proper effect upon our Congress." Wilson added an understatement when he noted that Congress would be wary about accepting any mandate. "My own judgment is that we should accept not only this mandate for Armenia, but also the mandate for Constantinople." That sentence came directly from his comments months before in the Supreme Council. To help this campaign, the President finally released a copy of the Harbord Mission report to the Senate. He continued to suppress the King-Crane document, which did not appear in print until late in 1922. His administration granted de facto recognition to the Erivan Republic, and qualified the act by saying it was in no way prejudicial to an integral Armenia.[62]

The President's determination to have a mandate over Armenia cheered missionaries and their friends. They felt they might salvage something from the Wilson-Lodge feud and the isolationist boom. Barton probably had known the President's intent for some time, as indicated by the missionary's statement in the New York *Times* of April 5, 1920. At any rate, Barton had anticipated the White House advice to Dodge, helping organize a group of Armenophiles called the American Friends of Armenia (later the Armenia-America Society). The new movement brought together leaders of Near East Relief, the former Congregational Committee on Armenia, and the American Committee for the Independence of Armenia. It functioned under the secretarial direction of missionary Ernest Riggs. Keeping out bickering individuals of Armenian background, it sought—as Barton told Bryce—a front among American Armenophiles. Gerard worked somewhat with the American Friends. The ACIA continued a separate institution, with its line that the United States should aid Armenia directly rather than take a mandate.[63]

While the Allies in the latter part of April 1920 were requesting the United States to take a mandate, the news was foreboding for Armenian independence. Since Cilicia had been eliminated from an integral Armenia by France's occupation, the Allies requested that Wilson set out boundaries for an Armenia restricted to four of the six so-called Turkish-Armenian vilayets. Even this large a definition was preposterous. After the British set up a military government in Constantinople in March as a way to press the Kemalists (who happened to be in the interior, not at the Straits), the Turkish nationalists assumed almost every aspect of governing Anatolia except the name. Bargaining with the Bolsheviks who were taking over Azerbaijan, the Kemalists put a psychological squeeze on the western frontier of the Erivan Republic. The Allied thought of an Armenian mandate larger than the little Erivan Republic was a cruel hoax.

Lloyd George, probably influenced by Bryce, was responsible for the Allied request to the United States for both an Armenian mandate and a Wilsonian boundary delimitation. The British particularly wanted America to provide a buffer against Soviet expansion and to neutralize French and Italian spheres in Asia Minor. Lloyd George desired Wilson to arbitrate Armenia's boundaries because he feared Muslim reaction in British India to a large cession of "Muslim" Turkish territory to "Christian" Armenia. The British government was cynical. Lloyd George had a document from his military general staff that a Turkish settlement and an integral Armenia with Wilson boundaries would be impossible until the Allies stopped backing the Greeks in Asia Minor. Since a stop seemed remote and since there were inadequate British troops to establish integral Armenia, the general staff had recommended abandonment of an enlarged Erivan Republic. Further, Foreign Minister Curzon had known since October 1919, through repeated reports from Ambassador Grey, that America's accepting a mandate was almost out of the question. Yet Lloyd George argued with the Allies that since the United States had been responsible for the delay in the Turkish treaty and had shunned military burdens in the Near East, the Wilson administration ought to be in a situation of assisting or refusing a commitment in the Ottoman Empire. The Prime Minister wanted to prevent a Sermon-on-the-Mount judgment from Wilson about the Allies' not helping the Armenians.[64]

The European leaders went through this ritual to try to live with their consciences. They were much more enamoured with economic interests in Ottoman territories than in the decimated, unattractive region of the Armenians. Considering their pro-Armenian statements, this disregard was unfair to a group which had done much to help the West defeat the Empire. European nations had petted the Armenians in their state papers for years; the Armenians were to get nothing. No one had petted the Turks; they were to get everything.

The Allied invitation for a mandate over Armenia did little to shake the American public. Many newspapers did not even mention this event. Isolationist organs, such as the Chicago *Tribune*, had already conditioned people to turn away from the untidy grab bag called Turkey. One newspaper editorialist illustrated how mission-relief publicity had failed to show businessmen any reason for a mandate: "It is Armenia's crowning misfortune, with a 'mandate' going begging, that it has no oil wells. . . . What a difference oil makes in the white man's burden."[65] A member of Barton's American Friends of Armenia, Hamilton Holt—editor of the *Independent* and founder of the League to Enforce Peace—did not alter the "Christian" image of Armenia in an article. He did mention a practical argument when he said a mandate would not require a large presence by the American Army (only one thousand United States officers to train Armenians). Holt veered off into opinions not designed to win Republican Senators' allegiance. He said Americans' pity for the martyred Christians would help Wilson and Lodge "sink their differences and join this great cause. If so, Armenia will be saved. The United States will enter the League of Nations, and the peace of the world will be assured."[66] Possibly

243

the last thing Lodge and the irreconcilables wanted to learn about was a side door to the League.

A final move by missionary diplomacy to establish an American mandate in Asia Minor came in a message from Dodge to Wilson. For apparently the first time, Dodge went to the center of the domestic political situation. He confronted his invalid friend with a suggestion of reconciliation with the Republicans. Using advice from Holt, he suggested that "if you will consent to accepting a reasonable modification of the Lodge reservations," an Armenian mandate would be possible. To help work out whatever would achieve this end, Wilson's companion from Princeton days promised his full ability and Near East Relief's "considerable influence through its large number of Committees throughout the country." [67] It was too little, too late, for both the League and the mandate. Throughout the entire friendship Dodge had not practiced trying to help Wilson with his poorer characteristics as well as reinforcing his better. The change in Dodge at this point made no difference. The sick President recklessly had his sights on something which no healthy person had ever been able to do in American history — conduct a referendum on foreign policy (in this case on the Covenant) in a presidential election.

Soon, events in the Senate showed that no matter what Dodge did, the Republicans were in no mood for a mandate. Through the winter the Harding subcommittee of the Foreign Relations Committee had contained the Williams Resolution. The subcommittee had heard testimony from such individuals as relief leader Walter Smith. On May 11, 1920, the subcommittee sent a resolution to the floor under Harding's name in a form which reduced the original Williams Resolution's permission for American soldiers in Armenia to a small gesture. The Harding Resolution flattered the Erivan Republic and asked for a warship to Batumi to protect Americans' lives and property, reportedly threatened by Bolsheviks. After the Senate piously adopted the Harding Resolution, there was little the President could do to make it mean anything. [68] A Navy vessel was already at Batumi picking up seventy women working with Near East Relief in the Caucasus.

Yet the United States government explored ways to carry out the oral commitments which the President had made at Paris. Cooperating with Gerard, Morgenthau, and Holt, Secretary of State Colby sought means for the administration to bypass Congress. At a meeting on May 18, Wilson and Colby reportedly met with Armenophiles to consider a Holt proposal that the United States send munitions, money, Armenian-American volunteers, and Army officers for training Armenians to the Erivan Republic. Concurrently, Colby asked the British Foreign Office if the Allies would reopen the possibility of the United States taking the Constantinople mandate.[69]

Apparently abandoning the Holt scheme, Wilson went ahead with tactics which seemed to invite the opposite of what he said he wanted. Perhaps he desired to blame the Republicans for what would be a scuttling of the mandate ship. In a statement to Congress of May 24, 1920, he asked for an Armenian mandate of undefined size and location. He did not even try to develop a toughminded analysis based upon Harbord's research. Barely hinting at the idea that attention to Old World situations would stiffen international order, Wilson instructed a Senate already antagonized by his pretentiousness. In his statement, he considered divine providence, relief offerings which had saved Armenians, wishes of the great body of Christian people in America to help Armenia, empathy for Armenian freedom springing from the unadulterated Christian faith of the United States, and acceleration of civilization by a mandate.[70] Lodge's Foreign Relations Committee, thinking more about the Republican party than religious internationalism, crumpled the President's message only three days after its arrival. The Committee sent to the Senate a resolution under Lodge's name against a mandate over Armenia.

Debate in the Upper Chamber showed the results of Wilson's disregarding public education about the Near East for more than a year. Most Senators appeared not to have read Harbord's report; nearly everyone overlooked the report's main point that it was a unified mandate over Anatolia and the Caucasus the report was considering, not an Armenian mandate. Showing isolationism's pervasiveness, no one noticed the report's favorable recommendations; many Senators picked up the unfavorable ones. Irreconcilables talked as if the Good Samaritan had been an imbecile to run the risk of being beaten by the man he befriended. Anti-mandate expressions included fear of breaking the Monroe Doctrine, fear of violating the Constitution, fear of Bolshevism, fear of war with Turkey, fear of financial cost, fear of an underdeveloped economy (Armenia was a poorhouse).

There were reasons, as Gates and Morgenthau and Bristol had been saying again and again, why a separate Armenian mandate was wrong. But there was no legislative voice crying: "Unless the United States does something for the transatlantic nations besides giving relief, collecting war debts, and conducting business as usual through the Open Door, there will be a second world war to pay." Such expanding industrial corporations as Standard Oil of New York, Ford Motor, and General Electric even during the debates were sizing up resources and markets in Arab areas and in Soviet Russia. Ford and General Electric sensed that Russia was about to annex the Erivan Republic anyway, so they did not want the United States to bother with a mandate. Apparently it did not occur to Republican nationalists in the Senate that Dollar Diplomacy and the Open Door might be poor long-range policies for the Old World — perhaps poorer than a mandate.[71]

Things looked terrible to Barton during the debates as he tried to postpone a vote on Lodge's resolution against a mandate. The Republican majority leader, at the same time, was moving for a roll call as quickly as possible and then adjournment. In his haste, the Senator, proud of his literary accomplishments, made a speech which showed that he had badly misread the Harbord document. The Senators on June 1, with the political conventions in mind, approved the Lodge Resolution by a vote of 52 to 23. [72]

◀ ▶

America thus spurned a possible opportunity. It rejected the only military obligation, outside of what might have happened through League membership, to take a step in hard learning about the ambiguities and responsibilities of European order; Britisher Harold Nicolson said for the Allies, after Wilson's departure from France, that the United States became the "ghost at all our feasts."[73] Imperceptions by the missionaries, relief leaders, and the President helped ruin their effort to make America's duty commensurate with its ability. They were creatures of the last heyday of the Protestant frontier era in America. Their language was often irrelevant to an increasingly pluralistic society. They saw dimly the intercontinental culture which in 1920 was already emerging.[74] But they had a vision of a cooperating, noncolonial relation among nations which had more of the future in it than the view of the isolationists.

Chapter *10*

"*Clamorous Armenianism*"

IT MUST have seemed in June 1920 to some missionary leaders that God had taken a vacation. There was little left of their peace plans. What remained of a century's investment in the Ottoman Empire was in such unsettled straits that obstacles to education and evangelism, except in the coastal mission colleges, were almost insuperable. For the American Board and Near East Relief, philanthropy and politics had to be the continued emphases. The Protestants turned to direct help for Armenians, while also looking for signs that Wilsonian foreign policy was not disappearing.

THE EASTERN RIDDLE

The defeat of the mandate was not the end but a midpoint in America's long affair with Armenia. Ever since massacres began in the 1890s, Armenianism was the main factor missionaries had used to influence United States relations with the Near East. At the end of the war the Protestants had involved the Wilson administration in the Eastern Question by urging protection of relief among Armenians. Barton was sure during the peace settlement that since more of Armenia's young people had studied in American schools than in those of all the other Western countries put together, the United States should have a mandate. In Paris, Wilson and

247

House talked regularly of an American mandate over Armenia. A touch-stone for the Morgenthau Memorandum and the King-Crane and Har-bord reports on Asia Minor was deliverance for the Armenians. No less a dispassionate appraiser of Anatolia than Gates declared to Secretary of State Colby before the mandate vote in the Senate: "Our desire is simply and solely that some way may be found of saving the unhappy Armenians from complete extermination." [1] Armenianism had such force that it would be the main issue in United States relations with Turkey for a dec-ade after the Treaty of Sèvres, which the Allies presented to their puppet government at Constantinople in June 1920.

If the reservoir of Armenianism in America was so expansive, why had the Senate said no to the mandate scheme? One reason, as noted, was the religiously romantic image which Near East Relief and Wilson had of Asia Minor. This maudlin idea had kept the Gates-Morgenthau view from coming to the fore until May 1919. By the time the King-Crane and Har-bord groups had given their support to the Morgenthau Memorandum, prospects for a favorable American opinion had already soured. Most Americans, including Wilson, Lodge, and Gerard, did not recognize that the Christian Armenians were not the good people or the Muslim Turks the bad. These American leaders did not emphasize that the millets and Westernization were causing communal warfare in the Ottoman Empire. British and French thinking, in contrast, often noted that a Christian Ar-menia among Turkey, Azerbaijan, Syria, and Mesopotamia would be an irritant to any French and British mandates over Muslim Arabs. The ex-perienced Allies did not get taken by the fact that their own and Armenian peoples both used Christian symbols. Mission-relief propaganda always had been careful to make sure that the American public would never know that the Dashnaktsuthiun was as much Marxist-socialist as Christian, or that a gulf separated Cilician Armenia from the Erivan Republic: Chris-tian Armenia was Christian Armenia. It was in the Near East somewhere, an indivisible unit. The average American admittedly did not need to have careful explanations of subtleties when the President himself did not un-derstand them well.

Then too, there was divided counsel from American supporters of Ar-menia, which helped turn the Senate toward a negative decision. Barton's effort for unity among Armenophiles through the Armenia-America So-ciety (formerly the American Friends of Armenia) had not worked. Fail-ure came partly because the ACIA (even though it had among its members

248

Near East Relief spokesmen Cleveland Dodge and Walter Smith) increasingly had come under the influence of such Republicans as Senator Lodge and extremist Armenian Americans as Yale University graduate Vahan Cardashian. Gerard thought Cardashian "crazy," [2] but Gerard did nearly everything Cardashian wanted him to do. Republican isolationism and Cardashian's conspiracy theory about Western treachery toward Armenia complemented each other to produce the idea that the Erivan Republic should help itself and accept aid but no mandate. Because of these goals and Gerard and Cardashian's desire to run their program, the ACIA did not join the mandate-oriented Armenia-America Society. The Armenia-America Society cooperated mostly with such Turkish Armenians as Boghos Nubar and excluded all Armenian Americans, trying to checkmate Cardashian. The executive committee members of the Armenia-America Society included its chairman Walter Smith, its secretary Ernest Riggs, George Montgomery of the King-Crane Commission, Stanley White of the Presbyterian Board, and Hamilton Holt. The group's prime motive was to secure a mandate over areas in Anatolia where there were American Board compounds.

In spite of disagreement among Armenophiles and the naiveté of the American government, a mandate over Armenia would not necessarily have failed. United States prestige and British prestige were still so high in the Erivan Republic and Caucasus in 1920 that the handful of American officers with Haskell and the British garrison at Batumi were enough to deter any armed clash between Kemalists and the Erivan Republic. Harbord's miniscule group earlier had helped diminish fears between Turks and Armenians for months. The peoples of Anatolia so respected the relative impartiality of the United States that America's potential for easing millet-conditioned tension was many times higher than that of France or Greece.

But the United States rejection of a mandate showed that Wilson's stress on Armenia had been inadequate. Americans had not been wise or steadfast enough to take on the Eastern riddle through Armenianism. The narrow perspective and mawkishness of the pro-Armenian stance helped mystify Wilson on broader matters related to Turkey after Italy had taken the first open step of resistance to his idealism in April 1919. United States principles of mandates and self-determination for Armenians and other ethnic groups in Turkey had been a fine start. But Wilson's hesitant, no more than token moves had confused the whole Near East reconstruction.

249

The Sèvres Treaty presented to the Porte in June 1920 showed that American diplomacy had saved neither Syria nor Armenia. Sèvres stipulated a separate, integral Armenia impossible to achieve without a United States mandate. This inclusion by the Allies was foolish, for they knew that the American Senate had eliminated such a contingency just a few days before the Treaty's delivery to the Porte. The Armenian fate was worse than that of any minority in the Ottoman Empire — and this minority deserved better. The Treaty also ended any thought of American guidance over Arabs. The French soon conquered Feisal's soldiers in July 1920, and the Arab leader fled to Mesopotamia, where the British made him king. Subject to confirmation by the League of Nations, the Treaty set aside a Syrian mandate for France, Palestinian and Mesopotamian mandates for Britain. Sèvres also gave economic concessions in Anatolia to the Allies and spheres of influence in Cilicia to France, in Smyrna to Greece, and in Adalia to Italy. Constantinople was to be an international territory.

The Allies had carried out the secret treaties in the Sèvres document, albeit with less harshness than if the United States had not entered the Turkish negotiations. (See Map 4, including inset, on p. 103.) American involvement had helped the possibility that the Arabs in Asia would establish their independence more quickly than their brothers in North Africa. It was an unsolicited compliment both for America's awkward procrastination and its principle of self-determination that Kemalist nationalism prospered so well that the Anatolian articles of Sèvres would soon be dead letters.

Even though the United States refused to accept a long-term connection with the Armenians, it continued to accept Armenianism. No small help was Sèvres, which made formal the desire of the Allies to have the American President arbitrate the boundaries of an integral Armenia. This duty, which Wilson was glad to carry out, encouraged missionaries to keep proclaiming Armenianism.

FANTASY AND PASSIVENESS

During the months after the United States Senate refused a mandate, the Protestant establishment searched for clues that the grandeur of an American protection of Armenians was not receding from view. Nostalgia increased. Would it be through the Erivan Republic or through the French sphere in Cilician Armenia that something would happen to reverse the trend? through events in Europe? in the United States? The religious aspects of Armenianism were so many in the American mind that it was hard for Armenophiles to let go of Armenianism. Whereas a salty Bristol in Constantinople could use a millet view to describe Armenians and their situation, most people in the United States used a Christian frame.

The Republican and Democratic national conventions of 1920 showed that Americans cherished Armenianism, but not the maelstrom of European quarrels supposedly connected with a mandate over Armenia. The Republicans defiantly condemned Wilson for even asking for a mandate over Armenia. Despite the President's move to get into the Democratic platform a plank favoring an American guardianship over what he thought was a hideously distressed Armenia, Wilson's party resolved on nothing more than sympathy and direct aid to Armenia. Sympathy and aid were also in the Republican platform. These words indicated what was possible in American help for Armenia.[3]

Actually, nothing much was possible except fantasy because of circumstances in the Near East. The Turkish nationalists, who were de facto rulers of much of Anatolia, were not fond of Sèvres' provisions for Asia Minor. Moreover, the Allies did not like them either in connection with an integral Armenia. Britain in July 1920 gave munitions to the Erivan Republic, and withdrew its last soldier from the Caucasus. Bristol warned Washington against an arbitration by Wilson and stated that if the West did not back the arbitral decision with troops, there would be Kemalist reprisals against Armenians and Near East Relief personnel. Riggs of the Armenia-America Society and Barton nevertheless encouraged the White House to establish boundaries for a nonexistent state. As Wilson and other Americans clung to the preposterous notion of an integral Armenia, Haskell in August resigned both as Allied high commissioner and as relief head, removing his military staff. Haskell saw that the West had abandoned the Erivan Republic. Also, the Kemalists and the Soviet government agreed to press the Erivan Republic militarily. Having lost the pretense of allegiance from Kemal and being coerced by the Allies, the Porte then signed the Treaty of Sèvres with its articles on Armenia.[4]

While the Erivan Republic was deteriorating, an internationalism in America conducive to missionary aims was declining. Many of the returned soldiers, seeing futility in the defeat of the Covenant, were already feeling like Lieutenant Henry in Ernest Hemingway's *A Farewell to Arms*

251

— Henry said that the sacrifices of the war were like the Chicago stock-yards, if nothing was done with the meat except to bury it. Frustration in America was large, as shown by police-state arrests of radicals, dozens of lynchings of black Americans, violent strikes, economic recession, and unemployment of millions of workers. Concern for internal matters was so general that there was little energy in America for dealing with foreign problems as remote as Armenia.

Presidential candidate Harding in a speech in Des Moines vowed to keep the United States out of the League and bloviated (his word) about starting a new association of nations. One leading Democrat observed that Harding was standing at Armageddon and straddling for the Lord. Henry King, Hamilton Holt, and many other Republicans in the League to Enforce Peace bolted their party after the Des Moines address. Senator Lodge and the irreconcilables rejoiced over the speech, for they virtually had been the authors. Lodge had stated to Harding in September 1920, almost as a threat against any Wilsonian inclinations within Harding, that Republicans would "refuse absolutely to go in . . . to the Wilson League." The Senate majority leader had said to Harding: "we want to beat Wilsonism and the League just as badly as possible and bury them as deeply as can be done." [5] Democratic candidate James M. Cox's final campaign comment, a tearful plea for the United States to use the League to salvage broken nations abroad, looked un-American in comparison with the Republicans' isolationism and nativism. Harding tapped the narrower moods of the country when he bloviated: "What America needs is not heroics but healing, not surgery but serenity." [6]

Serenity was the label for the election outcome, but incredibility was the word for Wilson's approach to the Turkish settlement. The Chief Executive earlier had established a committee under William Westermann (former head of the Western Asia Section of the Peace Commission) to prepare an arbitral description of an imaginary, integral Armenia's borders. Using statistics from American Board files, Riggs and Barton pressed the Westermann group. The missionaries wanted a generous grant of territory to an Armenia with no government (unless one granted authenticity to the goverment in the nearly extinct Erivan Republic). In October 1920, while the Westermann committee was completing its task, Turkish nationalists and Bolsheviks conducted forays against the wobbly Republic. The American Committee for the Independence of Armenia tried vainly to get an American warship to Batumi. The Armenia-America Society fruitlessly sought Elihu Root as legal counsel. Then in one of the most utopian steps in Near East peacemaking, Wilson on November 23, 1920, cabled to the Supreme Council an ideal boundary award for a paper Armenia (see Map 7 on p. 229); Kemalists responded by invading the Kars region of the Erivan Republic.[7]

Barton continued to push Wilson, partly because he felt that the future of missions in Asia Minor rested with Armenians. He wrote Ernest Riggs, who had resigned from the Armenia-America Society to become educational director for Near East Relief in Turkey, that it was uncertain whether there would be any Turks in power for long. Barton believed that missionaries like Riggs, who were working both in politics and relief, could re-establish evangelism and education among Armenians under protection of the West. He thought that Greece, backed by Britain, would not allow the Kemalists to push the Europeans out of Asia Minor. Barton knew it would be hard to continue the American Board under the Turkish nationalists — from Samsun a relief official in November 1920 notified Boston that Kemalists thought "Near East Relief exists solely as a political organization to further the aims of Armenia." [8] Bristol also got word to Barton that Kemal was going to put commissars with relief personnel in areas under his control to make sure they administered philanthropy to people regardless of race or religion. An indication that Barton's prognosis was inaccurate came in December 1920 when Kemalists expelled Harry Riggs (Ernest's brother) from Harput.

Administrators of independent missionary schools meanwhile had turned to security for their colleges under the new Allied governments in Constantinople and in Syria. President Gates of Robert College had written to House, who was in London at a League of Nations meeting. Gates asked for help in obtaining rights for his school, which he declared was a "strictly Christian Missionary institution." The several independent schools also coordinated and improved their business management and financial stability through the Near East College Association, incorporated in New York in 1919. Dodge led in the establishment of the College Association; clergyman Albert Staub was its executive head.[9]

American Board–Near East Relief forces were in a different position. They felt that without the Erivan Republic, there conceivably would be no Armenia and no missions or relief among Armenians. William Peet and Walter Smith in November 1920 lobbied at the League of Nations in Geneva. The League then invited mediation of the Erivan Republic and

Kemalist fighting. Barton and Howard Bliss' brother, Frederic J. Bliss, persuaded Wilson to propose good offices. The two men obtained the designation of Morgenthau as presidential mediator. Dodge corresponded with his friend at the White House, enclosing a letter which indicated that Barton had obtained from Senator Lodge a promise to approve an American loan of twenty million dollars for the Erivan Republic. Dodge asked Wilson to advise such an act in his annual message to Congress. "I really think, from what Dr. Barton told me," Dodge concluded, "that Mr. Lodge is sincere." [10] The President answered that he would take pleasure in recommending to Congress a loan to the Erivan Republic.

Reports from the Caucasus at the same time were militating against policies proposed by both Republican and Democratic platforms. The Erivan Republic early in December 1920 signed agreements with the Kemalists and Soviet Russia, authorizing an annexation of the Kars region by the Turkish nationalists and a new Erivan government which included a majority of Bolsheviks. This move was more than American isolationists could take. Senator Lodge informed Barton that since the Erivan Republic had gone into an alliance with Soviet Russia, a Congressional loan was almost out of the question. The Bolshevik Erivan government then annulled all foreign loans. That did it. Although the Armenia-America Society tried to press officials on the mediation plan, the League of Nations and Allied governments acknowledged the fait accompli in the Caucasus and did not respond to America's mediation offer. The unexpected picture of revolutionary Bolshevism in Armenia startled Americans, who had thought Armenia was Christian. In this instance, as in the past, United States Congressmen and other officials had almost no analytical data from which to make decisions. The American audience seldom got such views as the comment by American Board missionary Clarence Ussher (formerly at Van, currently with Near East Relief in the Caucasus). Ussher declared that the Armenian Bolsheviks in the Erivan Republic had been "very moderate and very different from what we were led to expect from the stories of Russia. If they continue as they have begun the country may soon be better satisfied than with the old rotten government." [11]

After the Erivan Republic came under Soviet domination, American and British Armenophiles hated to admit defeat. Since they believed their cause was righteous, they looked for a new course. Bryce remarked his anguish to Barton: the United States Congress "will vote no money for an expedition. Neither will the British government ask Parliament. The

League of Nations has no funds nor troops. France will not lift a finger, indeed she is said to be courting the Turks. Italy has been supplying munitions to Kemal and his Nationalists. . . . Every power has behaved ill." [12] Gerard of the ACIA visited Harding at Marion, Ohio, and ridiculously asked backing for Sèvres provisions for an integral Armenia. Harding equivocated. Gerard petitioned Wilson to protest attacks on Armenians to the Turkish governments at Constantinople and at Ankara, the Kemalist capital. The President finally saw that talk was useless.

It was the new secretary of the Armenia-America Society, George Montgomery, a son of missionaries to Armenia, who came up with a novel plan. Montgomery was both clergyman and attorney. From 1916 to 1920 he had served the American embassy at Constantinople, the Young Men's Christian Association, and the King-Crane Commission. He had taught at Yale. Late in 1920 he asked Barton whether a provisional government for Cilician Armenia under Boghos Nubar might not be a good idea. Montgomery thought such a government might help in maintaining the Sèvres Treaty. Thus was born a scheme upon which the American public could expend its Armenianism. Montgomery in January 1921 proposed to President Wilson and Senator Lodge a text for a Congressional resolution: "*Resolved* that the United States government be asked to take action alone or in association with other Powers to assure a protectorate over . . . portions . . . of the Ottoman Empire, with a view to the development of these portions into an Armenian home." [13]

After the lame-duck Wilson administration ignored Montgomery, Barton asked Bryce about a conference which the Allies had scheduled to revise the Treaty of Sèvres. Bryce cabled that Barton and Montgomery should attend the forthcoming Allied meeting. At the London Conference, to which the United States government did not send a representative, Barton and Montgomery cultivated such individuals as Lloyd George's private secretary, Kerr, and Foreign Secretary Curzon. Through the American ambassador to Great Britain, Barton sent Allied leaders documents on missionary interests in the Near East, particularly on the cause of an Armenian national home. The response at first was not promising. One Britisher before the meeting had stated that only the United States could relieve Armenians. The Americans did not know how to take tips from Lloyd George's office, partly because Bryce dismissed the British Prime Minister as a "scoundrel." [14]

As Soviet Russia moved to occupy and annex the Erivan Republic after a Dashnak government had displaced the Bolshevik, the London Conference took up the Barton-Montgomery idea. Putting Armenia on the agenda again, without serious intent to do anything, the Allies were perpetuating their irresponsible behavior toward Armenia since the Congress of Berlin in 1878. The West, by appearing to provide protection, helped prevent the direct negotiation between Turks and Armenians which might have produced a viable Erivan Republic. At any rate, the London Conference in March 1921 discarded an integral Armenia with boundaries arbitrated by Wilson, and prescribed a national home in Cilicia for Turkish Armenians. The Council of the League of Nations was to draw the boundaries. Missionary diplomacy at last got a victory that seemed to mean something.

While Barton was in England, the Nestorian question came up. The American Board secretary sought help for thirty thousand or more Urmia-area Nestorians who were in a refugee camp near Mosul. He met at the Colonial Office with T. E. Lawrence and Churchill, who explained that Britain did not have the resources to repatriate Nestorian refugees. Churchill asked Barton to seek a change in American immigration laws so the Nestorians could go to the United States. He promised that Britain would supply part of the transport cost. Churchill, who planned to leave for a conference in Cairo on Arab-Allied conflict, agreed to press later for assistance from America on the Nestorian affair. Returned to the United States, Barton and Presbyterian Board Secretary Robert Speer late in March 1921 both went to the new Secretary of State, Charles Evans Hughes, for aid on Churchill's recommendations. The two missionaries organized a fund to help emigration of Nestorians from Mesopotamia, and worked with Nestorian Americans to present the problem of their compatriots to President Harding. For months Nestorian matters remained unsettled. Speer explained to a correspondent that he had written as strongly as he could to Harding, but whether the United States would do anything was not clear. Speer feared that suffering among Christian people was to continue.[15]

As to an Armenian national home, Barton realized that Near East Relief increasingly had less power. Even with public support by Wilson (who before leaving office had stated that his heart jumped with feeling for Armenians), Near East Relief was losing its hold on the American people. Income in 1921 was about half what it had been late in 1919. Americans were weary of a cause which seemed to have no end. Overseas, United

States Army personnel were completing their tours with the relief staff. In the Caucasus, the resignation of Haskell and his aides had left Haskell's missionary successor, Ernest Yarrow, in a bad position. When the Soviets entered the Erivan Republic, Yarrow faced restrictions much like those which Kemal had imposed upon relief workers in Turkey. At Merzifon the Kemalists ordered all but two Americans to leave (Anatolia College had housed an orphanage in mid-1919; the college had functioned under George White's leadership both as a school and relief center since autumn 1919).[16]

The Armenia-America Society and the American Committee for the Independence of Armenia hoped optimistically that the Harding administration might bring better things for Armenia. Secretary of State Hughes had been one of the charter members of the ACIA. Barton, unofficial head of the Armenia-America Society, had a long conference with Hughes in March 1921 about an autonomous Armenia in Cilicia. Montgomery soon asked the Secretary to support government financing for an Armenian national home, declaring there would be no end to relief until Armenians were safe from the Turks. The ACIA disagreed. Gerard and its new secretary, Henry Jessup (whose father had been a pioneer Presbyterian missionary in Syria), rejected the national home scheme. Gerard wildly requested of Hughes de jure recognition for the Soviet Armenian Republic and equipment for ten thousand Armenian Americans so that together with Armenians in the Near East they might occupy the area specified for Armenia in the Treaty of Sèvres.[17]

The Armenia-America Society and the ACIA thus opposed each other. It was as if the ACIA had to be different to have a raison d'être. The new disagreement gave Gerard an excuse to drop his nominal membership in the Armenia-America Society. Difficulties between the organizations continued partly because Gerard and Jessup were under the enchantment of Cardashian. Gerard signed nearly anything this Armenian sent to him. Jessup became nervous because the "crowd headed by Barton" was willing to forsake a large Armenia. As for Cardashian, he was jealous of Barton forces for their access to Western officials and resented the Armenia-America Society for keeping him out. He published a theory in the booklet, *Wilson: The Wrecker of Armenia*, which charged that President Wilson, Near East Relief, and American missionaries were answerable for the long delay in the Ottoman treaty and for the crucifixion of Armenia.[18]

Barton did not obtain Hughes' endorsement of an Armenian national home. Hughes neglected both the Armenia-America Society and the ACIA. He took more account of Bristol's ideas than had the previous administration, and made the Open Door basic to American diplomacy in the area. Hughes' attitudes did not deter Barton from telling Senator Lodge in April 1921 that if the United States would supply funds, Britain would develop the structure for an Armenian national home. Lodge was not sympathetic. Sending Barton's letter to Hughes, Lodge declared that Congress was unlikely to lend money to establish any government anywhere; the Secretary of State acquiesced.[19]

Barton meanwhile began to sense that Wilsonianism was out and irreconcilability was in. After Senator Borah threatened to wreck the Harding administration if it led the United States into any association of nations, the new President in April 1921 capitulated to the tiny right-wing minority in his party which by then clearly included Lodge. For months the Massachusetts Senator had been drumming into Harding that the election was a referendum against America's entering the League. Having prevented passage of Wilson's Covenant, Lodge and Borah believed they had delivered the country from a witches' brew of dragon teeth in the transatlantic cauldron. Democratic Senator Williams mourned to Barton that the Republicans had made America so base that it was no longer its brother's brother. This turn away from the League was a disappointment to Hughes, who was a moderate internationalist. But the irreconcilables were in control, and Harding apparently did not have the strength to overcome them. Party unity was a norm by which policy was to be made. Since powerful Lodge was against direct aid for an Armenian national home, there was nothing Hughes felt he could do but neglect the home plan and turn to goals that had no trace of Wilsonianism in them. Lodge's obstructionism throughout the peace settlement had contributed much to America's ineptness in relations with the Near East.[20]

Barton was almost beside himself. The American government was passive while in Cilicia the French, under attack by the Kemalists, were considering a withdrawal from the area where an Armenian national home was to be. Barton asked Montgomery to see if something could not be done to stay the horror which menaced the American Board's Central Turkey field in Cilicia: "I hardly know which way to turn." [21] Leaders of the Protestant, Catholic, and Gregorian Armenians in the Near East declared to Barton that they trusted his activities would have the blessing of "our Heavenly Father who is now, more than ever, our only hope." [22] Relying on human appeals too, the missionary statesman besought the American government to oppose French designs in Cilicia. Barton and Montgomery prepared a booklet, *The United States Government and Help to Armenia*, which traced Western obligations to Armenians. Near East Relief in June 1921 distributed the booklet to every Congressman and hundreds of leaders and organizations in every state. The State Department soon responded to this propaganda by forwarding to Boston a Bristol dispatch which recommended missionaries' forbearance both in Turkey and in Armenia and abstention from an anti-Turkish campaign.[23]

KEMALIST MOMENTUM

Near East Relief and the American Board soon discovered that Armenianism no longer was going to move the United States government into Turkish peacemaking. The Harding administration was busy dismantling the United States military establishment built during the war and preparing for a grand conference on limitation of naval armaments. A lull came in mission-relief lobbying when Barton, whom an Armenian leader described as the intercessor between Western and Eastern Christians and "father" of the Armenians, surveyed the Far East for the American Board. Near East Relief's educational director, Ernest Riggs, who returned from Anatolia in late summer 1921 after expulsion by Kemalists for pro-Armenian policies, partly filled Barton's place.

In Asia Minor, important happenings had been foreshadowing a Kemalist conquest over the Allies. After the Porte lost most of its prestige among Turks by signing the Treaty of Sèvres, the Kemalists had evolved into the government representing Turkey. At the London Conference of spring 1921 which Barton attended, Italy had agreed with the Kemalists to withdraw from Adalia in return for economic concessions. The Greeks tried to check the Allies' move away from Sèvres by marching east into central Anatolia to capture Ankara. Just short of the Kemalist capital, the Greek advance halted. Mustafa Kemal and his troops then made ready for countering the Greeks while skirmishing against the French in Cilicia. At the end of the summer the Greeks lost fifteen thousand men in a desperate battle along the Sakarya River, and retired to the Baghdad railway. (See Map 1 on p. 16.) Weakened in Cilicia because of this Kemalist victory, France in October promised the Turkish nationalists to evacuate the area which the London Conference had set as an Armenian national home. Having more losses than any Western nation in the war, France decided that Syria was the only vital interest it could afford in the Near East. When the French left Cilicia, over one hundred fifty thousand Greeks and Armenians fled with them.

While the Kemalists were eliminating Italian and French occupation of Anatolia, the Harding administration cautiously looked over the Turkish nationalists. Bristol since January 1921 had been receiving evidence that the Ankara government wanted formal relations with the United States. At one point, a Near East Relief worker stationed at Samsun told Bristol that the Kemalists desired recognition by the United States and investment of American capital in Anatolia. After the French agreed to withdraw from Cilicia, Bristol persuaded Washington to send to Ankara a United States Department of Commerce official to discuss economic matters informally.[24]

During the Commerce official's stay in the Kemalist capital, the Armenia-America Society kept trying to get an Armenian national home. Montgomery got stimulation from a visit by Bryce to the United States; Bryce thought the Greeks could force a Turk evacuation of Cilician Armenia. Montgomery and Riggs drafted a resolution and persuaded Congressman John J. Rogers of Massachusetts to introduce it in December 1921. The Rogers Resolution requested that the United States call a conference to consider methods for establishing the Cilician Armenians as a nation. Back from the Far East, Barton set about getting Secretary of State Hughes to bring up the Cilician issue at the Washington Naval Conference. He had such a concern partly because the Kemalists had driven American Board personnel out of Cilicia. But Bristol summed up the State Department's reaction to Barton, writing that partiality for Christian minorities was an injury to them so long as the West did not supply the military forces required for Turkish compliance with a separate Armenia.[25]

Bristol's attitude irritated Barton and Montgomery, who sought to have Bristol removed as American high commissioner to Turkey, in part because Bristol had not defended Ernest Riggs when the Kemalists had expelled that missionary. Rather, Bristol had remonstrated with Riggs for favoritism to Armenians. Barton felt that Bristol's apparent accommodation to the Kemalists was "absolutely wrong." Riggs doubted the wisdom of an anti-Bristol position; "I confess that I fear," he confided to Montgomery, "that a new man going from America might be led to the same position which Admiral Bristol holds." [26] Yet Barton went ahead with a case against Bristol, which in March 1922 he presented to Secretary Hughes. The theme was that Bristol had not protected American interests in the Near East. Commending the Admiral for zeal and ability, Barton declared that Bristol "inclined to take the word of a Turk as of more value than the word of an American," and to defend the Turks more than the minorities. Barton noted a missionary letter from Turkey which charged Bristol with seeming approval of both the extirpation of Christian elements from the Asia Minor population and the removal of missionaries. Barton asked Hughes for an ambassador who had diplomatic experience, knowledge of the Near East, and an intent to work closely with the missionaries. The Board secretary understandably did not want to sit idle while what had been the best American Board program in the world lost its constituency. But attacking a fairly perceptive Bristol was trying to remove a symptom. The missionaries needed to think about coming to terms with the Kemalists. Relying on a West determined to behave irresponsibly about Asia Minor was not producing security for the Armenians or for the Protestants from the United States.[27]

Barton and other friends of Armenia could not obtain a State Department endorsement of the proposed dismissal of Bristol or of the Rogers Resolution. As the Allies in February and March 1922 postponed scrapping the Sèvres Treaty and reaffirmed a national home for Armenians, the American government remained aloof. Barton soon was apologetic about his political agitation in a letter to Hughes, but defensive about his attempt to prevent violence against Christian minorities in Anatolia. The Secretary in April 1922 wrote Barton at length: "I am very sorry to say that I see no way in which this Government can, in existing circumstances, act to the advantage of the Ottoman Greeks or of the Armenians. . . . In view of the sentiment of this country against participation in transatlantic affairs, and of the limits imposed upon our action, I do not feel that it is advisable for us to issue protests which we are not prepared to follow with practical support." Hughes wrote similarly to Henry Jessup of the ACIA.[28]

Then another flicker of hope. Barton acted vigorously when in May 1922 the British ambassador to Washington proposed a Western investigation of alleged Turkish atrocities. There had been reports of new deportations attending the Kemalist-Greek war. The executive committee of Near East Relief directed its chairman to ask Hughes to appoint a representative for the investigation. Telegrams went to Harding and Hughes. Barton had conferences with the Secretary of State and with Allen W.

Dulles, who was the Near East specialist in the State Department and a former assistant to Bristol in Constantinople. The American Board secretary reported to Caleb Gates that recent publicity by Near East Relief and the Federal Council of Churches had done something of worth for the Armenians: Washington had decided to join an international inquiry of Muslim-Christian relations in Asia Minor. Giving a sop to Armenianism, Hughes in June 1922 publicly announced America's commitment to the inquiry. The Secretary followed Barton's desire that James Harbord be the American representative. But the French and Italians balked at a move which might weaken their relations with the Ankara government; so the inquiry was put in the hands of the International Red Cross. Dulles in July told Barton that the idea of an international commission was unworkable.[29]

Meanwhile Near East Relief continued its philanthropy. It had transferred work out of such Kemalist areas as Kars (annexed from the Erivan Republic in December 1920) and Harput to Soviet Armenia and Syria. The relief group early in 1922 dismissed twenty-five thousand children from orphanages because of limited funds. Despite cutbacks, Near East Relief innovated a braille program for children (probably the first of its kind in the Caucasus), an agricultural school for orphans which used over seventeen thousand acres provided by the Soviet Armenian government, a maternity ward for refugee mothers in Beirut.[30]

It was in August 1922 that relief chairman Barton observed Kemalist momentum pushing all before it. The Turkish nationalists began an offensive against the Greeks, and within three weeks pushed their antagonists into the Aegean Sea. Kemalists soon controlled all of Asia Minor.

This drive to the Aegean outraged the American Board secretary, not least because a fire in Smyrna inflicted damage of more than one hundred thousand dollars to Board property. Foreseeing an Armageddon, Barton burst out against the Turks, whom he chose to blame for missionary problems: "The rights of Americans and of minorities are held in contempt and all civilized laws are defied," he wrote to Harding and Hughes, "as we must always expect from a distinctly Mohammedan Government. We are witnessing what promises to be the beginning of another European war, in which barbarianism will be arraigned against civilization." [31] He urged a Western ultimatum to the Kemalists, and troops to the Bosporus to save the Near East. Several church groups passed resolutions with similar language. But the thunder of the First World War's rhetoric was ineffective.

The view of Turks in Barton's message to Harding and Hughes was inappropriate, as remarked by President MacLachlan of International College. The Turks did not massacre Greeks, as Greeks had done to Turks in May 1919. About the worst the Turkish Army did was force captured Greek soldiers to shout "Long live Mustafa Kemal" as they marched into detention. Turkish soldiers protected International College during the disruption of the occupation; a Turkish cavalryman rescued MacLachlan from irregulars who nearly beat the missionary to death while trying to loot the agricultural buildings of the college (MacLachlan suffered broken ribs and badly injured arms and legs; it took him nearly two months to recover). A three-day Smyrna fire (September 13–15), which Turks made every effort to control, destroyed nearly a square mile in Greek and Armenian areas and made two hundred thousand people homeless. Included in this loss was the American Board's Collegiate Institute for Girls. MacLachlan's investigation of the fire's origins led to the conviction that Armenian terrorists, dressed in Turkish uniforms, fired the city. Apparently the terrorists were attempting to bring a Western intervention.[32]

Soon after the request for a Western ultimatum, the calmed American Board secretary reflected with Gates on events from the first Smyrna crisis of May 1919 to the crisis of September 1922. Gates thought that the United States could have prevented the disruption in Asia Minor which occurred after the Paris Peace Conference. He felt the inscription on America's flag should be the criticism Jesus pronounced against irresponsible peoples in the final judgment story of Matthew 25: Inasmuch as you did not help the needy, you did not help me. Barton suspected that Turkish nationalism rather than Western protection was to be the outcome of the Greek invasion blessed by the Supreme Council three years earlier. Informing Washington of a three-million-dollar claim by the American Board against the Ankara government, he requested through an aide that the United States participate in any conference planned by the Allies to rewrite the Treaty of Sèvres.[33]

THE LOOSENED GRIP

As the West talked of negotiating with the Kemalists, part of the American public began to realize that Armenianism and godliness were not identical. Ever since missionaries in the nineteenth century had become the dominant United States concern in the Ottoman Empire, opinion in

America increasingly favored Christian minorities. With the massacres of the 1890s, attitudes had become fixed on the stereotype of the terrible Turk.

It was Gates and Bristol who led in weakening Armenianism in the American mind. During his year in the United States at the end of the war, the Robert College president had not hesitated to give press interviews which included his equalitarian view toward ethnic groups in Turkey. He declared in his memoirs: "I had often told my students that I was pro-Turk just as I was pro-Armenian, pro-Bulgarian, pro-Greek, pro-Jew." [34] Bristol, though never disagreeing with missionaries that the United States should lead Ottoman reconstruction, had opposed their Armenianism. Believing Armenophile publicity "exaggerated, misconstrued, and abusive," Bristol early in 1920 told Barton that in some ways it had called forth the worst Turkish feelings. He said to the mission secretary that it was contrary to the American sense of fair play to kick a man when he was down and give him no chance to defend himself. Bristol sought firsthand studies of the Near East by United States newsmen, and a broad idea of ethnic relations in Turkey. Thinking that a diversity of American interests in Turkey would militate toward his aim, he welcomed business development in Turkey. With concurrence from Gates, Bristol repeated often in 1921 and 1922 that relief workers and minorities had provoked reprisals and were like the boy who "poked the hornets' nest and naturally was thoroughly stung"; Bristol thought the boy should be paddled. Troubled that killings by Armenians and Greeks did not get into the American press, the admiral wondered in his diary, "Why aren't the atrocities committed by a Christian nation more heinous than those committed by Moslem races," if Christianity is better than Islam? He worked on the feelings of William Peet, but decided Peet had an unchangeable resentment against Turks. Bristol acknowledged that since Turks had failed the missionary so many times, there was reason for his negativeness. [35]

Meanwhile, Bristol and the State Department had been indirectly seeking access for American business in Turkey. Since 1919 the State Department had reflected a worry over depleted domestic oil resources by resisting British and French attempts at exclusive oil contracts in Mesopotamia, Palestine, and Anatolia. The State Department not only defended equal opportunity for its nationals in the Near East, but asked American consuls to check on oil prospects. As noted, Bristol had gotten a United States Department of Commerce official to talk informally to the Kemalists about economic possibilities for Americans in Asia Minor. Amid this Open Door atmosphere but without explicit State Department support, members of the ill-fated prewar Chester Project planned anew for a railroad and mining concession in Asia Minor.[36]

In autumn 1922 a pro-Turk statement in an American periodical figured in a public debate about Asia Minor. Retired Rear Admiral Colby M. Chester, believing opinion against Turks was harmful to State Department backing for his revival of the earlier Chester Project (currently called the Ottoman-American Development Corporation), published "Turkey Reinterpreted." Trying to reverse thirty years of Armenianism in one dramatic attempt, the flighty, seventy-eight-year-old Chester produced an extreme model. He depicted Turks as moral, religious, and honest ("Although I have been much in Turkey I never have met a crooked Turk."). As for Armenian massacres, he not only stirred up history but made a little of his own: "Armenians were moved from the inhospitable regions where they . . . could not actually prosper to the most delightful and fertile part of Syria. . . . In due course of time the deportees, entirely unmassacred and fat and prosperous, returned." He claimed that an acquaintance had seen Armenian towns filled with astonishing live ghosts. What a pity, he remarked, "to upset the good old myth of Turkish viciousness . . . but in the interest of accuracy I find myself constrained to do so, although it makes me feel a bit like one who is compelled to tell a child that Jack the Giant Killer really found no monstrous men to slay." [37] The mission-relief reaction to the old man was as serious as to California Congressman A. M. Free's public charge a year earlier that Armenians had killed more Turks than vice versa (Free retreated when Near East Relief pressed him for evidence). The day Riggs of the American Board read Chester's piece, he mailed to the admiral his estimate that "Turkey Reinterpreted" was absolutely false. Within a few weeks Montgomery challenged Chester by an article presenting evidence from German and Turkish eyewitnesses of the massacres of 1915. A relief worker complemented Montgomery's effort by "Crimes of Turkish Misrule," in which he presented documentation for what he called a massacre of two thousand Armenians and Greeks which had taken place a few months before.[38]

The fat was in the flames. In addition to the Chester-Montgomery interchange, *Current History* carried an analysis of missionary and relief organizations by journalist Clair Price. For a series of four articles Price visited Ankara and Constantinople, including a talk with Bristol. The journalist stated that American missions, Armenian clauses in the Treaty of Berlin, and such societies as the Dashnaktsuthiun had alienated Armenians from Turks. After the war, he declared, missionaries to the Ottoman Empire sought to take over the country and to use Armenians for this vast political project. Price said that Near East Relief was at the time of his writing flooding the United States with Armenianism through its monthly, *New Near East* (successor to the *News Bulletin*). He noted that the editor of the periodical, Talcott Williams, had published a book pleading for America to adopt a protectorate over Asia Minor. Price believed that "Near East Relief's magazine alone would provide adequate political cause for the deportation of every one of its workers out of Asia Minor." [39] (Actually, Williams in his book, although showing special concern for the "great people" of Armenia, did recognize that both Christians and Muslims had committed atrocities against each other. Williams felt this factor was reason enough for Anatolian peoples to receive assistance under an experienced umpire like Uncle Sam. [40]) Price regarded Kemalist leaders as trustworthy and not implicated in the Armenian massacres. He thought that mission and relief workers should communicate with the Ankara government, stop "clamorous Armenianism," realize that the millet system made it almost impossible for Turks to regard Christianity as anything other than an unfriendly political program, and accept the Turkification of Asia Minor.

Friends of missionaries hastened to answer this journalist who was revealing what had been concealed. Refusing to compliment the accurate parts of Price's articles, Montgomery protested in *Current History* that American missionary schools were not divisive. Armenian revolutionary leaders criticized the American Board schools, Montgomery said, because they prohibited politics. He stated that the feeling of both Armenians and Arabs against the Turks stemmed from racialism and Ottoman despotism. Regarding reconstruction, he stressed that American officials in Turkey as well as missionaries recommended mandates by the United States. As to Price's comment on clamorous Armenianism, Montgomery pointed out that Near East Relief had worked to find a balance between helping people about to perish and aggravating politics in Anatolia. [41]

Another missionary defender less restrained than Montgomery was Everett P. Wheeler, who had helped relief among Armenians since the

266

1890s. Wheeler claimed it a perversion of patriotism to blame missionaries and Armenians for seeking victory over the Allied enemy, the Turks. History had praised the defense of the West against Muslim intrusion in the Middle Ages, he said, and Christian nations should receive credit for seeking protection of Christians in the Near East. Wheeler thought it an indelible disgrace for America to allow the killing of its citizens in Asia Minor and the destruction of their property without intervention.[42]

During all this public interaction, Barton was writing to Gates that at the end of the Relief Commission trip in 1919 he had come home to push Bristol's idea — namely, a United States responsibility for the whole Ottoman Empire. Meeting opposition, Barton said that the most effective appeal to Americans concerned aid to unprotected minorities. It was this propaganda "to which you refer," he told Gates, "and to which Admiral Bristol has repeatedly referred as an attack on the Turks. It might be so interpreted, but the intention and purpose was not to attack the Turk. [It was to involve America in the Near East.] Do you see the dilemma of the situation?" Turning to contemporary affairs, Barton admitted to Gates that the scheme of an Armenian national home probably would be unattainable. "I cannot get away from the feeling," he stated, "that the suggestion contained in your letter of the shifting of the populations of the Near East will have to be the ultimate conclusion of the Near Eastern question." [43]

An unorthodox view had arisen, and Barton saw that Bristol and Gates had helped bring it into being. The public debate of late 1922 loosened the grip of Armenianism upon Americans. It also helped threaten the monopoly of opinion about Asia Minor held so long by missionary and Armenian groups. The debate came at the same time that President Harding decided the United States would send observers to a conference at Lausanne, which the Allies were calling to negotiate a peace with the Kemalists.

◄ ►

Bristol's preaching about un-Christian elements in Armenianism never found its mark with Barton until Kemalist guns made it ridiculous for the American Board to snub Ankara any longer. The Turks eventually named a hospital at Istanbul (Constantinople) for Bristol in recognition of his sense of justice. The missionaries since the 1830s often had sustained their enterprise by being anti-Muslim and anti-Turk. The American Board also had been willing to idolize its institutions among Armenians more than to remember that God is no respecter of persons. If Barton had heeded Jesus' instruction about loving enemies and praying for those who are spiteful, the mission secretary might have seen the Christianity in Bristol's remarks long before the Greek evacuation of Smyrna.

Chapter 11

Xenophobic Asian Nationalism

MISSION-RELIEF people reluctantly admitted four years after the Armistice of Mudros that there was no alternative to talking with the Turks. The Kemalists determined not to be treated condescendingly. The Allies understood this attitude and did not start a war with Ankara. Some voices urged a United States mediation between the European nations and the Kemalists; Secretary Hughes stated in a speech in Barton's home city that the American government did not intend to intervene in Turkey.[1] President Harding did not go beyond sending destroyers to safeguard American lives in Asia Minor.

A MODERATELY BRAVE SURRENDER

Before the Lausanne Conference opened there was an interesting exchange between the Harding administration and Barton forces. The American Board secretary had pressed Washington for formal representation at the negotations. Harding on October 5, 1922, wrote that the United States "can be represented informally and properly safeguard American interests." [2] Believing full participation necessary, the American Board at its annual meeting so petitioned the Chief Executive. The appeal did not move the President (his refusal did not indicate hardheart-

269

edness toward Armenians; he previously had made donations to Near East Relief). But the request of the mission group did result in the selection of Barton as an adviser to the American delegation at the Conference. Barton thereby learned United States aims for Lausanne: continuance of the capitulations; protection for relief, education, and evangelism; security for minorities, possibly through an Armenian national home; equal commercial opportunity; freedom of the Straits; indemnity for American losses during the war.[3] Receiving permission from the State Department for Peet to assist him, Barton arrived in Switzerland on November 18 — two days before the conference opened. He represented the American and Presbyterian boards, Near East Relief, the Near East College Association (the service agency for the independent missionary colleges which Dodge had founded), and the Federal Council of Churches. Incidentally, the ACIA tried to turn the calendar back two years by requesting the government to defend the Sèvres provisions for Armenia.[4]

Official American observers at Lausanne were the minister to Switzerland, Joseph C. Grew; the ambassador to Italy, Richard W. Child, who directed the United States group; and Mark Bristol. A capable young careerist with dark bushy eyebrows and mustache, Grew had been the secretary-general of the American Peace Commission at Paris. Child, also a young man, had both large ability and arrogance. Grew and Child had little knowledge of the Near East, a factor Barton and Bristol deplored. Child did not work much with Bristol and tried to keep matters in his and Grew's hands. Bristol's chief assistant at the meeting was Gates. Bristol had asked the State Department earlier to designate the Robert College president as an adviser (Crane supported Bristol's request about Gates, having been a visitor at Constantinople Woman's College at the time). Montgomery of the Armenia-America Society was also at Lausanne, acting as a spokesman for the Armenians. Barton noted that Montgomery intended to be openly pro-Armenian; he himself planned to be circumspect so as not to increase Turk opposition to the American Board and to Near East Relief.[5]

The Americans at Lausanne decided at first that their informal status permitted policies no stronger than those of the Allies. Barton declared that the Turks were against an Armenian home and the Western nations were not backing the notion. Some comfort came to the missionary leader from a message of Secretary Hughes to Child, Grew, and Bristol: "It is the desire of the United States Government to support any constructive measure designed to obtain due consideration for the welfare of Christian minorities in Turkey. . . . But you should, on your part, avoid making any proposals." [6] Bristol estimated the home scheme in his diary: Kemalist insistence on the Turkification of Asia Minor probably would eventuate in the removal of Armenians from Anatolia.

Although Bristol's idea was correct, there were reasons for the United States to advocate a national home. Before the Lausanne Conference, the State Department had received over one thousand pro-Armenian letters, causing Hughes to remark to his observers at Lausanne about Americans' deep identification with minorities. Another factor was the plight of Near East Relief in saving orphans and refugees. Having reduced philanthropy in Asia Minor because of Kemalist obstruction and having met United States labor's objections to changing immigration laws for Armenian refugees, Barton and his colleagues felt an autonomous Armenia was an efficient answer to many relief problems. [7]

In spite of previous statements against splitting Asia Minor, Bristol and Gates at Lausanne approved the national home program. They so chose because there was a certain justice about a plan developed by Montgomery, who proposed an Armenian area of eighteen thousand square miles in Cilicia which would be neutral under international guarantee. Conversing with Montgomery, Bristol listened politely to the Armenia-America secretary's old arguments; Bristol noted: "I tried very hard not to show that I was bored. . . . I think I succeeded very well." [8] Bristol also told Barton that he preferred keeping Armenians, Greeks, and Turks together, but recently had concluded that the Armenians deserved a place of their own. Discussing America's humanitarianism in Turkey, Gates said: "Her charities are magnificent but they come short of being effective because they provide no terminal facilities, they do not lead to independence of the refugees." [9]

Also, there was Child's belief that opinion in the United States demanded some attempt to aid Armenians, no matter how impractical. Barton wrote to Boston headquarters that Child and Grew wanted what the Protestants wanted, that the two diplomats talked like mission board members. Barton was ever the optimist. [10]

Child actually was cynical. Causing missionaries to feel he was working for them, he privately thought the home program was a futile, religious goal. In his diary he stated that Near East Relief involved considerable nonsense, ignorant benevolence, and "men who claim to represent God, but whose credentials appear to me to be forged." Recognizing unselfish people among missionaries, he also noted that they were on his neck about an Armenian national home. Both Child and the near-deaf chief delegate of the Turks, Ismet Pasha (later known as Ismet Inönü), believed that there was as much chance for a separate Armenia as for a national home for Negroes in Mississippi or Georgia. Someone reminded Ismet of Indian reservations in America, and the Turk said: "Yes. What a happy experience for the Indian!" Child declared that if every group in the world got the freedom it desired "there would be thousands of peanut states and the map would look . . . like chickenpox." [11]

The United States drive for an Armenian home met high obstacles. Child delivered a speech on giving safety to minorities rather than merely succor. He asked the conference to create a territorial refuge for minorities. After British Foreign Minister Curzon announced in an Olympian manner that the Allies stood united on a national home for the Armenians, Ismet on December 14 stated Turkey would only agree to the League of Nation's standard on minority rights. From that point on, Curzon and the Allied delegates quietly backed down.

Not so the Americans. Barton, Peet, and Montgomery cabled Near East Relief headquarters about the need for decisiveness from Washington. The relief office forwarded this cable to the State Department. Secretary Hughes in turn asked Child, Grew, and Bristol on December 26 to inform him of specific, practical ideas on a territorial base for Armenians. The American observers replied that the Allies probably would use this question only for trading. Americans at Lausanne then obtained permission for Armenians to appear before the subcommission on minorities. Boycotting the Armenians' presentation, Turkish delegates prevented a record of it going into the subcommission's report and declared informally that they were "violently insistent that Turkey would give no territory for the Armenians. . . . They said let America, England, France give them a national home if they feel so solicitous about their dear Armenians." [12] On December 30 Grew released to the press a statement on an Armenian home; he also submitted mission-relief documents to the subcommission on minorities, including the Montgomery plan noted above. These moves so angered the Turks that one of them denounced missionaries as troublemakers. Hughes wrote that Turkish threats were not to affect a continued American effort. In the United States, the ACIA, which belatedly had adopted the Montgomery plan, besieged President Harding and Secretary

Hughes. The Secretary cabled his representatives to consider pressing the Turks or the French for an Armenian area in Cilicia or northern Syria.[13]

United States diplomacy sought little more than a moderately brave surrender to the Kemalists. Harding and Hughes did not expect more than an appeasement of domestic Armenianism. The President remarked to Hughes that Grew's press release ought to have satisfied American sentiment. Seeing the Turks' obsession with full independence, Hughes soon advised his observers to suggest that the Kemalists take initiative for an Armenian autonomy. But the Turks emerged triumphant over an Armenian home in the final report by the subcommission on minorities of January 11, 1923. Harding then epitomized the lameness of his government's strategy: "It is going to be a very keen disappointment to religious America that the Armenian Christians are to be dealt with in this manner, but I frankly do not see how we can do more than strongly appeal in their behalf." [14]

The general position of the Americans at Lausanne was so weak that Barton and Peet eventually gave up. The United States from the beginning had not planned to sign any treaty the Allies framed, or to spell out a separate treaty. American attempts to reinforce the capitulations and secure payment for claims had been unavailing. Ismet Pasha would go no further than oral promises to protect American schools and missions. After an interview with Ismet, Barton stated: "Neither Peet nor I think it amounted to a hill of beans. Ismet said . . . what he thinks the people of America would like to hear. . . . the breath he spends here in talking on this subject would not flare a candle in Angora [Ankara], I fear." [15]

Before the subcommission's defeat of an autonomous Armenia, Barton and Peet had departed Switzerland to survey relief in the Near East. Bristol provided a ship to visit Athens, Salonika, Smyrna, and Constantinople. Concentrating on the thousands of Armenians and Greeks fleeing Anatolia, the veteran missionaries decided to withdraw relief entirely from Asia Minor and Constantinople and to establish a new center in Athens.

Back in Lausanne late in January 1923, the American Board secretary discovered that the Allies had not been able to reach an understanding with the Turks over commercial issues and the capitulations. On February 4 there began a rupture of the Lausanne Conference which would last more than two months.

273

BOON AS WELL AS BANE

Barton thought that the decision at Lausanne on Armenians was abominable; but he and Peet felt relieved at the prospect of a stop to Christian-Muslim conflict in Anatolia. They believed that the elimination of Christian groups from Turkey would at least end the suspense about renewing the traditional mission program.[16]

The Armenian cause had become tiresome. Distressed during the first days at Lausanne that discussions turned on commerce, Barton had cried to Boston: "Oh, for an American leadership that would not flinch or put politics above right!" [17] Of course Barton, like men everywhere, tempered his description of "right" by his self-interest — Armenianism, not Turkish nationalism. The mission secretary in February 1923 stated to relief leader Everett Wheeler that in Europe he had "attempted to protect the Armenians by appealing to the nations of the world. This attempt goes back over my entire period of connection with Turkey. That attempt ingloriously failed at Lausanne. England, France, and Italy let it be understood that they would not unite in bringing physical pressure to bear upon Turkey, and the United States announced in advance that it would do nothing." The Allies failed, he said, to condemn Turkish atrocities, and tacitly approved the deportation of Armenian and Greek remnants from Asia Minor. Barton's anger about no punishment for the massacres was understandable. After the Second World War the Allies conducted the Nuremberg trials partly to judge the executioners of six million Jews. Yet Barton recognized that his own idea of right included the application of the Gospel to all men: "Must we believe that the Turk is so bad that he cannot be Christianized? . . . may we not hope that through the grace of God . . . conditions will be so changed that in another generation or more the Turk will cease to wish to destroy?" [18] Although paternalistic, he was acknowledging that the Turks could possibly be a boon to him as well as a bane.

The American Board secretary sought better relations not only with the Kemalists, but Bristol. At their confrontation in November 1922 at Lausanne, the two men had tried to smooth differences. Bristol put in his diary that they did not allude to the correspondence between the State Department and themselves.[19] Then in January 1923 Barton and Bristol brought past tensions into the open in an amicable conversation.

The Near East Relief chairman after his return to the United States restricted his pro-Armenian lobbying to a resettlement of refugees leaving

Turkey. For a time he considered sending Montgomery to explore in Moscow the possibility of the Soviet Armenian Republic as a haven. Instead, he let the Armenia-America Society pass out of existence. Barton and his relief associates decided that an international commission on refugees, a plan considered with Ambassador Child at Lausanne, was the best way to assist the Armenians. Barton stated to Secretary Hughes that an international group should study the number, condition, and need of Armenians who had left Turkey. Wearied by Armenianism, the Harding administration did not act.[20]

Events overseas confirmed that the American Board would have to revise its goals. Child, Grew, and Bristol had pleased the Kemalists at Lausanne by being more moderate than the Allies on the issue of capitulations. Believing the United States had sympathy for Asian self-determination and wanting to counter Europe's economic imperialism, the Ankara government renewed negotiations with the Chester business group. Hughes had a considerable reticence about this venture. The Turks early in 1923 approved the so-called Chester Concession, a project of the Ottoman-American Development Corporation (Ankara later annulled this concession, a plan to build a railroad across eastern Anatolia in exchange for mining privileges; the Development Corporation had financial problems and an unstable leadership). Meantime such pro-American Turkish nationalists as Adnan Bey, the husband of Halidé Edib and governor of Constantinople, wanted an updated treaty with the United States. Late in April 1923 a second session of the Lausanne Conference began, and the United States advised the Turks that Grew was ready to prepare a treaty of amity and commerce. In midsummer the Lausanne Conference ended, approving an Allied-Kemalist treaty which made no mention of minorities, capitulations, or reparations for losses in Western property and lives. Grew and Ismet by August had completed the similar and separate Treaty of Lausanne between the United States and Turkey.[21]

The treaty completions marked a dramatic turn within Anatolian social processes. The millets and capitulations were gone, and with them the source of so much past violence. Because of Greek blunders, Allied rivalries, American indecision, Bolshevik support, and Kemalist spirit, modern Turkish nationalism had come of age.[22]

Barton and Gates decided they would go along with the new context in Asia Minor and seek to interpret it to the relief and mission constituency. The Robert College president felt that it was time to understand accomplished facts. He helped Barton realize that if the Kemalists desired a reform government, the Protestants should assist such a laudable purpose. Arriving in the United States to defend the Turkish-American Lausanne Treaty, Gates was sentitive about public censure. He thought the average American evaluated being pro-Turk as "equivalent to eternal damnation." [23] He wondered if the United States would ever escape provincialism. In September 1923 Gates stated to Barton: "I hope that the Treaty will be ratified, not that it is a very good Treaty. It leaves out our schools and does not provide that our associations may hold property in their own corporate name. But it is a *Treaty*. It opens the way for the resumption of diplomatic relations and friendly intercourse. We cannot get a better treaty so long as we are not prepared to use force." [24] The American Board secretary in a letter to Senator Lodge sounded like Gates. "I hope," Barton declared, "that in the discussion of the treaty a great deal of wild talk will not be indulged in against the Turk. The Turk is bad enough the Lord knows, but if we have to live with him and cooperate with him we gain nothing by constantly reminding him and others that he is a scoundrel." [25] Armenianism was beginning to leave Barton's system and tolerance for Turks to enter.

Ernest Riggs wrote an article defending the American Board's official action to rebuild among Turks. He remarked that "we have made no adequate presentation of the Gospel to the Turkish people. We had been satisfied with the marvelous success among Armenians and Greeks. . . . Perhaps we Americans have been too happy to meet fawning and friendly people at home and abroad and hand to them a plush Bible and a Church system plainly marked 'Made in U.S.A.' Perhaps we have been cursed with too easy success." Riggs maintained a solid purpose, like that of Parsons and Fisk: "It is not confidence in favorable social or political conditions, but faith in this invincible power of God which presses the American Board to carry on in Turkey." [26]

Throughout the months before Secretary Hughes in January 1924 defended the Lausanne Treaty in a speech in New York City, Barton and Gates worked at changing American prejudice against the Turks. The Near East College Association released a statement by Gates which said that the Turkish-American Treaty allowed an opportunity for missionaries and educators to make the principles of righteousness known and practiced in Turkey; the Treaty also gave the businessman a field for his concerns. Knowing Barton's public endorsement of the Treaty, Bristol from

Constantinople congratulated the American Board spokesman. Bristol believed Barton had taken the true Christian attitude, the American idea of a square deal.[27]

The fairly sudden change in missionary policy was a little painful to the religionists. Armenophile longings were still close to the surface. Independent educators did not find it too difficult to make a transition. At Constantinople Woman's College Turks had been among its graduates for some time; several of these alumna were active feminists as well as wives of Kemalist leaders. It was no small tribute that when the Sultan fled Constantinople in November 1922, his adopted daughter had elected to remain at the Woman's College rather than depart with her father.[28] Whatever the experience of the Protestants in the Near East, they felt awkward defending the Lausanne Treaty in an America which still liked Armenianism.

THE DESTROYED CHRISTIAN BLOC

As the missionary program of a home for Armenians was ending, the scheme of Western protection for Nestorians was moving toward a similar climax. Not much had come of actions by Barton and Speer in 1921 to obtain American permission for the immigration of some thirty thousand Nestorians from a refugee camp near Mosul. Undaunted, the Presbyterian Board had said it would continue in cooperation with Near East Relief to attempt to secure the Nestorian remnant.[29]

Visiting the Near East in 1922, Speer labored for a return of the Nestorians to their homes. A Kurdish tribe held the area west of Lake Urmia, having overcome efforts of the Persians and the British to dislodge them. Speer noted that while he was in Persia new nationalist leaders under Reza Shah Pahlev were mobilizing about twelve thousand soldiers to invade the Kurdish stronghold. The nationalists appeared sure of themselves, partly because they had nullified the Anglo-Persian Agreement of 1919. The Presbyterian Board secretary received assurance that Persians would not only allow but encourage Nestorians to return to Urmia. Restrictions would be only in regard to the Nestorians who had advocated independence from Persia. "Of the many clear and unmistakable calls which we have heard in Persia," Speer wrote, "no one has seemed to us more indisputable than the call to reoccupy the very instant the way opens."[30]

Wherever Speer went among Nestorians in the Near East, he found gratitude for relief and disappointment that migration to America had proved impossible. A Nestorian at Tabriz said that he and his compatriots had had only one friend who had stayed with them in their exile, Near East Relief. He felt ashamed to be a burden to others. But what were the Nestorians to do, he asked, since America had closed its gates? Speer stated that if the United States had opened, the refugee camp near Mosul would have gone forth in a body.

The Presbyterian leader discovered among the Persians an expectation, raised by such ventures as the Persian Commission led by Harry Judson, of an American trusteeship over Persia. Speer declared that he heard nothing but sadness because America had not provided technical assistance, investment, and counsel after the Judson trip. Even as Speer heard these comments, the United States government helped arrange the private Millspaugh Mission of financial experts to the Tehran government. Serving in Persia in the 1920s and again in the early 1940s, the Millspaugh Mission followed the pattern of the prewar Shuster Mission.[31]

Returned to New York, Speer in July 1922 trusted that Persia would solve the Nestorian case. Next month Persia drove the Kurds out of the Urmia region, and in early autumn some Nestorians moved there. Near East Relief donated seeds and around eight hundred oxen to those Nestorians who at last were home again.[32]

This reoccupation did not satisfy missionary E. W. McDowell, the companion of William Shedd. McDowell did not believe that the Nestorians had found justice. Persia had shaky control of Urmia, and Kurds dominated the Nestorian area in Anatolian Turkey. Most refugees in Persia and Mesopotamia refused to go to Urmia. It certainly did not simplify matters for Nestorians to live under three different jurisdictions — Turkish, Mesopotamian, Persian. McDowell at the Lausanne Conference sought a home for Nestorians, either in a region at the conjunction of Turkey, Mesopotamia, and Persia, or in an Armenian region in Cilicia. Bristol obtained for him an interview with Curzon, which did not encourage McDowell. The final report of the subcommission on minorities, as with the Armenians, refused a national home for Nestorians.[33]

While Nestorians slowly left places of exile for Urmia, McDowell and Speer pressed London to secure the scattered minority. Involved in a border dispute with Turkey and embroiled with belligerent Kurds north of Mosul, Britain was not certain it could retain northern Mesopotamia. One man in the British Colonial Office recommended to Speer that the United States "kick up a row" with the Persian government and enlist American businessmen in Persia and experts with the Millspaugh Mission to trade Persia's interest in American aid for larger protection of Nestorians. Speer doubted that the State Department would follow this procedure. He put the responsibility for the Nestorians upon Britain. The Presbyterian Board secretary stated to an American colleague "that Great Britain officially made promises to the Assyrian [Nestorian] people which were not kept. That the nation has been in a fair way to being extinguished. That the British have been using and are using now Assyrian levies for their military operations north of Mosul. That if they withdraw from Mosul without making provision for the Assyrians they will be leaving them just where the French left the Armenians in Cilicia." Speer continued: Nestorians "will be sacrificed just because they are a small people." [34]

The Nestorian matter dragged on. As the Presbyterians early in 1924 began rebuilding in Urmia, McDowell went to London. Seeing that the British were not going to act, he turned to the idea that the League of Nations should supervise the boundary between Turkey and Mesopotamia and oversee an autonomous Nestorian region. McDowell asked Speer to use Near East Relief to stir up the American government about the new notion. Speer could not do much. Some months later a League of Nations decision which awarded territory north of Mosul to Iraq (formerly Mesopotamia) also split lands previously occupied by Nestorians. The Nestorian kettle was as uncovered as ever. Lobbying in Washington and Geneva, Speer and McDowell met no success for emigration of the Nestorians or for League intervention. The two men eventually stopped trying.

The new xenophobic nationalism of Iran (formerly Persia) later ended the Urmia station of the Presbyterians, one decade after its revival. By the beginning of the Second World War, Iran had eliminated Presbyterian schools throughout Iran and reduced the American Protestant enterprise to hospitals and clinics. Nestorians in the 1960s were a scattered minority, with most numbers in the following locations: Iraq (30,000); Tehran, Iran (8,000); Lebanon (5,000); and the United States (4,000). [35]

McDowell at one point showed how hard it was for the Presbyterian and American boards to revise the theories of Parsons, Fisk, Smith, and Dwight. "I think," McDowell wrote, "of the ante-bellum situation: A Christian bloc thrust — Providentially — right down through the midst of Islam, to its very heart"; Armenian and Nestorian, from Constantinople to the Persian Gulf; "touching closely Turks, Kurds, Arabs and Persians; giving point of vantage for every civilizing and Christianizing influence

. . . to be exerted from center to circumference." He added ruefully: "How changed the situation: That Christian bloc all but destroyed, from the Black Sea to Mosul . . . and with it in large measure the rights and privileges of Christian missions." [36] Poor McDowell. He was yearning for nineteenth-century conditions in which Asian nationalism had not asserted itself and in which the West could still ply non-Muslim minorities.

THE MOUNTAIN OF ILL WILL

Meanwhile, the anti-Turk feeling in America which mission-relief people had roused was helping prevent ratification of the Treaty of Lausanne. Whereas the Kemalist Grand National Assembly had approved the Treaty a few days after Grew and Ismet signed it, the United States government sensed that Armenianism was too strong to allow passage. Secretary Hughes put off submitting the Treaty to the Senate.

Many Armenophiles had objected heatedly to the Treaty. Such an individual was relief organizer E. H. Bierstadt, who published *The Great Betrayal*. In his book Bierstadt indicted Bristol and the State Department for a diplomacy of economic imperialism. The author said the Treaty "was signed in oil, and sealed with the blood of the Greeks and Armenians who were sacrificed to make the signing possible." [37]

The ACIA loudly repeated the cant and clichés of Armenianism. Instead of going out of business as the Armenia-America Society had done, the ACIA complained that Armenia would be sold out if the United States accepted the Treaty. But as historian James B. Gidney has stated, Armenia had been sold out as thoroughly as possible before the Lausanne Conference ever opened. That reality was of no moment to the ACIA. Morgenthau bolstered the ACIA instead of associates Barton and Gates, announcing that nothing can be settled until it is settled right. Gerard lashed at the State Department's supposed backing for the Chester Concession (already annulled by the time of his criticism) and the bad faith of the West toward Armenians. Vahan Cardashian in February 1924 explained to Barton: "I differ with you absolutely concerning the desirability or advisability of the ratification of the Treaty, and I do not in the slightest degree share your hope for influencing the Turk through any missionary effort. Ex-President Wilson, whose Near Eastern policy you have said that you have directed, has categorically denounced the Lausanne Treaty." Cardashian alleged that Barton could not understand the Turks and that the American

Board would not be able to rebuild under the Kemalists; he boasted that "We will get thirty-two votes to beat" the Lausanne Treaty. Cardashian was gleeful that events had provided a setting in which he could possibly get a revenge against Barton.[38]

The State Department behaved carefully. Fearing the Treaty's defeat, Allen Dulles of the State Department and Barton helped to hold up its submission to the Senate until May 1924. Bristol wrestled over pressing educational and other matters in Turkey without benefit of its ratification. Senator Lodge's successor as head of the Foreign Relations Committee, Borah, recognized that opposition to the Treaty was too large for approval and did not schedule hearings. During the summer of 1924 Alexander MacLachlan of International College worked for the State Department to identify poor arguments in ACIA's propaganda. In addition to Armenianism and ACIA's stubbornness, partisanship figured in the situation. Many Democratic Senators saw resistance to the Treaty as a retaliation against Republicans who had abused Wilson's peace plans. Gerard, both ACIA chairman and treasurer of the Democratic National Committee, helped get his language into the Democratic platform of 1924: "We condemn the Lausanne treaty. It barters legitimate American rights and betrays Armenia, for the Chester oil concessions." Adopting ACIA fantasy, the platform continued: "We favor . . . the fulfillment of President Wilson's arbitral award respecting Armenia." [39]

Bypassing the obstructionists, the State Department two years later (February 1926) established a modus vivendi commercial agreement with Ankara. It contained trade rights for the United States as in the Allied Treaty of Lausanne. About the same time the Foreign Relations Committee, without hearings, reported favorably on the American-Turkish Treaty. Joseph Grew gloomily guessed the Gerard interests would reduce the country to tears over Armenians and defeat the Treaty.[40]

During the delay Barton forces had marshalled many arguments against ideas of the American Committee Opposed to the Lausanne Treaty (transmutation of the ACIA). The arguments contended that only an army — which no nation would provide — could secure a home for the Armenians, that a pro-Armenian policy without military support could result in the liquidation of the few Christians in Anatolia, that the United States had not traded Armenian autonomy for the Chester Concession. Armenians had a certain security in the Soviet Armenian Republic. Further, Americans in Turkey favored ratification.[41]

The American Committee Opposed to the Lausanne Treaty hammered on the lack of protection for the Armenians. Gerard stated that Barton did not have the right to speak for relief personnel who disliked the Lausanne Treaty, an un-Christian and un-American document; he deplored the American Board secretary's putting himself in the position of jollying the Turk.[42]

The inordinate procrastination in the American settlement with Turkey touched Near East Relief lightly. After the Smyrna crisis of 1922, the philanthropic group had given leadership, along with the American Red Cross, to transferring over one million Greek and Armenian refugees from Anatolia to Greece and Syria. The United States and Greek governments provided ships. Near East Relief thereafter operated almost entirely outside of Turkey in Greece, Syria, and Soviet Armenia. It also shifted emphasis from stopgap provisions to foster homes for orphans, vocational training in some thirty trades, and technical assistance. Among outstanding tasks was reduction of trachoma cases among Soviet Armenian orphans from fourteen thousand in 1921 to three thousand in 1924. For Barton, withdrawal of orphanages from Anatolia had hurt. He had hoped that the orphans, who received Christian instruction from the relief staff, would become mission leaders in Turkey.[43]

The lack of formal relations between Ankara and Washington hampered the American Board. The Treaty itself did not explicitly provide rights for missions, yet its ratification would have increased the access of the State Department to Turkish officials and the potential for protection.

In the period after the Lausanne Conference, secular Kemalism restricted the Protestant emissaries. Nationalistic Turks criticized foreign religion, and their government passed laws forbidding schools from teaching Christianity. The American Board sent out young missionaries who concentrated on living their faith among Turks. There was no formal church ministry. Bristol enthusiastically approved the new approach; many clergymen in the United States blasted Barton as a compromiser with evil, an opportunist seeking to save Board properties. Turkey in 1924 closed French and Italian schools when they refused to remove Roman Catholic symbols from classrooms. Harassed but usually not closed, American Board schools remained small in number — fewer than ten, including one college (International at Izmir). The statistical contrast with the several hundred prewar schools was large. Undismayed, Barton stated: "Turkey, with its face turned toward the West and calling for help, looks especially and almost exclusively to America."[44] As with Board institutions, Robert College and Istanbul Woman's College (changed name of Constantinople Woman's College) were forced to become less obviously religious. Yet the personal style of most faculty members was in the missionary tradition, a mixture of piety and Puritan duty. Recruitment for staff still included using the Student Volunteer Movement and the churches. Having to suppress overt Protestantism, the colleges stressed character building among students.[45]

While missionaries and educators were encountering the regime headed by Atatürk (Mustafa Kemal), pro–Lausanne Treaty interests in America had stepped up their efforts. After the Foreign Relations Committee early in 1926 reported the Treaty to the Senate, Barton, Dulles, and Grew (then Under Secretary of State) had coordinated the drive. They released statements by Gates and other Americans in Turkeys. Barton corresponded with Congressmen and urged an associate editor of the New York *Times*, John H. Finley (also, vice chairman of Near East Relief), to back the Treaty. Returned to the United States, the Robert College president wrote and spoke. Surveys of colleagues convinced Senator Borah that Democrats, whom Gerard and Morgenthau were pressing, could defeat the Treaty. Borah waited for a showdown until the next Congress.

With a boost from the State Department, Barton in August 1926 helped organize the General Committee of American Institutions and Associations in Favor of the Treaty with Turkey. Dodge and Crane assisted. A New York attorney, Rayford W. Alley (chairman of the Council on Turkish-American Relations), directed the group. The Near East College Association, Near East Relief, Young Men's Christian Association, and various business firms had spokesmen on the Committee in Favor of the Treaty. Ernest Riggs formally represented the American Board. Alley distributed to editors, journalists, Congressmen, and other individuals a booklet, *The Treaty with Turkey: Why It Should Be Ratified*. With a vote in the Senate close at hand, Alexander MacLachlan lobbied in Washington with Democratic Senators, and got fourteen of them to consider changing their anti-Treaty stance. Barton also lobbied a week in December 1926 in cooperation with Alley and State Department officials. Morgenthau soon caucused with Democratic Senators and, as MacLachlan described it, used a partisan argument, "you [Republicans] killed my dog [the Covenant] — I'll kill your cat," to hold several wavering Democrats in line.[46]

Then occurred a consequence to the mountain of ill will piled up against Turks by Near East Relief. The Senate on January 18, 1927, failed by vote of fifty to thirty-four (six short of two thirds) to consent to the Treaty. Gerard and Cardashian reportedly had financed much of their extensive publicity through a rich New Yorker who had become a fanatic Armenophile. The leading Democratic Senator in the anti-Treaty fight, William King of Utah, had been an ardent spokesman for Armenia since 1918. During the interim, King had introduced several pro-Armenian resolutions in Congress (none endorsed).[47]

The sequel to the Senate decision of January 1927 showed both the decline and foolishness of Armenianism. "I have been tremendously criticized," Barton stated, "even in our own circle, for having been so conspicuous in promoting the treaty." Feeling the Senate had gone "daft" and trying to be more "undercover," [48] the American Board secretary urged the State Department to resume ambassadorial relations with Turkey. Bristol began an exchange with the Atatürk government which led in May 1927 to the selection of Grew as American ambassador. Believing since the Lausanne Conference that Grew was the man for the post, Gates and Barton had figured in this choice. When Turkish Ambassador Mouhtar Bey came to Washington, the United States government had to guard him heavily because Armenophiles declared they would assassinate him. The American Committee Opposed to the Lausanne Treaty helped hold off Senatorial consent to a commercial treaty with Turkey for three years after the exchange of ambassadors. Testifying to Cardashian's importance, the State Department complained that his purpose in life was to make ties with Turkey as difficult as possible. It took several more years before the American Board received $192,000 from Turkey as compensation for losses during the war and before the Senate approved provisions equivalent to the Lausanne Treaty.[49]

In 1927 nearly a century had passed since the American Board began evangelism among Armenians. During these decades education and social service became part of the Protestant movement in the Near East. Finally, relief and politics developed as focal points, with missionary internationalists neglecting the millet problem and Asian nationalism as they sought to shape United States policy. At the end, the religionists lost much after Kemalism had swept over Anatolia; the American Board was again at a junction comparable to that facing the pioneer team of Eli Smith and Harrison Gray Otis Dwight in 1830. The situation of 1927 brought from

Board leaders their traditional hope that the future would provide new opportunities. Board officials were not ready to surrender to adversity after massive setbacks during the First World War and its aftermath.

◄ ►

The story of United States religionists in Turkey and Persia is a tragedy like Thucydides' history of the war between Athens and Sparta. Missionary anguish in response to the massacres of 1915 and 1916 led to one of the largest philanthropic expeditions ever organized. This crusade's main slogan: "Save the Armenians." Unrecognized by participants in the struggle, events which mastered William Shedd and his Presbyterian station at Urmia were an omen. Anxiety among missionaries grew as both the bravery of the Near East Relief staff and the investment of millions of dollars did not win safeguards for Armenians and Nestorians. Then Wilson, whom missionaries saw as the heroic redeemer of Near East Christians and leader of the West, fell in battle. The final fate which overwhelmed both Protestant forces and minorities is reminiscent of the disaster which overtook the Athenian expedition to Sicily during the Peloponnesian War.

Chapter 12

A Remarkable Heritage

THE story of Protestant diplomacy and the Near East is not only a narrative of pathos. It is a case study of a powerful lobby which wanted the United States government to organize part of the Old World. Failing to achieve this aim, the religionists nevertheless had a continuing effect in diplomacy as well as missions, education, and philanthropy.

"THE SEARCH FOR ORDER"

Missionaries foreshadowed actions of the American government to help stabilize transatlantic affairs after the Second World War. Religionists developed Near East Relief, an aid and recovery program not unlike the Marshall Plan and Point Four. Through a leading lobby for the Versailles Treaty (the National Committee on the Churches and the Moral Aims of the War), they helped promote the League, prototype for the United Nations. They advocated a strategic presence for the United States in the Near East (mandates over Armenia or all of Asia Minor), a presence similar to the Truman administration's support for Iran, Greece, and Turkey against Soviet challenge. They favored a military commitment by the Wilson government within the European power balance, an idea which prefigured the American obligation in the North Atlantic Treaty Organization.

286

The largest mission and relief pressure on Washington to assist in securing the peace of the Near East occurred in the years from 1917 to 1923. Interests headed by Foreign Secretary James Barton of the American Board of Commissioners for Foreign Missions successfully promoted Ottoman-American neutrality, preventing expropriation of the Protestant enterprise in Turkey. The Persian Commission led by Harry Pratt Judson of the University of Chicago, helping Persian nationalism, came out of efforts by Barton interests. The Barton plan for a federated Ottoman Empire under United States tutelage received a considerable backing within the Wilson administration. State Department personnel in the Near East almost unanimously favored such a scheme. The Barton Relief Commission of 1919 was as much a program to obtain political safeguards for Armenians as a humanitarian venture to provide food and medicine. Missionaries reacted angrily to the disruption caused by the Greek landing at Smyrna in May 1919. They then had a crucial part in the Morgenthau Memorandum, a proposal for an American mandate over Asia Minor; this mandate was to soften strife caused by overlapping imperial and ethnic claims in Anatolia. The informal commitment of President Wilson and Colonel House at Paris to American territorial responsibilities in Asia Minor came directly from pushes by mission and relief interests to ensure civil order in Turkey. These interests also figured vitally in the calming efforts in the Caucasus led by United States Army officers William Haskell and James Harbord, and in retention of a British garrison at Batumi. One can trace to mission-relief people the King-Crane and Harbord recommendations for a United States mandate in Anatolia. After the Senate turned down the Versailles Treaty these people were the largest factor in several of Wilson's moves: submission of the Armenian mandate question to the Senate, arbitration of boundaries for an integral Armenia, and a proposal to Congress for a loan to the Erivan Republic. Hollow victories for the Protestants were acceptance by the Allies of the Armenian national home plan and Secretary of State Hughes' willingness to take part in a Western inquiry into alleged Turkish atrocities. In a last stand at the Lausanne Conference, Barton and his colleagues received support from the Harding administration for an autonomous Armenia.

How strong was the Protestant pull for a United States engrossment in Old World problems? It is hard to say exactly where the strength of missionaries and their institutions began and ended in ties with such relief figures as Henry Morgenthau, Herbert Hoover, and Haskell, public per-

287

sonages as Wilson, House, and Admiral Bristol, the American Armenophile James Gerard, the Britisher James Bryce. It is sure that Near East
Relief, although including nonmissionaries, was under Barton's control.
The policies of the United States toward the Near East usually reflected
the thinking of missionary spokesmen, who received invaluable assistance
from board chairmen of missionary colleges such as Cleveland Dodge and
Charles Crane, and from sons of missionaries such as George Montgomery
and Talcott Williams. Religionists probably had more influence than public servants in American diplomacy connected with the Ottoman settlement, at least through August 1919.

Before American intervention in the First World War, Barton and his
associates had not anticipated such an attempt to pacify the Near East.
But decisions by missionaries before 1917 pointed toward that end. One
choice of theirs was to identify with minorities, and another was to stress
education. Also, they chose to publicize the Armenian massacres of 1894–
1896 and 1915–1916, and to provide relief. It was just one step from their
supervising schools and philanthropy to seeking dependable political conditions, so that relief could proceed efficiently.

Further, coincidences related to the Eastern Question facilitated the
Protestant attempts to quiet Turkish turbulence. In the nineteenth century, Greeks and Bulgarians had received European aid against the Ottoman Empire — Armenians and Arabs tried to do the same. The First
World War brought fighting between minorities and the Young Turks,
and massacres of Armenians accompanied this battling. Then there was
Russia's unexpected withdrawal from the secret treaties. This pullout and
America's missionary aid to Armenians prepared the Allies to look upon
the United States as a nation for the areas promised the Russians.

In addition to these general developments, coincidences related to
Americans made possible missionary efforts to make the United States an
organizer of the Turkish peace. Americans became aware of mission concerns in Turkey partly because nonreligious investment by United States
nationals in the Near East was small. The Protestants had a monopoly on
American opinions about Turkey. Stimulated by wartime emotions, the
popular mood was a ready market for applying the idea of a world safe for
democracy to the Ottoman Empire; the long-held view that transatlantic
affairs were untidy helped the American Board and Near East Relief.
Overall United States foreign missions in the 1910s were unprecedentedly
vigorous. Nativist Protestant influence was at the peak of its strength, and

Wilson carried missionary diplomacy farther than any President before. Also, there was happenstance in Dodge's being an intimate of both Wilson and of missions. By chance, Foreign Secretary Barton of the American Board had done fieldwork among Armenians.

Mission-relief people struggled to benefit from these circumstances, and despaired when the United States government refused to carry out "the search for order"[1] across the Atlantic. Talcott Williams in 1921 wrote that the United States was certain to be drawn into some future European war. The American people had refused a mandate, Williams said, but would pay an inevitable penalty, sharing in the horror and destruction of a war greater than the Great War. "Already the mere delay of our Senate in advising the ratification of the covenant of peace . . . has cost at least a million lives by famine and by massacre in Central Asia, in Siberia, in Russia, in Central Europe, and in Asiatic Turkey. This has been the penalty of delay." Williams asked: "What will be the penalty of refusal altogether to act? . . . What the United States was asked to do was not wrecking . . . but salvage. It is not charity, it is insurance."[2] Concurrently, Barton declared that the "timidity of our American leaders and their unreasoning conservatism, bound hand and foot by tradition and worst of all politics," had permitted situations "extremely bad two years ago to proceed into conditions vastly worse." Unless the United States "wants to face another world war," he affirmed, "it must be ready to discuss national steps that will have for their end . . . the peace and good order of the world."[3] These men sensed the anachronism of American isolation from European difficulties.

The ideas of Barton, Williams, and their associates were like those of William Westermann (American expert on the Near East at the Paris Peace Conference). In 1921 Westermann felt that America should have accepted an Armenian mandate because the United States could no longer afford isolationism in a troubled, interdependent world.[4]

Missionaries to Turkey demonstrated political insight.[5] The Near East religionists wanted the United States to guide history in the Near East and in Europe rather than to follow. Desiring continuity between war and its aftermath, they tried to conserve American initiative gained in Wilson's Fourteen Points. Making peace in the Ottoman Empire was as important to them as fighting in France. The Protestants thought, albeit in an ill-defined way, that America should lead the Western victors in defense of the Versailles Treaty. Such ideas anticipated the cold war's Truman Doctrine for Greece and Turkey. Missionaries as private internationalists strained to draw the United States government into a responsible stance in the international system.

The religionists were part of the Progressive movement, which had brought bureaucratic control to some domestic excesses. They conceived the Near East to be anarchic, not unlike American industry before Congress enacted trade and banking regulations. To this overseas area rife with communal killings they hoped to bring stability — the stability of American reform.

The reliance of the United States in the 1920s and 1930s upon unilateral negotiations with European states, upon the Open Door, limitation of naval armaments, readjustment of reparations and war debts, moral suasion, and neutrality legislation was an approach not so prescient as the missionary view. Involvement by Washington in turbulent Asia Minor probably would have been better than no territorial or military duty in Europe at all. The Second World War came partly because the United States refused to take a tough obligation in the European power balance.

A presumptuous aspect of the Protestants' search for an American task abroad concerned their moralistic view of the United States. They saw America as the world's best savior, its judge, its policeman. This exaggeration helped produce difficulties of the 1960s — the morass of the Vietnam conflict, the overextension of United States power overseas.

If the broad ideas of the mission-relief lobby toward transatlantic order were quite sound, their tactics were not always so. The pressure group unnecessarily repressed news about atrocities by Armenians and Greeks. Commendably, Bristol and Caleb Gates of Robert College soon after the war opposed excessive emphasis, both in America and the Near East, on minorities. These two individuals perceived a fundamental problem: relief based too much on "clamorous" Armenianism caused as many hindrances as aids to stability in Anatolia. The mission-relief people obstructed a consensus in the United States by appealing much more to America's moral and philanthropic instincts than to economic and strategic possibilities. Robert Lansing's attitude in 1921 demonstrated that this approach failed to unify the American people on a duty in Asia Minor: "It is not too severe to say of those who engaged in this propaganda that the purpose was to take advantage of the unselfishness of the American people and of the altruism and idealism of President Wilson in order to impose on the United States the burdensome mandates." [6]

Incidentally, the virtual absence of collaboration between missionaries and businessmen for "imperial" purposes, not only during the peace negotiations but during the preceding century, contradicted Marxist-Leninist theory. This philosophy suggests that missionaries and investors from "capitalist" nations cooperate in colonial ventures.

As to missionary means for regulating the Near East, Barton helped set expectations too high when he proposed a United States protectorate over the Ottoman Empire. And there was undue optimism about a separate, integral Armenia. Regarding Syria, the on-the-spot inquiry promoted by Howard Bliss of the Syrian Protestant College was not the best scheme; Gates' opposition to this idea was laudable.

With all their mistakes, Barton and his associates sought methods for providing tranquillity in Asia Minor which were more realistic than Wilson's. By Point Twelve, the President declared to the Allies that they could not unreservedly use the secret treaties for Turkey's dismemberment. Beyond getting Supreme Council agreement to apply the mandate and self-determination principles to the Ottoman Empire, he did not set forth a clear and specific version of Point Twelve. During the first months of the Peace Conference he had backing in Asia Minor, Europe, and the United States for his leadership in the Turkish peace and for American involvement in Anatolia. The Morgenthau Memorandum offered the most practical modification of the secret treaties. The President vacillated when pressed by Lloyd George and others to accept formally a mandate over Asia Minor or mandates in Armenia and Constantinople. Orally the President committed his government to an Armenian mandate, an understanding which he did not publicly promote until the spring of 1920. Since he desired an American presence in Turkey, he would have done better to obligate his administration and the United States Army to an Asia Minor task in May 1919 or to a solely Armenian mandate as late as August 1919. Primarily because of his absorption with the League question and with the increasingly inflexible positions he and some of his opponents took, he made large errors. Wilson approved the divisive Greek landing at Smyrna; he sent the King-Crane and Harbord inquiries, which postponed a Turkish peace. These stalling tactics of the President made security in the Near East harder rather than easier.[7] In contrast, Barton asked almost monotonously — during the period from the Armistice of Mudros in October 1918 through his cable to Dodge in August 1919 — for an Allied or American occupation of Asia Minor and the Caucasus. He sensed all along that procrastination would not bring a United States mandate in the Near East.

Barton neglected much of his normal restraint about Church-State relations as he put all he could into his effort to establish an American hegemony over the whole or part of Turkey. He repeatedly twisted (perhaps broke) one of his own maxims: a missionary is a preacher of righteousness, not an instituter of public reform.[8] In his book on Near East Relief, Barton hid the diplomatic aspects of the philanthropic institution; he need not have followed that pretense. He could have pointed out that Christianity and culture had blended throughout Western history, that the Protestants to Turkey had political plans quite progressive and appropriate to values and events then current at home and abroad. This chief of the American Board and of Near East Relief took precedent from much of the best in the West's Christian heritage when he urged the United States to turn from its isolationism to a dependable position in a disjointed world.

AN EXCEPTION TO THE TREND

The prominence of missionaries in diplomacy toward the Near East raises a question about how the experiences of these Protestants compare with mission lobbying in American relations with other regions. Apparently, missionary influence on United States policy during the breakdown of the Ottoman Empire was larger than in any other time or place in American history.

In the founding of Liberia from the first decade of the nineteenth century to the 1860s, both the American Colonization Society (directed by churchmen and philanthropists) and missionaries involved public and private groups in an unofficial African colony. Through schools and churches, American Methodists and Episcopalians led in shaping a Protestant Americo-Liberian culture. Religionists obtained from Washington, for their own enterprises and for the Liberian government (independent after 1847), financial assistance, Navy transport and protection, disembarkation of captured slaves. Opinion on the slavery issue in the United States divided between colonization and abolition, helping postpone formal recognition of Liberia by the United States until 1862. The Protestant effect upon Liberia was broader than that of American Board and Presbyterian emissaries upon Ottoman affairs; but in the Near East, the hold of missionary diplomacy upon the United States government was larger than in the African situation.[9]

In another instance, American Board personnel in Hawaii from 1820 to 1863 established churches and schools, and Americanized the government. Sons of missionaries figured in the Revolution of 1893 and 1894, the Hawaiian Republic, and United States annexation. But American Board officials did not counsel the United States government in relation to Hawaii as systematically as Barton did in relation to the Near East.[10]

There are other cases for comparison. Missionaries and churches contributed to American expansion in Oregon. In Korea, missionary-diplomat Horace N. Allen helped shape United States thinking toward the competition of Japan and Russia over Korea until President Theodore Roosevelt in 1905 acceded to a Japanese protectorate there. As to Japan, American missionaries had their effect primarily through nondiplomatic means.[11] Concerning China, Paul A. Varg has written that "missionaries were unsuccessful as a pressure group to influence the Department of State, especially after 1900." In the nineteenth century, missionary effect on the Treaties of Wanghia and Tientsin was important. Missionaries generally sought protection (as in the Chinese riots of the 1890s) rather than lobbied for special United States policies. The religionists had a large place interculturally, affecting Chinese ideas (as in the Taiping Rebellion) or American opinion (pro-Open Door, pro-Nationalist Chinese, anti-Communist). Seemingly in none of the above situations did the proportion of missionary involvement with diplomacy match that of Barton and his associates.[12]

The missionary part in Wilsonian diplomacy toward the Near East was an exception to the historic trend in America. Although European states traditionally subsidized missionaries as agents of territorial imperialism, the United States had not done so. (This difference came partly because the New World republic, unlike Old World nations, had separated Church and State from its beginning.) Instead of being agents of the government, American Protestants abroad generally had to press Washington to be their agent. Missions were private ventures which often ran far ahead of the flag. The "grand" century of American missions in the decades before 1927 coincided with continental expansion, isolation from European alliances, and promotion of commercial opportunities. Thus, the American State Department usually sought nothing more for its religionists overseas than protection of lives and property. American economic and strategic interests after the 1920s became so much larger than the concerns of churchmen abroad that the United States continued to stress the rights of missionaries as citizens rather than as initiators or supporters of policy.[13]

Of course, there were aspects of American Board politics that were similar to Europe's missionary diplomacy. One observer of the relations of Western missions and colonialism has concluded that religious emissaries often longed for Western occupation of a territory as the only way to rescue peoples from extermination (especially in Africa and Asia). Also, missionaries often exhibited an imperial psychology.[14]

For all the status of missionary politics in United States relations with the Ottoman Empire, the American Board did not have the resources to accomplish what it had done in Hawaii. On the islands in mid-Pacific, the New England Puritans went through each step of the cycle of evangelism, education, and public affairs years before the Protestants in Turkey. In the former instance, the American Board came to have the blessing of the Hawaiian monarchy, with minor help from Washington; in the latter instance, the Kemalists almost ended the mission program in spite of major assistance from the Wilson government. Reasons for the outcomes were the different settings. Tribal, illiterate animistic Hawaii had little ability to resist Americans; Turkish and Armenian cultures had much. The American Board ministered in Hawaii to the whole society but in the Near East to minorities. In both regions there was constant Western interference, yet only in the Ottoman Empire was there a turbulent millet structure. Americanization in Hawaii brought eventual annexation to the United States; Americanization of Armenians helped bring emigration and massacres. Despite dissimilarities between the two cases, Barton apparently felt that Hawaii was a pattern for what could happen in Armenia. Eventually meeting stiff opposition from Turkish nationalism and American isolationism, the mission secretary increased his Armenophile action rather than re-evaluated. In the end, the formal United States support for the Barton-Dodge combination was not enough to make Armenia the success story Hawaii had been.

Actually, the American Board work in Anatolia was more like missions in China than Hawaii. Neither Turkish nor Chinese officials believed that American missionaries dealt satisfactorily with the generally recognized Asian feeling of technical and military inferiority to the West. Neither Turks nor Chinese appreciated the Americans so much for their considerable benevolence and aid as depreciated them for their ethnocentrism and for what they did not do. In neither place could the missionaries see that Asians most wanted ideology, skills, and capital necessary for a socioeconomic evolvement like the West's. More quickly than either missionaries or Western governments, Bolsheviks perceived the nature of modern nationalism in Turkey and China. For both Asian countries, missionaries created anti-Turkish and anti-Communist ideas in America which helped make United States adjustment to the triumphs of Mustafa Kemal and Mao Tse-tung painful and protracted. As an irony, in the two areas where the United States government most sought to safeguard its missionaries, destruction to its religionists was extensive.

The problem of the missionary effect upon the history of United States diplomacy is one which requires much more research. Historian John K. Fairbank has stated: "the missionary in foreign parts seems to be the invisible man of American history. His influence at home, his reports and circular letters, his visits on furlough, his symbolic value for his home church constituency seem not to have interested academic historians. . . . Mission history is a great and underused research laboratory for the comparative observation of cultural stimulus and response in both directions." [15]

GOD IS NO RESPECTER OF PERSONS

Whereas the Red Chinese government expelled American missions to China, many institutions established by American Protestants in the Near East survived. Not only did the mission institutions persist, they often recovered from the troubles of the First World War.

The American Board during post-Lausanne years sought to content itself with a new activity among Turks. In 1927 it was conducting a hospital at Gaziantep (formerly Aintab), eight primary and secondary schools, and International College. Some Muslim Turks continued to fear the Board's cultural imperialism; upset about Kemalist restrictions against Islam, these Turks could not tolerate a diluted Protestant activity. They fulminated against their enemy — insidious, "unnamed" Christianity. In 1928 officials arrested, tried, and convicted three missionary instructors on a charge of trying to convert several Muslim girls and closed the American Girls' Lycée in Bursa. Soon laws by the secularists at Ankara, who were almost making a religion of Turkish nationalism, prescribed government-appointed teachers and texts in the social sciences for all foreign and domestic schools. Harassment of International College by Turks eventually caused it to move in 1936 from Izmir to Beirut. Excessive Armenianism by missionaries had contributed to excessive fear of foreigners by the Kemalists. Amid the problems, there were pro-American Turks who exempted Board schools from certain taxes which would have closed them. After the Depression began in the United States, the religionists' chief difficulty was lack of money. Financial strictures discontinued several schools and in 1939 only four remained, in Istanbul, Izmir, Talas, and Tarsus.[16]

Board missionaries showed much of the character of Jesus, if not institutional Christianity, in their metamorphosis from an Armenian to a Turkish focus. They rejected bitterness about Kemalism and served people more than proclaimed beliefs. As Barton once put it, the Board decided to kiss and make up. Missionary talk with Turks as equals, not superior Westerners, ultimately brought appreciation from Ankara. In 1949 the government relaxed control of mission institutions. Turks thronged to mission schools. Periodicals prepared by the American Board provided valuable but not explicitly Christian literature to a wide audience. The Board published overtly Christian as well as secular books. In the 1960s there were nine times as many applicants to the mission's secondary schools at Istanbul, Izmir, and Tarsus as could be admitted (the school at Talas closed in 1967); the Gaziantep hospital continued. Concurrently, there were almost no Protestant congregations in Turkey. Religionists did not concentrate on bemoaning blocks to organized Christianity. Rather, the seventy Board missionaries were optimistic about opportunities to show behavioral Christianity (Turkey was again the largest Board field, as it had been earlier). The Board's report of 1960 declared: "Let the churches beware of demanding from the missionaries results in statistical form. . . . Ours is a mission of reinterpretation of Christianity to those who have known it as a political sword; it is a mission of fellowship and reconciliation to a people that have had bitter blows from the so-called Christian West; it is a mission of love and sharing with people who are trying to understand the sources of the West's power and strength." [17] Since Turkish laws helped restrict to this emphasis, American Protestants could take comfort that their Bible said applying the Word is more important than hearing it.[18]

The director of the American Bible Society in Turkey from 1925 to 1955, Lyman MacCallum (son of Board missionary Frederick MacCallum), demonstrated behavioral Christianity. The younger man strove to understand Turkish psychology and society, worshipped in mosques, became close to many Turks. He also adhered to orthodox Christian beliefs, helped several Turks become "informal" Christians (nonchurch members), and led in preparing an idiomatic Turkish translation of the Bible. His candidness, nonpietism, and wry humor were attractive.[19]

At long last, more than a century after Parsons and Fisk had tried to "demolish sin" in the Ottoman Empire, the Protestants were communicating freely with Turks. That was a step in integrity needed as much for the salvation of Americans as for Near Easterners. Many wounds had come before the missionaries realized that even though Christianity was unique, God's truth did not involve so sharp a discontinuity between Christian and other systems as they had thought. It was too bad that the American Board (renamed the United Church Board for World Ministries soon after its one hundred fiftieth anniversary in 1960) could not fully express itself by helping form local churches. Perhaps that would come when Westerners and Turks treated each other with sustained, generous respect.

In the meantime, educational institutions begun by the American Board offered beneficial programs for Arabs, Armenians, Turks, and others. International College in 1936 became the preparatory school for the American University of Beirut (new name for the Syrian Protestant College). Teaching mostly Arab pupils, International by the 1960s had become independent; it served over one thousand secondary students and had an aesthetically exciting campus plan in Beirut, with buildings designed by Edward Durell Stone. In 1937 former staff people of the American Board's Central Turkey College cooperated with a Presbyterian school in Syria to form Aleppo College. This institution in 1960 was run by a joint effort of the two original mission boards and of Armenian and Syrian evangelical churches. Developing a two-year curriculum in secretarial skills, business, arts, pre-medicine, and pre-engineering, Aleppo College had primarily an Armenian and Arab constituency.[20]

Robert College and American College for Girls (formerly Constantinople Woman's College) eventually adapted to Turkish nationalism. In the interwar years Kemalists expelled Robert's dean, Edgar Fisher, over a trivial incident. Laws required that Robert's vice president be a Turk. But the colleges were not opponents of Ankara, commending themselves increasingly to the Turkish government through technical programs in engineering (sometimes serving Ankara without fee), agriculture, and public health. One Turk alumnus of Robert College, Hassan Halet, became a

297

professor of electrical engineering at his alma mater and helped the Turkish Minister of Public Works design more than one hundred power plants; Dean Lynn Scipio of the Robert engineering school prepared a valuable ten-thousand-word Turkish-English technical dictionary. At the retirements of Caleb Gates and Mary Patrick in 1932, the administrations of the schools merged. When the Second World War began, the colleges had a total of nearly a thousand students. At the same time the institutions retained much from their missionary past. The well known Presbyterian clergyman of New York City, Henry Sloane Coffin, was chairman of Robert's board from the death of Dodge until 1945. The president of Robert for the eleven years after 1944, Floyd H. Black — like Gates, Washburn, and Hamlin — had been an American Board missionary (in Bulgaria).[21]

A new period opened for Robert (Yüksek Okulu, in Turkish) in the 1950s. By then its trustees and those of the American College had combined, with Robert becoming coeducational and American College becoming a girls preparatory school. Connected to Robert was a secondary academy for boys. Curricular emphases for Robert were engineering (over 2,500 degrees by 1963) and business administration. Graduate programs and a research center to provide expertness and facilities for industry and the professions began. In 1968 there were over two hundred faculty members and nearly two thousand students in the Robert system.

By this time the American University of Beirut (AUB) had become a pearl of United States educational internationalism. In contrast to Howard Bliss' fears about Roman Catholic restrictions under a French mandate, the university operated without interference. (Stricken with diabetes, then tuberculosis, Bliss died in 1920.) Under the long presidency of Bayard Dodge, which began in 1923, the school dropped most of the symbols but not the spirit of Protestantism. Dodge declared: "To develop the spiritual natures of our students, we do not propose to proselytize, or to emphasize names and forms. To us Protestantism means religious freedom. It is for the mosque, synagogue, or church to provide the practical formalities of organized religion, but the school should join with them in fostering a consciousness of God, and a desire to live in accordance with God's moral purpose." [22] AUB introduced coeducation in 1925, a first within the Arab world, and also appointed Asian and Western professors on the basis of full equality. The teaching staff received control of local administration. Here was an example of what Americans in the 1960s called dialogue, not just a mission to primitives nor a tactic to subvert another's assumptions. Supported by $1,500,000 from the Rockefeller Foundation between the world wars, the university by 1939 had grown to a student body of nearly two thousand. During the following decades it pursued its increasingly famous course, introducing schools of engineering, architecture, agriculture, and public health. A professor of history at the Founders' Day convocation in 1960 gave an address which reaffirmed the "abiding truths" of Daniel Bliss, urging the university to train for intellectual excellence, moral stature, and for personal faith and courage. Dodge remarked in his history of AUB that the school blended Orient and Occident, technical knowledge and spiritual idealism. Muslim and Christian young people from all over the Near East (mostly from Lebanon, Jordan, and Syria) liked this philosophy. About 3,500 of them by 1968 were attending this school, the largest overseas American school in the world.[23]

The American University of Beirut led a United States educational contribution to the Muslim world (from Morocco to Iran, Turkey to Sudan) bigger than all other foreign colleges combined. Of one hundred fourteen centers of higher learning in this region in 1960, twelve were American. Other non–Near Easterners had eight. All but two of the American schools either at that time or originally were missionary organizations. In Lebanon, Syria, and Turkey, there were ten American institutions with four thousand enrollees out of a total student population in these areas of sixty-five thousand. In Iran, where confiscation of missionary schools had taken place, there were no American colleges. In the United Arab Republic (Egypt), the American University in Cairo (begun in 1920) had over a thousand students. The Presbyterian-led American College for Girls, also at Cairo, had several dozen students. These statistics are lifeless, but they do show that United States internationalism, led by missionaries through the 1920s, had a continuing course.[24]

American education in the Near East not only instructed residents there but anticipated the United States government's Fulbright program and the work of the United States Information Agency. These formal efforts by the American government were part of its new cultural diplomacy after the Second World War. Robert College and the American University of Beirut since their origins had included many Armenians and Arabs on their faculties. The Fulbright program in the two decades after 1948 brought thousands of citizens from foreign countries to teach temporarily at schools within the United States. In reciprocation, American Fulbright scholars went to foreign institutions. The Fulbright scholars were like

299

many short-term appointees, such as Albert Lybyer of another era, who had taught at the missionary colleges in the Ottoman Empire. Just as thousands of Near East young people since the 1860s had gotten an American-style education at the schools developed by Protestants, so the Fulbright program subsidized study by overseas youth at United States colleges abroad; Robert College, the American University of Beirut, and the American University in Cairo participated in this phase of the Fulbright program. Anticipating also the United States Information Agency (USIA), missionaries and educators for decades unofficially had spread knowledge about their homeland – the USIA made more comprehensive and systematic what had been going on for a long time. As in other instances, private internationalism prepared the way for America's public internationalism.[25]

There was also the previously noted missionary precedent for a policy of continuous government foreign aid. Nineteenth-century activities of American Board religionists had established Bible study groups, churches and schools, hospitals, and relief. To help sustain Near East Relief, the government provided transport, personnel, diplomatic help, and financial assistance amounting to about $25,000,000 (approximately $12,000,000 through the American Relief Administration to Near East Relief enterprise in the Caucasus). The government gave semiofficial backing to the Persian Commission and the Barton Relief Commission. From help to Near East Relief by the President, State and Navy departments, and the Relief Administration in the Wilson era, it was just one more logical move to regular foreign aid by Washington. Calvin Coolidge made a link between Near East Relief's mission and the public interest: "The volunteer relief committee was, from the beginning, a National organization of the United States, manned by our people and incorporated by a special act of Congress. . . . It was National because it received its support from all our people and was endorsed by Congress and all our Presidents throughout its history." [26] Anticipating an idea the American government would use to begin systematic overseas aid, Coolidge in 1924 suggested that Near East Relief and the Relief Administration helped stave the spread of Bolshevism.[27]

By the end of fifteen years of service, Near East Relief had aided over a million refugees and had housed, clothed, and educated over one hundred thousand orphans. Education included the training of nearly two hundred nurses. All this philanthropy had come through an expenditure of $116,-

000,000 (including the $25,000,000 in government aid). The human expense added up to thirty relief workers who had lost their lives to disease and violence.[28]

Near East Relief became Near East Foundation in 1930. Among the Foundation's trustees was Barton, the only missionary executive on the board; when he died in 1936 another American Board official took his place. Absent from the trustees were politicians. The chairman of the new group at its inception and for thirty-eight years thereafter was Dodge's son, Cleveland E. Dodge. A former missionary to Iraq and a Presbyterian clergyman, John S. Badeau, succeeded Dodge in 1968 (Badeau's experience included being president of the American University in Cairo and United States ambassador to Egypt). The Foundation was, as Barton once stated, Christian but not ecclesiastical. It and the American Board cooperated, as when at the end of the Second World War a missionary physician served with the Foundation among Greek refugees. The Foundation viewed itself in the Presbyterian missionary tradition when in 1968 it began assistance to the Rezaieh Agricultural College, which used buildings on the old mission compound at Urmia. Because of persecution (even execution of some non-American staff members), the Foundation had discontinued work in Soviet Armenia in 1930. The main places of activity were Greece — with a major village program in Macedonia — Bulgaria, Albania, Syria, and Lebanon. It dropped Bulgaria and Albania and took on Iran and Jordan after 1945. Its stress was not sentimental publicity or temporary aid; the Foundation became the first American effort expressly designed for technical assistance abroad. It fashioned creative approaches in agricultural extension services ("the Gospel of the Plow"), social work, public health, home welfare, physical therapy, and recreation. Giving priority to the demonstration method, it paid about 10 per cent of a pilot project; the host government paid 90 per cent. This procedure encouraged local initiative. The chief architect of the shift to technical assistance through the demonstration method was Presbyterian clergyman Barclay Acheson, executive secretary of Near East Foundation from 1930 to 1937 (he later became associate editor of *Reader's Digest*).[29]

When President Truman in 1950 was discussing the Point Four plan of government aid, he cited the Near East Foundation: "Four years ago, the Government of Iran asked the Foundation to set up a demonstration project in a group of 35 villages not far from the capital, Tehran. The Foundation brought village leaders to a series of training courses. It won their confidence, and through these leaders it began to carry out agricultural and health improvements. The Foundation met a water shortage by drilling deep wells. It overcame water-borne diseases. It sprayed homes with DDT. It sprayed crops with insecticides. It helped to organize schools in each of the 35 villages. The effects of the Near East Foundation's work are spreading throughout Iran." [30] (The Foundation was partly fulfilling expectations raised by Judson's Persian Commission.) The President envisioned the Point Four program both to relieve misery and win friends in the cold war.

Thus, Near East Foundation was one among many models for United States foreign aid. A Foundation leader, Harold B. Allen, wrote in a book of 1953 that his organization had shown a way for the official American fight against Communism in underdeveloped lands.[31]

Not only was the Foundation a pacesetter, but it and American schools in the Near East came to receive or administer government assistance funds. The Agency for International Development (AID), the foreign aid organization of the 1960s, contracted with the Foundation to carry out AID programs in Afghanistan, Korea, Kenya, Tanzania, and other nations; AID finances to the Foundation amounted to over $700,000 in 1968. International College's preliminary work on its new campus was made possible by a grant of $2,600,000 from AID in 1965. The American University of Beirut handled United States technical assistance scholarships for students, beginning in 1952; hundreds of students received AID money. An AID grant in 1964 at AUB started the only graduate program in the Near East for English language teaching. AID cutbacks at the end of the 1960s began to force such a reduction in American education as a planned elimination of the senior college program at Robert College.[32]

Not only in the Near East but in the world at large there was a direct line between missionary humanitarianism and systematic United States assistance abroad. Merle Curti has traced this line, stating that before the year 1900 American philanthropy overseas was primarily spasmodic and private. Protestant missions and the American Red Cross were the only institutions providing continuity; government participation was almost nil. During the next forty years, fund-raising became professional. Helped by tax policies, business corporations entered overseas philanthropy, with Washington regularly assisting its citizens. After 1940 the government role moved toward ascendancy. Through this long process, motives were as mixed generally as were Near East Relief's motives. There was egotism

(Ralph Waldo Emerson once wrote that if egotism were taken out of giving, the benefactor would be castrated), self-righteousness, Judeo-Christian compassion, and humanism.[33]

A final illustration of missionary influence on United States cultural policy was in the appearance of the Peace Corps. Near East Foundation and other humanitarian and religious groups were examples for Peace Corps practices. Also, Near East Foundation in 1962 agreed to cooperate with the Peace Corps on rural education in Iran. Soon there were some forty Peace Corps volunteers there to coordinate with the Foundation. The young volunteers began a job not unlike that of American Board teachers in the villages of Turkey and Persia over one hundred years before.[34]

Of course, there were differences between the American Board frontiersmen and the Peace Corps volunteers. The volunteers did not bring heavy dogmatic baggage with them, as did nineteenth-century religionists. The first missionaries were more condescending and argumentative than the volunteers. The young Americans of the 1960s had more appreciation for foreign values than the religionists.

To point out distinctions is not to make the volunteers look good. Protestants to the Near East had been groundbreakers for understanding. Without the volunteers' advantages of jet airplanes, television, and special literature, missionaries had developed a regard for foreigners. Through many painful mistakes the Protestants learned after the First World War that God is no respecter of persons. That he desires relations with people of every culture without discrimination. That no one society deserves more of his grace than another. These principles had been in the missionaries' Bible all along, in the story of Jonah's stubborn refusal to acknowledge that Yahweh liked Assyrians and in Jesus' concern for Samaritans so despised by Jews. It took repeated encounters for the religionists to feel these principles. When the American and Presbyterian boards and the institutions which came out of their enterprise grasped equalitarian concepts, they passed their experience in a nonecclesiastical form — along with other influences — to the United States government.

All the while, the Presbyterian Board was developing its enterprise among the Arabs. During the 1920s in Syria and Lebanon it stopped seeking to convert members of ancient churches. It chose instead to serve the already existing evangelical churches and the community at large. This fraternal style helped guard the missionary organization against worshipping itself. The style also recognized that evangelism was the primary responsibility of Armenians and Arabs, not Americans. The Presbyterian Board concentrated on medicine, rural reconstruction, orphanages, schools. Its program by 1960 had come under direct control of the National Evangelical Synod of Syria and Lebanon. The Board started the Beirut College for Women, the only four-year girls' college in the Arab nations, which in 1960 numbered four hundred fifty enrollees. Aleppo College has already been mentioned. Together with Armenian evangelicals in Syria and with Anglicans, the Presbyterian Board in 1932 opened the Near East School of Theology at Beirut (affiliated with AUB), the only Protestant one in Western Asia; in 1960 there were seventeen seminarians. After the partition of Palestine, the Presbyterian Board returned to the old task of relief, this time among Arab refugees. By the end of the June War of 1967, the numbers of displaced persons had grown to over a million. For missionaries, it was a problem similar to the Armenian dislocations. The Commission on Ecumenical Mission and Relations (new name of the Presbyterian Board of Missions), with its fifty some fraternal workers, cooperated with the interchurch Near East Christian Council and the United Nations Relief and Works Agency to relieve some of the suffering. In these concerns the Presbyterians were trying to demonstrate that their enemy was not other ecclesiastical bodies or political entities. They were trying to demonstrate that God was at work in the Near East to bring justice and opportunity for all people — Christians, agnostics, Muslims, Jews.[35]

After a century and a half of mission activity, the indigenous Protestant movement was not large. The number of local Protestants nurtured by Americans had not grown much from the level of 1914. There were forty-eight independent Presbyterian congregations in Iraq, Lebanon, and Syria in 1960. The thirty-two hundred members of these congregations were a fourth of the entire Protestant membership of thirteen thousand in these countries. In Egypt over half of the fifty thousand Protestants there were Presbyterians. In Iran, more than half the four thousand Protestant church members were Presbyterians. A portion of the non-Presbyterians in the Near East were products of American missions directed by the Reformed Church, the Friends, the Christian and Missionary Alliance, the Seventh-Day Adventists, and other small groups.[36]

The dream of Levi Parsons and Pliny Fisk in the 1810s about converting the Ottoman Empire had not come true. In the 1960s there were only small indigenous Protestant communities in the Near East; they seemed to be holding their own within Arab and Iranian cultures.

AID TO ASIAN NATIONALISM

Distinctly Protestant monuments to missionary enterprise in the Near East were not imposing. But American religious groups and their successor organizations deserve recognition for aid they gave to Asian nationalism.

The Armenian revolution was not a total loss. Turkish-Armenian emigrants established colonies in the United States, Egypt, Lebanon, Syria (in 1968 there were over 250,000 Armenian Americans). Aleppo College, with its Armenian constituency, and the Evangelical Armenian Church of Syria were direct successors to American missions in eastern Anatolia (AUB had large numbers of Armenian enrollees). United States missionaries through Near East Relief preserved the lives of tens of thousands of people in the Caucasus, many of whom helped populate the Armenian Soviet Socialist Republic. The Protestants unwittingly made a larger contribution than any other Americans to the territorial and political structure of Soviet Russia. With its Gregorian Church, Soviet Armenia functioned as it did in the 1960s partly as a result of the philanthropy of American missionaries.[37]

Religious and philanthropic contributions to Bulgarian nationalism, like those to Armenian, met political obstacles. Between the wars the American Board developed the American College of Sofia, and Near East Foundation experimented in Bulgaria with rural education. Protestant congregations increased. After Axis occupation of Bulgaria in 1942, the Americans fled, never to return. American College's president, Floyd Black, through his post in the Department of State (1942–1944) sought to prevent Allied bombing of Sofia and to counter Soviet penetration of Bulgaria, but failed. After the Communist takeover, the missionary heritage continued in the Bulgarian Evangelical Church.[38]

Whereas Communist governments subsumed much of missionary enterprise in territorial Armenia and in Bulgaria, Protestant and independent United States schools helped Western culture dominate in Turkey. From the beginning of the Kemalist movement, its leader focused on democratic liberalism rather than Bolshevism. Kemal accepted Soviet assistance but not ideology. Factors not unrelated to America's educational internationalism in Turkey were that Ismet Inönü had employed a Robert College professor as secretary-interpreter at Lausanne, and soon after began the study of English. During the 1930s there were a few American firms (Ford and Curtiss-Wright, for example) and several technical experts (railways, mining, sanitation, economic planning) in Turkey. Ankara looked to the United States as a friend and considered mission and other American organizations as political assets. Increasingly Robert College alumni were becoming Turkish diplomats (the delegation head at the United Nations Conference in San Francisco) and cabinet ministers. In the 1960s Robert Academy boasted Turkey's national poet on its faculty; Robert's graduates were leading industrialists, engineers, journalists, playwrights. Applications for admission to American Board schools, as mentioned, became nine times the number that could be accepted. The American Board's Redhouse Press continued to have a large market for its Turkish-English dictionary.[39]

Private Americans thus had aided the friendship between Turkey and the United States. Adnan Menderes, who became Premier of Turkey in 1950, had been educated in an American institution. The year after he took office Menderes led his nation into formal alliance with the United States through NATO. The two countries in the later 1950s signed executive agreements related to the Central Treaty Organization, the anti-Russian alliance system in the Near East. American military bases and soldiers appeared in Anatolia. United States foreign aid facilitated development in Asia Minor, including one project which eventually made Turkey a wheat exporter. Barton would have been pleased that the United States Army had finally answered his call to help stabilize the Old World.[40]

A leading center for cultivation of Arab identity was the American University of Beirut. After the Second World War several Arab nations organized universities with a bigger student body than AUB, but none maintained a higher academic standard. (The United States institution also paid its professors the largest salaries in the Near East.) Demands for Arab graduates from AUB, often called the Queen of the Orient, were larger than it could fill. Out of fourteen thousand alumni by 1968, 80 per cent had chosen to remain in the Arab world. These graduates were active professionally as physicians, dentists, teachers, and public figures. By the same year, both the overwhelming majority of the thirty-five hundred students then enrolled and 70 per cent of the five hundred fifty faculty members were Arabs. The school remained aloof from many vicissitudes of

Arab politics. This aloofness made it possible for AUB to meet long-range needs no matter how inflamed the political divisions. Amid the anti-Americanism within Arab countries after the June War of 1967, enrollment at AUB increased 7 per cent. One set of parents from the Israeli-held west bank of Jordan gathered just enough money to travel to Beirut and to register their teenage girl at the American school. They said: "Please watch over her. She is our only daughter and we hand her over in your care. We don't know when we will be able to come back." The university's social concern went into such a task as rural reconstruction, started jointly with Near East Foundation in 1930. By the 1960s a two hundred fifty–acre agricultural center of AUB had produced a dryland wheat which promised a doubled yield with half the regular seed. Political contributions had come through training of young men like the crown prince of Iraq. At the United Nations Conference in San Francisco, thirty participants were graduates of AUB, more than from any other single educational institution. Charles Malik, an alumnus, after ten years as a Lebanese diplomat (including the presidency of the UN General Assembly in its thirteenth session), returned to AUB as the dean of graduate studies. In 1965 the UN ambassadors of seven Arab nations were alumni of the university.[41]

AUB graduates helped bring to maturity the efforts of American missionaries and other inaugurators of Arab nationalism. Using ideas such as those of Protestant-taught Butrus al-Bustani and those of the King-Crane Commission, Arab leaders pressed against their British and French rulers. Iraq and Egypt became nominally independent in the two decades after the Paris Peace Conference. During the Second World War and its aftermath, Syria and Lebanon freed themselves of French tutelage. In the Suez crisis of 1956, Western European control was broken actually and potentially throughout the entire Arab area.

During the triumph of Arab militancy, United States missionaries and educators found the American government modifying its pro-Arab views. Washington had retained the King-Crane report's warmness for Arab freedom and coldness for territorial Zionism several years after 1919. (Wilson's commitment to the Balfour Declaration was not matched by succeeding Republican administrations.) The American oil companies in the Near East, procuring concessions between 1927 and 1940, developed pro-Arab attitudes. Protestants, AUB people, and oilmen helped the State Department in the 1930s to resist Zionism within the United States. The Department's position was the historical one: protection of its citizens and

307

their interests. After Nazi extermination of Jews became known widely, Zionism became an open issue within America, in a way reminiscent of Armenianism. Zionist propaganda sensitized the White House and Congress to the idea of a Palestinian homeland for Jews. Spokesmen for oil investors, whose commodity had strategic value, sensitized State, War, and Navy departments to Arab anti-Zionist notions on Palestine. In 1945 mission and church groups helped found the Institute of Arab-American Affairs to combat Zionism. During the next two years what was named the Anglo-American Committee of Inquiry studied the Jewish homeland question. Testimony of American mission-related individuals was anti-Zionist, although one United States churchman, representing conservative Christians who saw a separate Jewish home as a fulfillment of biblical prophecy, was pro-Zionist. Both the British government and President Truman spurned vigorous pro-Arab advice from their executive departments and from lobbyists, and agreed with pro-Zionist public opinion.[42]

Americans after 1948 became emotional over Zionism, as they had earlier over Armenianism. In this climate, it was difficult for the United States public to develop an impartial regard for Near East problems. The anti-Arab idea became overdrawn, as the anti-Turk image years before. Many Americans failed to understand the rage of Arabs over what they believed was a Jewish theft of territory, backed by imperial money and munitions from the West; Arabs felt that just when they were mastering French and British colonialism, a new and more subtle Western imperialism in the guise of protection of Jews was taking its place.

Missionaries and churchmen sought to present views in the United States which showed Arab perspectives as well as Jewish. Polls after June 1967 indicated a large majority of the American populace was sympathetic to Israeli concerns. At the same time professional Christian religionists had reactions just about evenly divided between Arab and Israeli positions. The Christian religionists usually accepted Israel's right to exist, without harassment. However, their chief concern was a settlement of the Arab refugee question (this was like Near East Relief's concern for the deported Armenians).[43] Unlike missionaries from the Wilson period, they had no dramatic effect on United States policy.

◄ ►

The influence of American Protestant missionaries on Asian nationalism and on United States diplomacy had declined after the First World

War and nonecclesiastical forces had become powerful. Higher education and philanthropy were no longer dominated by churchmen, and economic concerns challenged the hold by missionaries and educators on American relations with the Near East. The cold war pushed strategic aims of the United States government to a place of prominence.

In the 1960s a life-size portrait of James L. Barton hung in an office of the United Church Board for World Ministries, reminding missionary executives of a grand past, of a vigorous American Board leader. Three years before Barton died he had written that "America's paramount influence and interest in the Near East was begun and has been perpetuated" by Christians.[44] Counting hundreds of missionaries and educators in regions from Albania to Persia and Turkey to Arabia, he anticipated a promising future. He characterized fifteen schools of higher learning which either had originated with Protestant leadership or continued to operate under mission boards as "Christian in spirit." He implied that the heritage of missions would often not be demonstrably Christian, but remarkable.

Indeed, an era had passed when the United States Senate rejected the Lausanne Treaty in 1927. The event signalled that both the ascendancy of Protestant diplomacy and the heroic age of Protestantism in the Near East had ended.

Notes

Notes

Chapter 1. "Christianize the Nations"

1. Kenneth Scott Latourette, *Christianity in a Revolutionary Age: A History of Christianity in the Nineteenth and Twentieth Centuries* (5 vols.; New York: Harper, 1958–1962), III, 242–246.

2. James L. Barton, *Daybreak in Turkey* (Boston: Pilgrim Press, 1908), 88.

3. Clifton Jackson Phillips, *Protestant America and the Pagan World: The First Half Century of the American Board of Commissioners for Foreign Missions, 1810–1860* (Cambridge, Mass.: East Asian Research Center of Harvard University, 1969), 1–31; Fred Field Goodsell, *They Lived Their Faith: An Almanac of Faith, Hope and Love* (Boston: American Board of Commissioners for Foreign Missions, 1961), 60–61.

4. James A. Field, Jr., *America and the Mediterranean World: 1776–1882* (Princeton, N.J.: Princeton University Press, 1969), 3–104.

5. Latourette, *Christianity in a Revolutionary Age*, I, viii–ix; Basil Mathews, *John R. Mott: World Citizen* (New York: Harper, 1934), 120–128; *Addresses and Papers of John R. Mott* (5 vols.; New York: Association Press, 1947), V, 7–12.

6. Henry Nash Smith, *The Virgin Land: The American West as Symbol and Myth* (Cambridge, Mass.: Harvard University Press, 1950).

7. Parsons to his father, February 1, 1820, and Parsons Diary, February 23, 1820, in Daniel O. Morton, ed., *Memoir of Rev. Levi Parsons: First Missionary to Palestine from the United States* (2nd ed.; Burlington, Vt.: C. Goodrich, 1830), 251, 283; also, Alvan Bond, *Memoir of the Rev. Pliny Fisk, A.M., Late Missionary to Palestine* (Boston: Crocker & Brewster, 1828); William E. Strong, *The Story of the American Board: An Account of the First Hundred Years of the American Board of Commissioners for Foreign Missions* (Boston: Pilgrim Press, 1910), 80–107.

8. A. L. Tibawi, *American Interests in Syria: 1800–1901, A Study of Educational, Literary and Religious Work* (London: Oxford University Press, 1966), 13–16; Phillips, *Protestant America and the Pagan World*, 133–135.

9. Quoted in David H. Finnie, *Pioneers East: The Early American Experience in the Middle East* (Cambridge, Mass.: Harvard University Press, 1967), 152.

10. Franklin Hamlin Littell, *From State Church to Pluralism: A Protestant Interpretation of Religion in American History* (Chicago: Aldine, 1962), 29–62.

11. American Board, *Annual Report*, 21 (1831), 48, quoted in Tibawi, *American Interests in Syria*, 60.

12. Eli Smith, *Researches of the Rev. E. Smith and Rev. H. G. O. Dwight in Armenia* (2 vols.; Boston: Crocker & Brewster, 1833), II, 70.

13. See n. 12.

14. Quoted in E. D. G. Prime, *Forty Years in the Turkish Empire; or, Memoirs of Rev. William Goodsell* (New York: Robert Carter, 1876), 18–21.

15. Finnie, *Pioneers East*, 274.

16. Latourette, *Christianity in a Revolutionary Age*, V, 279–298.

17. Quoted in Prime, *Forty Years in the Turkish Empire*, 185; also, Bernard F. Nordmann, "American Missionary Work among Armenians in Turkey (1830–1923)," unpublished Ph.D. thesis, University of Illinois (1927), 6, 12, 44; also, George A. Paboojian, "A History of Missionary Activity among Armenians in the Near East since 1819," unpublished B.S.T. thesis, Biblical Seminary in New York (1957), 16–23.

18. Eli Smith in *Missionary Herald* (June 1830), quoted in Leon Arpee, *A Century of Armenian Protestantism: 1846–1946* (New York: Armenian Missionary Association of America, 1946), 54.

19. Records of Syrian Mission, quoted in Tibawi, *American Interests in Syria*, 80.

20. Quoted in *ibid.*, 105.

21. Quoted in Nordmann, "American Missionary Work among Armenians in Turkey (1830–1923)," 199.

22. Robert L. Daniel, "American Influences in the Near East before 1861," *American Quarterly*, 16 (Spring 1964), 77; Julius Richter, *A History of Protestant Missions in the Near East* (New York: Revell, 1910), 111–113.

23. R. Pierce Beaver, "North American Thought on the Fundamental Principles of Missions during the Twentieth Century," *Church History*, 21 (1952), 345.

24. Phillips, *Protestant America and the Pagan World*, 234–256.

25. Sydney N. Fisher, "Two Centuries of American Interest in Turkey," in David H. Pinkney and Theodore Ropp, eds., *A Festschrift for Frederick B. Artz* (Durham, N.C.: Duke University Press, 1964), 119–120; Nordmann, "American Missionary Work among Armenians in Turkey (1830–1923)," 230–231.

26. Quoted in Finnie, *Pioneers East*, 131.

27. Quoted in Tibawi, *American Interests in Syria*, 121.

28. Albert H. Lybyer, "America's Missionary Record in Turkey," *Current History*, 19 (February 1924), 802–810.

29. Nordmann, "American Missionary Work among Armenians in Turkey (1830–1923)," 57–58.

30. Quoted in Tibawi, *American Interests in Syria*, 132.

31. Barton, *Daybreak in Turkey*, 171–178; Leland James Gordon, *American Relations with Turkey: 1830–1930, An Economic Interpretation* (Philadelphia: University of Pennsylvania Press, 1932), 222; Nordmann, "American Missionary Work among Armenians in Turkey (1830–1923)," 230–231.

32. Nordmann, "American Missionary Work among Armenians in Turkey (1830–1923)," 87.

33. James L. Barton, *Educational Missions* (New York: Student Volunteer Movement, 1913), 1–25.

34. Marshall McLuhan, *Understanding Media: The Extension of Man* (New York: McGraw-Hill, 1964), 81–88; Daniel Boorstin, *The Americans: The National Experience* (New York: Random House, 1965), 327–337; Elizabeth L. Eisenstein, "Some

Conjectures about the Impact of Printing on Western Society and Thought: A Preliminary Report," *Journal of Modern History*, 40 (March 1968), 38–41; Phillips, *Protestant America and the Pagan World*, 258.

35. Cyrus Hamlin, *My Life and Times* (2nd ed.; Boston: Congregational Sunday School and Publishing Society, 1893), 205–369; Richter, *A History of Protestant Missions in the Near East*, 126–128.

36. George Washburn, *Fifty Years in Constantinople and Recollections of Robert College* (2nd ed.; Boston: Houghton Mifflin, 1911), 1–13; K. M. Greenwood, "A Brief History of Robert College," unpublished centennial paper (1963), 1–13, Robert College's New York office; Robert College, *Catalog* (1967–1968).

37. Syrian Mission Report of 1962, quoted in Tibawi, *American Interests in Syria*, 161.

38. Daniel Bliss, *The Reminiscences of Daniel Bliss*, ed. by Frederick J. Bliss (New York: Revell, 1920), 198; also, brochure by Daniel da Cruz, *The American University of Beirut Celebrates Its Proud Centennial* (1966), American University of Beirut's New York office.

39. Mary Mills Patrick, *A Bosporus Adventure: Istanbul (Constantinople) Woman's College, 1871–1924* (Palo Alto, Calif.: Stanford University Press, 1934), 28–35.

40. Hester Donaldson Jenkins, *An Educational Ambassador to the Near East: The Story of Mary Mills Patrick and an American College in the Orient* (New York: Revell, 1925), 303.

41. Quoted in *ibid.*, 6.

42. "American Educational, Medical, Industrial, Benevolent and Religious Institutions in Turkey, 1915," enclosure in letter from James L. Barton to Robert Lansing, April 6, 1916, ABC 3.2, American Board of Commissioners for Foreign Missions Archives, Houghton Library, Harvard University (Archives hereafter cited ABC); Vahan M. Kurkjian, *A History of Armenia* (New York: Armenian General Benevolent Union of America, 1959).

43. George E. White, *Adventuring with Anatolia College* (Grinnell, Ia.: Herald-Register Publishing Company, 1940), 13–76; Goodsell, *They Lived Their Faith*, 101–103, 132–133, 154–155, 271; Alexander MacLachlan, "A Potpourri of Sidelights and Shadows from Turkey," 87–137, unpublished memoir, private holding.

44. Bernard Lewis, *The Emergence of Modern Turkey* (London: Oxford University Press, 1961), 73–125, 171–205.

45. See n. 56, this chapter, for sources on statistics.

46. Barton, *Educational Missions*, 1–25.

47. Quoted in *ibid.*, 162.

48. A. L. Tibawi, "The Genesis and Early History of the Syrian Protestant College," *Middle East Journal*, 21 (Winter & Spring 1967), 1–15, 199–212. For a general history of the Presbyterian Board, see Arthur Judson Brown, *One Hundred Years: A History of the Foreign Missionary Work of the Presbyterian Church in the U.S.A.* (New York: Revell, 1937).

49. Patrick, *A Bosporus Adventure*, 125.

50. Howard Sweetser Bliss, "The Modern Missionary," *Atlantic Monthly*, 125 (May 1920), 667, 671, 674.

51. John White, "Missions and Proselytism," *His*, 28 (November 1967), 10–14.

52. James L. Barton, *The Missionary and His Critics* (New York: Revell, 1906), 39; also, James L. Barton, *The Unfinished Task of the Christian Church: Introductory Studies in the Problem of the World's Evangelism* (New York: Layman's Missionary Movement, 1908).

53. "Missionary Temptations," *Nation*, 61 (November 21, 1895), 360–361.

54. Gordon, *American Relations with Turkey*, 311.

55. Reports of Howard S. Bliss, George A. Ford, and Franklin E. Hoskins to the

chairman of Commission I for the Edinburgh Conference, John R. Mott, in 1909, Edinburgh Conference MSS, Missionary Research Library, New York City.

56. For statistics on evangelistic, educational, and medical missions, see J. H. Greene, *Leavening of the Levant* (Boston: Pilgrim Press, 1916), Chs. 10–13; John A. DeNovo, *Ameircan Interests and Policies in the Middle East: 1900–1939* (Minneapolis: University of Minnesota Press, 1963), 31, 96; J. C. Hurewitz, *Middle East Dilemmas: The Background of United States Policy* (New York: Harper, 1953), 59–167; Paul A. Remick, "The Story of Christian Missions in the Near East," unpublished B.D. thesis, Butler University School of Religion (1954), 204–225; Richter, *A History of Protestant Missions in the Near East*, 416–419; Nordmann, "American Missionary Work among Armenians in Turkey (1830–1923)," 230–231; Barton, *Educational Missions*, 180–271. On the American Bible Society, see Constance E. Padwick, *Call to Istanbul* (London: Longmans, 1958), 52–53. And see Henry Harris Jessup, *Fifty-Three Years in Syria* (2 vols.; Chicago: Revell, 1910), Appendices 1–7.

57. Lloyd C. Griscom, *Diplomatically Speaking* (New York: Literary Guild of America, 1940), 134.

58. Norman Goodall, *Christian Mission and Social Ferment* (London: Epworth, 1964), 13–57.

59. Quoted in Tibawi, *American Interests in Syria*, 301.

Chapter 2. The Eastern Question

1. Quoted in Fisher, "Two Centuries of American Interest in Turkey," in Pinkney and Ropp, eds., *A Festschrift for Frederick B. Artz*, 117.

2. Field, *America and the Mediterranean World*, 104–140.

3. Robert L. Daniel, *American Philanthropy in the Near East: 1820–1960* (Athens: Ohio University Press, 1970), 5–16.

4. Quoted in Merle Curti and Kendall Birr, *Prelude to Point Four: American Technical Missions Overseas, 1838–1938* (Madison: University of Wisconsin Press, 1954), 22–24.

5. DeNovo, *American Interests and Policies in the Middle East*, 58–87.

6. Philip K. Hitti, *The Syrians in America* (New York: Doran, 1924), 54–55; Hurewitz, *Middle East Dilemmas*, 167.

7. S. B. L. Penrose, *That They May Have Life: The Story of the American University of Beirut, 1866–1941* (New York: Trustees of the American University of Beirut, 1941), 87; DeNovo, *American Interests and Policies in the Middle East*, 6, 20.

8. White, *Adventuring at Anatolia College*, 28–31; Edwin M. Bliss, *Turkey and the Armenian Atrocities* (Boston: H. L. Hastings, 1896), 337–344.

9. Bliss, *Turkey and the Armenian Atrocities*, 345–569; Avedis K. Sanjian, *The Armenian Communities in Syria under Ottoman Dominion* (Cambridge, Mass.: Harvard University Press, 1965), 278.

10. M. Vartan Malcom, *The Armenians in America* (Boston: Pilgrim Press, 1919), 65–77.

11. Bliss, *Turkey and the Armenian Atrocities*, 511, 551.

12. *Congressional Record*, 28 (January 22 and 24, 1896), 854, 959–960; also, Gabriel A. Almond, *The American People and Foreign Policy* (New York: Harcourt, 1950), 3–10.

13. Brochures, *The Story of a Nation's Martyrdom* (cartoons) and *Garden of Eden Defiled!* (c. 1896), Missionary Research Library.

14. Bliss, *Turkey and the Armenian Atrocities*, 1–4.

15. Cyrus Hamlin, "America's Duty to Americans in Turkey," *North American Review*, 163 (September 1896), 276–281; George E. Paulsen, "The Szechwan Riots

of 1895 and American 'Missionary Diplomacy,' " *Journal of Asian Studies*, 28 (February 1969), 285–298.

16. Merle Curti, *American Philanthropy Abroad: A History* (New Brunswick, N.J.: Rutgers University Press, 1963), 120, 131–133.

17. Angell and missionaries quoted in Tibawi, *American Interests in Syria*, 295–297.

18. Oscar S. Straus, *Under Four Administrations: From Cleveland to Taft* (Boston: Houghton Mifflin, 1922), 141–142; Penrose, *That They May Have Life*, 87.

19. Griscom, *Diplomatically Speaking*, 135, 172–174.

20. Penrose, *That They May Have Life*, 97.

21. Theodore Roosevelt to William Wingate Sewall, May 4, 1898, in Elting E. Morison, ed., *The Letters of Theodore Roosevelt* (8 vols.; Cambridge, Mass.: Harvard University Press, 1951–1954), II, 822.

22. Roosevelt to General Sickles, August 8, 1904, in *ibid.*, IV, 885.

23. Edward M. Earle, "American Missions in the Near East," *Foreign Affairs*, 7 (April 1929), 406–407.

24. Barton, *The Missionary and His Critics*, 106.

25. Kenneth Scott Latourette, "Colonialism and Missions: Progressive Separation," *Journal of Church and State*, 7 (Autumn 1965), 330–349.

26. DeNovo, *American Interests and Policies in the Middle East*, 49.

27. Ahmed Rustem to William Jennings Bryan, September 12, 1914, in *Papers Relating to the Foreign Relations of the United States: The Lansing Papers, 1914–1920* (2 vols.; Washington D.C.: Government Printing Office, 1939–1940), I, 68–69 (the general work hereafter cited *Foreign Relations*).

28. White, *Adventuring with Anatolia College*, 29, 31, 46–47; Goodsell, *They Lived Their Faith*, 125–126.

29. Louise Nalbandian, *The Armenian Revolutionary Movement: The Development of the Armenian Political Parties through the Nineteenth Century* (Berkeley: University of California Press, 1963); Sarkis Atamian, *The Armenian Community* (New York: Philosophical Library, 1955), Chs. 6–9; Simon Vratzian, "The Armenian Revolution and the Armenian Revolutionary Federation," *Armenian Review*, 3 (Autumn 1950 & Winter 1950–1951), 3–31, 58–66.

30. James G. Mandalian, trans. and ed., *Armenian Freedom Fighters: The Memoirs of Rouben der Minasian* (Boston: Hairenik Association, 1963); Firuz Kazemzadeh, *The Struggle for Transcaucasia (1917–1921)* (New York: Philosophical Library, 1951), 9–10.

31. Sanjian, *The Armenian Communities in Syria under Ottoman Dominion*, 280–282; Nordmann, "American Missionary Work among Armenians in Turkey (1830–1923)," 125–126; Strong, *The Story of the American Board*, 410–412.

32. Kamel S. Abu Jaber, "The Millet System in the Nineteenth-Century Ottoman Empire," *Muslim World*, 57 (July 1967), 212–223; Loofty Levonian, "The Millet System in the Middle East," *Muslim World*, 42 (April 1952), 90–96.

33. James B. Gidney, *A Mandate for Armenia* (Kent, Oh.: Kent State University Press, 1967), 15–23; Nordmann, "American Missionary Work among Armenians in Turkey (1830–1923)," 227; *The Joint Mandate Scheme* (New York: American Committee for the Independence of Armenia, c. December 1919), 52, Missionary Research Library.

34. Gidney, *A Mandate for Armenia*, 31; also, Roderic H. Davison, "The Armenian Crisis: 1912–1914," *American Historical Review*, 53 (April 1948), 481–505; Feroz Ahmad, *The Young Turks: The Committee of Union and Progress in Turkish Politics, 1908–1914* (London: Oxford University Press, 1969).

35. Quotation of Khorene Narbe De Lusignan in Gidney, *A Mandate for Armenia*, vi.

36. Washburn, *Fifty Years in Constantinople and Recollections of Robert College*,

164, 177–178, 180–183, 207, 295–299; Daniel, *American Philanthropy in the Near East*, 124–140.

37. Caleb F. Gates, *Not to Me Only* (Princeton, N.J.: Princeton University Press, 1940), 167–168; Griscom, *Diplomatically Speaking*, 135; Strong, *The Story of the American Board*, 390.

38. Enoch F. Bell to James L. Barton, June 12, 1919, ABC 3.2; Strong, *The Story of the American Board*, 403, 409–410; Goodsell, *They Lived Their Faith*, 450–452; Daniel, *American Philanthropy in the Near East*, 141–144.

39. Spencer Lavan, "Four Christian Arab Nationalists: A Comparative Study," *Muslim World*, 57 (April 1967), 114–125.

40. Tibawi, *American Interests in Syria*, 303.

41. George Antonius, *The Arab Awakening: The Story of the Arab National Movement* (Philadelphia: Lippincott, 1939), 43.

42. Quotation of Ameen Rihani, in DeNovo, *American Interests and Policies in the Middle East*, 50–51.

43. Muyhee Al-Din Hatoor Al-Khalidi, "A Century of American Contribution to Arab Nationalism: 1820–1920," unpublished Ph.D. thesis, Vanderbilt University (1958), 144–164; Philip K. Hitti, *The Near East in History* (Princeton, N.J.: Van Nostrand, 1961), 847–848; Alan R. Taylor, "The American Protestant Mission and the Awakening of Modern Syria: 1820–1870," unpublished Ph.D. thesis, Georgetown University (1957); William R. Polk, *The United States and the Arab World* (Cambridge, Mass.: Harvard University Press, 1965), 100–107.

44. Laurence Evans, *United States Policy and the Partition of Turkey: 1914–1924* (Baltimore: Johns Hopkins Press, 1965), 24.

Chapter 3. "Prelude to Point Four"

1. W. D. P. Bliss, "Armenia's Struggle for Independence," *Current History*, 11 (October 1919–March 1920), 138–144; Garegin Pasdermadjian, *Why Armenia Should Be Free* (Boston: Hairenik Association, 1918); Simon Vratzian, *Armenia and the Armenian Question* (Boston: Hairenik Association, 1943).

2. Clarence D. Ussher, *An American Physician in Turkey: A Narrative of Adventures in Peace and War* (Boston: Houghton Mifflin, 1917), 279, 285; also, Onnig Mekhitarian, "The Defense of Van (Part Five)," *Armenian Review*, 2 (Spring 1949), 131–141; Grace Higley Knapp, *The Mission at Van: In Turkey in War Time* (n.p.: privately printed, 1916), 11–48.

3. Speech of James Bryce to the House of Lords on October 6, 1915, in Arnold J. Toynbee, *Armenian Atrocities: The Murder of a Nation* (London: Hodder & Stoughton, 1915), 10–11. For the experience of a Protestant Armenian clergyman at Marash, see Abraham H. Hartunian, *Neither to Laugh nor to Weep: A Memoir of the Armenian Genocide* (Boston: Beacon Press, 1968), 51–76.

4. James Bryce (with Arnold J. Toynbee), ed., *The Treatment of Armenians in the Ottoman Empire, 1915–16; Documents Presented to Viscount Grey of Fallodon, Secretary of State for Foreign Affairs* (London: Joseph Causton, 1916), 645–648.

5. Franz Werfel, *The Forty Days of Musa Dagh* (New York: Viking Press, 1934).

6. Anonymous letter of August 3–16, 1915, conveyed out of Turkey in the sole of a refugee's shoe, in Bryce, ed., *The Treatment of Armenians in the Ottoman Empire*, 20–21.

7. Grace H. Knapp, *The Tragedy of Bitlis* (New York: Revell, 1919), 44–87.

8. White, *Adventuring with Anatolia College*, 82–89.

9. Bryce, ed., *The Treatment of Armenians in the Ottoman Empire*, 617–633; notation on March 16, 1919, of discussion between Clarence Ussher and Edgar J. Fish-

er, Edgar J. Fisher Diary, Ohio State University Library; Richard G. Hovannisian, *Armenia on the Road to Independence: 1918* (Berkeley: University of California Press, 1967), 40–68; Howard M. Sachar, *The Emergence of the Middle East: 1914–1924* (New York: Knopf, 1969), 87–103; Ulrich Trumpener, *Germany and the Ottoman Empire: 1914–1918* (Princeton, N.J.: Princeton University Press, 1968), 202–205.

10. Henry Morgenthau Diary, August 8, 1915, Henry Morgenthau, Sr., MSS, Library of Congress.

11. There is no way of knowing how many Armenians died. Estimates range as high as 1,500,000. An American consul in Aleppo, J. B. Jackson, did some careful figuring and concluded "about 1,000,000 persons lost up to this date." Jackson to Morgenthau, September 29, 1915, *ibid.* See Bryce ed., *The Treatment of Armenians in the Ottoman Empire*, 650–651; Herbert Hoover, *An American Epic* (4 vols.; Chicago: Regnery, 1959–1964), II, 203–204.

12. Morgenthau Diary, April 24 and 26, 1915, Morgenthau MSS.

13. Henry Morgenthau, *All in a Lifetime* (New York: Doubleday, 1922), 175–177, 203–204.

14. Gates, *Not to Me Only*, 122; Syrian Protestant College, *Annual Report* (1914–1915).

15. Gates, *Not to Me Only*, 115–119; also, Gates to his father-in-law, S. M. Moore, November 7, 1895, and Gates to "Friends," November 13, 1895, Caleb F. Gates MSS, private collection.

16. Mary Ellen Moore Gates Diary, April 27, 1915, Gates MSS.

17. James L. Barton to Morgenthau, December 22, 1916, ABC 3.2; also, Louise J. Peet, *No Less Honor: The Biography of William Wheelock Peet* (n.p.: privately printed, 1939); Nordmann, "American Missionary Work among Armenians in Turkey (1830–1923)," 161.

18. Ahmed Djemal Pasha, *Memories of a Turkish Statesman: 1913–1919* (New York: Doran, 1922), Ch. 9.

19. Morgenthau Diary, May 10, June 19, July 12, and July 18, 1915, Morgenthau MSS; also, Henry Morgenthau, *Ambassador Morgenthau's Story* (New York: Doubleday, 1918), 299ff.

20. Morgenthau, *Ambassador Morgenthau's Story*, 327–328.

21. Peet to James L. Barton, August 17, 1915, ABC 16.9.3.

22. Curti, *American Philanthropy Abroad*, 620–622.

23. *Ibid.*, 120–131; Leon Arpee, *A History of Armenian Christianity from the Beginning to Our Own Time* (New York: Armenian Missionary Association, 1946), 299; Nordmann, "American Missionary Work among Armenians in Turkey (1830–1923)," 163.

24. Robert L. Daniel, "From Relief to Technical Assistance in the Near East, A Case Study: Near East Relief and Near East Foundation," unpublished Ph.D. thesis, University of Wisconsin (1953), 11–12.

25. File 1761, Box 520, Presbyterian Board of Foreign Missions Archives (part of the Commission on Ecumenical Mission and Relations Archives), Presbyterian Historical Soicety, Philadelphia (hereafter cited Presbyterian Board Archives).

26. Morgenthau to the Department of State, September 3, 1915, Morgenthau MSS.

27. Peet to Barton, September 6, 1915, ABC 16.9.3; also, Cleveland Dodge to Edward M. House, October 11, 1915, Edward M. House MSS, Yale University Library; James L. Barton, *Story of Near East Relief (1915–1930): An Interpretation* (New York: Macmillan, 1930), 8–10.

28. Charles Herbert Levermore, *Samuel Train Dutton: A Biography* (New York: Macmillan, 1922), 75–77, 159–164, 206.

29. Many missionaries called the new group the Dodge Relief Committee, accord-

ing to a letter of retired missionary Luther R. Fowle to me, March 27, 1961. The organization also had other names, including Committee on Armenian Atrocities. See New York *Times*, September 27, 1915.

30. Crane to "JCB," October 5, 1915, Charles R. Crane MSS, offices of the American Universities Field Staff and the Institute of Current World Affairs, New York City; Leo J. Bocage, "The Public Career of Charles R. Crane," unpublished Ph.D. thesis, Fordham University (1962), 1–103; cover story of *Time* magazine, March 9, 1931, 16–17. I talked about Crane in 1961 with the former director of the Institute of Current World Affairs, Walter Rogers, a close friend of Crane's for several decades.

31. Morgenthau to State Department, September 25, 1915, Morgenthau MSS.

32. New York *Times*, September 17, 21, 25, and 27–30, 1915; newspaper release for October 4, 1915, James L. Barton MSS, part of the American Board Archives (ABC 55).

33. W. E. Strong to Barton, February 10, 1919, ABC 3.2; also, unpublished, typewritten (399 pp.) Barton "Autobiography," Barton MSS; publications of Barton's noted earlier; Goodsell, *They Lived Their Faith*, 183–184, 248–249.

34. Barton to James Bryce, June 6, 1916, ABC 3.2; also, Crane to JCB, March 2, 1916, Crane MSS.

35. Barton to Morgenthau, August 1, 1916, ABC 3.2; also, Barton to Samuel Dutton, June 24, 1916, *ibid*.

36. Quotation of Elkus to Joseph Tumulty, November 18, 1916, in DeNovo, *American Interests and Policies in the Middle East*, 104.

37. James Bryce, *Transcaucasia and Ararat: Being Notes of a Vacation Tour in the Autumn of 1876* (London: Macmillan, 1877), 406–420.

38. H. A. L. Fisher, *James Bryce (Viscount Bryce of Dechmont, O.M.)* (2 vols.; New York: Macmillan, 1927), I, 181–184, 300–302; II, 119, 145; James B. Gidney, "Cold War in the Eighties," *Ararat*, 9 (Fall 1968), 6–13.

39. See n. 4, this chapter.

40. ACASR bulletins, *Latest News Concerning the Armenian and Syrian Sufferers* (January 25, 1916), *Armenia* (February 21, 1916), *Latest News* (April 5, 1916), and *Latest News* (May 24, 1916), Missionary Research Library.

41. Barton to Wilson, August 16, 1916, ABC 3.2; also, Box 498 (relief propaganda) in Series 4 of the Woodrow Wilson MSS, Library of Congress.

42. The ACASR published each of Rockwell's booklets in 1916; copies are in the Missionary Research Library. See ACASR materials in the William Walker Rockwell MSS, Missionary Research Library; also, see a publicity piece of December 1915 in the Barton MSS.

43. *Independent*, 84 (October 18, 1915), 96.

44. DeNovo, *American Interests and Policies in the Middle East*, 103.

45. James L. Barton, "The Near East Relief: A Moral Force," *International Review of Missions*, 18 (1929), 501–502.

46. Barton to D. L. Pierson, April 15, 1918, ABC 3.2.

47. Curti, *American Philanthropy Abroad*, 248; also, ACASR bulletin, *Armenia* (February 21, 1916).

48. Barton to Lansing, April 6, 1916, ABC 3.2; also, Barton to Everett P. Wheeler, March 9, 1916, *ibid*.

49. Barton to William Rockwell, March 11, 1916, *ibid*.

50. Quoted in Daniel, "From Relief to Technical Assistance in the Near East," 37.

51. Oscar S. Straus, "Americans in Turkey: Their Notable Work for Education," *Review of Reviews*, 26 (December 1914), 710–713.

52. See Ch. 2, n. 4 (p. 316).

Chapter 4. An Unofficial Cabinet

1. New York *Times*, June 24, 1926; also, "The Near East Loses Its Greatest Friend," *News Letter of the Near East College Association* (September 1926), New York City offices of the Near East College Association.

2. Wilson to Dodge, July 12, 1914, Cleveland H. Dodge MSS, Princeton University Library; also, Wilson to Dodge, February 18, 1911, *ibid.*

3. Edith Wilson to Dodge, October 9, 1920, *ibid.*

4. Wilson to Dodge, October 4, 1923, *ibid.*

5. Edith Wilson to Dodge, June 11, 1924, *ibid.*

6. Ray Stannard Baker, *Woodrow Wilson: Life and Letters* (8 vols.; New York: Doubleday, 1927–1939), II, 240; also, Robert L. Daniel, "The Friendship of Woodrow Wilson and Cleveland H. Dodge," *Mid-America*, 43 (July 1961), 182–196; my article, "Cleveland H. Dodge, Woodrow Wilson, and the Near East," *Journal of Presbyterian History*, 48 (Winter 1970), 249–264.

7. Wilson to Dodge, June 21, 1906, Dodge MSS.

8. Wilson to Dodge, August 4, 1907, *ibid.*

9. Minutes of board quoted in Baker, *Woodrow Wilson: Life and Letters*, II, 261.

10. Dodge to Wilson, December 18, 1907, quoted in *ibid.*, 267.

11. Dodge to Wilson, December 28, 1909, quoted in *ibid.*, 319.

12. Wilson to Dodge, February 7, 1910, Dodge MSS.

13. Wilson to Dodge, July 1, 1910, quoted in Baker, *Woodrow Wilson: Life and Letters*, II, 353.

14. Dodge to Wilson, January 27, 1911, quoted in Arthur S. Link, *Wilson: The Road to the White House* (Princeton, N.J.: Princeton University Press, 1947), 235.

15. Quoted in Baker, *Woodrow Wilson: Life and Letters*, III, 365.

16. Wilson to Dodge, July 29, 1912, Dodge MSS.

17. Link, *Wilson: The Road to the White House*, 336, 403, 485.

18. Draft of Dodge letter to Wilson, February 1917, Dodge MSS; also, Mathews, *John R. Mott*, 138, 437.

19. Baker, *Woodrow Wilson: Life and Letters*, IV, 253.

20. On the indictment and misappropriation charges, see Frank Harris Blighton, *Woodrow Wilson and Co.* (New York: Fox Printing House, 1916). During the 1916 campaign Blighton, a muckraking Arizona newspaperman, and others claimed that Phelps Dodge had misappropriated 6,400 acres of public land in New Mexico and Arizona and that the United States attorney general failed to prosecute. Cleveland Dodge denied these charges. Robert Glass Cleland, *History of Phelps Dodge: 1834–1950* (New York: Knopf, 1952) does not mention these matters.

21. Dodge to Wilson, July 13, 1914, Dodge MSS.

22. Dodge to Wilson, January 14, 1916, Wilson MSS.

23. Wilson to Dodge, January 17, 1916, Dodge MSS.

24. Wilson to Dodge, April 4, 1917, Wilson MSS.

25. Several of these ideas come from a letter of Dodge's son, Cleveland E. Dodge, to me on May 29, 1968.

26. Wilson to Dodge, December 27, 1909, October 23, 1914, and December 21, 1910, Dodge MSS.

27. Baker, *Woodrow Wilson: Life and Letters*, II, 2.

28. Dodge to Wilson, November 8, 1920, Wilson MSS.

29. Arthur S. Link, "Woodrow Wilson and the Life of Faith," *Presbyterian Life*, 16 (March 1, 1963), 11.

30. Wilson to Dodge, July 1, 1907, Dodge MSS.

31. Alexander L. and Juliette L. George, *Woodrow Wilson and Colonel House: A Personality Study* (New York: Day, 1956), 113.

32. Quoted in Arthur S. Link, *Wilson: The New Freedom* (Princeton, N.J.: Princeton University Press, 1956), 93.

33. Quoted in *ibid.*, 68–69.

34. Charles W. Vickrey, "Dodge Would Not Keep 'Blood Money,'" *Outlook*, 143 (May–August 1926), 566–567; also, Dodge to House, October 11, 1915, House MSS.

35. Arthur S. Link, *Wilson the Diplomatist: A Look at His Major Foreign Policies* (Baltimore: Johns Hopkins Press, 1957), 23.

36. Wilson to Dodge, February 6, 1917, Wilson MSS.

37. Barton to Lansing, February 8, 1917, ABC 3.2.

38. Quoted in Evans, *United States Policy and the Partition of Turkey*, 29.

39. Elkus to Lansing, March 2, 1917, *Foreign Relations: Lansing Papers*, I, 787–791; also, Barton to James Bryce, August 7, 1917, ABC 3.2.

40. Howard M. Sachar, "The United States and Turkey, 1914–1927: The Origins of Near Eastern Policy," unpublished Ph.D. thesis, Harvard University (1953), 26.

41. American Board, *Annual Report*, 107 (1917), 72; Robert L. Daniel, "The Armenian Question and American-Turkish Relations: 1914–1927," *Mississippi Valley Historical Review*, 46 (September 1959), 258–259; Barton to Wilson, November 2, 1917, and Barton to Dodge, November 3, 1917, ABC 3.2.

42. Bayard Dodge corroborated these ideas in a letter to me, May 19, 1968.

43. Dodge to Wilson, December 2, 1917, Wilson MSS; also, Dodge to Barton, December 7, 1917, Barton MSS.

44. Evans, *United States Policy and the Partition of Turkey*, 38–39.

45. Wilson to Dodge, December 5, 1917, Dodge MSS.

46. Barton to Dodge, December 8, 1917, ABC 3.2.

47. Dodge to Wilson, December 8, 1917, Wilson MSS.

48. Barton to Senator Lodge, December 10, 1917, ABC 3.2; also, Barton to Lodge, December 14, 1917, and Barton to James Bryce, March 12, 1918, *ibid.*

49. *Missionary Herald*, 114 (January 1918), 3.

50. Albert H. Lybyer to Dodge, September 20, 1917, also, Dodge to Lybyer, September 21, 1917, Albert H. Lybyer MSS, University of Illinois Library.

51. Evans, *United States Policy and the Partition of Turkey*, 37–38.

52. Barton to James Bryce, March 25, 1918, ABC 3.2.

53. Paul von Hindenburg, *Out of My Life* (2 vols.; New York: Harper, 1921), II, 95–96.

54. Lodge to Barton, April 8, 1918, ABC 14.2; also, Lodge to Barton, April 17, 1918, *ibid.*; Barton to Lodge, April 15, 1918, ABC 3.2; Roosevelt speech in Portland, Maine, March 28, 1918, in Morison, ed., *The Letters of Theodore Roosevelt*, VIII, 1294.

55. Peet to Barton, May 3 and May 9, 1918, ABC 16.9.3; Mary Ellen Moore Gates Diary, April 7, 1917, Gates MSS; Levermore, *Samuel Train Dutton*, 171–172, 177–181.

56. Roosevelt to Barton, May 13, 1918, ABC 14.2.

57. Theodore Roosevelt, *Fear God and Take Your Own Part* (New York: Doran, 1916), 21, 383; also, Roosevelt to Carl Schurz, September 8, 1905, and Lodge to Roosevelt, October 2 and November 26, 1918, in Henry Cabot Lodge, ed., *Selections from the Correspondence of Theodore Roosevelt and Henry Cabot Lodge: 1884–1918* (2 vols.; New York: Scribners, 1925), II, 197–199, 538–539, 546–548.

58. Roosevelt to Dodge, May 11, 1918, in Morison, ed., *The Letters of Theodore Roosevelt*, VIII, 1316–1318; also, Roosevelt to his father (mention of seeing Dodge at a football game), April 29, 1877, and Roosevelt to Dodge, June 16, 1902, *ibid.*, I, 27–28, III, 275.

59. Lansing to Wilson, May 8, 1918, *Foreign Relations: Lansing Papers*, II, 124–126; also, House Diary, May 4, 1918, House MSS.

60. Dodge to House, May 10, 1918, House MSS; also, Barton to Roosevelt, May 9, 1918, ABC 3.2.

61. Wilson to Dodge, May 23, 1918, Dodge MSS; also, House Diary, May 19, 1918, House MSS.

62. Dodge to Barton, June 12, 1918, ABC 14.2.

63. House Diary, June 15, 1918, House MSS.

64. H. K. Moderwell, "America's Dilemma on War with Turkey," New York *Tribune*, June 23, 1918.

65. William Yale, "Ambassador Henry Morgenthau's Special Mission of 1917," *World Politics*, 1 (April 1949), 308–320; Morgenthau, *All in a Life Time*, 274; Morgenthau to Wilson, September 15, 1917, Morgenthau MSS.

66. Barton to House, July 18, 1918, House Diary of July 19, 1918, Barton to House, July 20, 1918, and House Diary of August 29 and September 15, 1918, House MSS; Barton to House, July 18, 1918, ABC 3.2; Dodge to Wilson, December 2, 1917, Wilson MSS; Gates, *Not to Me Only*, 180; Edward C. Moore, *Twenty-Five Years with the Board* (Boston: American Board of Commissioners for Foreign Missions, Envelope Series, 1925).

67. Roosevelt to Lodge, October 24, 1918, in Morison, ed., *The Letters of Theodore Roosevelt*, VIII, 1380; also, Barton to Vahan Cardashian, September 11, 1918, and Barton to Dodge, October 1, 1918, ABC 3.2.

68. House Diary, September 24, 1918, House MSS.

69. Wilson to Assistant Secretary of State William Phillips, July 29, 1916, Wilson MSS; also, Morgenthau Diary, February 23, 1916, Morgenthau MSS.

70. Bayard Dodge in letters to me of May 19, 1968, and January 29, 1969.

71. Barton to Bryce, January 25, 1917, ABC 3.2; also, Barton to Bryce, August 23, 1916, March 3, 1917, and June 20, 1917, *ibid.*

72. Decimal File 860J.01, State Department Archives, National Archives; Barton to William Phillips, May 3, 1917, and Barton to Bryce, November 14, 1917, ABC 3.2; document on Armenia by William L. Westermann, December 28, 1918, unpublished records of The Inquiry, National Archives; Ralph E. Cook, "The United States and the Armenian Question: 1894–1924," unpublished Ph.D. thesis, Fletcher School of Diplomacy (1957), 116–149; Charles Trowbridge Riggs Diary, February 18, March 12, May 31, June 20, July 4–5, October 16, and December 6, 1918, private holding.

73. Harry N. Howard, *The Partition of Turkey: A Diplomatic History, 1913–1923* (Norman: University of Oklahoma Press, 1931), 182.

74. Evans, *United States Policy and the Partition of Turkey*, 49–70.

75. *Foreign Relations: Paris Peace Conference*, I, 86; Barton to State Department official Albert H. Putney, November 8, 1917, Barton to William Hall, November 23, 1917, and Barton to Bryce, November 5, 1917, ABC 3.2.

76. Inquiry memorandum of December 22, 1917, *Foreign Relations: Paris Peace Conference*, I, 43; "Report from [Hall] Committee on Turkish Survey," February 20, 1918, Inquiry Papers; Morgenthau Diary, April 27, 1918, Morgenthau MSS; Barton to Bryce, March 22 and May 21, 1918, also, Barton to House, January 8, 1918, ABC 3.2; Peet to Barton, April 13, 1918, ABC 16.9.3; Barton to Peet, May 20, 1918, ABC 3.2.

77. Mezes to Barton, June 3, 1918, Sidney E. Mezes MSS, Columbia University Library. See Ch. 5 for discussion of Barton's federation plan.

78. James L. Barton, "Introduction," in Bertha S. Papazian, *The Tragedy of Armenia: A Brief Study and Interpretation* (Boston: Pilgrim Press, 1918), ix–xii.

79. Peet to Barton, March 30 and April 24, 1918, ABC 16.9.3; Barton to Schmavonian, January 30 and March 8, 1918, Barton to Lansing, April 4, 1918, Barton to Dodge, April 15, 1918, and Barton to Elihu Root, April 15, 1918, ABC 3.2.

80. Lawrence E. Gelfand, *The Inquiry: American Preparations for Peace, 1917–1919* (New Haven, Conn.: Yale University Press, 1963), 28–31, 105–106.

Chapter 5. Transatlantic Visions and Doings

1. Peet to Barton, June 8, 1918, ABC 16.9.3; Barton to Schmavonian, February 14, 1918, ABC 3.2; Pasdermadjian to Lansing, March 4, 1918, Inquiry Papers; Kazemzadeh, *The Struggle for Transcaucasia*, 109–172.

2. Atamian, *The Armenian Community*, 165–172; Vahan Cardashian, "The Armenian Revolutionary Federation," *Armenian Review*, 2 (Winter 1949–1950), 65–69; Gidney, *A Mandate for Armenia*, 75.

3. Quoted in Malcom, *The Armenians in America*, xix.

4. Barton, Dodge, and Peet to Lansing, October 31, 1918, Decimal File 867.48/1075, State Department Archives; Barton to Peet, October 1, 1918, ABC 3.1; Peet to Barton, October 25, 1918, ABC 16.9.3; Barton to Boghos Nubar, October 16, 1918, ABC 3.2.

5. Decimal File 860J.01, State Department Archives; Barton to Cardashian, October 16, October 22, and November 27, 1918, ABC 3.2; James W. Gerard, *My First Eighty-Three Years in America: The Memoirs of James W. Gerard* (Garden City, N.Y.: Doubleday, 1951), 285–286.

6. *Missionary Herald*, 114 (April 1918), 164; Barton to Cardashian, October 22, 1918, ABC 3.2.

7. Barton to Lansing, November 21, 1918, ABC 3.2; also, Howard, *The Partition of Turkey*, 204–205.

8. Barton to Boghos, November 22, 1918, and Barton to Bryce, December 9, 1918, ABC 3.2.

9. See Ch. 2, n. 1 (p. 316). The ACIA published part of Pasdermadjian's booklet under the title *Armenia, a Leading Factor in the Winning of the War*.

10. Avedis Aharonian, "Death Knell," *Armenian Herald*, 1 (June 1918), 389.

11. Bryce to House, January 24, 1917, and Bryce to Lowell, April 8, 1917, in the James Bryce MSS, Bodleian Library, Oxford University; Bryce to Roosevelt, October 30, 1918, quoted in Fisher, *James Bryce*, II, 195–197.

12. James Bryce, *The Future of Armenia* (London: National Press Agency, 1918); Arnold J. Toynbee, *"The Murderous Tyranny of the Turks"* (London: Hodder & Stoughton, 1917).

13. New York *Times*, September 7, 1918; also, Roosevelt to Bryce, August 7, 1918, in Morison, ed., *The Letters of Theodore Roosevelt*, VIII, 1358–1359.

14. *Congressional Record*, 57 (December 10, 1918), 237; Bliss, "Armenia's Struggle for Independence," *Current History*, 11 (October 1919–March 1920), 143; Gidney, *A Mandate for Armenia*, 65–67; Hovannisian, *Armenia on the Road to Independence*, 247–254.

15. Merze Tate, *The United States and the Hawaiian Kingdom: A Political History* (New Haven, Conn.: Yale University Press, 1965), 1–26.

16. Edward McNall Burns, *The American Idea of Mission: Concepts of National Purpose and Destiny* (New Brunswick, N.J.: Rutgers University Press, 1957).

17. Clifton E. Olmstead, *History of Religion in the United States* (Englewood Cliffs, N.J.: Prentice-Hall, 1960), 495–506; William Archibald Karraker, "The American Churches and the Spanish American War," unpublished Ph.D. thesis, University of Chicago Divinity School (1940); Kenneth Scott Latourette, *Missions and the American Mind* (Indianapolis: National Foundation Press, 1949), 33; Charles Howard Hopkins, *The Rise of the Social Gospel in American Protestantism: 1865–1915* (New Haven, Conn.: Yale University Press, 1940), 318, 322.

18. Cornelius H. Patton, *World Facts and America's Responsibility* (New York: Association Press, 1919).

19. Phillips, *Protestant America and the Pagan World*, 261–262; John Edwin Smylie, "Protestant Clergymen and America's World Role: 1865–1900, A Study of Christianity, Nationality, and International Relations," unpublished Th.D. thesis, Princeton Theological Seminary (1959), 118–119.

20. Reprint of James L. Barton, "The War and the Mohammedan World," *Biblical Review* (January 1919), 28–46, Missionary Research Library; also, James L. Barton, *The Christian Approach to Islam* (Boston: Pilgrim Press, 1918), 97–312.

21. Quoted in Barton, "Survey of the Fields: 1917–1918," *Missionary Herald*, 114 (1918), 513–524.

22. Smylie, "Protestant Clergymen and America's World Role," 97–128, 154–159, 163–227; also, Valentin H. Rabe, "The American Protestant Mission Movement, 1880–1920," unpublished Ph.D. thesis, Harvard University (1965), to be published in revised form.

23. William E. Leuchtenberg, *The Perils of Prosperity: 1914–32* (Chicago: University of Chicago Press, 1958), 34; also, Albert K. Weinberg, *Manifest Destiny: A Study of Nationalist Expansionism in American History* (Baltimore: Johns Hopkins Press, 1935); Frederick Merk, *Manifest Destiny and Mission in American History: A Reinterpretation* (New York: Knopf, 1963), 261 266; Carl N. Degler, *Out of Our Past: The Forces That Shaped Modern America* (New York: Harper, 1959), 338–378.

24. *Cosmopolitan*, 65 (June 1918), 17, reprinted in Perry E. Gianakos and Albert Karson, eds., *American Diplomacy and the Sense of Destiny* (4 vols.; Belmont, Calif.: Wadsworth Publishing Company, 1966), II, 76. For Wilson's war message and "Over There" see *ibid.*, 60–66, 75.

25. Ray H. Abrams, *Preachers Present Arms* (New York: Round Table Press, 1933), iii, 79, 99, 246; Olmstead, *History of Religion in the United States*, 509–512; also, John F. Piper, Jr., "Robert E. Speer: Christian Statesman in War and Peace," *Journal of Presbyterian History*, 47 (September 1969), 201–225.

26. Jerome D. Frank, "The Face of the Enemy," *Psychology Today*, 2 (November 1968), 24–29; Harold D. Lasswell, *Propaganda Technique in the World War* (New York: Peter Smith, 1927), 211–222.

27. Warren F. Kuehl, *Hamilton Holt: Journalist, Internationalist, Educator* (Gainesville: University of Florida Press, 1960), 65–133; Selig Adler, *The Isolationist Impulse: Its Twentieth Century Reaction* (New York: Abelard-Schuman, 1957), 9–40; Edward H. Buehrig, *Woodrow Wilson and the Balance of Power* (Bloomington: Indiana University Press, 1955); John Morton Blum, *Woodrow Wilson and the Politics of Morality* (Boston: Little, Brown, 1956), 110–156; Robert H. Wiebe, *The Search for Order: 1877–1920* (New York: Hill & Wang, 1967), 262–274.

28. James L. Lancaster, "The Protestant Churches and the Fight for Ratification of the Versailles Treaty," *Public Opinion Quarterly*, 31 (Winter 1967–1968), 597–607; also, Ruhl J. Bartlett, *The League to Enforce Peace* (Chapel Hill, N.C.: University of North Carolina Press, 1944), 97; Warren F. Kuehl, *Seeking World Order: The United States and International Organization to 1920* (Nashville, Tenn.: Vanderbilt University Press, 1969), 245–246.

29. Walter Lippmann to Sidney Mezes, September 5, 1918, Mezes MSS; also, Arno J. Mayer, *Political Origins of the New Diplomacy: 1917–1918* (New Haven, Conn.: Yale University Press, 1959).

30. Dodge to Wilson, September 28, 1918, Wilson MSS.

31. Barton to Dodge, October 1, 1918, ABC 3.2.

32. House Diary, October 13, 1918, House MSS; Dodge to Wilson, November 19, 1918, Wilson MSS.

33. Barton to Dodge, October 15, 1918, ABC 3.2.

34. Wilson to Morgenthau, November 9, 1918, Wilson MSS; also, see Ch. 3, n. 9 (p. 318).

35. Quoted in Gelfand, *The Inquiry*, 173.

36. Link, *Wilson the Diplomatist*, 17; Robert E. Osgood, *Ideals and Self-Interest*

in America's Foreign Relations: The Great Transformation of the Twentieth Century (Chicago: University of Chicago Press, 1953), 17–20, 111–113.

37. *Foreign Relations: 1918, Supplement 1*, I, 405–413; also, Evans, *United States Policy and the Partition of Turkey*, 71–77.

38. Gelfand, *The Inquiry*, 145–146, 227–257.

39. William Yale, "An Analysis of the Syrian-Palestine Situation in 1919: The American Point of View," unpublished M.A. thesis, University of New Hampshire (1928); William Yale, "The Syrian Question," February 11, 1918, and Franklin Hoskins et al., "Syria: The Situation in Lebanon," n.d., Inquiry Papers.

40. Mezes to Lippmann, November 16, 1918, Mezes MSS; also, Bryce to Barton, July 10, 1918, ABC 14.2.

41. See the last section of Chapter 4 for the origins of the Hall Committee. The ACASR published the Hall report in a long 243-page and a short 7-page form; William H. Hall edited the former with the title, *Reconstruction in Turkey: A Series of Reports Compiled for the American Committee of Armenian and Syrian Relief* (1918); Hall and Harold A. Hatch edited the latter, *Recommendations for Political Reconstruction in the Turkish Empire* (November 1918).

42. James L. Barton, "Suggested Possible Form of Government for the Area Covered by the Ottoman Empire at the Outbreak of the War, Exclusive of Arabia but Inclusive of the Trans-Caucasus," May 21, 1918, Barton, "The Turkish Government: Analysis of Its Inherent Evils," n.d., Hall Committee, "Report from Committee on Turkish Survey," February 20, 1918, and Hall Committee, "Turkish Survey: Recommendations for Political Reconstruction," June 18, 1918, Inquiry Papers; Mezes to Barton, June 4, 1918, Mezes MSS; Barton to The Inquiry member and Princeton professor, Dana C. Munro, April 12 and June 5, 1918, ABC 3.2; Barton, *Story of Near East Relief*, 108.

43. Selig Adler, "The Palestine Question in the Wilson Era," *Jewish Social Studies*, 10 (October 1948), 303–334; Richard Ned Lebow, "Woodrow Wilson and the Balfour Declaration," *Journal of Modern History*, 40 (December 1968), 501–523.

44. Dodge to Wilson, November 19, 1918, Wilson MSS; Albert H. Lybyer, "Turkey under the Armistice," *Journal of International Relations*, 12 (1922), 456.

45. Barton to Bryce, December 9, 1918, ABC 3.2; also, Gates to Barton, November 3, 1918, and Bryce to Barton, November 6, 1918, ABC 14.2.

46. Gates, *Not to Me Only*, 252–253.

47. H. K. Moderwell in the New York *Tribune*, June 23, 1918, wrote that the "office in the Congregational Building in Boston is a sort of state department, . . . it has taken on an almost diplomatic character."

48. Barton to Peet, September 27, 1918, Barton to Dodge, October 1, 1918, and Barton to Bryce, October 22, 1918, ABC 3.2; Peet to Barton, October 4, 1918, ABC 16.9.3; Padwick, *Call to Istanbul*, 3, 27; Goodsell, *They Lived Their Faith*, 96–97.

49. Materials on relief, Barton MSS; Daniel, "From Relief to Technical Assistance in the Near East," 47ff.; *Missionary Herald*, 114 (March–October 1918), 110, 482; Barton memorandum, "Work of the American Committee for Armenian and Syrian Relief," enclosed in a letter to D. L. Pierson, April 15, 1918, ABC 3.2; relief organization handbook, November 1917, news release, November 12, 1917, auditing report, June 4, 1918, and Sunday School War Council news releases, November 1 and December 12, 1918, Missionary Research Library; Bertha Spafford Vester, *Our Jerusalem: An American Family in the Holy City, 1881–1949* (Garden City, N.Y.: Doubleday, 1950), 230–283; Fisher Diary, March 5, 1919.

50. Riggs Diary, January 22, January 29–30, February 23 and 27, March 7 and 19, April 8 and 27, June 14, August 25, September 13 and 27, October 15, December 7, 14, and 19, 1918, and January 12, 26, and 28, 1919.

51. Barton, *Story of Near East Relief*, 58–97; MacLachlan, "A Potpourri of Sidelights and Shadows from Turkey," 87–137.

52. Barton to Boghos, May 21, 1918, ABC 3.2; also, Sachar, *The Emergence of the Middle East,* 115.

53. Henry Morgenthau, "The Greatest Horror in History," *Red Cross Magazine,* 13 (March 1918), 7–15.

54. Morgenthau, *Ambassador Morgenthau's Story,* 321–322.

55. Barton to Bryce, March 12, 1918, ABC 3.2.

56. *Foreign Relations: 1919,* II, 817; also, Peet to Barton, November 2, 4, 14, and 16, 1918, ABC 3.2; Herbert Hoover, *The Memoirs of Herbert Hoover* (3 vols.; New York: Macmillan, 1951), I, 385–389; ACRNE, *News Bulletin* (March 1919), Barton MSS; unsigned letter probably written by Morgenthau to Hoover, November 15, 1918, Morgenthau MSS; Hoover cable to ACRNE, January 7, 1919, in ACRNE, *News Bulletin* (January 1919), Missionary Research Library.

57. Dodge to Wilson, November 19, 1918, also, the President's proclamation, November 29, 1918, Wilson MSS.

58. Barton to Bryce, December 9, 1918, ABC 3.2; also General Letter (Stanley White) to the Syria Mission, May 26, 1919, Box 101, Presbyterian Board Archives.

59. ACRNE booklet, *Practicing Bible Precepts in Bible Lands: Handbook for Busy Pastors, Campaign for $30,000,000, January 12th to 19th, 1919,* Missionary Research Library.

60. Dodge to Wilson and Wilson to Dodge, undated cables in the period from January 5 to 12, 1919, Wilson MSS; *Foreign Relations: 1919,* II, 819; Barton, *Story of Near East Relief,* 109–111; New York *Times,* January 29, 1919; ACRNE, *News Bulletin* (January 1919).

61. The relief mission to Turkey had no regularly used name. People generally called it a committee or commission of the ACRNE. I have named it for the leader.

62. Barton to his wife Flora, January 12 and 24, 1919, and Bryce to Barton, January 7, 1919, Barton MSS; Barton to House, January 21, 1919, House MSS; Department of State to ambassadors at London, Paris, and Rome, December 21, 1918, ABC 16.5; Peet to Barton, December 24, 1918, ABC 16.9.3.

63. Quoted in Mary Ellen Moore Gates Diary, March 6, 1918, Gates MSS; also, Lynn A. Scipio, *My Thirty Years in Turkey* (Rindge, N.H.: Richard R. Smith, 1955), 97–158; Hoover, *An American Epic,* II, 213.

64. DeNovo, *American Interests and Policies in the Middle East,* 97; James L. Barton, "Memorandum: Requesting the Safeguarding of the Rights, Privileges, and Properties of American Missions and American Institutions in the Capitulation Areas of the Near East," January 28, 1919, and Howard Bliss and Arthur Curtiss James to Westermann, February 10, 1919, Inquiry Papers.

65. *Missionary Herald,* 115 (February 1919), 58; also, Barton to his wife, January 12, 1919, Barton MSS.

66. Barton, "Survey of the Fields: 1917–1918," *Missionary Herald,* 114 (November 1918), 522.

67. I Corinthians 9:22.

Chapter 6. The Nestorian Kettle

1. Robert E. Speer and Russell Carter, *Report on India and Persia of the Deputation Sent by the Board of Foreign Missions of the Presbyterian Church in the U.S.A. to Visit These Fields in 1921–22* (New York: Presbyterian Board of Foreign Missions, 1922), 315–326; John Joseph (himself of Nestorian background), *The Nestorians and Their Muslim Neighbors: A Study of Western Influence on Their Relations* (Princeton, N.J.: Princeton University Press, 1961), 43–44.

2. The names *Chaldean* and *Assyrian* in recent years have been out of favor because research has shown Nestorians racially are a mixed people. They are often

known in the West as Nestorians to distinguish them more clearly from Arabic-speaking Syrians, even though they call themselves Syrians.

3. Princeton Professor David Magie, "Report on the Assyrian Christians," August 24, 1918, Inquiry Papers; Finnie, *Pioneers East*, 232–241; Mary Alice Shepard, *Doctor's Care: Medical Mission in Turkey* (Istanbul: Redhouse Press, 1970), 1–2.

4. Abraham Yeselson, *United States–Persian Diplomatic Relations: 1883–1921* (New Brunswick, N.J.: Rutgers University Press, 1956), 25–64.

5. DeNovo, *American Interests and Policies in the Middle East*, 34–35; Joseph, *The Nestorians and Their Muslim Neighbors*, Ch. 6; Yeselson, *United States–Persian Diplomatic Relations*, 68–104.

6. Yeselson, *United States–Persian Diplomatic Relations*, 133; Speer and Carter, *Report on India and Persia*, 461ff.

7. Mary Lewis Shedd, *The Measure of a Man: The Life of William Ambrose Shedd, Missionary to Persia* (New York: Doran, 1922), 144–145.

8. William Reginald Wheeler, *A Man Sent from God: A Biography of Robert E. Speer* (New York: Revell, 1956).

9. Quoted in Shedd, *The Measure of a Man*, xii.

10. Barton to the secretary of the ACASR, Samuel T. Dutton, April 5, 1916, ABC 3.2; Morgenthau Diary, April 22, 1915, and Lansing to Morgenthau, October 19, 1915, Morgenthau MSS; Shedd, *The Measure of a Man*, Chs. 8–11; Rockwell, *The Pitiful Plight of the Assyrian [Nestorian] Christians in Persia and Kurdistan*, 7–24, and Mary Schauffler Platt, *The War Journal of a Missionary in Persia* (New York: Presbyterian Board of Foreign Missions, c. 1916), Missionary Research Library.

11. Harry Pratt Judson to John Timothy Stone, March 4, 1919, Harry Pratt Judson MSS in the Presidents' Papers, University of Chicago Library; Shedd, *The Measure of a Man*, Chs. 13–14; Speer and Carter, *Report on India and Persia*, 464.

12. Shedd, *The Measure of a Man*, 271; also, Harry Pratt Judson, "Report of the Director of the American-Persian Relief Commission," January 19, 1919, Judson MSS; Joseph, *The Nestorians and Their Muslim Neighbors*, 144; Presbyterian Board, *Annual Report*, 83 (1920), 47.

13. Edward M. Dodd, "Near East Vortex," unpublished MS of 107 pages, Presbyterian Historical Society.

14. Shedd, *The Measure of a Man*, 249–251; Judson to John Timothy Stone, March 4, 1919, Judson MSS; Robert E. Speer, *"The Hakim Sahib": The Foreign Doctor, A Biography of Joseph Plumb Cochran, M.D., of Persia* (New York: Revell, 1911), 295–317.

15. *A Century of Mission Work in Iran (Persia): 1834–1934* (Beirut: American Press, 1936), 4; also, Yeselson, *United States–Persian Diplomatic Relations*, 133.

16. See in the Barton MSS a typewritten, three-page, undated statement: "Commission to Persia."

17. Mezes to Judson, May 7, 1918, Judson MSS; Peet to Barton, May 9, 1918, ABC 16.9.3; Dodge to House, May 10, 1918, House MSS.

18. Mezes to House, June 7, 1918, Mezes MSS; also, Judson to Mezes, May 10, 1918, Judson MSS; Peet to Barton, May 25, 1918, ABC 16.9.3.

19. Judson to Charles Vickrey, June 13, 1918, Vickrey to Judson, June 13, 1918, and State Department official William Phillips to Judson, June 19, 1918, Judson MSS; Barton to Bryce, June 10, 1918, ABC 3.2.

20. Judson to Vickrey, June 8, 1918, and an exchange of letters between relief leader Frederick W. MacCallum and Judson, June 24–26, 1918, Judson MSS.

21. Vickrey to Judson, June 13 and 14, 1918, Vickrey to Mrs. Judson, September 30, 1918, Judson to a member of the expedition, Joseph W. Cook, February 19, 1919, and Judson, "Report," January 19, 1919, *ibid.*; Crane to J.C.B., July 14, 1918, Crane MSS.

22. ACRNE, *News Bulletin* (June 1918), Barton MSS.

23. Persian official quoted in ACRNE, *News Bulletin* (August 1918), *ibid.*; also, Barton to Bryce, August 24, 1918, ABC 3.2; Jackson party to Vickrey, July 10, 1918, and Jackson to Judson, August 27, 1918, Judson MSS.

24. DeNovo, *American Interests and Policies in the Middle East*, 53–55, 278; Yeselson, *United States–Persian Diplomatic Relations*, 105–129; William Morgan Shuster, *The Strangling of Persia* (New York: Century, 1912).

25. Presbyterian Board, *Annual Report*, 83 (1920), 55; Speer and Carter, *Report on India and Persia*, 465; Judson, "Report," January 19, 1919, Judson MSS.

26. Judson to Gordon Paddock, November 26, 1918, Judson MSS.

27. Quoted in Yeselson, *United States–Persian Diplomatic Relations*, 138; also, Judson speech in Tehran, November 14, 1918, Judson MSS; Barton, *Story of Near East Relief*, 99.

28. Three Judson letters to Mezes, January 2, 4, and 21, 1919, and a diary reference to Judson, January 8, 1919, House MSS; Judson, "Report on Mesopotamia," n.d., Inquiry Papers; McDowell to Judson, December 19, 1918, Judson MSS. "Long talk with President Judson and the American Commission which had just returned from India, Persia and Mesopotamia. A very able, clear-sighted man. . . . I have accounts of Judson's remarks by . . . Westermann." George L. Beer Diary, December 30, 1918, George L. Beer MSS, Library of Congress; Gates, *Not to Me Only*, 252; Yeselson, *United States–Persian Diplomatic Relations*, 144–151.

29. Wertheim discussed his published interview with the New York *Evening Post*, February 13, 1919, in a letter to Judson, February 20, 1919, Judson MSS.

30. Speer to Judson, March 4, 1919, File 1761, Box 520, Presbyterian Board Archives; Judson to Speer, March 6, 1919, Judson to a Nestorian working with the ACRNE, Paul Shimmon, February 24, 1919, and Judson to Stone, March 4, 1919, Judson MSS.

31. Mezes to Speer, April 9, 1919, File 1761, Box 520, Presbyterian Board Archives; also, Speer's letters in February 1919 to Mezes, Speer to Wilson, March 3, 1919, secretary of the Peace Commission Joseph Grew to Speer, March 19, 1919, Mezes to Speer, March 5, 1919, and memorandum of May 3, 1919, Judson MSS; File 867S.01/3, records of the American Commission to Negotiate Peace, National Archives; Speer to Mezes, February 8 and 24, 1919, House MSS; Presbyterian Board, *Annual Report*, 82 (1919), viii, 48.

32. David Magie, "Report on the Assyrian Christians," Inquiry Papers and File 1761, Box 520, Presbyterian Board Archives; Theodore Roosevelt to Paul Shimmon, July 10, 1918, in Morison, ed., *The Letters of Theodore Roosevelt*, VIII, 1348.

33. For Yohannan's relation to The Inquiry see *Foreign Relations: Paris Peace Conference*, I, 87; also, see Abraham Yohannan, *The Death of a Nation or the Ever Persecuted Nestorians or Assyrian Christians* (New York: Putnam, 1916); Yohannan, "The Assyrians," n.d., Inquiry Papers; Speer to Mezes (introduction of Yohannan), May 8, 1919, File 1761, Box 520, Presbyterian Board Archives.

34. Yohannan and Jesse M. Yonan, "Petition of the Persian Assyrians to the Peace Conference," June 1919, and Yohannan to Speer (mention of help from Westermann), June 12, 1919, Presbyterian Board Archives.

35. Mimeographed press release of American Peace Commission, March 6, 1919, Ray Stannard Baker MSS, Princeton University Library.

36. Yohannan to Speer, June 12, 1919, File 1761, Box 520, Presbyterian Board Archives.

Chapter 7. Missionary Internationalism

1. "Howard Bliss, Pres. of the Syrian Prot. College Beyrut is here. Mr. Dodge cabled him to meet me here. We are getting on well." Barton to his wife, January 24, 1919, Barton MSS; also, Penrose, *That They May Have Life*, 166.

2. House Diary, February 4, 1919, House MSS.

3. "Howard Sweetser Bliss," *News Letter of Robert College and the Syrian Protestant College* (June 1920), American University of Beirut Library, Beirut, Lebanon.

4. Quoted in Evans, *The United States and the Partition of Turkey*, 112; also, Henry H. Cumming, *Franco-British Rivalry in the Post-War Near East: The Decline of French Influence* (New York: Oxford University Press, 1938), 75. For a general treatment, see Sydney Nettleton Fisher, *The Middle East: A History* (New York: Knopf, 1959), Ch. 29.

5. William Yale, "The Syrian Question," February 11, 1918, Inquiry Papers.

6. Bliss to D. Stuart Dodge, December 4, 1918, American University of Beirut Library.

7. George A. Ford to Stanley White, March 15, 1915, Franklin E. Hoskins to White, April 17, 1919, White to William S. Nelson, December 13, 1915, Hoskins to Dear Friends, December 31, 1918, White to James H. Nicol, January 29, 1918, Ford to White, May 31, 1919, Arthur B. Fowler to White, June 9, 1919, and Nelson to White, June 2, 1919, Box 101, Presbyterian Board Archives.

8. William S. Nelson, *Habeeb the Beloved: A Tale of Life in Modern Syria* (Philadelphia: Westminster Press, 1913), xi; William S. Nelson, *Silver Chimes in Syria: Glimpses of a Missionary's Experiences* (Philadelphia: Westminster Press, 1914), 173–174; also, Robert E. Speer, *Missions and Politics in Asia* (New York: Revell, 1898), 13–66.

9. George A. Ford to White, October 24, 1918, and White to Hoskins, November 23, 1914, Box 101, Presbyterian Board Archives.

10. White to Friends of the Syria Missionaries, June 22, 1917, William Jessup to White, October 21, 1918, Nelson to White, June 2, 1919, and White to C. A. Dana, November 4, 1919, *ibid.*

11. H. I. Katibah, "Syria for the Syrians under the Guardianship of the United States," *Syrian National Bulletin*, 1 (February 28, 1919); A. H. Rihbany, *America, Save the Near East* (Boston: Beacon Press, 1918), ix–x, 95; also, Lybyer Diary, April 3, 1919, Lybyer MSS.

12. Bliss to Lansing, January 28, 1919, 185.5137/54, American Peace Commission Papers.

13. Evans, *The United States and the Partition of Turkey*, 89–104; Barton to his wife, February 1, 1919, Barton MSS.

14. Lansing to Wilson, January 31, 1919, 184.017/2, Peace Commission Papers.

15. Quoted in Barton to his wife, February 1, 1919, Barton MSS.

16. Barton to Boston, February 3, 1919, *ibid.*; Wilson to Barton, February 1, 1919, Wilson MSS; also, typewritten, five-page, undated statement, "The Syrian Commission," and Peace Commission to Barton, February 7, 1919, Barton MSS; Barton to Lansing, February 3, 1919, House MSS.

17. There was no official name for the investigation to be led by Barton, so this appellation is as appropriate as any.

18. Frederic C. Howe, *The Confessions of a Reformer* (New York: Scribners, 1925), 300–306.

19. William L. Westermann to Howe, February 8, 1919, Barton MSS; House Diary, February 6, 1919, House MSS; Barton to Peace Commission, February 18, 1919, 184.017/15, and Minutes of the Peace Commission, February 21, 1919, 184.00101/18, Peace Commission Papers.

20. Bliss to Barton, February 8, 1919, Barton MSS.

21. Bliss to Wilson, February 7, 1919, quoted in Harry N. Howard, "An American Experiment in Peacemaking: The King-Crane Commission," *Moslem World*, 32 (1942), 124–125.

22. *Foreign Relations: Paris Peace Conference*, III, 1016–1018; also, Wilson to Bliss, February 11, 1919, and Bliss to Wilson, February 11, 1919, Wilson MSS.

23. *Foreign Relations: Paris Peace Conference*, XI, 76–77; also, Zeine N. Zeine, *The Struggle for Arab Independence: Western Diplomacy and the Rise and Fall of Faisal's Kingdom in Syria* (Beirut: Khayats, 1960), 189–208.

24. "Department interested to know if American officer [Hoskins?] was appointed on Commission as suggested by Dodge." Frank L. Polk to Peace Commission, March 18, 1919, Decimal File 763.72119/4179, State Department Archives; also, Harold Hoskins to me in a letter of November 30, 1961.

25. C. A. Dana and Franklin Hoskins to State Department, March 17, 1919, 883.00/87, Peace Commission Papers.

26. Crane to Dodge, February 26, 1919, Decimal File 763.72119/3881, State Department Archives; also, Dodge to Mrs. Albert Lybyer, March 31, 1919, Lybyer MSS.

27. Ray Stannard Baker, *Woodrow Wilson and World Settlement* (3 vols.; New York: Doubleday, 1922), I, 72–77; *Foreign Relations: Paris Peace Conference*, V, 1–14.

28. House Diary, March 26, 1919, House MSS; Harry N. Howard, *The King-Crane Commission: An American Inquiry in the Middle East* (Beirut: Khayats, 1963), 31–38; Donald M. Love, *Henry Churchill King of Oberlin* (New Haven, Conn.: Yale University Press, 1956), 282; also, Henry Churchill King, *For a New America in a New World* (Paris: Young Men's Christian Association, 1919).

29. Unsigned letter to King and Crane, April 1, 1919, 181.91/69–70, and memorandum of Christian Herter, April 3, 1919, 181.91/76, Peace Commission Papers; Gidney, *A Mandate for Armenia*, 144.

30. David Lloyd George, *Memoirs of the Peace Conference* (2 vols.; New Haven, Conn.: Yale University Press, 1939), II, 691.

31. New York *Times*, January 9 and 29, February 15 and 17, March 30, and May 12, 1919; ACRNE, *News Bulletin* (November 1918, January 1919), Missionary Research Library.

32. Barton to House, January 21, 1919, House MSS.

33. Barton to his wife, February 1, 1919, Barton MSS.

34. *Foreign Relations: 1919*, II, 819–820; document on the American Relief Administration, April 16, 1919, 180.05501/17, Peace Commission Papers; Barton, *Story of Near East Relief*, 108–111; New York *Times*, January 12, 17, and 26, 1919; ACRNE, *News Bulletin* (February 1919); Fisher Diary, February 12–13 and April 21, 1919; Riggs Diary, February 17, 1919.

35. Riggs Diary, February 23–March 9, 1919.

36. Barton, "Data on the Work of the American Commission for Relief to the Near East, 1919," Barton MSS; also, Mark L. Bristol Diary, February 7, 12, 14, and 25, 1919, Mark L. Bristol MSS, Library of Congress.

37. Joseph C. Grew, *Turbulent Era: A Diplomatic Record of Forty Years, 1904–1945*, ed. by Walter Johnson (2 vols.; Boston: Houghton Mifflin, 1952), I, 503–504, 539; also, *Foreign Relations: 1919*, II, 810–813; Thomas A. Bryson, "Mark Lambert Bristol, U.S. Navy, Admiral-Diplomat: His Influence on the Armenian Mandate Question, 1919–1920," *Armenian Review*, 21 (Winter 1968), 3–22; Fisher Diary, January 30, February 22 and 26, March 20 and 22, May 23, June 4, and July 15, 1919; Peter M. Buzanski, "Admiral Mark L. Bristol and Turkish-American Relations: 1919–1922," unpublished Ph.D. thesis, University of California (1960).

38. Barton to his wife, February 26–March 5, 1919, Barton MSS; Walter George Smith, "Journal of a Journey to the Near East," February 18–May 31, 1919, unpublished diary of 1919, private holding (hereafter cited "Journal").

39. Main's letter of April 14, 1919, reprinted in ACRNE, *News Bulletin* (May 1919), Barton MSS.

40. Tiflis to Charles Vickrey and relayed by Barton, March 14, 1919, ABC 16.5 also, New York *Times*, April 23, 1919.

41. Riggs Diary, March 10–25, 1919.

42. Moore Gates Diary, March 29, 1919, and Caleb Gates to his wife, March 23, 1919, Gates MSS.

43. Gates' address in Bristol Diary, April 29, 1919, Bristol MSS; also, Lewis Heck (State Department Commissioner in Constantinople) to Washington, April 11, 1919, Decimal File 860J.01/5, State Department Archives; Gates, *Not to Me Only*, 260; Fisher Diary, April 13 and 23, and July 15, 1919; Riggs Diary, April 13, 1919.

44. Barton to the editor of *Missionary Herald*, W. E. Strong, May 27, 1919, ABC 16.5; also, Riggs Diary, May 5, 1919.

45. Strong to Barton, January 20, February 26, and March 14, 1919, ABC 3.2.

46. Albert Lybyer to his wife, January 22, 1919, Lybyer MSS.

47. Barton to his wife, January 24, 1919, Barton MSS.

48. James L. Barton, "Today in Turkey," *Missionary Herald*, 115 (June 1919), 231–235; also, Barton's nine-point plan, January 28, 1919, 867B.00/29, and Barton et al. to Peace Commission, March 1, 1919, 181.91/42, Peace Commission Papers; Barton to House, February 26, March 27, and April 9, 1919, House MSS.

49. Barton to House, June 21, 1919, F.W. 767.68/17, also, State Department Commissioner in Constantinople (including Barton's ideas) to Peace Commission, June 13, 1919, 867B.00/134, Peace Commission Papers; message about Barton to State Department, June 13, 1919, Decimal File 860J.01/9, State Department Archives.

50. *Missionary Herald*, 115 (March 1919), 91–96, 117; Luther Fowle's interview mentioned in Board Secretary H. E. B. Case to Barton, June 12, 1919, and Armenian Evangelical Alliance resolution mentioned in Board Secretary Enoch F. Bell to Barton, June 12, 1919, ABC 3.2.

51. Henry W. Jessup, "The Future of the Ottoman Empire," and Talcott Williams, "The Disposition of the Turkish Empire," *Annals of the American Academy of Political and Social Science*, 84 (July 1919), 6–29, 41–50; Talcott Williams, "America's Duty in Turkey," *Independent*, 99 (1919), 215–216; New York *Times*, March 30, 1919; Henry W. Jessup to the Secretary of State, Decimal File 860J.01/404, State Department Archives.

52. MacLachlan, "A Potpourri of Sidelights and Shadows from Turkey," 45; MacLachlan before the Peace Commission, June 6, 1919, 767.68/17, Peace Commission Papers.

53. Mary Mills Patrick, "Fourteen Reasons for an American Mandatory over Turkey," *Outlook*, 123 (September 1919), 32–33; also, Patrick, *A Bosporus Adventure*, 208; John E. Merrill quoted in *Missionary Herald*, 115 (April 1919), 159.

54. Vahan Cardashian, ed., *Should America Accept Mandate for Armenia?* (New York: American Committee for the Independence of Armenia and Armenian National Union, 1919), 13; also, Gerard, Lodge, and Senator John Sharp Williams to Wilson, February 18, 1919, and ACIA to Wilson, March 19, 1919, Decimal File 860J.01/2,8, State Department Archives.

55. Gates to Albert Lybyer, March 2, 1919, House MSS; also, copy of Wilson to Lybyer, April 23, 1919, enclosed in Lybyer to his wife, April 26, 1919, Lybyer MSS; Leon Dominian to Joseph Grew, April 26, 1919, 867B.00/104, Peace Commission Papers.

56. Fisher Diary, January 28, March 1, June 14 and 17, and December 12, 1919.

57. Bristol Diary, June 22, 1919, Bristol MSS.

58. Memorandum was prepared officially by three men: Morgenthau, William H. Buckler (a career diplomat, archaeologist to the Near East, half-brother to American Commissioner Henry White), and Philip M. Brown. Morgenthau to Wilson, May 21, 1919, Wilson MSS; also Morgenthau, *All in a Life Time*, 323, 336–337; Ly-

byer Diary, April 29, 1919, Lybyer MSS; Philip M. Brown, *Foreigners in Turkey: Their Juridical Status* (Princeton, N.J.: Princeton University Press, 1914).

59. Notes on a conversation between House and Feisal, March 29, 1919, House MSS; also, Howard, *The King-Crane Commission*, 35; Lybyer Diary, April 1, 1919, Lybyer MSS.

60. Lybyer to his wife, April 12, 1919, Lybyer MSS; also, Scipio, *My Thirty Years in Turkey*, 162–168; Albert H. Lybyer, *The Government of the Ottoman Empire in the Time of Suleiman the Magnificent* (Cambridge, Mass.: Harvard University Press, 1913).

61. Westermann to a leading fellow expert, Isaiah Bowman, April 29, 1919, 181.91/96, Peace Commission Papers.

62. House Diary, April 14, 1919, House MSS; Lybyer to his wife, April 16, 1919, and Lybyer Diary, April 17 and 18, 1919, Lybyer MSS; Howard, *The King-Crane Commission*, 47–50; Evans, *United States Policy and the Partition of Turkey*, 143–146.

63. Frank E. Manuel, *The Realities of American-Palestine Relations* (Washington, D.C.: Public Affairs Press, 1949), 70–71, 85, 115–116, 120, 215.

64. Felix Frankfurter to Wilson, May 8, 1919, and Wilson to Frankfurter, May 16, 1919, in E. L. Woodward, Rohan Butler, and J. P. T. Bury, eds., *Documents on British Foreign Policy: 1919–1939* (30 vols.; London: H.M.S.O., 1946–1963), 1st series, IV, 260–262 (general work hereafter cited *British Documents*).

65. House Diary, April 21, 1919, House MSS.

66. Lybyer to his wife, April 23, 1919, Lybyer MSS; Lybyer to Joseph Grew, April 23, 1919, 181.91/84, Peace Commission Papers.

67. Wilson to Dodge, January 25, 1919, Wilson MSS; also, Gidney, *A Mandate for Armenia*, 78–87.

68. Fisher, *James Bryce*, II, 206–212; Evans, *United States Policy and the Partition of Turkey*, 105.

69. Quoted in New York *Times*, February 24, 1919; also, Wilson to Frank Polk, March 12, 1919, Decimal File 763.72119/4433, State Department Archives.

70. New York *Times*, February 27, 1919.

71. Herbert Hoover, *The Ordeal of Woodrow Wilson* (New York: McGraw-Hill, 1958), 225–226; Lodge to White, December 2, 1918, and White to Lodge, February 10, 1919, quoted in Allan Nevins, *Henry White: Thirty Years of American Diplomacy* (New York: Harper, 1930), 355, 376.

72. Morgenthau Diary, March 25, 1919, Morgenthau MSS; *Foreign Relations: Paris Peace Conference*, II, 147–157; House to Wilson, March 7, 1919, in Charles Seymour, ed., *The Intimate Papers of Colonel House* (4 vols.; Boston: Houghton Mifflin, 1928), IV, 358–359; British Armenia Committee resolution in New York *Times*, March 1, 1919. Leon Dominian reported to Joseph Grew that Wilson had told Clemenceau that America desired a mandate over Armenia, April 28, 1919, 867B.00/105, Peace Commission Papers.

73. Baker, *Woodrow Wilson and World Settlement*, II, 187–203.

74. Lybyer to his wife, May 6, 1919, Lybyer Diary, May 8, 1919, Lybyer MSS.

75. *Foreign Relations: Paris Peace Conference*, V, 465–468, 482–485; MacLachlan, "A Potpourri of Sidelights and Shadows from Turkey," 45–49.

76. Gates' visit to House in the latter's Diary, May 13, 1919, House MSS; Lybyer Diary and letter to his wife, both May 11, 1919, Lybyer MSS; Gates, *Not to Me Only*, 261–262; Gidney, *A Mandate for Armenia*, 93–95; Fisher Diary, May 17, 1919.

77. *Foreign Relations: Paris Peace Conference*, V, 582–584, 614–616.

78. MacLachlan before the Peace Commission, June 6, 1919, 767.68/17, Peace Commission Papers; also, MacLachlan, "A Potpourri of Sidelights and Shadows from Turkey," 76–78; Halidé Edib, *The Turkish Ordeal* (New York: Century, 1928), 22–23.

79. Fisher Diary, May 17–24, and August 7, 1919.

80. Washburn to Lybyer, n.d., also, Lybyer Diary and letter to his wife, both May 20, 1919, Lybyer MSS; New York *Times*, June 4, 1919.

81. Morgenthau to Wilson, May 21, 1919, also Wilson to Morgenthau, May 22, 1919, Wilson MSS; Gidney, *A Mandate for Armenia*, 95–96; Riggs Diary, May 13, 1919.

82. Paul Mantoux, *Les Délibérations du Conseil des Quatre (24 mars–28 juin 1919): Notes de l'Officier Interprète* (2 vols.; Paris: Éditions du Centre National de la Recherche Scientifique, 1955), II, 142; also, *Foreign Relations: Paris Peace Conference*, V, 756–766.

83. "Questions Remaining to Be Settled after German and Austrian Peace Treaties," in House to Wilson, May 22, 1919, House MSS; Hoover, *The Ordeal of Woodrow Wilson*, 228–229.

Chapter 8. Commissions amid Conflicts

1. Strong to Barton, January 3 and 20, 1919, ABC 3.2.

2. *Missionary Herald*, 115 (May–August 1919), 177–179, 316–317; American Board, *Annual Report*, 109 (1919), 32–33.

3. Board Secretary Enoch F. Bell to Barton, June 12, 1919, ABC 3.2.

4. Timothy L. Smith, *Revivalism and Social Reform in Mid-Nineteenth-Century America* (New York: Abingdon Press, 1957); H. Richard Niebuhr, *Christ and Culture* (New York: Harper, 1951), 1–44.

5. Leo Pfeffer, *Church, State and Freedom* (rev. ed.; Boston: Beacon Press, 1967), 221–320.

6. Smylie, "Protestant Clergymen and America's World Role," 126–129, 558–566.

7. John Higham, *Strangers in the Land: Patterns of American Nativism, 1860–1925* (New Brunswick, N.J.: Rutgers University Press, 1955), 194–233; Winthrop Hudson, *American Protestantism* (Chicago: University of Chicago Press, 1961), 124–127.

8. Barton, *Story of Near East Relief*, ix, 55.

9. Morgenthau to Wilson, May 21, 1919, Wilson MSS; also, Gates, *Not to Me Only*, 260.

10. Bliss to Wilson, February 11, 1919, Wilson MSS; Gates, *Not to Me Only*, 261; Barton to House, March 27 and April 9, 1919, House MSS; Barton to House, June 21, 1919, F.W. 767.68/17, Peace Commission Papers.

11. Quoted in House Diary, April 1 and 28, 1919, House MSS; also, Paul Birdsall, *Versailles Twenty Years After* (New York: Harcourt, 1941), 4–21.

12. John A. Garraty, *Woodrow Wilson: A Great Life in Brief* (New York: Knopf, 1956), 163; also, Edwin A. Weinstein, "Woodrow Wilson's Neurological Illness," *Journal of American History*, 57 (September 1970), 324–351.

13. Louis A. R. Yates, *United States and French Security: 1917–1921* (New York: Twayne, 1957); Thomas A. Bailey, *Woodrow Wilson and the Lost Peace* (New York: Macmillan, 1944), 179–192; Walter Lippmann, *U.S. Foreign Policy: Shield of the Republic* (Boston: Little, Brown, 1943), 71–77; Daniel M. Smith, *The Great Departure: The United States and World War I, 1914–1920* (New York: Wiley, 1965), 157–160; Arno J. Mayer, *Politics and Diplomacy of Peacemaking: Containment and Counterrevolution at Versailles, 1918–1919* (New York: Knopf, 1967), 875–893.

14. Lansing Diary, December 17, 1918–February 14, 1919, Robert Lansing MSS, Library of Congress.

15. Joseph Grew to William Phillips, April 13, 1919, in Grew, *Turbulent Era*, I; also, Lansing to State Department official Frank Polk, July 26, 1919, Frank L. Polk

MSS, Yale University Library; Lybyer to his wife, May 14, 1919, Lybyer MSS; Gelfand, *The Inquiry*, 134–135, 176–180.

16. Sachar, "The United States and Turkey," 212–213.

17. House Diary, April 1, 1919, House MSS.

18. *Foreign Relations: Paris Peace Conference*, V, 468, 756–766.

19. "Wilson Defers Action on Armenian Mandate," (the article states that Wilson personally favors a mandate but will not make a formal commitment until he submits the question to Congress; it mentions that Dodge and Christian missions are involved in the mandate question), New York *Times*, March 30, 1919.

20. Quoted in Adler, *The Isolationist Impulse*, 99 (see also pp. 32–117).

21. Barton to Boston office, February 3, 1919, Barton MSS.

22. Gates, *Not to Me Only*, 261, Lybyer to his wife, February 12, 1919, and Lybyer Diary, May 23, 1919, Lybyer MSS; Crane to M. N. Page, March 9, 1919, Crane MSS; Lansing Diary, February 14, 1919, Lansing MSS; House Diary, May 30, 1919, House MSS; Beer Diary, March 21 and 25, 1919, Beer MSS.

23. House Diary, May 20, 1919, House MSS; also, Seymour, ed., *The Intimate Papers of Colonel House*, IV, 468.

24. *Foreign Relations: Paris Peace Conference*, V, 766, 812.

25. King to House, May 22, 1919, House MSS; Lybyer Diary and letter to his wife, both May 22, 1919, Lybyer MSS; Baker, *Woodrow Wilson and World Settlement*, II, 203.

26. Crane to his son, John O. Crane, May 10, 1919, Crane MSS; also, House Diary, May 23, 1919, House MSS; Howard, *The King-Crane Commission*, 59–80.

27. Barton to King, May 4, 1917, and King to Barton, May 18, 1918, Henry Churchill King MSS, Oberlin College Library.

28. Smith, "Journal," June 4, 1919.

29. Crane to M. N. Page, July 9, 1919, also, Crane to John O. Crane, July 27, 1919, Crane MSS.

30. Feisal to Wilson, July 9, 1919, quoted in Evans, *United States Policy and the Partition of Turkey*, 155.

31. William Yale, *The Near East: A Modern History* (Ann Arbor: University of Michigan Press, 1958), 336; also, Howard, *The King-Crane Commission*, 87–154.

32. Crane to Wilson, July 10, 1919, Crane MSS; King and Crane to Wilson, July 10, 1919, F.W. 181.9102/3, and Lybyer to Peace Commission, July 1, 1919, 181.-9102/2, Peace Commission Papers.

33. Handwritten notebook on the relief trip in 1919, Barton MSS; also, Crane to C.S.C., July 29, 1919, Crane MSS; Riggs Diary, May 23, June 4, June 26, June 30, and July 9, 1919.

34. Lybyer to his wife, August 3, 1919, Lybyer MSS; Barton to his wife, August 3, 1919, Barton MSS.

35. Howard, *The King-Crane Commission*, 183–188; Fisher Diary, July 26, 1919.

36. John Patrick (Lord Kinross), *Ataturk: A Biography of Mustafa Kemal, Father of Modern Turkey* (New York: Morrow, 1965), 217; Fisher Diary, February 1 and August 5, 1919.

37. Howard, *The King-Crane Commission*, 155–183, 189–194, 287–291; Roderic H. Davison, "Turkish Diplomacy from Mudros to Lausanne," in Gordon A. Craig and Felix Gilbert, eds., *The Diplomats: 1919–1939* (Princeton, N.J.: Princeton University Press, 1953); Edib, *The Turkish Ordeal*, 4–23; Evans, *The United States and the Partition of Turkey*, 170–189; Gidney, *A Mandate for Armenia*, 97–133; Fisher Diary, August 3, 6, and 7, 1919.

38. Barton to House, June 21, 1919, F.W. 767.68/17, Peace Commission Papers; also, Smith, "Journal," June 11–July 3, 1919.

39. Barton to Bristol, June 14, 1919, enclosed in letter of Barton to Arshag Schmavonian, October 17, 1919, Decimal File 860J.01/542, ACIA to Wilson, June 22, 1919,

NOTES TO PAGES 207-212

Decimal File 860J.01/12, on Dodge's influence consult Elizabeth Marbury of the ACIA to Wilson, August 30, 1920, Decimal File 860J.48/44, State Department Archives; *Foreign Relations: 1919*, II, 824.

40. Morgenthau to Harbord, June 25, 1919, Morgenthau MSS; Frank Polk to Charles Evans Hughes, July 12, 1919, Decimal File 860J.01/13, State Department Archives.

41. Morgenthau to Barton, December 26, 1919, Morgenthau MSS; *Foreign Relations: Paris Peace Conference*, VI, 729-730, 741, VII, 30-31; John Philip Richardson, "The American Military Mission to Armenia," unpublished M.A. thesis, George Washington University (1964), 13-19; MacLachlan, "A Potpourri of Sidelights and Shadows from Turkey," 49-50.

42. Harbord to Morgenthau, June 28, 1919, James G. Harbord MSS, Library of Congress; M. P. A. Hankey to Morgenthau, June 28, 1919, Morgenthau MSS; *Foreign Relations: Paris Peace Conference*, VII, 28, XI, 261-264; Barton to Boston, June 28, 1919, ABC 16.5; Smith, "Journal," July 2-6, 1919.

43. Morgenthau to Dodge, n.d., Morgenthau MSS; also, telephone message from American Peace Commission to Harbord, July 31, 1919, Harbord MSS; Morgenthau, *All in a Life Time*, 324-343.

44. Polk to Lansing, July 31, 1919, Polk MSS; also, James L. Barton, "Turkey the Morning After," *Missionary Herald*, 115 (August 1919), 316, 332-333; Gerard to Lansing, July 28, 1919, Decimal File 860J.01/22, State Department Archives; Gidney, *A Mandate for Armenia*, 169-170, 193-194.

45. Peace Commission to State Department as paraphrased in Peace Commission telephone message to Harbord, July 31, 1919, Mary Mills Patrick to Harbord, n.d., Harbord MSS; Hoover to Polk, July 30, 1919, and Mary Mills Patrick to Polk, July 30, 1919, Polk MSS; Tiflis consul to American Peace Commission, July 30, 1919, 867B.00/193, Peace Commission Papers; Smith, "Journal," August 5 and 10, 1919.

46. James G. Harbord, *America in the World War* (Boston: Houghton Mifflin, 1933), 3; also, Polk to Harbord, August 13, 1919, Harbord MSS; *Foreign Relations: 1919*, II, 828, 842.

47. Wilson to Lansing, August 4, 1919, Decimal File 860J.01/26½, State Department Archives.

48. Wilson to Dodge, August 14, 1919, also, Dodge to Wilson, August 10, 1919, Wilson MSS.

49. Smith, "Journal," August 6-19, 1919; also, British embassy official to Curzon, August 16 and 25, 1919, in *British Documents*, 1st series, IV, 730, 738; Riggs Diary, August 5-6, and September 24, 1919; Thomas A. Bryson, "Walter George Smith and the Armenian Question at the Paris Peace Conference: 1919," *Records of the American Catholic Historical Society of Philadelphia*, 81 (March 1970), 3-26.

50. Wilson to Williams, August 12, 1919, Wilson MSS; also, Howard, *The King-Crane Commission*, 247-248; *Foreign Relations: 1919*, II, 831-841.

51. Wilson to Williams, August 2, 1919, and Williams to Wilson, August 9, 1919, John Sharp Williams MSS, Library of Congress; Gerard (discussing Lodge, Hughes, and Root) to Lansing, August 28, 1919, Decimal File 860J.01/70, State Department Archives.

52. Barton to his wife, July 27, July 31, August 3 and 4, 1919, Barton MSS.

53. Barton and Peet to Dodge, August 23, 1919, Decimal File 860J.01/62 (Learning of the Barton-Peet telegram, Bristol aimed to neutralize it by telling the State Department to beware of sentimental propaganda which slighted the relation of the Armenian question to matters of Asia Minor as a whole.), September 4, 1919, Decimal File 860J.01/73, State Department Archives; also, Barton to his wife, August 22, 1919, Barton MSS; Fisher Diary, August 27, 1919.

Chapter 9. The Isolationist Revival

1. New York *Sun*, August 27, 1919, quoted in Gidney, *A Mandate for Armenia*, 197; Polk to House, August 13, 1919, Polk MSS; Evans, *United States Policy and the Partition of Turkey*, 184–185.

2. Correspondence of an Anglo-Irish reformer and economist, Moreton Frewen, with Lodge and David Lloyd George, March 7, 1919–August 17, 1920, Moreton Frewen MSS, Library of Congress; John A. Garraty, *Henry Cabot Lodge: A Biography* (New York: Knopf, 1953), 345–366.

3. House Diary, May 10 and June 29, 1919, House MSS.

4. Dodge to Wilson, August 10, 1919, Wilson MSS.

5. Quoted in Allan Nevins, ed., *American Press Opinion: Washington to Coolidge; A Documentary Record of Editorial Leadership and Criticism, 1785–1928* (New York: Heath, 1928), 556.

6. Quoted in Garraty, *Henry Cabot Lodge*, 345; also, Smith, *The Great Departure*, 177–201; Link, *Wilson the Diplomatist*, 132–156; John Chalmers Vinson, *Referendum for Isolation: Defeat of Article Ten of the League of Nations Covenant* (Athens: University of Georgia Press, 1961), 86–95.

7. Elmer Ellis, *Mr. Dooley's America: A Life of Finley Peter Dunne* (New York: Knopf, 1941), 117–118, 251.

8. Lodge to White, August 19, 1919, quoted in Nevins, *Henry White*, 465–466.

9. Crane to Wilson, August 31, 1919, Crane MSS.

10. House Diary, September 21, 1919, House MSS.

11. Thomas A. Bryson, III, "Woodrow Wilson, the Senate, Public Opinion and the Armenian Mandate Question, 1919–1920," unpublished Ph.D. thesis, University of Georgia (1965), 76–97.

12. Wilson to State Department official William Phillips, received September 17, 1919, Decimal File 860J.01/82, also, Gerard to Lansing, n.d. but in September 1919 after Williams Resolution introduced, Decimal File 860J.01/78, State Department Archives.

13. Phillips to Wilson, September 20, 1919, Decimal File 860J.01/82, *ibid.*; Edward Grey to Curzon, October 7, 1919, in *British Documents*, 1st series, IV, 797; article on John Sharp Williams by Thomas A. Bryson, to be published.

14. *Congressional Record*, 58 (September 11, 1919), 5219–5225.

15. Marian C. McKenna, *Borah* (Ann Arbor: University of Michigan Press, 1961), 162.

16. Blum, *Woodrow Wilson and the Politics of Morality*, 190–192; Lloyd George, *Memoirs*, II, 818; Gene Smith, *When the Cheering Stopped: The Last Years of Woodrow Wilson* (New York: Morrow, 1964), 105–114.

17. Polk to Bristol, October 14, 1919, Polk MSS; also, Peet to Barton, September 30, 1919, ABC 16.9.3; missionary E. A. Yarrow in Tiflis (about Haskell) to a correspondent in America (probably Morgenthau), October 14, 1919, Morgenthau MSS.

18. Quoted in *Missionary Herald*, 115 (November 1919), 434.

19. *Ibid.*, 429; American Board, *Annual Report*, 109 (1919), 7; Barton to Bryce, October 29, 1919, ABC 3.2; Gidney, *A Mandate for Armenia*, 222–223; Edward Grey to Curzon, October 7, 1919, in *British Documents*, 1st series, IV, 797; Smith, "Journal," October 24, 1919.

20. Lancaster, "The Protestant Churches and the Fight for Ratification of the Versailles Treaty," *Public Opinion Quarterly*, 31 (Winter 1967–1968), 608–609; Kuehl, *Seeking World Order*, 324.

21. Quoted in Garraty, *Henry Cabot Lodge*, 378.

22. Quoted in *ibid.*, 379; Claudius O. Johnson, *Borah of Idaho* (New York: Longman, 1936), 244–245.

23. Lodge to Gerard, November 17, 1919, quoted in Cook, "The United States and the Armenian Question," 230.

24. Handwritten, undated notebook on Barton Relief Commission of 1919, Barton to his wife, September 12, 1919, and Bryce to Barton, October 10, 1919, Barton MSS.

25. Atamian, *The Armenian Community*, 208–234; Howard, *The King-Crane Commission*, 248; *Foreign Relations: Paris Peace Conference*, II, 147–157.

26. King-Crane report in *Foreign Relations: Paris Peace Conference*, XII, 745–863; Donald Brodie, "American Section of the International Commission on Mandates in Turkey," October 19, 1919, Crane MSS; Winston Churchill, *The Aftermath: Being a Sequel to the World Crisis* (London: Macmillan, 1941), 362–363.

27. Howard, *The King-Crane Commission*, 249–256, 276–280; Evans, *United States Policy and the Partition of Turkey*, 216–234, 237–247; Crane to Henry Churchill King, December 3, 1919, Crane MSS; Barton to his wife, September 12, 1919, and Barton memorandum, "The Syrian Commission," n.d., Barton MSS.

28. Peter M. Buzanski, "The Interallied Investigation of the Greek Invasion of Smyrna: 1919," *Historian*, 25 (May 1963), 325–343.

29. Richardson, "The American Military Mission to Armenia," 26–49; Barton to Bryce, November 29, 1919, ABC 3.2; Bryson, "Mark Lambert Bristol," *Armenian Review*, 21 (Winter 1968), 3–22; Fisher Diary, September 3–5, 1919.

30. Riggs Diary, September 6, 1919; James G. Harbord, "Investigating Turkey and Trans-caucasia," *World's Work*, 40 (May–July 1920), 35–47, 176–193, 271–280.

31. *Ibid.*, 189.

32. Patrick, *Ataturk*, 218–219.

33. Harbord Mission report, *Foreign Relations: 1919*, II, 841–889, and 184.-02102/1–19, Peace Commission Papers; the thirteen-part series by James Tashjian, "The American Military Mission to Armenia," *Armenian Review*, 2–5 (1949–1952); Gidney, *A Mandate for Armenia*, 171–191.

34. Howard, *The King-Crane Commission*, 281; Grey to Curzon, October 23, 1919, in *British Documents*, 1st series, IV, 843.

35. *Foreign Relations: Paris Peace Conference*, XII, 843–847.

36. Lybyer to his wife, July 26, 1919, Lybyer MSS; Bristol Diary, August 18, 1919, Bristol MSS.

37. *Foreign Relations: Paris Peace Conference*, XII, 845; also, Crane to M. N. Page, July 29, 1919, Crane MSS.

38. *Foreign Relations: 1919*, II, 874; also, Harbord, "Investigating Turkey and Trans-caucasia," 190.

39. *Foreign Relations: 1919*, II, 871.

40. Fisher Diary, January 17, and September 4, 1919; Riggs Diary, March 9–December 31, 1919.

41. William Phillips to Crane, October 30, 1919, Crane MSS; Grey to Curzon, November 23, 1919, in *British Documents*, 1st series, IV, 901.

42. Hamilton Holt, "Armenia and America," *Independent*, 102 (1920), 205–208; *Foreign Relations: 1919*, II, 824; Charles Vickrey to State Department, March 21, 1920, Decimal File 860J.48/26, and memorandum on Near East Relief of June 29, 1921, Decimal File 860J.4016/143, State Department Archives; Barton, *Story of Near East Relief*, 124–127.

43. Daniel, "From Relief to Technical Assistance in the Near East," 56–65; James H. Nicol to Stanley White, December 31, 1919, Box 101, Presbyterian Board Archives.

44. Barton to Bryce, January 28, 1920, ABC 3.2; also, Barton to Bryce, November 29, 1919, December 17, 1919, and February 26, 1920, and Barton to Morgenthau, December 29, 1919, *ibid.*; Bryce to Barton, November 27, 1919, ABC 16.5;

Morgenthau to Barton, December 26, 1919, Morgenthau MSS; Gates, *Not to Me Only*, 263.

45. Fisher Diary, November 19, 1919, and May 22, 1920; Edgar J. Fisher, "From Bad to Worse in Constantinople," New York *Times Magazine*, January 11, 1920.

46. New York *Times Magazine*, November 9, 1919; Fisher Diary, February 26, 1920; also, King to Harding, December 13, 1919, King MSS; *Foreign Relations: Paris Peace Conference*, XII, 847.

47. William H. Hall, *The Near East: Crossroads of the World*, including James L. Barton, "Shall the Land Be Healed?" (New York: Presbyterian Board of Foreign Missions, 1920), 190–191, 212–213; also, Bryce to Barton, November 5, 1919, Barton MSS; Fisher Diary, November 25, 1919, and April 11, 1920.

48. Bristol Diary, November 9, 1919, Bristol MSS; also, Bristol to the Secretary of State, February 21, 1920, Decimal File 860J.01/214, State Department Archives.

49. *The Joint Mandate Scheme* (New York: American Committee for the Independence of Armenia, c. December 1919), Missionary Research Library.

50. William Jessup to Harry Jessup, December 5, 1919, and typed copy of article entitled "Opportunities in Syria," c. November 1919, Box 101, Presbyterian Board Archives.

51. Margaret McGilvary, *Dawn of a New Era in Syria* (New York: Revell, 1920), 298–299.

52. Margaret McGilvary, *A Story of Our Syria Mission* (New York: Presbyterian Board of Foreign Missions, 1920), 29; also, Evans, *United States Policy and the Partition of Turkey*, 247–257; Presbyterian Board, *Annual Report*, 83 (1920), 70–71.

53. Speer to Jesse Yonan, March 13, 1920, also, Yohannan to Speer, November 18, 1919, File 1761, Box 520, Presbyterian Board Archives.

54. Quotation of Barton in "American Churchmen Are Eager to Help Armenia," *Current Opinion*, 67 (December 1919), 313–314.

55. *Independent*, 101 (February 28, 1920), 314.

56. Mabel E. Elliott, *Beginning Again at Ararat* (New York: Revell, 1924), 115; also, Evans, *United States Policy and the Partition of Turkey*, 257–261.

57. Gates to Barton, March 8, 1920, ABC 14.2; also, Barton to Dodge, March 9, 1920, and Barton to the Secretary of State, March 8, 1920, ABC 3.2.

58. Barton to Wilson, March 18, 1920, also, Barton to Lodge, March 9, 1920, Barton to Bryce, March 12, 1920, Barton to Morgenthau, March 13 and 19, 1920, ABC 3.2; Lodge to Barton, March 15, 1920, ABC 16.9.1.

59. House Diary, December 11, 1919, and January 5 and February 18, 1920, House MSS.

60. Kuehl, *Hamilton Holt*, 144; Near East Relief pamphlet, *Has America Responsibility for Protecting Armenia?*, Judson MSS.

61. For an interpretation more pro-Wilson than mine, see Thomas A. Bryson, "Woodrow Wilson and the Armenian Mandate: A Reassessment," *Armenian Review*, 21 (Autumn 1968), 10–29.

62. Wilson to Dodge, April 19, 1920, Wilson MSS; also, *British Documents*, 1st series, XIII, 60; Howard, *The King-Crane Commission*, 295–298. The King-Crane report came out unofficially in *Editor and Publisher*, 5 (December 2, 1922).

63. Barton to Bryce, April 23, 1920, ABC 3.2; Gidney, *A Mandate for Armenia*, 223.

64. Gidney, *A Mandate for Armenia*, 217–218; *British Documents*, 1st series, IV, 797–798, 815, 842–843, 1st series, VI, 1, 43, 1st series, VII, 20–21, 31–34, 46, 61–63, 118, 145, 156–168, 216–219, 1st series, XIII, 55–56; Thomas A. Bryson, "An American Mandate for Armenia: A Link in British Near Eastern Policy," *Armenian Review*, 21 (Summer 1968), 23–41.

65. Editorial quoted in Bryson, "Woodrow Wilson, the Senate, Public Opinion and the Armenian Mandate Question," 228.

66. Holt, "Armenia and America," *Independent*, 102 (1920), 205–208.

67. Dodge to Wilson, April 29, 1920, Dodge MSS.

68. *Congressional Record*, 59 (May 11 & 13, 1920), 6844, 6979; Riggs Diary, May 10, 1920.

69. *British Documents*, 1st series, XIII, 66, 70–76; Fisher Diary (conversation with Cleveland Dodge), May 22, 1920.

70. Woodrow Wilson, "The United States and the Armenian Mandate," *International Conciliation*, 151 (June 1920), 271–274.

71. Bryson, "Woodrow Wilson, the Senate, Public Opinion and the Armenian Mandate Question," 113–249; Richardson, "The American Military Mission to Armenia," 105–108.

72. *Congressional Record*, 59 (May 29 & June 1, 1920), 7876, 8072–8073.

73. Quoted in Elizabeth Monroe, *Britain's Moment in the Middle East: 1914–1956* (Baltimore: Johns Hopkins Press, 1963), 61–62.

74. Kenneth E. Boulding, *The Meaning of the Twentieth Century: The Great Transition* (New York: Harper, 1964).

Chapter 10. "Clamorous Armenianism"

1. Gates to Colby, May 4, 1920, Decimal File 860J.4016/23, State Department Archives; also, handwritten notebook on the Barton Relief Commission, Barton MSS.

2. Gerard to Colby, May 6, 1920, Decimal File 860J.01/266, State Department Archives; also, Barton to Riggs, April 26 and 29, 1920, ABC 3.2.

3. Gidney, *A Mandate for Armenia*, 238–239.

4. *British Documents*, 1st series, XII, 610–611, 631–634.

5. Lodge to Harding, September 2 and 15, 1920, Warren G. Harding MSS, Ohio Historical Society, Columbus, Ohio; also, Bartlett, *The League to Enforce Peace*, 187–188.

6. Quoted in Wesley M. Bagby, *The Road to Normalcy: The Presidential Campaign and Election of 1920* (Baltimore: Johns Hopkins Press, 1962), 158.

7. Barton to Riggs, July 19, 1920, August 13 and September 2, 1920, ABC 3.1; Riggs to Barton, July 30, 1920, August 11, 1920, ABC 14.2; Barton to George Montgomery, November 19, 1920, ABC 3.2; Bristol to Colby, September 24, 1920, Decimal File 860J.01/349, Consul C. K. Moser in Tiflis to State Department, October 29, 1920, Decimal File 860J.48/61, and Near East expert Warren D. Robbins to Secretary Charles Evans Hughes, May 16, 1921, Decimal File F.W. 860J.01/502, State Department Archives.

8. Relief official quoted in State Department official Alvey A. Adee to Barton, November 29, 1920, ABC 16.9.1; also, Adee to Barton, December 21, 1920, *ibid.*; minutes of the Armenia-America Society, September 30, 1920, ABC 14.2; Barton to Riggs, September 2, 1920, ABC 3.1; *Missionary Herald*, 116 (October 1920), 441; Riggs Diary, December 22, 1920.

9. Gates to House, June 23, 1920, also, Dodge to House, June 17, 1920, House MSS; Riggs Diary, December 31, 1919.

10. Dodge to Wilson, December 1, 1920, also, Wilson to Dodge, December 2, 1920, Wilson MSS; Dodge to Barton, December 4, 1920, and Morgenthau to Barton, December 8, 1920, ABC 14.2; Barton to Morgenthau, December 3, 1920, Morgenthau MSS; *British Documents*, 1st series, XII, 655–659; Riggs Diary, November 5 and December 3, 1920.

11. Ussher's comments enclosed in Consul Moser in Tiflis to Colby, January 13, 1921, Decimal File 860J.48/75, State Department Archives; also, Lodge to Barton, December 13, 1920, ABC 16.9.1.

12. Bryce to Barton, January 5, 1921, Barton MSS.

13. Montgomery to Wilson, January 13, 1921, Decimal File 860J.01/375, State Department Archives; also, Montgomery to Barton, December 28, 1920, ABC 14.2.

14. Barton, "Autobiography," 269–278, and handwritten notebook entitled "London Conference; 1921," Barton MSS; Barton to Bryce, January 29, 1921, and Barton to Montgomery, February 4, 1921, ABC 3.2; Barton memorandum, "America and the Council of Premiers in London," March 1921, ABC 16.9.1; Montgomery to Charles Evans Hughes, March 2, 1921, Decimal File 860J.01/491, State Department Archives; Gidney, *A Mandate for Armenia*, 255.

15. Speer to Abraham Moorhatch, August 22, 1921, File 1761, Box 520, Presbyterian Board Archives.

16. Wilson to relief official John B. Larner, March 1, 1921, Wilson MSS; James L. Barton, *Survey of the Fields: 1920–1921* (Boston: Congregational House, 1921); minutes of the Near East Relief committee in Armenia, enclosed in a letter of Moser to the State Department, December 29, 1920, Decimal File 860J.48/77, State Department Archives; White, *Adventuring with Anatolia College*, 95–109; Riggs Diary, March 24, 1921.

17. Barton to Hughes, March 29, 1921, Barton to Bryce, March 24, 1921, and Barton to Montgomery, January 22, 1921, ABC 3.2; Decimal File 860J.01/404, 425, 426, 434, and 860J.51/5, State Department Archives.

18. Barton to Bristol, May 6, 1921, ABC 3.2; Jessup to Hughes, July 15, 1921, Decimal File 860J.01/512 (heads of Protestant, Catholic, and Gregorian Armenians in the Near East labeled Cardashian's booklet "senseless and false," and State Department officials thereafter ignored Cardashian's lobbying), Bristol to Hughes, June 8, 1921, Decimal File 860J.01/451, also, 860J.01/447 and 470, State Department Archives.

19. Barton to Lodge, April 22, 1921, ABC 3.2; Lodge to Barton, April 25, 1921, ABC 14.2; Lodge to Hughes, April 25, 1921, Decimal File 860J.01/498, State Department Archives.

20. Lodge to Harding, November 10, 1920, December 24, 1920, and January 4, 1921, and Harding to Lodge, December 29, 1920, and January 10, 1921, Harding MSS; Kurt and Sarah Wimer, "The Harding Administration, the League of Nations, and the Separate Peace Treaty," *Review of Politics*, 29 (January 1967), 13–24; Adler, *The Isolationist Impulse*, 114–124; Williams to Barton, May 11, 1921, Barton MSS.

21. Barton to Montgomery, April 27, 1921, ABC 3.2.

22. Armenian churchmen to Barton, April 29, 1921, ABC 16.5.

23. Bristol to State Department, July 27, 1921, forwarded to Boston, ABC 16.9.1; Barton to British Armenophile Aneurim Williams, May 18, 1921, ABC 3.2; memorandum on Near East Relief, June 29, 1921, Decimal File 860J.4016/143, Montgomery to Hughes, April 29, 1921, Decimal File 860J.01/425, Montgomery to Robbins, July 25, 1921, Decimal File 860J.01/456, and Robbins to Hughes, May 16, 1921, Decimal File 860J.01/502, State Department Archives.

24. Evans, *United States Policy and the Partition of Turkey*, 329–333.

25. Paraphrase of Bristol in Cook, "The United States and the Armenian Question," 311; Vickrey and Montgomery to Hughes, November 10, 1921, Decimal File 860J.01/477, State Department Archives; Bryce to Montgomery, September 5, 1921, Bryce MSS.

26. Riggs to Montgomery, January 6, 1922, ABC 3.2; also, Barton to Montgomery, January 5, 1922, *ibid.*; Montgomery to Hughes, January 6, 1922, Decimal File 123B.773/31, State Department Archives.

27. Barton to Hughes, March 27, 1922, ABC 3.2.

28. Hughes to Barton, April 5, 1922, ABC 16.9.1; also, Barton to Hughes, March 27, 1922, ABC 3.2; Hughes to Jessup, April 4, 1922, Decimal File 860J.01/518,

State Department Archives. On the lack of Harding administrative initiative on the Rogers Resolution, see *Congressional Record*, 62 (June 15, 1922), 1879–1880.

29. Harding to Hughes, July 21, 1922, Harding MSS; Evans, *United States Policy and the Partition of Turkey*, 341–344.

30. Daniel, "From Relief to Technical Assistance in the Near East," 57, 60, 65; Barton, *Story of Near East Relief*, 128–151.

31. Barton to Hughes and Harding, September 18, 1922, ABC 3.2.

32. MacLachlan, "A Potpourri of Sidelights and Shadows from Turkey," 7–27, 52–53, 81–82.

33. Riggs to Hughes, September 25, 1922, ABC 3.2; Gates to his brother Herbert Gates, October 15, 1922, Gates MSS.

34. Gates, *Not to Me Only*, 260.

35. Bristol Diary, December 16 and 29, 1921, and October 13, 1922, Bristol MSS.

36. Evans, *United States Policy and the Partition of Turkey*, 292–322, 344–348; DeNovo, *American Interests and Policies in the Middle East*, 167–191.

37. Colby M. Chester, "Turkey Reinterpreted," *Current History*, 16 (April–September 1922), 939–947.

38. The Free incident, Decimal File 860J.48/104–1112, State Department Archives; also, Riggs to Chester, September 8, 1922, ABC 3.2; George R. Montgomery, "The Massacres of Armenians in 1915," *Current History*, 17 (October 1922–March 1923), 25–28; Albert Mackenzie, "Crimes of Turkish Misrule," *Current History*, 17 (1922–1923), 28–31.

39. Clair Price, "Mustapha Kemal and the Americans," *Current History*, 17 (1922–1923), 116–125; also, Bristol Diary, December 1, 1921, Bristol MSS.

40. Talcott Williams, *Turkey, A World Problem of Today* (Garden City, N.Y.: Doubleday, 1921), 211–212.

41. George R. Montgomery, "Turkey and the Americans," *Current History*, 17 (1922–1923), 300–302.

42. Everett P. Wheeler, "American Missionaries in Turkey," *Current History*, 17 (1922–1923), 303–304; also, Everett P. Wheeler, *The Duty of the United States of America to American Citizens in Turkey* (New York: Revell, 1896); Albert W. Staub, "American School Work in the Near East," *Current History*, 17 (1922–1923), 596–600.

43. Barton to Gates, August 15 and September 6, 1922, ABC 3.2.

Chapter 11. Xenophobic Asian Nationalism

1. Harding to Under Secretary of State William Phillips, September 5 and 15, 1922, Harding MSS; Evans, *United States Policy and the Partition of Turkey*, 373–374.

2. Harding to Barton, October 5, 1922, also, Barton, "Autobiography," 287–308, Barton MSS; James L. Barton, "American Interests and Rights in the Near East," *Homiletic Review*, 85 (January 1923), 3–10.

3. American Board petition to Harding and Hughes, October 26, 1922, ABC 16.9.1; Barton to Gates, October 19, 1922, ABC 3.2; DeNovo, *American Interests and Policies in the Middle East*, 128–153; Evans, *United States Policy and the Partition of Turkey*, 393–399; *Foreign Relations: 1923*, II, 884–888; George B. Christian, Jr. to J. B. Larner, April 13, 1921, Harding MSS.

4. Bristol Diary, November 27, 1922, Bristol MSS; Barton to Hughes, October 18, 1922, ABC 3.2; Barton, "Report on Lausanne," February 3, 1923, ABC 16.9.1; Charles S. Farn to Barton, November 11, 1922, and Stanley White to Barton, November 5, 1922, Barton MSS; ACIA to Harding, September 5, 1922, Decimal File 860J.01/546, State Department Archives.

5. Barton to Boston, November 18–December 1, 1922, ABC 16.5; Bristol Diary,

November 10–23, 1922, Bristol MSS; Box 18–19 (one container), Lausanne Papers in the National Archives at Washington; Gates to his brother Herbert Gates, December 23, 1922, Gates MSS; Crane to his son John O. Crane, November 15, 1922, Crane MSS.

6. *Foreign Relations: 1923*, II, 900–904.

7. Cook, "The United States and the Armenian Question," 309; Barton to Gates, October 19, 1922, ABC 3.2; Decimal File 860J.48, State Department Archives.

8. Bristol Diary, November 27, 1922, Bristol MSS; also, *Foreign Relations: 1923*, II, 944–946.

9. Gates to Herbert Gates, October 15, 1922, Gates MSS; also, Gates, "The Armenians in Turkey," December 5, 1922, Box 18–19, Lausanne Papers; Barton, "Report on Lausanne," February 3, 1923, ABC 16.9.1.

10. Barton to Boston, December 1, 1922, ABC 16.5; *Foreign Relations: 1923*, II, 910; Richard W. Child, *A Diplomat Looks at Europe* (New York: Duffield, 1925), 116.

11. Child, *A Diplomat Looks at Europe*, 103–115.

12. Paraphrase of Turks in Barton to Boston, December 21, 1922, ABC 16.5; also, *Foreign Relations: 1923*, II, 922, 934, 939.

13. Grew, *Turbulent Era*, I, 524–525; *Foreign Relations: 1923*, II, 940–946, 971; Gerard to Harding, January 10, 1923, Decimal File 860J.01/562½, State Department Archives; Boxes 15, 18–19, Lausanne Papers.

14. Harding to Hughes, January 15, 1923, Harding MSS; also, Harding to Hughes, January 1, 1923, and Hughes to Harding, January 12, 1923, *ibid.*; *Foreign Relations: 1923*, II, 947–948; Roderic H. Davison, *Turkey* (Englewood Cliffs, N.J.: Prentice-Hall, 1968), 125–127.

15. Barton to Boston, December 7, 1922, ABC 16.5.

16. Barton to Boghos Nubar, February 13, 1923, ABC 3.2; Bristol Diary, December 27, 1922, Bristol MSS.

17. Barton to Boston, December 19, 1922, ABC 16.5.

18. Barton to Wheeler, February 21, 1923, ABC 3.2.

19. Bristol Diary, November 27, 1922, Bristol MSS.

20. Barton to Hughes, February 13, 1923, ABC 3.2.

21. On the Chester Concession see DeNovo, *American Interests and Policies in the Middle East*, 210–228; also see *Foreign Relations: 1923*, II, 1152–1171.

22. Elaine Smith, *Turkey: Origins of the Kemalist Movement and the Government of the Grand National Assembly (1919–1923)* (Washington, D.C.: Judd & Detweiler, 1959), 120–123.

23. Gates to Herbert Gates, December 29, 1922, Gates MSS; also, Gates, *Not to Me Only*, 289; Barton, "Report on Lausanne," February 3, 1923, ABC 16.9.1.

24. Gates to Barton, September 11, 1923, ABC 14.2.

25. Barton to Lodge, September 17, 1923, ABC 3.2.

26. Ernest W. Riggs, "The American Board and the Turks," *Moslem World*, 14 (January 1924), 1–4.

27. Statement by Gates, November 15, 1923, and Bristol to Barton, January 12, 1924, ABC 14.2.

28. Jenkins, *An Educational Ambassador to the Near East*, 299–301; Patrick, *Under Five Sultans*, 341.

29. Presbyterian Board, *Annual Report*, 85 (1922), 49–50.

30. Speer and Carter, *Report on India and Persia*, 355–356, 465–611.

31. DeNovo, *American Interests and Policies in the Middle East*, 281–283; Arthur C. Millspaugh, *The American Task in Persia* (New York: Century, 1925).

32. Near East Relief in Tabriz to Vickrey, October 23, 1922, File 1761, Box 520, Presbyterian Board Archives; Presbyterian Board, *Annual Report*, 86 (1923), 223–224.

33. Bristol Diary, December 10, 1922, Bristol MSS; Box 15 and Box 16–17 (one container), especially Syro-Chaldean [Nestorian] Delegation at Paris, "Report," April 15, 1922, Lausanne Papers; Barton, "Report on Lausanne," February 3, 1923, ABC 16.9.1.

34. Speer to E. C. Carter, November 12, 1923, File 1761, Box 520, Presbyterian Board Archives; also, Allen Dulles to Speer, July 10, 1923, Speer to Carter, October 5, 1923, and Carter to Speer, October 8 and 11, 1923, ibid.

35. A Century of Mission Work in Iran (Persia), 4ff.; DeNovo, American Interests and Policies in the Middle East, 291–297; Edward Every, "The Assyrians," in A. J. Arberry, ed., Religion in the Middle East: Three Religions in Concord and Conflict (2 vols.; Cambridge: Cambridge University Press, 1969), I, 521–533.

36. McDowell to Speer, December 3, 1924, File 1761, Box 520, Presbyterian Board Archives.

37. E. H. Bierstadt, The Great Betrayal: A Survey of the Near East Problem (New York: McBridge, 1924), 175.

38. Cardashian to Barton, February 5, 1924, also, speech by Gerard in New York City, January 24, 1924, ABC 16.9.1; Barton, "Autobiography," 307–308, Barton MSS; Gidney, A Mandate for Armenia, 251.

39. Quoted in DeNovo, American Interests and Policies in the Middle East, 159; also, MacLachlan, "A Potpourri of Sidelights and Shadows from Turkey," 52–53.

40. DeNovo, American Interests and Policies in the Middle East, 159–163.

41. There is a full discussion of both sides of the debate in James Gerard et al., The Lausanne Treaty: Should the United States Ratify It? (New York: Foreign Policy Association, 1924).

42. Gerard to Barton, November 17 and December 8, 1925, Barton MSS.

43. Frank A. Ross, C. Luther Fry, and Elbridge Sibley, The Near East and American Philanthropy (New York: Columbia University Press, 1929); Paul Monroe, R. R. Reeder, and James I. Vance, Reconstruction in the Near East (New York: Near East Relief, 1924); relief official L. W. Archer to Dulles, December 19, 1924, Decimal File 860J.48/191, State Department Archives; Daniel, "From Relief to Technical Assistance in the Near East," 89–103; Barton, Story of Near East Relief, 154–162; Near East Relief pamphlet, The Missionary Value and Missionary Educational Value of Near East Relief (c. December 1923), Missionary Research Library.

44. James L. Barton, Changing Turkey: Political and Religious Revolution (Boston: American Board of Commissioners for Foreign Missions, Envelope Series, 1926), 17; Roger R. Trask, " 'Unnamed Christianity' in Turkey during the Atatürk Era," Muslim World, 55 (January & April 1965), 66–76; Bristol to Barton, May 31, 1923–June 23, 1924, ABC 16.9.1.

45. Fisher Diary, May 25 and June 22, 1919, and January 4, 1920.

46. MacLachlan, "A Potpourri of Sidelights and Shadows from Turkey," 56–58; also, Barton to Bristol, August 6, 1926, Barton to Dulles' successor G. Howland Shaw, August 18, 1926, Barton to Alley, August 20, 1926, Riggs to Alley, September 1, 1926, Barton to President Calvin Coolidge, December 6, 1926, and Riggs to Borah, December 28, 1926, ABC 3.2; Borah to Barton, February 17, 1926, Dulles to Barton, February 5, 13, and 19, 1926, Shaw to Barton, April 15 and June 4, 1926, letters from Shaw to Riggs, August 20–October 23, 1926, and Alley to Riggs, November 16, 1926, ABC 14.2.

47. Gerard to Barton, December 8, 1924, Barton MSS; Alley to Barton, March 26, 1927, ABC 3.2; Vahan Cardashian, ed., The Lausanne Treaty: Turkey and Armenia (New York: American Committee Opposed to the Lausanne Treaty, 1926).

48. Barton to F. W. Allen, March 3 and 21, 1927, ABC 14.2.

49. Barton to Shaw, January 24, 1927, and Gates to Barton, September 11, 1923, ibid.; memorandum by Near East Division in State Department, May 8, 1929, Decimal File 860J.01/591, and Gerard to Secretary of State Henry L. Stimson, April 4,

1929, Decimal File 860J.01/589, State Department Archives; DeNovo, *American Interests and Policies in the Middle East*, 237–239.

Chapter 12. Midcentury Heritage

1. Wiebe, *The Search for Order*, 224–302.
2. Williams, *Turkey, A World Problem of Today*, 5–6.
3. Barton to Everett P. Wheeler, January 24, 1921, ABC 3.2.
4. William L. Westermann, "The Armenian Problem and the Disruption of Turkey," in Edward M. House and Charles Seymour, eds., *What Really Happened at Paris: The Story of the Peace Conference, 1918–1919* (New York: Scribners, 1921), 179–180.
5. Paul A. Varg, *Missionaries, Chinese and Diplomats: The American Protestant Missionary Movement in China, 1890–1952* (Princeton, N.J.: Princeton University Press, 1958), 322.
6. Robert Lansing, *The Peace Negotiations: A Personal Narrative* (Boston: Houghton Mifflin, 1921), 159.
7. Elie Kedourie, *England and the Middle East: The Destruction of the Ottoman Empire, 1914–21* (London: Bowes & Bowes, 1956), 147.
8. James L. Barton, "Some Missionary Activities in Relation to Governments," *International Review of Missions*, 13 (July 1924), 355.
9. P. J. Staudenraus, *The African Colonization Movement: 1816–1865* (New York: Columbia University Press, 1961); Mary Antoinette Brown, "Education and National Development in Liberia: 1800–1900," unpublished Ph.D. thesis, Cornell University (1967); John Walter Cason, "The Growth of Christianity in the Liberian Environment," unpublished Ph.D. thesis, Columbia University (1963); Werner T. Wickstrom, "The American Colonization Society in Liberia: A Historic Study in Religious Motivation and Awakening, 1817–1867," unpublished Ph.D. thesis, Hartford Seminary (1968); Mary Anne Rodolf, "American Missionary Influence in Liberia: 1816–1862," unpublished M.A. thesis, Illinois State University (1970); Raymond W. Bixler, *The Foreign Policy of the United States in Liberia* (New York: Pageant Press, 1957).
10. Tate, *The United States and the Hawaiian Kingdom*; Harold Whitman Bradley, *The American Frontier in Hawaii, The Pioneers: 1789–1843* (Palo Alto, Calif.: Stanford University Press, 1942); Sylvester K. Stevens, *American Expansion in Hawaii: 1842–1898* (Harrisburg: Archives Publishing Company of Pennsylvania, 1945); William Adam Russ, *The Hawaiian Revolution: 1893–1894* (Selinsgrove, Penn.: Susquehanna University Press, 1959); William Adam Russ, *The Hawaiian Republic (1894–98) and Its Struggle to Win Annexation* (Selinsgrove, Penn.: Susquehanna University Press, 1961); Gavan Daws, *Shoal of Time: A History of the Hawaiian Islands* (New York: Macmillan, 1968), 1–292.
11. Foster Rhea Dulles, *Yankees and Samurai: America's Role in the Emergence of Modern Japan* (New York: Harper, 1966); Edwin O. Reischauer, *The United States and Japan* (2nd ed.; Cambridge, Mass.: Harvard University Press, 1957); Fred Harvey Harrington, *God, Mammon and the Japanese: Dr. Horace N. Allen and Korean-American Relations, 1884–1905* (Madison: University of Wisconsin Press, 1944); Donald Kenneth Gorrell, "American Churches and American Territorial Expansion: 1830–1850," unpublished Ph.D. thesis, Western Reserve University (1960).
12. Varg, *Missionaries, Chinese and Diplomats*, 324; also, Chao-Kwang Wu, *The International Aspect of the Missionary Movement in China* (Baltimore: Johns Hopkins Press, 1930), 209–238; John M. H. Lindbeck, "American Missionaries and the Policies of the United States in China: 1898–1901," unpublished Ph.D. thesis, Yale University (1948); Paulsen, "The Szechwan Riots of 1895 and American 'Mission-

ary Diplomacy,' " *Journal of Asian Studies,* 28 (February 1969), 285–298; Te-kong Tong, *United States Diplomacy in China: 1844–1860* (Seattle: University of Washington Press, 1964); John K. Fairbank, *China: The People's Middle Kingdom and the U.S.A.* (Cambridge, Mass.: Harvard University Press, 1967), 131–138.

13. Latourette, "Colonialism and Missions: Progressive Separation," *Journal of Church and State,* 7 (Autumn 1965), 330–349.

14. Stephen Neill, *Colonialism and Christian Missions* (New York: McGraw-Hill, 1966), 412–417.

15. John K. Fairbank, "Assignment for the '70's," *American Historical Review,* 74 (February 1969), 877–878.

16. Trask, " 'Unnamed Christianity' in Turkey during the Atatürk Era," *Muslim World,* 55 (January & April 1965), 101–108; Roger R. Trask, "Joseph C. Grew and Turco-American Rapprochement: 1927–1932," in Sidney Devere Brown, ed., *Studies in Asia* (Lincoln: University of Nebraska Press, 1967), 150–156; DeNovo, *American Interests and Policies in the Middle East,* 254–259; American Board, *Annual Report,* 129 (1939), 51–52; Waldo H. Heinrichs, Jr., *American Ambassador: Joseph C. Grew and the Development of the United States Diplomatic Tradition* (Boston: Little, Brown, 1966), 129–139.

17. American Board, *Annual Report,* 150 (1960), 47; also, United Church Board for World Ministries, *Annual Report,* 157 (1968), 20–21; Latourette, *Christianity in a Revolutionary Age,* V, 291–292; W. Stanley Rycroft and Myrtle M. Clemmer, *A Factual Study of the Middle East* (New York: United Presbyterian Church in the U.S.A., 1962), 139; Fred Field Goodsell, *You Shall Be My Witnesses* (Boston: American Board of Commissioners for Foreign Missions, 1959), 25–27; Frank A. Stone, *Communities of Learning: People and Their Programs, the American Board Schools in Turkey from 1920 to 1970* (Istanbul: Redhouse Press, 1970), 1–26; Jean-Michel Hornus, "The Lutheran and Reformed Churches," in Arberry, ed., *Religion in the Middle East,* I, 539.

18. James 1:22.

19. Padwick, *Call to Istanbul,* 49–209.

20. Francis Boardman, *Institutions of Higher Learning in the Middle East* (Washington, D.C.: Middle East Institute, 1961), 26, 29; George Miller, "Aleppo College: Failure or Fulfilment?" *Muslim World,* 57 (January 1967), 42–45.

21. DeNovo, *American Interests and Policies in the Middle East,* 260–263; Scipio, *My Thirty Years in Turkey,* 132–133, 314–318, 364; Robert College, *Catalog* (1967–1968), Robert College centennial pamphlet, *Robert College of Istanbul, Turkey: Honors the Past, Faces the Future* (1963), and mimeographed guide of 1967–1968, "The American Colleges in Istanbul: Information for the Prospective Teacher," Robert College's New York office.

22. da Cruz, *The American University of Beirut Celebrates Its Proud Centennial.*

23. DeNovo, *American Interests and Policies in the Middle East,* 327–331; Constantine K. Zurayk, *Abiding Truths,* Founders' Day Convocation Address at the American University of Beirut, April 28, 1960, printed by the Near East College Association; Dodge, *The American University of Beirut,* 56–116.

24. Boardman, *Institutions of Higher Learning in the Middle East,* 2, 6; John K. Cooley, "Multinational University, Filling a Special Need [American University in Cairo]," *Christian Science Monitor,* January 11, 1969.

25. Walter Johnson and Francis Colligan, *The Fulbright Program: A History* (Chicago: University of Chicago Press, 1965), 3, 138, 311–320; Dodge, *The American University of Beirut,* 98.

26. Calvin Coolidge, "Introduction," in Barton, *Story of Near East Relief,* viii.

27. Coolidge speech in New York *Times,* October 25, 1924.

28. Barton, "The Near East Relief: A Moral Force," *International Review of Missions,* 18 (1919), 500; Barton, *Story of Near East Relief,* vii.

29. John S. Badeau and Georgiana G. Stevens, eds., *Bread from Stones: Fifty Years of Technical Assistance* (Englewood Cliffs, N.J.: Prentice-Hall, 1966); Daniel, "From Relief to Technical Assistance in the Near East," 100, 134–336; James L. Barton, "American Educational and Philanthropic Interests in the Near East," *Moslem World*, 23 (April 1933), 127; Goodsell, *They Lived Their Faith*, 113–114; Harold B. Allen, *Come Over into Macedonia: The Story of a Ten-Year Adventure in Uplifting a War-Torn People* (New Brunswick, N.J.: Rutgers University Press, 1943), ix–xviii; interview I had with Harold B. Allen, December 30, 1968; Laird Archer, *Balkan Journal* (New York: Norton, 1944), 8–9; Near East Foundation, *News*, 5 (Spring 1969); Sidney Gordon, *He Shot an Arrow: Barclay Acheson and the Concept of Helping People to Help Themselves* (New York: Near East Foundation, n.d.).

30. Quoted in Near East Foundation, *News* (July 1968); also, Curti, *American Philanthropy Abroad*, 609.

31. Harold B. Allen, *Rural Reconstruction in Action: Experience in the Near and Middle East* (Ithaca, N.Y.: Cornell University Press, 1953), xiii.

32. Near East Foundation, *Annual Report* (1968); International College, *Newsletter* (Fall 1965–1966); American University of Beirut, *Catalog* (1968–1969), 29; Mary Strout, "Grad Work in English at Beirut," *Christian Science Monitor*, February 15, 1969; Dodge, *The American University of Beirut*, 98; Sam Cohen, "American Academy in Turkey Forced to Trim Activities," *Christian Science Monitor*, December 7, 1970; Daniel, *American Philanthropy in the Near East*, 248–270.

33. Curti, *American Philanthropy Abroad*, especially 623ff.; Scott M. Cutlip, *Fund Raising in the United States: Its Role in America's Philanthropy* (New Brunswick, N.J.: Rutgers University Press, 1965).

34. Roy Hoopes, *The Complete Peace Corps Guide* (New York: Dial Press, 1965), 39–45; Badeau and Stevens, eds., *Bread from Stones*, 55.

35. Commission on Ecumenical Mission and Relations, *Annual Report*, 2 (1960), 72–77, and 8 (1966), 59–61; DeNovo, *American Interests and Policies in the Middle East*, 332–334; Boardman, *Institutions of Higher Learning in the Middle East*, 19; Latourette, *Christianity in a Revolutionary Age*, V, 292–295; Arthur Glasser, "Who Controls the Missionary?" *His*, 28 (May 1968), 15–16, 21–24; A. C. Forrest, "A Special Report on Arab Refugees," *Presbyterian Life*, 20 (October 1, 1967), 7–21; Goodall, *Christian Missions and Social Ferment*, 94–119; John K. Cooley, "Two Million Refugees: A Key to the Mideast Crisis, Arab Stand," *Christian Science Monitor*, April 30, 1969; Charles S. Malik, "The Orthodox Church," in Arberry, ed., *Religion in the Middle East*, I, 323–324.

36. Rycroft and Clemmer, *A Factual Study of the Middle East*, 139–141.

37. Marjorie Housepian, "The Unremembered Genocide," *Ararat*, 8 (Winter 1967), 2–11; "Armenia: Modern and Ancient," *Soviet Life*, No. 138 (March 1968), 9–63; K. V. Sarkissian, "The Armenian Church," in Arberry, ed., *Religion in the Middle East*, I, 482–520.

38. Interview I had with Floyd H. Black, August 30, 1961.

39. Roger R. Trask, "The United States and Turkish Nationalism: Investments and Technical Aid during the Atatürk Era," *Business History Review*, 38 (Spring 1964), 65–77; Kimmis Hendrick, "Couple Sparks Cultural Boom," *Christian Science Monitor*, October 15, 1968; Robert Avery, *Ink on Their Thumbs: The Antecedents of the Redhouse Press* (Istanbul: Redhouse Press, 1970), 7–8.

40. Robert L. Daniel, "The United States and the Turkish Republic before World War II: The Cultural Dimension," *Middle East Journal*, 21 (Winter 1967), 52–63.

41. DeNovo, *American Interests and Policies in the Middle East*, 327–333; Associated Press article by Elias N. Antar on AUB, in Canton (Ohio) *Repository*, February 28, 1968; Dodge, *The American University of Beirut*, 65, 106; American University of Beirut news releases, May 9, July 22, and September 13, 1968, AUB New

York office; William M. Bickers, "American University of Beirut," *Journal of the American Medical Association*, 200 (June 26, 1967), 1162–1168; Jack Long, "The First 100 Years of the AUB," *Lamp*, 47 (Winter 1965), 19–21.

42. Hurewitz, *Middle East Dilemmas*, 123–132; Manual, *The Realities of American-Palestine Relations*, 215, 280, 322–323; DeNovo, *American Interests and Policies in the Middle East*, 344.

43. Judith H. Banki, *Christian Reactions to the Middle East Crisis*, a pamphlet by the American Jewish Committee of New York City, late autumn 1967; also, *Presbyterian Life*, 20 (October 1, 1967), 7–21; John K. Cooley, "Semitic Union for Mideast?" *Christian Science Monitor*, June 16, 1969. Compare with a work by the chairman of Near East Foundation: John S. Badeau, *The American Approach to the Arab World* (New York: Harper, 1968).

44. Barton, "American Educational and Philanthropic Interests in the Near East," *Moslem World*, 23 (April 1933), 121–136.

Essay on Sources

Essay on Sources

EARLY in the research for this book I sensed that large gaps existed in publications about American relations with the Near East. Most general surveys of diplomatic history gave the impression that before the Second World War the page of United States interests in the eastern Mediterranean was nearly blank. Missionaries were invisible. (It seems that when professional American historians first appeared in the late nineteenth century, they and their successors not only had abandoned a religious interpretation of history but also much of the history of religion.) In special works on the Near East there were references to missionaries, including comments on the lobbying of religionists at the Paris Peace Conference. Some authors used annual reports of mission institutions; yet no one had read extensively in manuscript evidence. The search for unpublished papers took me eventually into varied repositories, from the air-conditioned Houghton Library at Harvard to a watery basement in a private residence. Since I started on this study, monographs have appeared which fill some of the empty places in accounts of American ties with the Near East from the 1770s to the 1960s. Despite the important contributions of late, considerable need for further investigation remains.

The bibliographical essay below concerns problems in gathering data and the nature and use of most of the sources I have employed. There is evidence in the notes which is not discussed in the essay (usually citations of pamphlets, articles, and such contextual materials as those cited for section two of Chapter 12).

351

PROTESTANT DIPLOMACY AND THE NEAR EAST

MANUSCRIPT SOURCES

Archives

Most historians of American concerns in the Near East have given little or no attention to the archives of the American Board of Commissioners for Foreign Missions (Houghton Library). I have found these papers of inestimable value for the religious and political experiences of missionaries, making use of several files: ABC 3.1 (correspondence from overseas missionaries), ABC 3.2 (correspondence originating at Boston), ABC 14.2 (miscellaneous letters), ABC 16.5 (Near East materials), ABC 16.9.1 and ABC 16.9.3 (Turkey documents); the most productive file has been ABC 3.2. (The James L. Barton MSS and several shelves of photographs, which used to be at American Board offices in Boston, have been taken to Houghton Library since I researched in them.) These extensive, apparently unabridged archives are well preserved and carefully organized. The American Board (now the United Church Board for World Ministries) deserves recognition for being not only the first overseas mission institution in the United States, but also one of the most responsible in preserving its records.

Crucial to the writing of the Syrian and Persian aspects of this narrative has been the manuscript collection of the Presbyterian Board of Foreign Missions (now part of the Commission on Ecumenical Mission and Relations Archives, located in the Presbyterian Historical Society at Philadelphia). I spent time in these papers, both when they were at Presbyterian Board headquarters in New York City and since they have been in Philadelphia. They reflect only a portion of the Presbyterian Board's history. Most materials dated before the year 1910 have been destroyed (some were microfilmed before their destruction); much of the post-1910 record has been conserved, but important sections are gone. A helpful guide to some files is a card index prepared years ago by Presbyterian Board secretaries in New York City. Considerable information on the Nestorians and the activities of missionaries to Persia is in Box 520 (File 1761). Important for Syria is Box 101 (no file number).

The New York City offices of the Syrian Protestant College (now the American University of Beirut), Robert College, and International College, among other things contain mimeographed papers, brochures, news releases, and photographs.

Near East Relief disposed of tons of records. One of its former officials explained to me that the agency felt at one point that it could no longer afford storage costs. Its successor organization, Near East Foundation (New York City headquarters), has retained photographs and financial statements from the period before 1930.

Interestingly, documents of the Department of State, located in the National Archives, have provided more data on Protestant lobbying than any of the above institutional manuscripts except the ABC files. I have extracted evidence of mission-relief influence upon The Inquiry and the American Commission to Negotiate Peace by methodically using, for example, the detailed card index of the American Peace Commission. Classifications 860J.01 and 860J.48 in the Decimal Files from 1910 to 1939 demonstrate much about the interests of the American Board, Near East Relief, and the American Committee for the Independence of Armenia. I have used only a few of the Lausanne Conference records.

Personal Papers

The papers of a leading missionary figure in this book, James L. Barton, are in the American Board Archives. I have investigated the entire collection: typewritten "Autobiography" (over 300 pages), essays, notebooks, correspondence (mostly letters received), articles, publicity pieces of Near East Relief. Barton's scribblings and his messages to his wife during his trip to Europe and the Near East in 1919 have been of exceptional assistance.

According to a member of the Howard S. Bliss family, the main Bliss MSS are in the American University of Beirut Library. One of the staff members of AUB Library went over them; he reported finding only two documents related to the pro-Arab activities of Bliss at the end of the First World War, which the staff member copied and sent to me.

Mark L. Bristol's rambling diary and correspondence (Library of Congress) have provided information on mission-government interaction for the years from 1919 to 1926.

Since James Bryce did not usually keep copies of his own letters, I have received little help from his papers in the Bodleian Library at Oxford. Apparently he retained no record of his communications with Barton. See Dennis S. Porter, *Papers of James Bryce: Calendar of Papers Relating to the United States of America* (1959). There are several of Bryce's letters in the Barton MSS; the American Board Archives apparently contain all of Barton's messages from Boston to Bryce. I have seen microfilm of Bryce's correspondence to Nicholas Murray Butler, A. Lawrence Lowell, Edward M. House, and George R. Montgomery, but not reproductions of material in six boxes on Armenia in the Bryce records (the boxes have not been catalogued or filmed).

The Charles R. Crane documents, in the New York City offices of the American Universities Field Staff and the Institute of Current World Affairs, include typewritten copies of his letters. Crane's correspondence has illuminated Near East Relief's origins, the King-Crane Commission, and the relation of Crane to President Wilson, Colonel House, Cleveland H. Dodge, and Henry Morgenthau, Sr.

Missionary physician Edward M. Dodd's typewritten memoir, "Near East Vortex," presents a nonpietistic view of the frightful events in northwest Persia from 1917 to 1919. This memoir of 107 pages, written in the 1930s and deposited in the Presbyterian Historical Society, is full of wit and humanity; Dodd constructed it largely from his correspondence.

Indispensable manuscripts showing how the missionaries affected the White House are the Cleveland H. Dodge–Woodrow Wilson letters. There are one hundred twenty letters by Wilson and five by Dodge in the Dodge papers

(Princeton University Library). As for the Wilson MSS (Library of Congress), I have sought to discover all exchanges between the two men during the period from 1914 to 1920 (amounting to around fifty). To help ferret out this correspondence, people microfilming the Wilson materials (under Arthur S. Link's direction) generously let me consult their index. Many more Dodge letters are in the Wilson MSS than in the Dodge collection. (According to one of Dodge's children, Dodge kept so few of his own records that after his death his family decided there were not enough to prepare a biography.)

The diary of missionary-educator Edgar J. Fisher, in the Ohio State University Library, covers several decades after the year 1899; I have read it for 1919 and 1920. Fisher had doctoral work in history, and was a penetrating observer of public matters. His outlook on Protestant diplomacy from beneath the top strata of mission-relief leaders has been revealing, both for events in Turkey and in the United States.

It is unfortunate that the manuscripts of Robert College's president, Caleb F. Gates, have a breach at the time of the First World War and the peace settlement (I have been able to find only two Gates letters for this period). These materials — a private collection — include hundreds of items during the years between 1910 and 1915 and the two decades or so after 1921. Of most assistance has been Gates' correspondence with his family (1895, 1921–1922), his son's diary (1918–1919), and his wife's diary (1914–1919), which she reportedly buried in a garden to preserve it from Turkish confiscation.

The James G. Harbord papers (Library of Congress) include only a few pieces of import for the present volume. Yet these few have been crucial for identifying mission-relief strength on the beginnings of the Haskell and Harbord missions.

At the Ohio Historical Society in Columbus I have researched the Warren G. Harding MSS for the transition from Wilsonianism to isolationism and for the Lausanne Conference. The records on Lausanne clearly set forth the Armenianism in American policy.

Among the Edward M. House papers in the Yale University Library are the political recommendations of the Persian Commission. Letters and cables between Barton and House (among other materials) and comments in House's typewritten, doublespaced diary have pointed out much about the political efforts of the missionaries; the House MSS have given fundamental evidence on the Protestants' role in Turkish reconstruction.

In the University of Chicago Library, amid the documents of Harry Pratt Judson (part of the Presidents' Papers), are four manila folders on the Persian Commission. At one point in 1919 Judson decided to dispose of these records; fortunately, he changed his mind. Without the Judson MSS it would have been almost impossible to construct the story of the relief expedition to Persia.

The Henry Churchill King papers at the Oberlin College Library have aided understanding of the Barton-King friendship. There is a lacuna at the point of the King-Crane Commission.

354

To get insight to the personal and administrative difficulties of Wilson, I have read the diary of Robert Lansing in the Library of Congress.

For the part taken by missionaries during the Paris Peace Conference and for the King-Crane Commission, the Albert H. Lybyer diary and correspondence (University of Illinois Library) have been vital.

The president of International College, Alexander MacLachlan, completed an unpublished memoir in 1938 — "A Potpourri of Sidelights and Shadows from Turkey." This document of over a hundred pages, a mimeographed private holding, is primarily an edition of reflections written during the sixteen years after 1922; it has been indispensable for the history of International College and for the Smyrna incidents of 1919 and 1922.

Sidney E. Mezes' correspondence in the Columbia University Library has indicated effects of Dodge, Barton, and other individuals in the Protestant lobby upon The Inquiry and the American Commission to Negotiate Peace.

I have used the Henry Morgenthau, Sr., papers in the Library of Congress (particularly the diary) about the relation of missionaries to public affairs during the Armenian massacres of 1915 and during the Peace Conference. There are important data herein.

A member of William W. Peet's family has written to me that the diary and papers of Peet are unavailable, or lost.

The diary of American Board missionary Charles Trowbridge Riggs, for the years 1918 through 1922, has provided the same kind of perspective as the diary of Edgar Fisher. The Riggs journal, in the possession of his family, has shown many indirect ways in which religious leaders sought to promote their postwar goals. It also has helped me grasp the climate of day-to-day missionary living.

In the William Walker Rockwell materials (Missionary Research Library, New York City) there is a file of Near East Relief propaganda for the organization's early years.

The Robert E. Speer MSS at the Speer Memorial Library in Princeton, New Jersey, seemingly include nothing relevant to the present book. This absence is regrettable, since Speer was the chief Presbyterian figure in American relations with the Near East.

Walter George Smith kept an account of his trip with the Barton Relief Commission — "Journal of a Journey to the Near East." A typewritten 78-page copy of the "Journal" has been made available to me by a colleague who plans to publish a biography of Smith. Smith's diary demonstrates how American missionary diplomacy influenced the British government during 1919.

The Wilson MSS contain interchanges of letters between the President and Crane, Morgenthau, and Dodge — in Series 2, 4, and 5 for the period 1914–1920. Container 498 in Series 4 concerns Armenia.

I have benefited from several other manuscript sources: Ray Stannard Baker MSS (Princeton University Library), George Louis Beer Diary (Library of Congress), Moreton Frewen MSS (Library of Congress), Frank L. Polk MSS

(Yale University Library), and John Sharp Williams MSS (Library of Congress).

Correspondence
Participants in events related in this book have written to me. Correspondents whose letters have been cited in the notes are Bayard Dodge, Cleveland E. Dodge, Luther Fowle, and Harold Hoskins.

INTERVIEWS
It has aided me to talk with a number of participants. Several of these individuals have directly contributed to this study: Harold B. Allen (Near East Foundation), Floyd H. Black (formerly, president of the American College in Sofia and of Robert College), Cleveland E. Dodge, Walter Rogers (associate of Charles Crane for decades).

PRINTED ARCHIVAL SOURCES
Documentary publications of both the United States Department of State and the British Foreign Office have set out aspects of the part taken by missionaries in the Ottoman peace. In the grand continuing series of the State Department, *Foreign Relations of the United States*, I have profited from regular volumes for the years 1918–1923 and special volumes for the Paris Peace Conference and for Secretary of State Lansing. In E. L. Woodward, Rohan Butler, and J. P. T. Bury, eds., *Documents on British Foreign Policy: 1919–1939* (30 vols.; London: H.M.S.O., 1946–1963), five volumes of the first series associate missionary pressure with British policy, particularly on the Armenian mandate question.

PERIODICALS AND NEWSPAPERS
Religious periodicals include the American Board's *Annual Report*, its monthly *Missionary Herald*, and the *Annual Report* of the Presbyterian Board. The Hartford (Conn.) Seminary Foundation's quarterly, *Muslim World* (formerly *Moslem World*), has many articles of interest.

The American offices of Robert College, the American University of Beirut, the Near East College Association, and other institutions begun by Protestants have files of newsletters, annual reports, catalogues.

In various repositories and collections – Missionary Research Library, Presbyterian Historical Society, and the Barton and Judson MSS – I have discovered many of the bulletins published by the American Committee for Armenian and Syrian Relief and its successor organizations (American Committee for Relief in the Near East, Near East Relief, Near East Foundation). During the years 1915–1917 intermittent bulletins usually were called *Latest News*; in 1918 and 1919 they came out each month and were entitled *News Bulletin*. The monthly continued in 1920 as *New Near East*. For the 1960s there is the Near East Foundation's *News* and its *Annual Report*.

Vital to tracing the propaganda effect of mission-relief interests during the period 1915–1923 have been the New York *Times, Independent,* and *Current History.* The New York *Times* carried full reports on relief interests and also articles by relief spokesmen. The editorial staff of the *Independent* had a close liaison with Barton and his colleagues. A debate in *Current History* in 1922 signalled the first large challenge to the hold of Armenianism on the American press.

A number of additional periodicals have been of assistance at various points, particularly the *American Historical Review, Congressional Record, Journal of American History,* and *Middle East Journal. Armenian Review* has proved the most productive Armenian-American periodical.

BIOGRAPHICAL MATERIALS

Two general works which provide vignettes on missionary personalities are David H. Finnie, *Pioneers East: The Early American Experience in the Middle East* (Cambridge, Mass.: Harvard University Press, 1967) and Fred Field Goodsell, *They Lived Their Faith: An Almanac of Faith, Hope and Love* (Boston: American Board of Commissioners for Foreign Missions, 1961). Finnie gives sketches of the first generation of American Board personnel; Goodsell (an American Board missionary to Turkey and executive successor to Barton) treats a dozen or more Board figures in the Near East, including Elias Riggs of the nineteenth century and Floyd Black of the twentieth.

The leading personality in the establishment of Near East Foundation's technical assistance approach is the subject of Sidney Gordon's *He Shot an Arrow: Barclay Acheson and the Concept of Helping People to Help Themselves* (New York: Near East Foundation, n.d.).

Lord Kinross (John Patrick), *Ataturk: A Biography of Mustafa Kemal, Father of Modern Turkey* (New York: Morrow, 1965) notes the place of Crane, Halidé Edib, and James Harbord in consideration of an American mandate by Turkish nationalists.

There is no biography of James L. Barton. His unpublished papers include short essays on missionary diplomacy in Syria and Persia; his long "Autobiography" stresses religion and education more than politics. Barton's writings exhibit his theories, his journalistic and organizational skills, his optimism and aggressiveness: *The Missionary and His Critics* (New York: Revell, 1906); a textbook on missions, *The Unfinished Task of the Christian Church: Introductory Studies in the Problem of the World's Evangelization* (New York: Layman's Missionary Movement, 1908); a survey of the American Board in the Near East, *Daybreak in Turkey* (Boston: Pilgrim Press, 1908); a worldwide overview, *Educational Missions* (New York: Student Volunteer Movement, 1917); a call for a large-scale united drive by Christians to evangelize Muslims, *The Christian Approach to Islam* (Boston: Pilgrim Press, 1918); the booklets, *Survey of the Fields: 1920–1921* (Boston: Congregational House, 1921) and *Changing Turkey: Political and Religious Revolution* (Boston:

American Board of Commissioners for Foreign Missions, Envelope Series, 1926); *Story of Near East Relief (1915–1930): An Interpretation* (New York: Macmillan, 1930). Barton wrote the introduction in Bertha S. Papazian, *The Tragedy of Armenia: A Brief Study and Interpretation* (Boston: Pilgrim Press, 1918) and "Shall the Land Be Healed?" in William H. Hall, *The Near East: Crossroads of the World* (New York: Presbyterian Board of Foreign Missions, 1920). There is a spate of articles by Barton: "Survey of the Fields: 1917–1918," *Missionary Herald*, 114 (November 1918), 513–524; an application of Christian internationalism, "The War and the Mohammedan World," *Biblical Review* (January 1919), 28–46; suggestions that the United States take responsibility for Asia Minor, "Today in Turkey," *Missionary Herald*, 115 (June 1919), 231–235, and "Turkey the Morning After," *Missionary Herald*, 115 (August 1919), 331–333; a challenge to the United States government to protect missions, "American Interests and Rights in the Near East," *Homiletic Review*, 85 (January 1923), 3–10; views on Church-State relations, "Some Missionary Activities in Relation to Governments," *International Review of Missions*, 13 (1924), 340–359; "The Near East Relief: A Moral Force," *International Review of Missions*, 18 (1929), 495–502; the missionary tradition, "American Educational and Philanthropic Interests in the Near East," *Moslem World*, 23 (April 1933), 121–136.

For Howard S. Bliss, see his obituary in the *News Letter of Robert College and the Syrian Protestant College* (June 1920), located in the American University of Beirut Library, and – a sort of autobiography – "The Modern Missionary," *Atlantic Monthly*, 125 (May 1920), 664–675.

Concerning Mark L. Bristol there is Peter M. Buzanski's "Admiral Mark L. Bristol and Turkish-American Relations: 1919–1922" (unpublished Ph.D. thesis, University of California, 1960), and Thomas A. Bryson's "Mark Lambert Bristol, U.S. Navy, Admiral-Diplomat: His Influence on the Armenian Mandate Question, 1919–1920," *Armenian Review*, 21 (Winter 1968), 3–22.

H. A. L. Fisher, *James Bryce (Viscount Bryce of Dechmont, O.M.)* (2 vols.; New York: Macmillan, 1927) inspects Bryce's Armenophile activities and quotes letters which illustrate his promotion of a United States mandate for Armenia. Bryce recorded the beginnings of his fascination with Armenia in his travel journal, *Transcaucasia and Ararat: Being Notes of a Vacation Tour in the Autumn of 1876* (London: Macmillan, 1877).

On William E. Borah's opposition to the Versailles Treaty and to an American duty in the Ottoman Empire, Claudius O. Johnson, *Borah of Idaho* (New York: Longmans, 1936), and Marian C. McKenna, *Borah* (Ann Arbor: University of Michigan Press, 1961), have been useful.

Richard W. Child, in *A Diplomat Looks at Europe* (New York: Duffield, 1925), makes scornful comments about missionaries and their policies at the Lausanne Conference.

The cover article of *Time*, March 9, 1931, is on Charles R. Crane. Leo J. Bocage, "The Public Career of Charles R. Crane" (unpublished Ph.D. thesis,

Fordham University, 1962), helps set Crane's Near East concerns within his Chicago experiences and his interests in Russia, Czechoslovakia, and China.

Materials on Cleveland H. Dodge, outside of manuscript collections, are meager. The first scholarly treatment of Dodge has been Robert L. Daniel, "The Friendship of Woodrow Wilson and Cleveland H. Dodge," *Mid-America*, 43 (July 1961), 182–196. Ray Stannard Baker, *Woodrow Wilson: Life and Letters* (8 vols.; New York: Doubleday, 1927–1939) quotes frequently from Dodge's correspondence. A brief article on contributions by the industrialist to Near East Relief is Charles W. Vickrey, "Dodge Would Not Keep 'Blood Money,'" *Outlook*, 143 (May–August 1926), 566–567. Frank Harris Blighton wrote a muckraking attack on Dodge, based on circumstantial evidence, in the booklet, *Woodrow Wilson and Co.* (New York: Fox Printing House, 1916). There are references to Dodge in the general literature on the Wilson years. Also, see my article, "Cleveland H. Dodge, Woodrow Wilson, and the Near East," *Journal of Presbyterian History*, 48 (Winter 1970), 249–264.

Members of the mission-relief lobby were often part of the internationalist movement in the United States, as demonstrated in the book on Near East Relief's board secretary by Charles H. Levermore, *Samuel Train Dutton: A Biography* (New York: Macmillan, 1922).

In *The Turkish Ordeal* (New York: Century, 1928), Halidé Edib discussed her connections with missionary educators, the Wilsonian League, the King-Crane Commission, and the rise of Kemalism.

Physician Mabel E. Elliot worked with Near East Relief at Marash, Ismit, and Erivan. A dramatic feature of her book, *Beginning Again at Ararat* (New York: Revell, 1924), is the escape of Armenians from Kemalists at Marash in February 1920.

A substitute for the hiatus in the Gates MSS from 1915 to 1921 is the memoir of Caleb F. Gates, *Not to Me Only* (Princeton, N.J.: Princeton University Press, 1940), which devotes considerable attention to philanthropic and political affairs of missionaries during the First World War and its aftermath.

There is almost no mention of the American Committee for the Independence of Armenia in *My First Eighty-Three Years in America: The Memoirs of James W. Gerard* (Garden City, N.Y.: Doubleday, 1951).

I have used Joseph C. Grew, *Turbulent Era: A Diplomatic Record of Forty Years, 1904–1945*, ed. by Walter Johnson (2 vols.; Boston: Houghton Mifflin, 1952), for the Paris Peace Conference and the Lausanne Conference. In addition, there is Waldo H. Heinrichs, Jr., *American Ambassador: Joseph C. Grew and the Development of the United States Diplomatic Tradition* (Boston: Little, Brown, 1966).

James G. Harbord's published lectures, *America in the World War* (Boston: Houghton Mifflin, 1933), state nothing on his Near East mission. For that mission there is his three-part article, "Investigating Turkey and Transcaucasia," *World's Work*, 40 (May–July 1920), 35–47, 176–193, 271–280, which details his close relation to the Protestant religionists.

Probably the best biographical work on the Armenian massacres, covering the holocausts of both the 1890s and the 1910s, is the graphic diary of an evangelical Armenian clergyman, Abraham H. Hartunian, *Neither to Laugh nor to Weep: A Memoir of the Armenian Genocide* (Boston: Beacon Press, 1968).

During the Progressive period no individual labored more continuously or energetically for some form of world federation than did Hamilton Holt. This thesis appears in Warren F. Kuehl, *Hamilton Holt: Journalist, Internationalist, Educator* (Gainesville: University of Florida Press, 1960). Through Holt's article, "Armenia and America," *Independent*, 102 (1920), 205–208, and other sources, I have been able to link Holt's promotion of the league idea to his collaboration with Barton-Dodge forces.

The publications of Herbert Hoover show his involvement with Near East Relief and the Armenian policy of the Wilson administration: *The Memoirs of Herbert Hoover* (3 vols.; New York: Macmillan, 1951); *The Ordeal of Woodrow Wilson* (New York: McGraw-Hill, 1958); *An American Epic* (4 vols.; Chicago: Regnery, 1959–1964).

As for Edward M. House, there are interesting perceptions in Alexander L. and Juliette L. George, *Woodrow Wilson and Colonel House: A Personality Study* (New York: Day, 1956). Charles Seymour, ed., *The Intimate Papers of Colonel House* (4 vols.; Boston: Houghton Mifflin, 1926–1928), contains almost none of the abundant evidence in the House MSS on missionary diplomacy.

An explanation for the abrupt end of the Barton Inquiry is in Frederic C. Howe, *The Confessions of a Reformer* (New York: Scribners, 1925).

When Donald M. Love wrote *Henry Churchill King of Oberlin* (New Haven, Conn.: Yale University Press, 1956), he did not have access to the part of the King papers dealing with the King-Crane Commission – papers which Harry N. Howard did use in *The King-Crane Commission: An American Inquiry in the Middle East* (Beirut: Khayats, 1963). King's approach to Christianity and public affairs at the time of his service in the eastern Mediterranean is in the booklet *For a New America in a New World* (Paris: Young Men's Christian Association, 1919).

Missionary Grace H. Knapp's recollection of the Armenian deportation of 1915 can be found in two works: *The Mission at Van: In Turkey in War Time* (n.p.: privately printed, 1916) and *The Tragedy of Bitlis* (New York: Revell, 1919).

There is less illumination on Protestant designs for the Near East in David Lloyd George, *Memoirs of the Peace Conference* (2 vols.; New Haven, Conn.: Yale University Press, 1929) than in *British Documents*.

On the role of Henry Cabot Lodge in the revival of isolationism and in Armenian matters, I have used John A. Garraty, *Henry Cabot Lodge: A Biography* (New York: Knopf, 1953), and the Lodge-White letters in Allan Nevins, *Henry White: Thirty Years of American Diplomacy* (New York: Harper, 1930).

A description of missions at their finest is contained in Constance E. Padwick's portrayal of Lyman MacCallum (director of the American Bible Society in Turkey), *Call to Istanbul* (London: Longmans, 1958).

Henry Morgenthau, *Ambassador Morgenthau's Story* (New York: Doubleday, 1918), devotes several chapters to the Young Turk assault on the Armenians. In his *All in a Lifetime* (New York: Doubleday, 1922) Morgenthau remarks on the American missionaries. There is need for a scholarly treatment of Morgenthau.

The study *John R. Mott: World Citizen* (New York: Harper, 1934) by Basil Mathews points out ties between this missionary statesman and Dodge. See also John R. Mott, ed., *Addresses and Papers of John R. Mott* (6 vols.; New York: Association Press, 1947).

In *Silver Chimes in Syria: Glimpses of a Missionary's Experiences* (Philadelphia: Westminster Press, 1914), Presbyterian emissary William S. Nelson illustrated both his humanitarianism and his paternalism.

A propagandistic and personal résumé of Dashnak operations during the First World War appears in the booklet by Garegin Pasdermadjian, *Why Armenia Should be Free* (Boston: Hairenik Association, 1918).

Mary Mills Patrick's two works — *Under Five Sultans* (New York: Century, 1929) and *A Bosporus Adventure: Istanbul (Constantinople) Woman's College, 1871–1924* (Palo Alto, Calif.: Stanford University Press, 1934) — and Hester Donaldson Jenkins' *An Educational Ambassador to the Near East: The Story of Mary Mills Patrick and an American College in the Orient* (New York: Revell, 1925) are helpful for the history of the Woman's College but not American diplomacy during the collapse of the Ottoman Empire. Miss Patrick lobbied for postwar goals, as noted by her article "Fourteen Reasons for an American Mandatory over Turkey," *Outlook*, 123 (September 1919), 32–33.

No Less Honor: The Biography of William Wheelock Peet (n.p.: privately printed, 1939), written by Peet's daughter, Louise Jenison Peet, includes little of this American Board figure's political activities.

Theodore Roosevelt had commitments to American missions in Turkey. These commitments and his attitudes and decisions concerning Armenia, the Eastern Question, and United States intervention in Turkey appear in Henry Cabot Lodge, ed., *Selections from the Correspondence of Theodore Roosevelt and Henry Cabot Lodge: 1884–1918* (2 vols.; New York: Scribners, 1925); Elting E. Morison, ed., *The Letters of Theodore Roosevelt* (8 vols.; Cambridge, Mass.: Harvard University Press, 1951–1954); and Theodore Roosevelt, *Fear God and Take Your Own Part* (New York: Doran, 1916).

The memoir of Lynn A. Scipio (Robert College's dean of the engineering school), *My Thirty Years in Turkey* (Rindge, N.H.: Richard R. Smith, 1955), is a tribute to Christianity and education. This work deals with mission problems during the First World War and the adjustment of Robert College to Turkish nationalism.

I have drawn on Mary Lewis Shedd, *The Measure of a Man: The Life of*

William Ambrose Shedd, Missionary to Persia (New York: Doran, 1922), for events in Urmia from 1915 to 1918.

A vivid telling of the missionary turmoil at Van during 1915 is in Clarence D. Ussher's *An American Physician in Turkey: A Narrative of Adventures in Peace and in War* (Boston: Houghton Mifflin, 1917).

William Reginald Wheeler, *A Man Sent from God: A Biography of Robert E. Speer* (New York: Revell, 1956), does not include Speer's involvement in Nestorian nationalism. Political concerns are in Robert E. Speer and Russell Carter, *Report on India and Persia of the Deputation Sent by the Board of Foreign Missions of the Presbyterian Church in the U.S.A. to Visit These Fields in 1921–22* (New York: Presbyterian Board of Foreign Missions, 1922). Speer's unwillingness to be an enthusiastic supporter of American intervention in the First World War appears in John F. Piper, Jr., "Robert E. Speer: Christian Statesman in War and Peace," *Journal of Presbyterian History,* 47 (September 1969), 201–225.

The place of an American Board school in the Armenian tangle, from 1887 to 1921, is presented in George E. White, *Adventuring with Anatolia College* (Grinnell, Ia.: Herald-Register Publishing Company, 1940).

Talcott Williams, journalist and missionary son, was prominent as an internationalist and publicist for Protestant goals in the Near East. See his "America's Duty in Turkey," *Independent,* 99 (1919), 215–216; "The Disposition of the Turkish Empire," *Annals of the American Academy of Political and Social Science,* 84 (July 1919), 41–50; *Turkey, A World Problem of Today* (Garden City, N.Y.: Doubleday, 1921).

William Yale's minority opinion within the King-Crane Commission is stated in his "An Analysis of the Syrian-Palestine Situation in 1919: The American Point of View" (unpublished M.A. thesis, University of New Hampshire, 1928). Echoes of this thesis are in his *The Near East: A Modern History* (Ann Arbor: University of Michigan Press, 1958).

There are valuable biographical materials for the period before the First World War: Daniel Bliss, *The Reminiscences of Daniel Bliss,* ed. by Frederick J. Bliss (New York: Revell, 1920); Robert E. Speer, *"The Hakim Sahib": The Foreign Doctor, A Biography of Joseph Plumb Cochran, M.D., of Persia* (New York: Revell, 1911); Alvan Bond, *Memoir of the Rev. Pliny Fisk, A.M., Late Missionary to Palestine* (Boston: Crocker & Brewster, 1828); E. D. G. Prime, *Forty Years in the Turkish Empire; or, Memoirs of Rev. William Goodell* (New York: Robert Carter, 1876); Lloyd C. Griscom, *Diplomatically Speaking* (New York: Literary Guild of America, 1940); Cyrus Hamlin, *My Life and Times* (2nd ed.; Boston: Congregational Sunday School and Publishing Society, 1893); Cyrus Hamlin, "America's Duty to Americans in Turkey," *North American Review,* 163 (September 1896), 276–281; Henry Harris Jessup, *Fifty-Three Years in Syria* (2 vols.; Chicago: Revell, 1910); James G. Mandalian, tr. and ed., *Armenian Freedom Fighters: The Memoirs of Rouben der Minasian [1903 to 1908]* (Boston: Hairenik Association, 1963); Daniel O. Morton, ed., *Memoir of Rev. Levi Parsons: First Missionary to Palestine from the United States* (2nd ed.; Burlington, Vt.: C. Goodrich, 1830); Eli Smith, *Researches of the Rev. E. Smith and Rev. H. G. O. Dwight in Armenia* (2 vols.; Boston: Crocker & Brewster, 1833); Oscar S. Straus, *Under Four Administrations: From Cleveland to Taft* (Boston: Houghton Mifflin, 1922); Oscar S. Straus, "Americans in Turkey: Their Notable Work for Education," *Review of Reviews*, 26 (December 1914), 710–713; George Washburn, *Fifty Years in Constantinople and Recollections of Robert College* (2nd ed.; Boston: Houghton Mifflin, 1911).

GENERAL AND SPECIAL WORKS

Two broad surveys of the Near East are Sydney Nettleton Fisher, *The Middle East: A History* (New York: Knopf, 1959), and Philip K. Hitti, *The Near East in History* (Princeton, N.J.: Van Nostrand, 1961).

On Ottoman and Turkish history in general see Kamel S. Abu Jaber, "The Millet System in the Nineteenth-Century Ottoman Empire," *Muslim World*, 57 (July 1967), 212–223; Bernard Lewis, *The Emergence of Modern Turkey* (London: Oxford University Press, 1961); Elaine Smith, *Turkey: Origins of the Kemalist Movement and the Government of the Grand National Assembly (1919–1923)* (Washington, D.C.: Judd & Detweiler, 1959); Lord Kinross (John Patrick), *Ataturk: A Biography of Mustafa Kemal, Father of Modern Turkey* (New York: Morrow, 1965); Feroz Ahmad, *The Young Turks: The Committee of Union and Progress in Turkish Politics, 1908–1914* (London: Oxford University Press, 1969); Roderic H. Davison, *Turkey* (Englewood Cliffs, N.J.: Prentice-Hall, 1968).

The demise of the Ottoman Empire, from both Western and Near East views, is presented in Harry N. Howard, *The Partition of Turkey: A Diplomatic History, 1913–1923* (Norman: University of Oklahoma Press, 1931); Henry H. Cumming, *Franco-British Rivalry in the Post-War Near East: The Decline of French Influence* (New York: Oxford University Press, 1938); Winston S. Churchill, *The Aftermath: Being a Sequel to the World Crisis* (London: Macmillan, 1941); Firuz Kazemzadeh, *The Struggle for Transcaucasia (1917–1921)* (New York: Philosophical Library, 1951); Roderic H. Davison, "Turkish Diplomacy from Mudros to Lausanne," in Gordon A. Craig and Felix Gilbert, eds., *The Diplomats: 1919–1939* (Princeton, N.J.: Princeton University Press, 1953); Elie Kedourie, *England and the Middle East: The Destruction of the Ottoman Empire, 1914–21* (London: Bowes & Bowes, 1956); Elizabeth Monroe, *Britain's Moment in the Middle East: 1914–1956* (Baltimore: Johns Hopkins Press, 1963); Howard M. Sachar, *The Emergence of the Middle East: 1914–1924* (New York: Knopf, 1969).

John Joseph, a Nestorian, has written a careful treatment of the Christian minority of northwestern Persia and eastern Turkey: *The Nestorians and their Muslim Neighbors: A Study of Western Influence on Their Relations* (Princeton, N.J.: Princeton University Press, 1961).

For the rise of Arab nationalism there is George Antonius' classic, *The Arab*

PROTESTANT DIPLOMACY AND THE NEAR EAST

Awakening: The Story of the Arab National Movement (Philadelphia: Lippincott, 1939); an article which considers missionary protégé Butrus al-Bustani — Spencer Lavan, "Four Christian Arab Nationalists: A Comparative Study," *Muslim World*, 57 (April 1967), 114–125; and the publication by Zeine N. Zeine, *The Struggle for Arab Independence: Western Diplomacy and the Rise and Fall of Faisal's Kingdom in Syria* (Beirut: Khayats, 1960).

The Armenian question has an explanation from an ideological and class-conflict basis in Sarkis Atamian, *The Armenian Community* (New York: Philosophical Library, 1955). Avedis K. Sanjian, *The Armenian Communities in Syria under Ottoman Dominion* (Cambridge, Mass.: Harvard University Press, 1965), represents a fine effort to appraise Armenian affairs in a scholarly way. Leon Arpee, *A History of Armenian Christianity from the Beginning to Our Own Time* (New York: Armenian Missionary Association, 1946), gives a Protestant Armenian perspective. Other sources are Simon Vratzian, *Armenia and the Armenian Question* (Boston: Hairenik Association, 1943), and Vahan M. Kurkjian, *A History of Armenia* (New York: Armenian General Benevolent Union of America, 1959).

Dealing specifically with the Armenian independence movement are the following: the first comprehensive work in English on the revolutionary groups, Louise Nalbandian, *The Armenian Revolutionary Movement: The Development of Armenian Political Parties through the Nineteenth Century* (Berkeley: University of California Press, 1963); a study of the Erivan Republic's origins, Richard G. Hovannisian, *Armenia on the Road to Independence: 1918* (Berkeley: University of California Press, 1967); a work on the period from 1903 to 1908, James G. Mandalian, tr. and ed., *Armenian Freedom Fighters: The Memoirs of Rouben der Minasian* (Boston: Hairenik Association, 1963); a booklet, James Bryce, *The Future of Armenia* (London: National Press Agency, 1918); W. D. P. Bliss, "Armenia's Struggle for Independence," *Current History*, 11 (October 1919–March 1920), 138–144; Onig Mekhitarian, "The Defense of Van (Part Five)," *Armenian Review*, 2 (Spring 1949), 131–141; Vahan Cardashian, "The Armenian Revolutionary Federation," *Armenian Review*, 2 (Winter 1949–1950), 65–69; Simon Vratzian, "The Armenian Revolution and the Armenian Revolutionary Federation," *Armenian Review*, 3 (Autumn & Winter 1950–1951), 3–31, 58–66.

American religionists and their friends published pieces on the Armenian massacres (see below). Sanjian, *The Armenian Communities in Syria under Ottoman Dominion*, and other titles already mentioned include comment on the episodes of 1894 to 1896, of 1909, and of the First World War. For the war, the most thorough coverage is in James Bryce (with Arnold J. Toynbee), ed., *The Treatment of Armenians in the Ottoman Empire, 1915–16; Documents Presented to Viscount Grey of Fallodon, Secretary of State for Foreign Affairs* (London: Joseph Causton, 1916). From German sources there is Ulrich Trumpener, *Germany and the Ottoman Empire: 1914–1918* (Princeton, N.J.: Princeton University Press, 1968). Other evidence is in Morgenthau, *Ambassador Morgenthau's Story*; Arnold J. Toynbee's two short books, *Ar-*

menian Atrocities: The Murder of a Nation (London: Hodder & Stoughton, 1915) and *"The Murderous Tyranny of the Turks"* (London: Hodder & Stoughton, 1917); a brief section in Herbert Hoover, *An American Epic* (4 vols.; Chicago: Regnery, 1959–1964), II; and Marjorie Housepian, "The Unremembered Genocide," *Ararat*, 8 (Winter 1967), 2–11. Abraham H. Hartunian, *Neither to Laugh nor to Weep: A Memoir of the Armenian Genocide* (Boston: Beacon Press, 1968), and Garegin Pasdermadjian, *Why Armenia Should Be Free* (Boston: Hairenik Association, 1918), are striking personal recollections. A Turkish apology is Ahmed Djemal Pasha's *Memories of a Turkish Statesman: 1913–1919* (New York: Doran, 1922). Novelist Franz Werfel memorialized an Armenian group in *The Forty Days of Musa Dagh* (New York: Viking Press, 1934).

For Christianity, Islam, and Judaism in the eastern Mediterranean generally, there is A. J. Arberry, ed., *Religion in the Middle East: Three Religions in Concord and Conflict* (2 vols.; Cambridge: Cambridge University Press, 1969). Probably the best brief survey of American missions is the chapter by Jean-Michel Hornus, "The Lutheran and Reformed Churches," I, 534–569. Of special interest are the following chapters: Edward Every, "The Assyrians," I, 521–533; K. V. Sarkissian, "The Armenian Church," I, 482–520; Charles S. Malik, "The Orthodox Church," I, 297–346.

As to religion in the United States, I have emphasized the overlap of Christianity and culture. Franklin Hamlin Littell, *From State Church to Pluralism: A Protestant Interpretation of Religion in American History* (Chicago: Aldine, 1962), and Leo Pfeffer, *Church, State and Freedom* (rev. ed.; Boston: Beacon Press, 1967), remark on this subject.

One of my purposes has been to regard the Protestant agents to the Near East interculturally, an approach advocated by John K. Fairbank in his December 1968 presidential address at the American Historical Association annual meeting: "Assignment for the '70's," *American Historical Review*, 74 (February 1969), 861–879. Several studies on missions and society have facilitated this approach: H. Richard Niebuhr, *Christ and Culture* (New York: Harper, 1951); Eugene A. Nida, *Message and Mission: The Communication of the Christian Faith* (New York: Harper, 1960); Alan Geyer, *Piety and Politics: American Protestantism in the World Arena* (Richmond, Va.: John Knox Press, 1963); Norman Goodall, *Christian Missions and Social Ferment* (London: Epworth, 1964); Stephen Neill, *Colonialism and Christian Missions* (New York: McGraw-Hill, 1966); "Missionary Temptations," *Nation*, 61 (November 21, 1895), 360–361; Kenneth Scott Latourette, "Colonialism and Missions: Progressive Separation," *Journal of Church and State*, 7 (Autumn 1965), 330–349; John White, "Missions and Proselytism," *His*, 28 (November 1967), 10–14.

On American missions there is Kenneth Scott Latourette, *Missions and the American Mind* (Indianapolis: National Foundation Press, 1949); the extraordinary synthesis which has material on missions in the United States, by the same author, *Christianity in a Revolutionary Age: A History of Christiani-*

ty in the Nineteenth and Twentieth Centuries (5 vols.; New York: Harper, 1958–1962); Clifton E. Olmstead, *History of Religion in the United States* (Englewood Cliffs, N.J.: Prentice-Hall, 1960); R. Pierce Beaver, "North American Thought on the Fundamental Principles of Missions during the Twentieth Century," *Church History*, 21 (1952), 345–364; and three books mentioned earlier — Barton's *The Unfinished Task of the Christian Church* and *Educational Missions* and Mathews' *John R. Mott.*

There are special works on American missions. Clifton Jackson Phillips, *Protestant America and the Pagan World: The First Half Century of the American Board of Commissioners for Foreign Missions, 1810–1860* (Cambridge, Mass.: East Asian Research Center of Harvard University, 1969), has excellent chapters about the missionary view of foreign cultures before the Civil War. Valentin H. Rabe, "The American Protestant Foreign Mission Movement: 1880–1920," a Ph.D. thesis at Harvard (1965) to appear in print in revised form, looks at the *Weltanschauung* of missionary agencies in relation to United States expansionism. The Ph.D. thesis by Donald Kenneth Gorrell, "American Churches and American Territorial Expansion: 1830–1850" (Western Reserve University, 1960), investigates the influence of churchmen and missionaries in United States expansion in Oregon, Texas, and California.

Accounts of the American Board, in addition to the one just noted by Clifton Phillips, are William E. Strong, *The Story of the American Board: An Account of the First Hundred Years of the American Board of Commissioners for Foreign Missions* (Boston: Pilgrim Press, 1910), and books by Fred Field Goodsell: *You Shall Be My Witnesses* (Boston: American Board of Commissioners for Foreign Missions, 1959) and *They Lived Their Faith: An Almanac of Faith, Hope and Love* (Boston: American Board of Commissioners for Foreign Missions, 1961). For the Presbyterian Board, there is Arthur Judson Brown, *One Hundred Years: A History of the Foreign Missionary Work of the Presbyterian Church in the U.S.A.* (New York: Revell, 1937). The author of each of these surveys is a missionary official.

Until the twentieth century, missionaries and other private interests set the pace in philanthropy and technical assistance overseas. This interpretation is developed in Merle Curti, *American Philanthropy Abroad: A History* (New Brunswick, N.J.: Rutgers University Press, 1963), and Merle Curti and Kendall Birr, *Prelude to Point Four: American Technical Missions Overseas, 1838–1938* (Madison: University of Wisconsin Press, 1954).

Protestant morality was of large consequence in the Progressive Era. Reform programs received much of their impulse from the Social Gospel movement, for which see Charles Howard Hopkins, *The Rise of the Social Gospel in American Protestantism: 1865–1915* (New Haven, Conn.: Yale University Press, 1940). Ray H. Abrams, *Preachers Present Arms* (New York: Round Table Press, 1933), shows that clergymen constituted a basic element in the martial spirit of the First World War. A creative analysis, John Edwin Smylie, "Protestant Clergymen and America's World Role: 1865–1900, A Study of Christianity, Nationality, and International Relations" (unpublished Th.D.

thesis, Princeton Theological Seminary, 1959), demonstrates that many assumptions and aims of missionary diplomacy during the early twentieth century came out of the churches. James L. Lancaster showed in his article, "The Protestant Churches and the Fight for Ratification of the Versailles Treaty," *Public Opinion Quarterly*, 31 (Winter 1967–1968), 597–619, that Christian internationalist spokesmen, led by the National Committee on the Churches and the Moral Aims of the War (which included the League to Enforce Peace), were a basic force for United States acceptance of the Versailles Treaty. Ruhl J. Bartlett, *The League to Enforce Peace* (Chapel Hill: University of North Carolina Press, 1944), and Warren F. Kuehl, *Seeking World Order: The United States and International Organization to 1920* (Nashville, Tenn.: Vanderbilt University Press, 1969), have statements similar to Lancaster's. Religion is implicit in Robert E. Osgood, *Ideals and Self-Interest in America's Foreign Relations: The Great Transformation of the Twentieth Century* (Chicago: University of Chicago Press, 1953). The isolationist revival of 1919 and 1920 took part of its strength from Protestant nativism, a force studied in John Higham, *Strangers in the Land: Patterns of American Nativism, 1860–1925* (New Brunswick, N.J.: Rutgers University Press, 1955).

Turning to American relations with the Near East, I have employed three overviews: J. C. Hurewitz, *Middle East Dilemmas: The Background of United States Policy* (New York: Harper, 1953), William R. Polk, *The United States and the Arab World* (Cambridge, Mass.: Harvard University Press, 1965), and John S. Badeau, *The American Approach to the Arab World* (New York: Harper, 1968).

For the pre-1939 American involvement in the Near East there are several accounts. David H. Finnie, *Pioneers East: The Early American Experience in the Middle East* (Cambridge, Mass.: Harvard University Press, 1967), regards missionaries, merchants, travellers, explorers, and government officials in the period before 1850 through previously neglected printed materials; Finnie has a fine style, flavoring his narrative with personality idiosyncrasies. James A. Field, Jr., *America and the Mediterranean World: 1776–1882* (Princeton, N.J.: Princeton University Press, 1969), traces the outworking of Manifest Destiny ("new order") ideas in commercial, naval, evangelical, and political activities. Helpful for business, mission, and diplomatic enterprises is Leland James Gordon, *American Relations with Turkey: 1830–1930, An Economic Interpretation* (Philadelphia: University of Pennsylvania Press, 1932), and Sydney Nettleton Fisher, "Two Centuries of American Interest in Turkey," in David H. Pinkney and Theodore Ropp, eds., *A Festschrift for Frederick B. Artz* (Durham, N.C.: Duke University Press, 1964), 113–138. The best single analysis of the diversity of American interaction with the Near East before the Second World War is John A. DeNovo, *American Interests and Policies in the Middle East: 1900–1939* (Minneapolis: University of Minnesota Press, 1963). Its author brings together a remarkable number and variety of sources and topics.

367

For Persia, Abraham Yeselson published *United States–Persian Diplomatic Relations: 1883–1921* (New Brunswick, N.J.: Rutgers University Press, 1956), relying on the State Department Archives.

As to Palestine and the development of Zionism in the United States, Frank E. Manuel, *The Realities of American-Palestine Relations* (Washington, D.C.: Public Affairs Press, 1949), is a helpful work.

Among general materials on the Protestant emissaries to the Near East, probably the first book to consult is by a German church historian, Julius Richter, *A History of Protestant Missions in the Near East* (New York: Revell, 1910). There are articles by historians in the United States, such as Albert H. Lybyer, "America's Missionary Record in Turkey," *Current History*, 19 (February 1924), 802–810, and Edward M. Earle, "American Missions in the Near East," *Foreign Affairs*, 7 (April 1929), 398–417. Religionists have written broad treatments, including J. H. Greene, *Leavening of the Levant* (Boston: Pilgrim Press, 1916), and such titles noted above as Barton's *Daybreak in Turkey* and *The Christian Approach to Islam*. An unpublished Ph.D. thesis of considerable aid on evangelism among Armenians is Bernhard Nordmann, "American Missionary Work among Armenians in Turkey (1830–1923)" (University of Illinois, 1927). On Nordmann's subject, there is also Leon Arpee, *A Century of Armenian Protestantism: 1846–1946* (New York: Armenian Missionary Association of America, 1946), and George A. Paboojian, "A History of Missionary Activity among Armenians in the Near East since 1819" (unpublished B.S.T. thesis, Biblical Seminary in New York, 1957). A multilingual and multiarchival work, A. L. Tibawi, *American Interests in Syria: 1800–1901, A Study of Educational, Literary and Religious Work* (London: Oxford University Press, 1966), deals principally with the place of missionaries in the ecclesiastical competition among Syrian religious bodies and in Arab society in general. Tibawi's study supersedes Alan Ros Taylor, "The American Protestant Mission and the Awakening of Modern Syria: 1820–1870" (unpublished Ph.D. thesis, Georgetown University, 1957). For Persia, there is *A Century of Missions Work in Iran (Persia): 1834–1934* (Beirut: American Press, 1936).

Francis Boardman's *Institutions of Higher Learning in the Middle East* (Washington, D.C.: Middle East Institute, 1961) and Barton's *Educational Missions* and "American Educational and Philanthropic Interests in the Near East," *Moslem World*, 23 (April 1933), 121–136, are evidence on Protestant-initiated education in the eastern Mediterranean. For Robert College, there are the autobiographies of its leaders: Cyrus Hamlin, *My Life and Times*; George Washburn, *Fifty Years in Constantinople and Recollections of Robert College*; Caleb Gates, *Not to Me Only*; and Lynn A. Scipio, *My Thirty Years in Turkey*. For Constantinople Woman's College, see biographical materials on Mary Mills Patrick cited earlier. The history of the American University of Beirut (AUB), formerly the Syrian Protestant College, has been traced by three of its presidents: S.B.L. Penrose, *That They May Have Life: The Story of the American University of Beirut, 1866–1941* (New York: American University of Beirut, 1941); Bayard Dodge, *The American University of Beirut: A Brief History of the University and the Lands Which It Serves* (Beirut: Khayats, 1958); Daniel Bliss, *The Reminiscences of Daniel Bliss*, ed. by Frederick J. Bliss (New York: Revell, 1920). Articles on AUB include A. L. Tibawi, "The Genesis and Early History of the Syrian Protestant College," *Middle East Journal*, 21 (Winter & Spring 1967), 1–15, 199–212; Jack Long, "The First 100 Years of the AUB," *Lamp*, 47 (Winter 1965), 19–21; William M. Bickers, "American University of Beirut," *Journal of the American Medical Association*, 200 (June 26, 1967), 1162–1168. For a view of two other schools there is a memoir by George E. White, *Adventuring with Anatolia College* (Grinnell, Ia.: Herald-Register Publishing Company, 1940), and an article by George Miller, "Aleppo College: Failure or Fulfilment?" *Muslim World*, 57 (January 1967), 42–45. Two booklets put out by and about American Board educational efforts are Frank A. Stone, *Communities of Learning: People and Their Programs, the American Board Schools in Turkey from 1920 to 1970* (Istanbul: Redhouse Press, 1970), and Robert Avery, *Ink on Their Thumbs: The Antecedents of the Redhouse Press* (Istanbul: Redhouse Press, 1970).

The main stimulus for Protestant involvement in politics was the series of Armenian massacres from the 1890s through the 1920s. These woeful events drew many reports from missionaries and their associates: Edwin M. Bliss, *Turkey and the Armenian Atrocities* (Boston: H. L. Hastings, 1896); Rose Lambert, *Hadjin and the Armenian Massacres* (New York: Revell, 1911); James Bryce, ed., *The Treatment of Armenians in the Ottoman Empire*; Grace Knapp, *The Mission at Van* and *The Tragedy of Bitlis*; Clarence Ussher, *An American Physician in Turkey*; Morgenthau, *Ambassador Morgenthau's Story*; and Mabel Elliott, *Beginning Again at Ararat*. The American Committee for Armenian and Syrian Relief put out booklets on the massacres of 1915 and 1916. Publications edited by William Walker Rockwell in 1916 were *The Deportation of the Armenians* and *Ravished Armenia: The Story of Aurora Mardigonian*. There are copies of the Rockwell booklets in the Missionary Research Library.

Near East Relief was the second largest philanthropic movement in American history. For the First World War years, there are biographical works cited above and such booklets and pamphlets as William Walker Rockwell, ed., *The Pitiful Plight of the Assyrian (Nestorian) Christians in Persia and Kurdistan* (New York: American Committee for Armenian and Syrian Relief, 1916) and as *Practicing Bible Precepts in Bible Lands: Handbook for Busy Pastors, Campaign for $30,000,000, January 12th to 19th, 1919* (n.p.: American Committee for Relief in the Near East, 1919). Books which show Near East Relief's metamorphosis from an emergency-aid to a self-help agency are Paul Monroe, R. R. Reeder, and James I. Vance, *Reconstruction in the Near East* (New York: Near East Relief, 1924), and Frank A. Ross, C. Luther Fry, and Elbridge Sibley, *The Near East and American Philanthropy* (New York: Columbia University Press, 1929). James L. Barton, *Story of Near East Relief*

PROTESTANT DIPLOMACY AND THE NEAR EAST

(1915–1930): An Interpretation (New York: Macmillan, 1930), stresses humanitarianism, not politics. A thoroughly researched Ph.D. thesis is Robert L. Daniel, "From Relief to Technical Assistance in the Near East, A Case Study: Near East Relief and Near East Foundation" (University of Wisconsin, 1953). Daniel identified antecedents to twentieth-century relief in "American Influences in the Near East before 1861," *American Quarterly*, 16 (Spring 1964), 72–84. Daniel's principal contribution is *American Philanthropy in the Near East: 1820–1960* (Athens: Ohio University Press, 1970). Curti, *American Philanthropy Abroad*, and Curti and Birr, *Prelude to Point Four*, already mentioned, inform both on Near East Relief and on its context. Near East Foundation has helped prepare for United States cultural diplomacy, as indicated in accounts by Foundation participants: Laird Archer, *Balkan Journal* (New York: Norton, 1944); Harold B. Allen, *Come Over into Macedonia: The Story of a Ten-Year Adventure in Uplifting a War-Torn People* (New Brunswick, N.J.: Rutgers University Press, 1943); Harold B. Allen, *Rural Reconstruction in Action: Experience in the Near and Middle East* (Ithaca, N.Y.: Cornell University Press, 1953); John S. Badeau and Georgiana G. Stevens, eds., *Bread from Stones: Fifty Years of Technical Assistance* (Englewood Cliffs, N.J.: Prentice-Hall, 1966). A source which notes Foundation influence in the origin of the Peace Corps is Roy Hoopes, *The Complete Peace Corps Guide* (New York: Dial Press, 1965).

There are materials concerned with American diplomacy in the First World War period which have contributed to the present book: a fine interpretive essay, Daniel Smith, *The Great Departure: The United States and World War I, 1914–1920* (New York: Wiley, 1965); a theory about American motivation, Robert H. Wiebe, *The Search for Order: 1877–1920* (New York: Hill & Wang, 1967); a work on peace planning, Lawrence E. Gelfand, *The Inquiry: American Preparations for Peace, 1917–1919* (New Haven, Conn.: Yale University Press, 1963). Paul Mantoux, *Les Délibérations du Conseil des Quatre (24 mars–28 juin 1919): Notes de l'Officier Interprête* (2 vols.; Paris: Éditions du Centre National de la Recherche Scientifique, 1955), has aided me on Wilson's view of an Armenian mandate. On the isolationist revival I have used Selig Adler, *The Isolationist Impulse: Its Twentieth Century Reaction* (London: Abelard-Schuman, 1957); John Chalmers Vinson, *Referendum for Isolation: Defeat of Article Ten of the League of Nations Covenant* (Athens: University of Georgia Press, 1961); Wesley M. Bagby, *The Road to Normalcy: The Presidential Campaign and Election of 1920* (Baltimore: Johns Hopkins Press, 1962); Arno J. Mayer, *Politics and Diplomacy of Peacemaking: Containment and Counterrevolution at Versailles, 1918–1919* (New York: Knopf, 1967).

Historians have given attention to Wilsonian diplomacy on the Eastern Question. Concentrating on government documents, Laurence Evans has produced *United States Policy and the Partition of Turkey: 1914–1924* (Baltimore: Johns Hopkins Press, 1965). Evans has covered many sections of the State Department Archives. Of help has been Howard M. Sachar, "The United

370

States and Turkey, 1914–1927: The Origins of Near Eastern Policy" (unpublished Ph.D. thesis, Harvard University, 1953). Harry N. Howard, *The King-Crane Commission: An American Inquiry in the Middle East* (Beirut: Khayats, 1963), is a well-done monograph based on the papers of members of the American investigation; this publication and Howard's article, "An American Experiment in Peacemaking: The King-Crane Commission," *Moslem World*, 32 (1942), 122–146, fill many blank places. My two-part piece, "Missionary Influence on American Relations with the Near East: 1914–1923," *Muslim World* (January & April 1968), 43–56, 141–154, briefly sets out some ideas in the present study. These is also Peter M. Buzanski, "The Interallied Investigation of the Greek Invasion of Smyrna: 1919," *Historian*, 25 (1963), 325–343.

Studies on the American place in the Armenian matter have been prepared primarily from political evidence. James B. Gidney, *A Mandate for Armenia* (Kent, Oh.: Kent State University Press, 1967), is deftly written and especially strong in relating the mandate issue to European and Near East diplomacy. Robert L. Daniel made some use of mission-relief MSS in his "The Armenian Question and American-Turkish Relations: 1914–1927," *Mississippi Valley Historical Review*, 46 (1959), 252–275. Ralph E. Cook, "The United States and the Armenian Question: 1894–1924" (unpublished Ph.D. thesis, Fletcher School of Diplomacy, 1957), is a traditional, solid history, built on State Department files. Focusing on the part of isolationist opinion and of the Senate in a new departure is Thomas A. Bryson, III, "Woodrow Wilson, the Senate, Public Opinion and the Armenian Mandate Question, 1919–20" (unpublished Ph.D. thesis, University of Georgia, 1965). Bryson has followed his thesis with several articles: "An American Mandate for Armenia: A Link in British Near Eastern Policy," *Armenian Review*, 21 (Summer 1968), 23–41; "Woodrow Wilson and the Armenian Mandate: A Reassessment," *Armenian Review*, 21 (Autumn 1968), 10–29; "Mark Lambert Bristol, U.S. Navy, Admiral-Diplomat: His Influence on the Armenian Mandate Question, 1919–1920," *Armenian Review*, 21 (Winter 1968), 3–22; "Walter George Smith and the Armenian Question at the Paris Peace Conference: 1919," *Records of the American Catholic Historical Society of Philadelphia*, 81 (March 1970), 3–26. Aspects of the Armenian issue are treated by a participant-observer, William L. Westermann, "The Armenian Problem and the Disruption of Turkey," in Edward M. House and Charles Seymour, eds., *What Really Happened at Paris: The Story of the Peace Conference, 1918–1919* (New York: Scribners, 1921), 176–203; by James Tashjian, "The American Military Mission to Armenia," *Armenian Review*, 2–5 (1949–1952); and by Roderic H. Davison's student, John Philip Richardson, "The American Military Mission to Armenia" (unpublished M.A. thesis, George Washington University, 1964).

The Protestant lobby offered ideas which either intimated or asked a United States part in Turkish reconstruction. Besides previously mentioned works there are four other books. Aimed specifically at the American Peace Commission was William H. Hall, ed., *Reconstruction in Turkey: A Series of Reports Compiled for the American Committee of Armenian and Syrian Relief* (n.p.:

privately printed, 1918). American Board Secretary Cornelius H. Patton accented the Near East in *World Facts and America's Responsibility* (New York: Association Press, 1919). Missionary-educator Hall argued that the United States should "heal" the eastern Mediterranean in *The Near East: Crossroads of the World* (New York: Presbyterian Board of Foreign Missions, 1920). Talcott Williams stated that a United States military presence in the Old World was necessary to stabilize it in *Turkey, A World Problem of Today* (Garden City, N.Y.: Doubleday, 1921). Articles include Williams, "America's Duty in Turkey," *Independent*, 99 (1919), 215–216; Henry W. Jessup, "The Future of the Ottoman Empire," and Williams, "The Disposition of the Turkish Empire," *Annals of the American Academy of Political and Social Science*, 84 (July 1919), 6–29, 41–50; Edgar J. Fisher, "From Bad to Worse in Constantinople," New York *Times Magazine*, January 11, 1920.

Armenianism was a prime element in most mission-relief propaganda, as indicated by "American Churchmen Are Eager to Help Armenia," *Current Opinion*, 67 (December 1919), 313–314. Armenian Americans, aided by religionists, promoted Protestant interests: Bertha S. Papazian, *The Tragedy of Armenia: A Brief Study and Interpretation* (Boston: Pilgrim, 1918); Vahan Cardashian, ed., *Should America Accept Mandate for Armenia?* (New York: American Committee for the Independence of Armenia and Armenian National Union, 1919); M. Vartan Malcom, *The Armenians in America* (Boston: Pilgrim Press, 1919).

As "clamorous" Armenianism faded in the United States after the year 1920, pointed opinions appeared in print. There was a debate in *Current History* during the last part of 1922, between pro-Kemalist Colby M. Chester and Clair Price on the one side, George R. Montgomery and Everett P. Wheeler on the other. The conflict became intense in the book by relief figure E. H. Bierstadt, *The Great Betrayal: A Survey of the Near East Problem* (New York: McBride, 1924), and in James W. Gerard et al., *The Lausanne Treaty: Should the United States Ratify It?* (New York: Foreign Policy Association, 1924).

To supplement Howard's *The King-Crane Commission* and Manuel's *The Realities of American-Palestine Relations* on the Arab-Zionist aspects of the Ottoman peace, there is Muyhee Al-Din Hatoor Al-Khalidi, "A Century of American Contribution to Arab Nationalism: 1820–1920" (unpublished Ph.D. thesis, Vanderbilt University, 1958); Selig Adler, "The Palestine Question in the Wilson Era," *Jewish Social Studies*, 10 (October 1948), 303–334; William Yale, "Ambassador Henry Morgenthau's Special Mission of 1917," *World Politics*, 1 (April 1949), 308–320; Richard Ned Lebow, "Woodrow Wilson and the Balfour Declaration," *Journal of Modern History*, 40 (December 1968), 501–523.

At the end of the First World War Protestants called for an American redemption of Syria. Among missionary appeals then were Hall, *The Near East*, and Margaret McGilvary, *Dawn of a New Era in Syria* (New York: Revell, 1920). Protestant, Syrian-American clergymen A. M. Rihbany and H. I. Katibah set forth, respectively, *America, Save the Near East* (Boston: Beacon Press, 1918) and "Syria for the Syrians under the Guardianship of the United States," *Syrian National Bulletin*, 1 (February 28, 1919). In *A Story of Our Syria Mission* (New York: Presbyterian Board of Foreign Missions, 1920), Miss McGilvary expressed regret that the United States government did not take advantage of its opportunity in Syria. An Arab instructed by missionaries, Philip K. Hitti, is the author of *The Syrians in America* (New York: Doran, 1924).

Except for John DeNovo, historians have done little to complement Yeselson, *United States–Persian Diplomatic Relations: 1883–1921* (Yeselson neglects the role of missionaries). On this role during the war and its aftermath, see Mary Schauffler Platt, *The Journal of a Missionary in Persia* (New York: Presbyterian Board of Foreign Missions, c. 1916); Abraham Yohannan, *The Death of a Nation, or The Ever Persecuted Nestorians or Assyrian Christians* (New York: Putnam, 1916); Shedd, *The Measure of a Man: The Life of William Ambrose Shedd*; Speer and Carter, *Report on India and Persia*; and *A Century of Mission Work in Iran* (full citations above).

For adaptation of the American Board and United States business to Kemalism after the Lausanne Conference, there are several articles: Ernest W. Riggs, "The American Board and the Turks," *Moslem World*, 14 (January 1924), 1–4; Roger R. Trask, "The United States and Turkish Nationalism: Investments and Technical Aid during the Atatürk Era," *Business History Review*, 38 (Spring 1964), 58–77; Roger R. Trask, " 'Unnamed Christianity' in Turkey during the Atatürk Era," *Muslim World*, 55 (January & April 1965), 66–76, 101–111; Robert L. Daniel, "The United States and the Turkish Republic before World War II: The Cultural Dimension," *Middle East Journal*, 21 (Winter 1967), 52–63. Also, see Roger R. Trask, *The United States Response to Turkish Nationalism and Reform: 1914–1939* (Minneapolis: University of Minnesota Press, 1971).

BIBLIOGRAPHICAL AIDS

There is no single, comprehensive guide to American relations with the Near East. Lists and comments on sources in the following works proved especially useful at the beginning of research for this study: Richard Ettinghausen, ed., *A Selected and Annotated Bibliography of Books and Periodicals in Western Languages Dealing with the Near and Middle East with Special Emphasis on Medieval and Modern Times* (Washington, D.C.: Middle East Institute, 1952); John A. DeNovo, "American Relations with the Middle East: Some Unfinished Business," in George L. Anderson, ed., *Issues and Conflicts: Studies in Twentieth Century American Diplomacy* (Lawrence: University of Kansas Press, 1959), and by the same author, *American Interests and Policies in the Middle East: 1900–1939* (Minneapolis: University of Minnesota Press, 1963); Ralph E. Cook, "The United States and the Armenian Question: 1894–1924" (unpublished Ph.D. thesis, Fletcher School of Diplomacy, 1957); Robert L.

Daniel, "From Relief to Technical Assistance in the Near East, A Case Study: Near East Relief and Near East Foundation" (unpublished Ph.D. thesis, University of Wisconsin, 1953). Howard M. Sachar, "The United States and Turkey, 1914–1927: The Origins of Near Eastern Policy" (unpublished Ph.D. thesis, Harvard University, 1953). A helpful guide to the American context of relations with the Near East during the Wilson period is Arthur S. Link and William M. Leary, Jr., comps., *The Progressive Era and the Great War: 1896–1920* (New York: Appleton, 1969). Several monographs published since the mid-1960s have extensive bibliographies, which aided in identifying recent works. An excellent paper to be part of a book on sources about United States foreign relations, published by the National Archives, is John A. DeNovo, "Researching American Relations with the Middle East: The State of the Art, 1970."

Index

Index

Abdul Hamid the Second, 28, 40–53, 67
Abeih (Lebanon), 15
Abeih Academy, 20, 24, 29
Abrams, Ray H., 119
Acheson, Barclay, 301
Adalia (Turkey), 181, 183, 185, 195, 207, 250, 259
Adams, John Quincy, 14, 37
Adana (city, Turkey), 15, 167, 200, 227
Adana (vilayet, Turkey), 50, 109
Adler, Selig, 215
Adnan Bey, 275
Adriatic Sea, 181
Adventists, 33, 304
Afghanistan, 111, 302
Afro-Americans, 47, 252, 272, 292
Agency for International Development, 302
Aharonian, Avetis, 112, 181, 224
Aintab (Turkey), 15, 26, 41, 295
Albanians, 47, 53–54, 187, 202–203, 301, 309
Aleppo (Syria), 40, 61, 71, 75, 129, 167, 169
Aleppo College, 26, 297, 304–305
Alexandretta (Turkey), 40, 94–95, 110, 126
Alexandria (Egypt), 6, 108
Alexandropol (Russia), 166–167

Allah, 22
Allen, Harold B., 302
Allen, Horace N., 293
Allenby, Edmund, 95, 99, 158, 163, 167, 179, 200, 226
Alley, Rayford W., 283
Allies (Great Britain and France), 59, 63–65, 78, 88, 91, 94–99, 101–102, 106–107, 110–118, 121, 123, 127,132–133, 155, 157, 175–184, 191–197, 205, 210, 219, 225, 241–261, 267, 269–275, 287–288, 291, 305
Ambassador Morgenthau's Story, 129
America, Save the Near East (by A. H. Rihbany), 158
American Bar Association, 131
American Bible Society, 33, 66, 296
American Board of Commissioners for Foreign Missions, 5–42, 46, 54–55, 60–78, 86, 90–101, 105, 109, 111, 114–116, 127–139, 145, 150, 165–169, 171, 186–191, 199, 202, 222–223, 232, 238, 242, 247, 249, 252–254, 258–270, 275–276, 279–284, 287–288, 292–301, 303–306, 309
American College (Van), 26, 60
American College for Girls (Cairo), 299
American College for Girls (Constanti-

377

Browne, Louis E., 205
Bryan, William Jennings, 89, 240
Bryce, James, 74–75, 95, 101–102, 112, 124, 126, 130–132, 152–153, 180–181, 184, 190, 211, 222, 236, 239, 242, 254–255, 260, 288
Bryn Mawr College, 81
Buddhism, 115, 117
Bulgarian Constituent Assembly, 54
Bulgarians: evangelism among, 18–19; education among, 19–28, 298; massacres of, 42; nationalism among, 47, 53–54, 264, 288, 305; and possible war with or mediation by the United States, 92–100; American protection of, 121, 187; philanthropy among, 201, 301
Bursa (Turkey), 167, 295
Business, 5, 10, 35–38, 46, 78–79, 84, 114–116, 119, 157, 236, 243, 245–246, 252, 259–260, 264–265, 270, 273–277, 279–284, 288, 290–291, 302, 306, 307–309
Bustani, al-, Butrus, 15, 18, 54–56, 307

Cairo (Egypt), 56, 64, 98, 124, 167, 179, 256
Caix, Robert de, 177
de Caix Note, 177
Caldwell, J. L., 78, 149
California, 67, 70, 220, 265
Canada, 113
Canning, Stratford, 14
Cardashian, Vahan, 110–111, 173, 249, 257, 280–281, 284
Caribbean Sea, 40, 45, 114, 117
Carnegie, Andrew, 31
Carnegie Foundation for International Peace, 86
Catholics. See Roman Catholics
Caucasus, 53, 61, 63, 69, 95, 107–108, 111, 126, 129, 147, 150, 165–167, 207–214, 220, 227–233, 244–245, 251, 254, 257, 262, 287, 291, 300, 305
Central Treaty Organization, 306
Central Turkey College (Aintab and Marash), 26, 47–48, 127, 173, 297
Cesarea (Turkey). See Kayseri
Ceyhan (Turkey). See Adana
Ceylon, 73
Chaldeans, 136
Chester, Colby M., 265
Chester Concession, 37, 46, 265, 275, 280–281

Chicago, 30, 38, 83, 146, 152, 221, 252
Chicago, Burlington, and Quincy Railroad, 66
Chicago *Daily News*, 205
Chicago Theological Seminary, 26, 65
Chicago *Tribune*, 243
Child, Richard W., 270–272, 275
China, 6, 19, 27, 36, 44, 70–71, 73, 84, 114–115, 200, 293–295
Christian and Missionary Alliance, 33, 304
Christian Herald, 77
Christian Internationalism, 120
Christianizing the Social Order (by Walter Rauschenbusch), 189
Church Missionary Society (Anglican), 4–5, 7, 9, 33, 136, 138, 152–153
Church-State relations, 14, 34–35, 46, 97, 100, 105, 114–122, 133–134, 186–191, 213, 292–293. *See also* Culture-religion
Churchill, Winston, 225, 256
Cilicia, 50, 61, 94, 102, 108–109, 126, 162, 173, 177, 183–185, 215, 220–221, 225–227, 239, 242, 248, 250–251, 255–260, 271, 273, 278–279
City College of New York, 102
Civil War, 31
Clay, Henry, 36
Clemenceau, Georges, 157, 161–163, 177, 184, 192–199, 207, 215, 220, 225–226, 232
Cleveland, Grover, 41, 43, 67
Cleveland, 160
Cobb, Frank I., 123, 125
Cobb-Lippmann Memorandum, 123–124, 126, 175
Cochran, Joseph Plumb, 144
Coffin, Henry Sloane, 298
Colby, Bainbridge, 241, 244, 248
Collegiate and Theological Institute (Samokov), 26, 54
Collegiate Institute for Girls (Smyrna), 263
Columbia University, 65, 69–70, 146, 152, 164, 174
Commission on Ecumenical Mission and Relations. *See* Presbyterian Board of Foreign Missions
Committee of Union and Progress. *See* Young Turks
Communism, 11, 191, 302, 305. *See also* Bolsheviks; Marxism
Communist International, 191

393